ESSAYS IN
AGRARIAN HISTORY

ESSAYS IN AGRARIAN HISTORY

VOLUME II

Reprints edited for
The British Agricultural History Society

by

W. E. MINCHINTON

Professor of Economic History
University of Exeter

DAVID & CHARLES
NEWTON ABBOT

© The British Agricultural History Society 1968

Printed in Great Britain by
Latimer Trend & Company Limited
Plymouth & Whitstable
for David & Charles (Publishers) Limited
Newton Abbot Devon

CONTENTS

	PAGE
THE AGRICULTURAL REVOLUTION IN ENGLISH HISTORY: A RECONSIDERATION G. E. Mingay Reprinted from *Agricultural History*, XXVI (1963), 123–33	9
THE LAND MARKET IN THE NINETEENTH CENTURY F. M. L. Thompson Reprinted from *Oxford Economic Papers*, IX (1957), 285–300	29
AN ENQUIRY INTO THE RENT OF AGRICULTURAL LAND IN ENGLAND AND WALES DURING THE NINETEENTH CENTURY R. J. Thompson Reprinted from *Journal of the Royal Statistical Society*, LXX (1907), 587–625	55
THE COMMISSIONERS OF ENCLOSURE M. W. Beresford Reprinted from *Economic History Review*, XVI (1946), 130–40	89
AGRICULTURAL RETURNS AND THE GOVERNMENT DURING THE NAPOLEONIC WARS W. E. Minchinton Reprinted from *Agricultural History Review*, I (1953), 29–43	103
AGRICULTURAL WAGES IN ENGLAND AND WALES DURING THE LAST HALF CENTURY A. Wilson Fox Reprinted from *Journal of the Royal Statistical Society*, LXVI (1903), 273–348	121
LIVESTOCK PRICES IN BRITAIN, 1851–93 E. H. Whetham Reprinted from *Agricultural History Review*, XI (1962), 102–19	199
THE CHANGING CATTLE ENTERPRISES OF ENGLAND AND WALES, 1870–1910 E. H. Whetham Reprinted from *The Geographical Journal*, CXXIX (1963), 378–80	211

	PAGE
THE CHANGING BASIS OF AGRICULTURAL PROSPERITY, 1853–73 E. L. Jones Reprinted from *Agricultural History Review*, X (1962), 102–19	217
THE GREAT DEPRESSION OF ENGLISH AGRICULTURE, 1873–96 T. W. Fletcher Reprinted from *Economic History Review*, 2nd series, XIII (1961), 417–32	239
THE DISTRIBUTION OF FARM INCOME IN THE U.K., 1867–1938 J. R. Bellerby Reprinted from *Journal of Proceedings of the Agricultural Economic Society*, X (1953)	259
OWNER-FARMING IN ENGLAND AND WALES, 1900–1950 S. G. Sturmey Reprinted from *Manchester School*, XXIII (1955), 245–68	281

PREFACE

The growth of interest in agrarian history in Britain was marked by the foundation of the British Agricultural History Society in 1952 which at once began to publish a journal, the *Agricultural History Review*. As the number of volumes lengthened on the shelves, it was proposed to make a selection of its contents available to a wider public by the publication of a collection of essays in agrarian history, the term 'agrarian' rather than 'agricultural' being used to indicate that interest in the subject ranged wider than the conduct of agriculture as an industry and included also a concern with the problems of rural society. After discussion the original plan to produce a single volume drawn entirely from the pages of the *Agricultural History Review* was replaced by the present scheme for two volumes drawn from a wide range of journals. Various alternative arrangements of material by topic were discussed but it was finally decided that the most workable division was a chronological one with the first volume concerned with the history of British agriculture and rural society before 1750 or thereabouts and the second concerned with the post-1750 situation.

Within these two volumes an attempt has been made to collect those essays which have proved most useful to students and teachers with one important proviso—that none of the essays relating to English agrarian history which have been reprinted in the three volumes of *Essays in Economic History* published for the Economic History Society by Edward Arnold have been reprinted. The present volumes therefore complement the other set of essays. For each volume a list of twenty or more possible articles was drawn up by the General Editor and these lists were circulated to members of the committee of the British Agricultural History Society and to other university teachers knowledgeable in this field who were asked to say which essays they would most like to see reprinted. They were also invited to make additions to the list if they so desired. In the event there was a surprisingly high degree of unanimity about the possible contents of both volumes. From these lists the contents of both volumes were drawn up. In the process some attempt was made to secure a reasonable coverage both by chronology and topic. Once the choice was made all the authors were invited, if they wished, to add a short postscript to their articles which could draw attention to more recent contributions to the same subject or to changes in the author's own views. In Volume II six contributors—J. R. Bellerby, M. W. Beresford, T. W. Fletcher, Eric Jones, W. E. Minchinton and G. E. Mingay—took advantage of this offer. Otherwise the articles represent the views of the authors at the time at which they were written. Since most of the articles have been reproduced by photo-lithography, apart from the correction of occasional misprints, the articles are reprinted as they first appeared. The article by J. R. Bellerby has, however, been extensively revised for this volume. In Volume II two articles—those by R. J. Thompson and A. Wilson-Fox—are printed posthumously.

The British Agricultural History Society is greatly indebted to the authors of all papers who willingly gave permission for their articles to be reprinted. Some of the articles were drawn from its own journal, but others came from different sources. It would therefore like to express its thanks in Volume II to the editors of *Agricultural History* for the article by G. E. Mingay, to the editors of the *Manchester School* and to Kraus Reprint Ltd for S. G. Sturmey's article, to the editors of *Oxford Economic Papers* for F. M. L. Thompson's article, to the Economic History Society for M. W. Beresford's and T. W. Fletcher's articles to the Royal Geographical Society for Edith H. Whetham's note, to the Royal Statistical Society for the articles by A. Wilson-Fox and R. J. Thompson, and the to *Journal of Agricultural Economics* for the article by J. R. Bellerby.

I am grateful to Roger Burt for his help with collecting the material for the volume and to the staff of the library of the University of Exeter for making available the requisite volumes of the journals.

The British Agricultural History Society proposes to issue, if occasion warrants, a further volume of essays in agrarian history in due course and the editor would be happy to receive suggestions of articles to be included in that volume.

Exeter, June 1967 W. E. MINCHINTON

THE AGRICULTURAL REVOLUTION IN ENGLISH HISTORY: A RECONSIDERATION

G. E. Mingay

The Agricultural Revolution in English History: A Reconsideration

G. E. MINGAY

'Revolution' is a word which has gone much out of fashion in the popular terminology of economic history. To talk nowadays of 'revolution' is to risk being considered a dangerous reactionary, or at least an incautious obscurantist. Indeed, it is clear from the scholarly preference for 'accelerated pace of economic development' or 'quickening of the growth process', that no matter how cumbrous the alternative we must eschew the convenience of 'revolution'—overlooking, incidentally, that the dictionary has it that revolutionary changes need only be radical and need not be sudden.

The old idea of an Agricultural Revolution ran parallel, and indeed was closely associated with that of an Industrial Revolution. Both were once seen as remarkable inter-related changes in the methods, organization, and levels of production which took place in a relatively short period of some seventy years between 1760 and 1830. For a long time now, however, the process of industrial change has been seen as extending much further back—some would say to the sixteenth century—and seen also as reaching forward, to at least the later nineteenth century; and many would pitch on the middle years of the nineteenth century as the most vital period of development. The 'agricultural revolution' has undergone a rather similar if less severe stretching process. Its roots in the seventeenth century, and even earlier, are now well-established, and as with industrialization, many authorities would place the period of most significant technical change in the middle nineteenth century, not long before the Great Depression (another term whose days are numbered?) swept away the old order of things and changed fundamentally the character and emphasis of English farming.

The traditional story of the agricultural revolution placed its crucial stages firmly in the later eighteenth and early nineteenth centuries, and the revolutionary character of the changes of that period was thought to spring from two developments: first, the original work of a number of pioneers whose names have become almost canonical in the textbooks, and by whom the inefficiency of existing farming methods was greatly modified—that celebrated quartet of agriculturists, Tull, Townshend, Coke, and Bakewell; and secondly, the large-scale enclosure of open fields by private Acts of Parliament, which not only made possible the adoption of improved farming methods but radically changed the agrarian structure, driving out small farmers and cottagers who lived out a comfortably static existence by farming mainly for subsistence, and replacing them with enterprising capitalist farmers who produced for the market.

I

The eighteenth-century innovations and the enclosure movement thus stood at the core of the old idea of the Agricultural Revolution, and it is illuminating to examine, if only very briefly, the basis from which this interpretation of English agricultural history derived. In the main, it depended on two major works, Lord Ernle's *English Farming Past and Present*, first published in 1912, and J. L. and Barbara Hammond's *The Village Labourer*, which appeared in the same year. Both books, of course, soon acquired a great reputation; the one came to be recognized as the single standard work for English agricultural history, and still has not been dislodged from this pedestal after half a century; the other has largely determined the interpretation of the social changes in the countryside, and has stamped on the minds of countless teachers and students an apparently indelible picture of social disintegration involving the exploitation by the few of the mass of humble peasantry.

Now, the influence achieved by these two works is in some ways very curious. Lord Ernle's classic was in many respects ill-balanced and defective when it first appeared, and the passage of time merely made it the more so, for in the later editions little or no effort was made to repair the omission of important contributions such as those of Tawney, Gonner, Clapham, and even the Hammonds. Ernle used, in fact, only the sources with which he was thoroughly familiar—particularly the contemporary farming books of Arthur Young, William Marshall and the reports of the Board of Agriculture—and he ignored the local histories, topographical writings, diaries and publications of record societies that were available in his time.[1] In short, his was a book based almost entirely on a partial selection of secondary sources, and it was especially weak in the analysis of the economic forces bearing on agriculture.

This is not to say, of course, that *English Farming* was an entirely bad book. There are long passages in it which even today can be read with pleasure and profit—his discussions of the enclosure movement and of the decline of owner-occupiers, for example, are still useful. But Ernle, while certainly not unaware of the plodding and uneven character of agricultural development, leaned towards a heroic view of the great figures of the eighteenth and nineteenth centuries. Turnip Townshend, he argued, revolutionized the condition of his estate, consisting originally only of 'rush-grown marshes, or sandy wastes where a few sheep starved and "two rabbits struggled for every blade of grass",' to such effect that

---

[1] Lord Ernle, *English Farming Past and Present* (6th ed.; London: Heinemann; Cass, 1961), Introduction by G. E. Fussell, p. xxii.

in a short time he quadrupled his rents. Coke of Norfolk, said Ernle, did even better, raising his rents almost ten-fold, and as the champion of 'the new system of large farms and large capital' replaced 'a barbarous system of cropping' by forcing upon the notice of Norfolk farmers 'the practice of drilling turnips and wheat, and the value of sainfoin, swedes, mangel-wurzel and potatoes'.[1] The assumption that Norfolk farming in Townshend's time, and even as late as Coke, was in a barbarous condition is the more curious because the agricultural writers well known to Ernle, and widely quoted by him, themselves recognized that the Norfolk system was not a recent innovation. And of course even a casual reading of Defoe's *Tour* (also quoted by Ernle) brings out the fact of a developed commercial farming embracing widespread improvements, and impresses the reader with the vigour and activity of the early eighteenth-century countryside.

The Hammonds's book, while in some ways a more thorough and perceptive piece of work than Ernle's, had something of the same defects. In effect, the Hammonds elaborated the Marxist view of enclosure as the transformation of a settled peasantry into a landless proletariat, driven by want and class legislation to face the choice of either leaving the countryside to become the exploited tools of the factory masters, or of remaining there as the degraded, under-employed and underpaid hands of the capitalist farmers. The Hammonds, it must be said, took the trouble to research among the contemporary letter-writers and pamphleteers, the Enclosure Acts and Awards, and the Home Office 'blue books'. But the advantage of knowing at the outset what the conclusion of the research was likely to be, made it convenient to be selective in the choice of material. This at any rate is the conclusion of those scholars like Mr. W. E. Tate who have made a painstaking survey of the same ground.[2] And it is borne out by the Hammonds's failure to make use of the statistical material for the early nineteenth century which Clapham subsequently deployed to such devastating effect, and even more by their neglect of the scholarly and detailed work of Gonner, whose book appeared in 1911, or that of A. H. Johnson who wrote two years earlier.[3] There is no doubt that had they taken these writers into account their story must have been greatly modified.

Now it may be asked, how was it that these two celebrated but seriously imperfect books came to establish their apparently unwarranted hegemony? There is no doubt that some part of Ernle's strength lay in the

[1] Ibid., pp. 174–5, 217–19.
[2] W. E. Tate, 'Opposition to Parliamentary Enclosure in the Eighteenth Century,' *Agricultural History*, XIX (July 1945), 137–41; 'Parliamentary Counter Petitions During Enclosures of the Eighteenth and Nineteenth Centuries,' *English Historical Review*, LIX (September 1944), 392–403.
[3] E. C. K. Gonner, *Common Land and Inclosure* (London: Macmillan and Co., 1912); Arthur Henry Johnson, *The Disappearance of the Small Landowner* (Oxford: The Clarendon Press, 1909).

quality of his prose: he commanded a style at once distinctive, lucid and elegant and he had remarkable powers of description. But, more important, was the fact that his was the only book which, on a large canvas and with considerable detail, covered the whole of English farming from the Middle Ages to his own time. It still remains so, and the latest sixth edition, which appeared so recently as 1961, has been supplemented by a long bibliographical introduction which seeks to bring the text up to date with 'a guide to the findings and direction of recent scholarship'.[1] A perusal of this *Introduction*, however, will have the effect of convincing most people that it is a waste of time to continue to read Ernle.

A book which for want of any better fills the place of a standard work is bound to have much influence, although that of Ernle must by now be approaching vanishing point. But one reason why the traditional idea of the Agricultural Revolution has remained so firmly entrenched is the apparent absence of anyone willing to stand forth as the new Ernle and able to draw up into one comprehensive volume all the devious threads of the writing of half a century. The Hammonds's book is in different case. Following in the footsteps of Engels, Marx and Thorold Rogers, the Hammonds represented the radical tradition, and they brought to bear all their considerable eloquence to present a case, which while logical and well-argued, persuaded primarily through its appeal to the reader's emotions and its power to convey the conviction of its authors. Historically the case was weak, relying as it did on a limited range of sources and on a relatively small body of supporting evidence. Indeed, many of the chief contentions had no sort of support at all, and the Hammonds were not the writers to bring down their readers' temperature with the kind of sobering statistics that were the tools of Gonner and Clapham. However, the Hammonds did not write for historians but for the educated public at large; and although the historians long ago rejected much of their case, the public continued to read and be convinced.

II

The gradual accumulation of new material has now reached the stage, despite certain gaps, of making it possible to reconsider the whole question of agricultural revolution in the eighteenth and nineteenth centuries. Some of this material is indeed not so new, for it involves a recognition of the work published by Clapham in the 1920s and even a reconsideration of the writings of Gonner, Johnson and others who were contemporary with Ernle and the Hammonds. The 'new' lines of thought can be said to have resulted mainly from two fields of research, one of which consists of a much more thorough and comprehensive investigation of the old sources known to Ernle, the Hammonds, and their contemporaries. The other, a new field—or at least little exploited before the last twenty-five

[1] Ernle, *English Farming Past and Present*, Introductions by G. E. Fussell and O. R. McGregor.

years—consists mainly of the investigation of estate records, particularly rentals, accounts, surveys and estate correspondence, the testamentary inventories left by farmers and cottagers, and (mainly for the nineteenth century) farmers' diaries, autobiographies and farm accounts. In the space of an essay we cannot do more, of course, than look very briefly at this very large volume of material, but an attempt to summarize the main conclusions which have emerged from it may prove a useful undertaking. In order to achieve some sort of system in presentation we shall group the material around three main themes, the general background to agricultural development, the changes in farming methods (including those of open-field farming), and of course that subject of perennial fascination and controversy—enclosure.

The general background to agricultural development from the later seventeenth to the later nineteenth centuries has been illuminated from two directions. From one of these the historians' searchlight has been turned on the structure of landownership and the effects of this structure on agricultural development. In the first of a series of well-known essays, Professor Habakkuk showed that the late seventeenth and early eighteenth centuries saw the growth in the English countryside of large accumulations of property in the hands of great landlords, accumulations created mainly at the expense of smaller owners, the lesser gentry and owner-occupiers. A number of the small estates were bought up also by newcomers such as retired merchants and lawyers, city and professional men.[1] In his subsequent essays Professor Habakkuk has elaborated on some of the aspects of this change, particularly the importance of the strict marriage settlement and the easier conditions for borrowing on mortgage. These developments enabled the great owners to keep their empires intact, by mitigating the risks necessarily attached to the propensity of great landlords to live beyond their incomes, and by guarding against the eventual appearance in the succession of a spendthrift, rake or imbecile—something which happened in the best of blue-blooded families.[2]

The growth and consolidation of large estates in the eighteenth and nineteenth centuries had important implications for agricultural progress. The development helps to explain the prominence of certain large owners in the propagation of improved farming—notably Coke of Norfolk, the Dukes of Bedford, the Egremonts, Rockingham and others—although there is now a tendency to think that the role of great owners in

[1] H. J. Habakkuk, 'English Landownership, 1680–1740,' *Economic History Review*, X (February 1940), 2–18.

[2] H. J. Habakkuk, 'Marriage Settlements in the Eighteenth Century,' *Transactions of the Royal Historical Society*, XXXII (London, 1950), 15–30; 'The English Land Market in the Eighteenth Century,' in *Britain and the Netherlands*, eds. J. S. Bromley and E. H. Kossman (London: Chatto & Windus, 1960). See also G. E. Mingay, *English Landed Society in the Eighteenth Century* (London: Routledge and Kegan Paul, 1963), chaps. 1–4, 7, 8.

this respect has been exaggerated and that the farming country gentlemen, the better owner-occupiers and large tenant-farmers formed the real spearhead of technical advance. But at least it is certain that landlords' capital was vital in providing a favourable environment for agricultural progress, the right conditions in which farmers of substance and enterprise could succeed; and these conditions included the creation of enclosed and compact farms, with adequate and suitably-sited buildings, with soil kept in good condition by drainage, marling, manuring and other means, by the commutation of tithes and a low burden of poor rates, by a moderate level of rents, and possibly—but not of necessary importance—by the provision of long leases.[1] It would be absurd to suggest that all large owners provided all these conditions, and even more absurd to suppose that they could all be provided at once. Agricultural improvement was a work of time, and its pace was limited to some extent by the availability of the necessary technical knowledge (for example, of cheap methods of under-drainage, not developed until the 1840's), as well as by the landowners' ability and willingness to spare income for investment. But the huge expenditures on enclosure in the eighteenth and early nineteenth centuries—which must have involved landlords in an investment of something over £10 million—and on drainage and buildings later in the nineteenth century, approaching £20 million, give some indication of the volume of landlords' rents that went back into improvement of the land. It should not be overlooked that the capital—and enterprise —of the landlords did much to stimulate the local economy, by the improvement of roads and the building of canals and railways, by exploiting minerals and establishing ironworks, and by developing manufactories of metal goods such as nails and agricultural implements, quarries, lime-kilns, brick-kilns and similar projects. The general lines of this aspect of English landownership have been traced by Professor Habakkuk, by two general surveys presented before the First International Conference of Economic History, in 1960, and in other writings.[2]

[1] The provision of long leases was related partly to the size and value of the farms and partly to regional practice. Leases did not necessarily include detailed clauses laying down the farming practice to be followed, and where they did it is difficult to tell how far they were followed by the tenants. In any case, leases went much out of fashion in the nineteenth century with the severe price fluctuations and periods of depression. Many farmers wanted freedom to vary their farming as prices and other circumstances changed, and the lack of leases did not usually mean lack of security. Good landlords had a reputation for keeping their tenants, and many families carried on for generations on annual tenancies. The growth of a customary tenant right of compensation for unexhausted improvements also worked in this direction.

[2] H. J. Habakkuk, 'Economic Functions of English Landowners in the Eighteenth Century,' *Explorations in Entrepreneurial History*, VI (December 1953), 92–102; G. E. Mingay, 'The Large Estate in Eighteenth-Century England,' and F. M. L. Thompson, 'English Great Estates in the Nineteenth Century,' First International Conference of Economic History, Stockholm, 1960, *Contributions* (The Hague: Mouton & Co, 1960), pp. 367–83; 385–97. See also Mingay, *English*

The gathering of land into few hands also has obvious implications for the development of larger farming units and the decline of that mystical rustic—the 'yeoman'. Professor Habakkuk agrees with earlier writers like Davies and Johnson, that the yeoman, or as the term is usually and more precisely understood, the smaller owner-occupier, was largely bought out in the period of active building up of great estates in the later seventeenth and early eighteenth centuries. It seems certain on the basis of the land tax assessments that the subsequent period of prosperous farming conditions enabled the surviving owner-occupiers to hold their own and even to multiply, until the big fall in prices of the 1820's. Then a further period of slow decline set in, until by the end of the nineteenth century small owner-cultivators had only about 12 per cent of the farm acreage.[1] On the whole it seems that the level of prices and the prosperity of farming had more impact on owner-occupiers than had enclosure.

Large estates, of course, had no necessary connection with large farms. In fact, it happened that many large estates had the major part of their land in undeveloped farming areas, and predominantly in small units. But the accumulation of land in the hands of large owners often encouraged consolidation, if only as a preliminary to enclosure, although again this was a slow process. It has been suggested by the present writer that the growth of larger farm units was a continuing secular process, which was under way long before the eighteenth century and did not stop with the fading out of enclosure in the nineteenth century. It was the result of a variety of influences—technical advantages of larger farms, landlords' preference for substantial tenants who could farm well and who gave less trouble in management, and the greater viability of large farmers in periods of depression. Enclosure encouraged and accelerated the process but it is clear that the engrossing of farms went on quite independently of enclosure. Indeed there is evidence to suggest that farms grew in size more rapidly in the early eighteenth century when enclosure was limited but times were difficult, than in the later eighteenth century when en-

---

Landed Society, chaps. 7, 8; David Spring, 'The English Landed Estate in the Age of Coal and Iron, 1830–1880,' *Journal of Economic History*, XI (Winter, 1951), 3–24; F. M. L. Thompson, 'English Landownership: the Ailesbury Trust, 1832–56,' *Economic History Review*, XI (August, 1958), 121–33; F. M. L. Thompson, 'The End of a Great Estate,' *Economic History Review*, VIII (August 1955), 36–52; David Springs, 'The Earls of Durham and the Great Northern Coalfield, 1830–1880,' *Canadian Historical Review*, XXXIII (September 1952), 237–53; 'A Great Agricultural Estate: Netherby under Sir James Graham, 1820–1845,' *Agricultural History*, XXIX (April 1955), 73–81.

[1] In 1800 they owned about a fifth of the cultivated acreage. See Habakkuk, 'English Landownership, 1680–1740'; Johnson, *Disappearance of the Small Landowner*; E. Davies, 'The Small Landowner, 1780–1832, in the Light of Land Tax Assessments,' *Economic History Review*, I (January 1927), 87–113; H. G. Hunt, 'Land-ownership and Enclosure, 1750–1830,' *Economic History Review*, XI (April 1959), 497–505; John H. Clapham, *Economic History of Modern Britain* (3 vols., Cambridge: The University Press, 1926–38), Vol. I, p. 105.

closure went on apace but prices were rising.¹ In any event, only those who like Cobbett refused to believe official statistics could hold that small farmers disappeared in the eighteenth century, for the figures show that in 1831 nearly a half of all farmers were small.²

The movements of prices not only influenced the survival of owner-occupiers and small farmers but affected land use and the whole course of agricultural change. The changes in the general levels of prices meant a periodical movement from prosperity into depression and back again, with consequent influences on activity in enclosure and other agricultural investment; and in addition, differential changes in the prices of the various agricultural products determined in the long run the relative profitability of grass and arable, and hence changes in land use. Ernle and other writers of his time were aware of the general course of prices and their significance, but they failed to follow through the implications for farmers of changing market conditions. Similarly, the consequences for agricultural specialization of the growth of towns and the increasing demand of urban populations for meat, milk, dairy produce, vegetables, fruit, and poultry were not fully considered; and neither was the impact of industrial growth on the demand for secondary products like wool, hides, tallow, and timber. There was among the writers before Clapham the same tendency towards an excessive concern with wheat, and with arable farming in general, which characterized the contemporary pamphleteers and Corn Law debates; although, as Caird pointed out, by the middle-nineteenth century the area under grass and the annual value of pasture products were approaching equality with the area and annual value of arable farming. In recent years this historical imbalance has been redressed, and much of current writing on the eighteenth and nineteenth centuries (as for earlier periods) has centered around agricultural price movements and effects on agricultural production in general, and indeed on their wider implications for the economy at large.³

III

Just as the investigations of eighteenth-century estate records and prices have tended to direct more attention to the earlier part of that cen-

---

[1] G. E. Mingay, 'The Size of Farms in the Eighteenth Century,' *Economic History Review*, XIV (April 1962), 469–88.

[2] Jonathan David Chambers, *The Workshop of the World* (London: Oxford University Press, 1960), p. 75; Clapham, op. cit., Vol. I, pp. 450–1, Vol. II, pp. 263–4.

[3] See A. H. John, 'The Course of Agricultural Change,' in *Studies in the Industrial Revolution*, ed. Leslie S. Pressnell (London: University of London, Athlone Press, 1960); 'Aspects of English Economic Growth in the First Half of the Eighteenth Century,' *Economica* (May 1961), pp. 180–3; G. E. Mingay, 'The Agricultural Depression, 1730–1750,' *Economic History Review*, VIII (April 1956), 323–38; T. W. Fletcher, 'The Great Depression of English Agriculture, 1870–1896,' *Economic History Review*, XIII (April 1961), 417–432; W. Ashworth, *An Economic History of England: 1870–1939* (London: Methuen, 1960), chap. 3.

tury, so similarly have the studies concerned with farming methods shifted the focus back in time. The system of alternate husbandry—that is, the celebrated Norfolk system of alternating roots and clover with corn crops—it is now recognized, had developed long before the days of those bucolic Norfolk gentlemen, Townshend and Coke. On the neighbouring estates of the Walpole family, for example, alternate husbandry has been traced back to 1673. The basic features of Norfolk farming, the large farms, long leases, the four-course rotation and the treatment of the soil with marl, were all well-established long before Coke was born.[1] Moreover, the practice of alternate husbandry, or some local version of it, was not confined to Norfolk or even eastern England. Turnips and clover came over from the Low Countries in the seventeenth century, if not earlier, and large areas of English farmland were influenced by the intensive methods of the Netherlands.[2] Wherever light or freely draining soils of sand or light loams were present, legumes, roots, and artificial grasses made headway, even in open-field areas.[3] On the chalk and limestone uplands, too, the early introduction of fodder crops into the rotations made it possible to reduce the formerly indispensable flocks of the ancient sheep-and-corn husbandry, and thus to plough up downland for crops.[4]

Alternate husbandry had thus become widespread even in the seventeenth century. Its failure to penetrate much of the Midlands and Western districts, however, sprang not so much from the obtuse conservatism of the farmers, as earlier writers supposed, but because the successful growing of roots was possible only on light land and was not adaptable to the wet, cold clays. On the more amenable clay soils of the Midlands, however, fallowing was abolished by the introduction of ley-farming or convertible husbandry; that is, the periodical alternation of white crops with legumes or artificial grasses (and sometimes roots), each field being cropped for three

---

[1] R. A. C. Parker, 'Coke of Norfolk and the Agricultural Revolution,' *Economic History Review*, VIII (December 1955), 156–66; J. H. Plumb, 'Sir Robert Walpole and Norfolk Husbandry,' *Economic History Review*, V, No. 1 (1952), 86–9; G. E. Fussell, Introduction to Ernle, *English Farming Past and Present*, pp. lxvi–lxxi. The importance of Coke lies mainly in his improvements of the system, his advances in the breeds of sheep and cattle kept in Norfolk, his encouragement of irrigation, under-drainage and new manures, and the demonstration effect of his 'sheep-shearings', or annual shows.

[2] G. E. Fussell, 'Low Countries' Influence on English Farming,' *English Historical Review*, LXXIV (October 1959), 611–22; B. H. Slicher van Bath, 'The Rise of Intensive Husbandry in the Low Countries,' in *Britain and the Netherlands*, eds. J. S. Bromley and E. H. Kossmann; E. Kerridge, "Turnip Husbandry in High Suffolk,' *Economic History Review*, VIII (April 1956), 390–2.

[3] M. A. Havinden, 'Agricultural Progress in Open-Field Oxfordshire,' *Agricultural History Review*, IX, Part 2 (1961), 75.

[4] E. L. Jones, 'Eighteenth-Century Changes in Hampshire Chalkland Farming,' *Agricultural History Review*. VIII, Part 1 (1960), 5–19; R. Molland, 'Agriculture c. 1793–c. 1870,' Wiltshire, *V.C.H.* IV (ed. E. Critall, 1959), 70–1.

or four years in succession, and then laid down to sainfoin or rye-grass for a similar period before being cropped again.¹ Ley-farming was far from being an eighteenth-century innovation, and was already in practice in the sixteenth century. The really evil clays—the cold, wet kind which Arthur Young advised 'every friend of mine to have nothing to do with' —remained throughout the eighteenth and at least part of the nineteenth century very largely unimproved and unimprovable. For lack of adequate drainage the two corn crops and fallow continued on them long after enclosure. In the south-west of England, lastly, where grass grows readily in the winter months and the shortage of fodder was not a serious problem, small areas of turnips were sufficient, and farmers were sensibly loth to incur the heavy labour costs of the full Norfolk rotation.²

Progress in arable farming was thus a matter of adapting the invaluable turnip, clover, sainfoin, or rye grass to local conditions of soil and climate. Farmers were not merely stupid in failing to take over the Norfolk system, lock, stock and barrel. Indeed, there became evident in the course of the nineteenth century a retreat from the classical four-course rotation, when the rising incidence of 'finger and toe' disease in turnips and of cloversick soil which refused to grow red clover properly, provided clear warning signs. Moreover, many farmers varied their rotations endlessly, not only in order to avoid these problems, but also to take advantage of fluctuations in market conditions. The East Lothians of Scotland, with its highly flexible system, displaced Norfolk as the home of the best arable farming, and the failure after the 1820's of the general level of grain prices to rise substantially, brought about over the years another subtle change of emphasis: the growing of grain crops purely for fodder purposes, the end-product of much arable farming now being stall-fed bullocks.³

To complete this brief survey of developments in arable farming we should note in passing that Jethro Tull's importance has now shrunk very considerably. He was not perhaps such a crank as some writers have supposed, for he recognized that his own pet system of monoculture without manures or fallows was not applicable to all soils, and was particularly unsuitable for 'wet clayey land . . . Many, it is like,' he said, 'will think, this repetition of wheat crops rather a curiosity than profitable, and in some circumstances it may be so.' Furthermore, there was real merit in his advocacy of sowing in drills and systematic hoeing to produce a fine tilth and to destroy weeds. These ideas, however, were not new, and even Tull's design for a horse-drawn drill had been anticipated by Worlidge, who suggested a practical machine some sixty years earlier. And it seems

---

¹ For a contemporary description see W. Marshall, *Rural Economy of Midland Counties* (1790), Vol. I, pp. 184–7.
² E. L. Jones, 'English Farming Before and During the Nineteenth Century,' *Economic History Review*, XV (August 1962), 146.
³ *Ibid.*, p. 147; Molland, 'Agriculture c. 1793–c. 1870,' pp. 74–5.

clear that while recognizing the value of turnips as cattle food, Tull failed to perceive that it was alternate husbandry, and not the intensive pulverization of the soil, which was the real answer to bare fallows and shortage of manure.[1]

One important consequence of the wider use of roots and artificial grasses was the increased supply of livestock. There is no doubt that the market for cattle and sheep was growing throughout the eighteenth and nineteenth centuries, and that this expanding demand lay behind the attempts to improve livestock husbandry. In his valuable books on the subject, Trow-Smith has collected for us the existing information about the earlier attempts to improve the old kinds of livestock. The principle of selective breeding had been known and put into practice for generations before Robert Bakewell appeared on the scene, and by the early eighteenth century there existed a number of well-known herds and flocks of high-quality animals. Bakewell did not begin from nothing with totally unimproved beasts, as is sometimes assumed. His place in agricultural history rests therefore not on the introduction of selective breeding, but rather on his successful exploitation of the advantages to be gained by breeding in and in, using only the best animals he could find for his purpose of fixing their desirable qualities in a new breed, on the lines of the highly-bred racehorses produced for the eighteenth-century aristocracy. Earlier breeders had not been able to do this, because they had not had the foresight, patience and resources to breed exclusively from the finest animals, as Bakewell did. Even Bakewell's success, however, was a limited one, for his longhorn cattle were soon destined to give way before the Collings brothers' improved shorthorns, while the flesh of his more long-lived New Leicesters was so fat that it was described as unsuitable 'for genteel tables', or more explicitly as 'coal-heavers' mutton'.[2]

The creation of new breeds that gave general satisfaction was essentially a long process, and the ousting of the old native varieties, or rather, as in many cases, their improvement by crossing with the newer varieties, took even longer. It was well into the nineteenth century before the recognition of the importance of quality in livestock spread from the progressive few to the general run of farmers.[3]

[1] E. R. Wicker, 'A Note on Jethro Tull: Innovator or Crank?' *Agricultural History*, XXXI (January 1957), 47–8; T. H. Marshall, 'Jethro Tull and the "New Husbandry" of the Eighteenth Century,' *Economic History Review*, II (January 1929), 41–60; G. E. Fussell, *The Farmers' Tools, 1500–1900* (London: Andrew Melrose, 1952), pp. 93–102.

[2] Robert Trow-Smith, *A History of British Livestock Husbandry to 1700* (London: Routledge and K. Paul, 1957); *A History of British Livestock Husbandry, 1700–1900* (London: Routledge and K. Paul, 1959), pp. 26–9, 36, 56–64.

[3] *Ibid.*, and G. E. Fussell, 'The Size of English Cattle in the Eighteenth Century,' *Agricultural History*, III (October 1929), 160–181; 'Eighteenth Century Estimates of English Sheep and Wool Production,' *Agricultural History*, IV (October 1930), 131–51; and 'Animal Husbandry in Eighteenth Century England,' *Agricultural History*, XI (April 1937), 96–116.

The lesser branches of farming, such as the large and important dairying industry (with which was connected much of the production of pork, hams and bacon), hops, fruit, market-gardening and poultry, we must pass over, as also the lesser technical advances in such matters as water-meadows, marling and manures. Much remains to be added to the work already produced on these subjects, but we can say at this stage that evidently they were all of considerable importance at the beginning of the eighteenth century, when English farming was already diversified and progressive. Of implements and machinery the story is different, for apart from improvements in the design of ploughs and the supplementing of the two-wheel carts by four-wheel wagons, there were few important advances that were widely adopted before the late eighteenth century. Then the developments of the Industrial Revolution eventually brought about the replacement of implements of local design, constructed of wood, stone or wrought iron, by the standardized factory product made of cast iron. It was about the 1780's that machines began to become important for lightening some of the laborious tasks of the farm, and the earliest ones included threshing machines, chaff cutters, root slicers and crushers. Many of these were first worked by hand or by horses, but eventually they were adapted to steam. However, the advance of the machines was slow, partly because many farmers were too small and too poor to buy them, partly because of the diversified output and varied growing conditions of English farming—the early American reapers, for instance, often failed in England—and partly because labour was plentiful and cheap. Only from about the 1850's did machinery become commonplace (although steam power was still highly exceptional), and only from that period could it be said to play a very significant part in agricultural output. It was about that time, too, that the invention of cheap methods of producing pipes and tiles made it possible to undertake large-scale under-drainage, the most important and most capital-absorbing of the productive improvements of the nineteenth century, comparable in these respects with the enclosure movement which was just drawing to a close.[1]

The marketing of agricultural produce remains one of the least explored areas of modern agricultural history. For much of our knowledge we are still obliged to Daniel Defoe, whose *Tour of England and Wales*, while tending perhaps to over-emphasize the importance of the London market, evokes a comprehensive picture of a bustling, highly commercialized agriculture catering considerably for distant markets—a picture that we cannot ignore.[2] Fussell has used this and other sources to give

---

[1] *History of Technology*, eds. Charles Singer, et al. (5 vols, New York: Oxford University Press, 1956–8), Vol. IV, chaps. 1, 2; Fussell, *The Farmers' Tools;* Clapham, *Economic History of Modern Britain*, Vol. I, pp. 458–62, Vol. II, pp. 267–73.

[2] D. Defoe, *A Tour Through England and Wales* (Everyman's edition; London: J. M. Dent & Sons, 1928).

us a valuable but inevitably vague account of eighteenth-century traffic in farm produce and of trade routes; and Mathias has thrown useful light on the important market offered by the brewing and distilling industries.[1] The rest is silence.

However, it is possible to say that we know much more about open-field farming than we did even a dozen years ago. Young, of course, exaggerated the backwardness of the 'goths and vandals' of open-field farmers, as he did so much else; but, as Professor Tawney once commented, it is now well understood that the open fields were not 'a miracle of squalid petrifaction', nor their cultivators 'the slaves of organized torpor'. Of course, there were plenty of villages with only two fields, one of which was always bare-fallowed, with inconveniently dispersed and highly-fragmented holdings, and with overstocked commons that periodically saw the livestock decimated by epidemic disease. But by the eighteenth century or earlier, many open-field villages had gradually overcome or mitigated these defects. In some areas the number of fields was increased to three, four, or even more, in order to diversify the rotations and reduce the area of fallow. Often there was no longer a rigid succession of crops, and the introduction of clover, sainfoin and turnips into the rotations, or as leys, largely obviated fallowing and made it possible to support a larger number of beasts. The area under white crops consequently declined but there was now more manure to keep the arable in better heart.[2] Thus the 'open-field system' was adapted to reap the advantages of alternate husbandry, and the age-old problem of inadequacy of winter fodder was at least partially solved. Dr. Hoskins found evidence that convertible husbandry in the open fields (i.e. leys) goes 'well back into the sixteenth century, and probably earlier than that'.[3] The sources of fodder were augmented by always keeping one of the fields in grass (or preferably in clover or sainfoin, which were far more nutritious), by leaving leys in the open fields, and furthermore by establishing water-meadows and by permanently enclosing large pieces of the open fields for

---

[1] G. E. Fussell and C. Goodman, 'The Eighteenth-Century Traffic in Livestock,' *Economic History*, III (February, 1936), 214–36; 'Traffic in Farm Produce in Eighteenth-Century England,' *Agricultural History*, XII (October 1938), 355–68; P. Mathias, 'Agriculture and the Brewing and Distilling Industries in the Eighteenth Century,' *Economic History Review*, V, No. 2 (1952), 249–57.

[2] Havinden, 'Agricultural Progress in Open-Field Oxfordshire,' pp. 75–82.

[3] William G. Hoskins, 'The Leicestershire Farmer in the Seventeenth Century,' *Agricultural History*, XXV (January 1951), 14–17, 20; also his *The Midland Peasant* (London: Macmillan, 1957), pp. 162–4, 235–6. Dr. Hoskins's examination of testamentary inventories has thrown light not only on the development of open-field farming but also on housing conditions and the distribution of wealth in rural communities. For further discussions see E. M. Gardner, 'East Sussex Inventories,' *Sussex Notes and Queries*, XV (1959); G. H. Kenyon, 'Kirdford Inventories, 1611–1776,' *Sussex Archaeological Collections*, XCIII (1955); Francis W. Steer, *Farm and Cottage Inventories of Mid-Essex, 1635–1749* (Chelmsford: Essex County Council, 1950).

additional stocking or dairying closes. The eventual enclosure of the open-field leys and the creation of closes for permanent pasture were factors in the piecemeal process by which the open-field area of many 'unenclosed' villages was reduced to quite a small proportion of the total cultivated land. At the same time there was often a good deal of consolidation and engrossing, and open-field farms grew larger, more compact and easier to work.

IV

Open-field farming thus developed towards a more flexible and efficient husbandry employing turnips, legumes and artificial grasses on increasingly larger and more compact farms, which often included a fair proportion of enclosed permanent pasture or ley ground. It follows, of course, that many enclosures merely speeded up and completed this process, and the view that all enclosures brought about a transformation of the farming system and represented the sudden overthrow of a traditional and completely obsolete structure is untenable. This is extremely important because it makes clear the hazards of generalizing about a process, the character and effects of which were in fact highly diverse. Each village had its own peculiar features in relation to soil and topography, markets and communications, the area of commons and waste and the size of the remaining open-fields, the existing system of cultivation, whether developed or still backward, and the structure of landownership and farm sizes, to mention only the more obvious variables, and each of these had some influence on the course taken by enclosure.

In so far as we may risk generalization, we can say that the great weight of modern evidence leads us to believe that the earlier writers like the Hammonds grossly exaggerated the influence of enclosure and ascribed to it consequences that derived more from price movements, industrialization, population growth, and other factors. The clearest reason for reconsidering the importance of enclosure is that the evils popularly thought to have been its peculiar results, such as rural unemployment and poverty, the engrossing of farms, decline of small owners and large rent increases, were very often found equally in villages quite untouched by the enclosures of the eighteenth and nineteenth centuries. Indeed, pauperism was more marked in counties like Kent and Sussex, where enclosure was negligible, than in some other areas which were exposed to the full flood of the movement, and in the last labourers' revolt of 1830 it is clear that enclosures were not an important factor.[1]

On the purely agricultural effects we can say with assurance that enclosure did not always have an immediate or very drastic effect on the system of cultivation. This was partly because much progress had been

---

[1] Compare Gonner's table of expenditure on poor relief (*Common Land and Inclosure*, p. 448) with Hammonds's account of the revolt, in *The Village Labourer*, p. 105, and chaps. 11, 12.

made already in developing the open-field husbandry, and partly because some heavy soils could not depart from the traditional two crops and fallow until cheap under-drainage was available. In general, enclosure naturally had the effect of accelerating the spread of improved farming and helped to achieve greater efficiency by creating compact farms in individual occupation, but perhaps the expansion of the cultivated acreage by the intake of commons and wastes was at least as important for the increase of total output. We have seen already that there was a secular trend towards larger farms and the displacement of owner-occupiers, which proceeded independently of enclosure although it may have been accelerated by it.[1] To suppose a sudden wholesale engrosing of farms as the result of enclosure is absurd in view of the nineteenth-century figures of farm sizes; and indeed such a supposition involves a further absurdity, for it assumes that lurking somewhere in the hedgerows were large numbers of capitalist farmers, all boasting capitals of £1,000 or more, and impatiently waiting for the enclosure commissioners to do their work that they might step in and gobble up the peasant holdings. Furthermore, the customary fairness of the enclosure commissioners, the moderate levels of enclosure costs, and the wide possibilities of borrowing which existed in the eighteenth-century countryside, are all recently-established considerations which collectively must throw great doubt on the supposed grounds for the collapse of the 'yeomen'.[2] Of course, there were undoubtedly *some* enclosures which brought about rapid changes in the farming system, the structure of ownership, the size of farms, and in employment. The extent of these changes was largely determined by local or regional circumstances, particularly those of soil, availability of waste lands, and the most profitable use of the land. But it seems unlikely that the changes unfavourable to the small peasantry which were the results of enclosure in some areas, were the typical consequences of enclosure in general.

The effects of enclosure on the labouring population, however, are perhaps more disputable. On the side of loss we have the enclosure of commons and the possibility that increased areas of permanent pasture caused local unemployment. But between 1760 and 1815, when the bulk of Parlimanetary enclosures were carried out, market considerations make it likely that much more of the newly-enclosed land went under the plough than down to grass, and Clapham pointed out a generation ago the fallacy in thinking that every labourer lost a cow, or indeed lost anything at all of much value when the commons were enclosed. It is even more fallacious to visualize the creation of an agricultural proletariat as

---

[1] See Mingay, 'Size of Farms,' Habakkuk, 'English Landownership,' and further references in fn. 1, p. 17.

[2] W. E. Tate, 'Opposition to Parliamentary Enclosure,' 'Parliamentary Counter Petitions,' and 'The Cost of Parliamentary Enclosure in England (with special reference to Oxfordshire),' *Economic History Review*, V, No. 2 (1952), 258–65.

dating from the Enclosure Acts, for even in 1690, as Clapham again noted, there were already nearly two landless labourers to every occupier, and in 1831 still only a proportion of two and a half to one.[1] Finally, in one of the most important contributions of recent years, J. D. Chambers has examined the connections between rural employment, migration, enclosure and population growth. His main conclusions are that enclosure greatly increased employment by expanding the area under cultivation and by extending the growing of labour-absorbing crops like turnips and the legumes; the total numbers employed in farming were rising, but it was the more rapid growth of population which created the surplus of labour from which the industrial labour force was drawn.[2]

The effect of all this new work on enclosure compels us to reassess its significance in modern agricultural history. The early twentieth-century generation of historians over-estimated its importance, first because both before and since Marx it had loomed large in the story of agricultural change; secondly, because it provided a ready-made explanation of changes that were not otherwise easily explicable; and lastly, perhaps, because the readily accessible material in Enclosure Acts and Awards made it an easy and obvious subject to study. It must be conceded that the far more complex picture which we now have lacks the unity of the old one, as it lacks also its appeal of monolithic simplicity; but the modern explanation bears much more the appearance of truth and historical probability. It is of course in the nature of history that the evidence produced by more detailed investigation of a wider range of sources will tend eventually to overthrow the more conjectural assessments of an earlier generation. Indeed, in view of the great volume of new evidence now in print it is remarkable that the romantic attraction of the traditional story should remain so durable. But then we have still to find our new Ernle and our new Hammonds.

V

What remains of the traditional Agricultural Revolution? Mainly, the still remarkable fact that even in 1870, when the population had grown to become some five times as large as it was in 1700, 80 per cent of the people could still be fed from home-produced food—from land cultivated by only 14 per cent of the labour force. The implications of this for industrial development and economic growth are evident and need not be laboured. This striking increase in agricultural output resulted, in brief, from greatly improved farming methods applied to a considerably in-

---

[1] Clapham, *Economic History of Modern Britain*, Vol. I, pp. 113–21.

[2] J. D. Chambers, 'Enclosure and Labour Supply in the Industrial Revolution,' *Economic History Review*, V, No. 3 (1953), 322–4. This supplements the point made by Redford in his *Labour Migration in England* (1926), pp. 59–60, that the migration of labour from the countryside into the towns was responsive more to the state of industrial employment than to agricultural conditions.

creased farm acreage, the major part of the land being cultivated in fairly large units under a system of landownership and management, which despite some failings, nevertheless encouraged a heavy investment of capital and achieved a high degree of efficiency. Does this amount to 'agricultural revolution'? The full development of this varied, intricate and highly productive system of agriculture took much longer to evolve than we used to think; this is the main lesson of the new evidence. Nevertheless, if we consider the enormous magnitude of the change and the complexity of its diverse advance—rather than merely the time-period involved—we may yet come to think that 'agricultural revolution' should not be relegated to the historians' lumber room of discarded terminology.

POSTSCRIPT

On a re-reading of this essay (written in 1962) there appear only one or two minor changes of emphasis or detail that I would now make. In fact, the materials on which it was based are expanded and brought more nearly up to date in J. D. Chambers and G. E. Mingay, *The Agricultural Revolution, 1750–1880* (1966). It would be true to say, however, that while it has been possible in the space of a volume to elaborate considerably the views expressed above, they have been but little modified. The two most significant changes of emphasis concern the early and final phases of the 'agricultural revolution': recent research makes it possible to trace back more positively convertible husbandry and other evidence of improved agricultural output to the sixteenth century and late Middle Ages; at the other end of the story the degree of technical perfection, variety, and flexibility achieved in the period of 'high farming' may now be more thoroughly demonstrated.

G. E. MINGAY

January 1967

THE LAND MARKET
IN THE NINETEENTH CENTURY

F. M. L. Thompson

THE LAND MARKET IN THE NINETEENTH CENTURY

By F. M. L. THOMPSON

THE nineteenth century witnessed the establishment or full development of organized markets for every variety of commodity, of money market and capital market, even of some semblance of a labour market. A land market alone seemed to remain persistently, obstinately, absent. Its absence was felt as a matter of organization and institutions. 'Where is the so-called "Property Market"?—and what of its quotations?' wrote a contributor to the *Estates Gazette* in 1895, having in mind an analogy with a commodity market as a particular place in which prices were made that governed dealings in that commodity.[1] Its absence was felt as an affront to harmony and symmetry, a nagging flaw in the perfection of the structure of markets which seemed to translate the theory of the self-regulating economy into the practice of impersonal allocation of resources to the economically most efficient use. Its absence was felt by some to be a social as well as an economic evil, a reflection of an artificially restricted circulation of land which produced the socially and politically undesirable, perhaps dangerous, effect of preventing a wide distribution of landed property among the middle and lower classes.[2]

It is plain that no national land market existed in the sense that the London Stock Exchange, the Mark Lane corn market, or the Liverpool cotton market existed. The press, daily and weekly, could locate the other markets and produce its reports of the level of activity and the ruling prices of money, securities, wheat, meat, cotton, indigo, and so on; it could not find the land market, in general it only began to carry real estate intelligence in the last quarter of the century, and it could not produce the ruling price of land. It is simple to state the reasons for this.

The amount of land changing hands by buying and selling was never sufficiently large to make possible the great specialization in function in dealing and jobbing, and the continuous transaction of business, which are essential features of a highly developed market. Land lacks uniformity of quality; it cannot be leased or sold by sample, one acre is not as good as another. Not only does the value of land depend on a variety of local and individual qualities of geology, climate, situation, and accessibility, but also the value put upon it varies with the tastes and interests of individual prospective possessors. By no means all competitors for land

---

[1] 'The Property Market, by an Old Hand', *Estates Gazette*, 5 Jan. 1895, p. 19.
[2] These opinions were common currency among contemporary law reformers, economists, liberals, and radicals who concerned themselves with the free trade in land issue.

look on it as a factor to be employed in production of one sort or another; many, perhaps at times most, value it for the fulfilment of non-economic satisfactions, social security, social advancement, or political influence. In such a situation it is difficult to visualize a dominant central market with the function of allocating resources not between competing uses differing only in degree, but between competing uses and satisfactions differing in kind. London might absorb much business, but in the nature of things local and personal land markets remained important means of transfer, and the centralized market could not emerge.

However, even if market institutions were imperfect or rudimentary, something like a market in the economists' sense might exist if general influences produced general effects on the level of land transfers. Technical writers agreed that the price of land was uniform and moved regularly in response to the price of Consols, though this faith was somewhat undermined by the end of the century.[1] They did not argue from price to the amount of business being done. The land reformers were concerned with showing that there were artificial, legal restrictions on the supply of land for sale, and to a lesser extent on the demand for land, and denied that there was a fluctuating and therefore at least partially free market in land. Sir John Clapham accepted their view in stating that 'the land was not effectively mobilised,' at least before the 1880's.[2]

The intention of this article is to examine the level of land transfers in the nineteenth century in an attempt to establish the long-period movements in the amount of land sold. Fluctuations in land sales do not in themselves prove that the market was freely open to economic influences. If they were produced mainly by alterations in the conditions of supply, such as the Settled Land Act of 1882 which empowered life tenants to sell settled estates, they might prove the opposite. The second object, therefore, is to suggest the probable reasons for these fluctuations.

No official, compulsory registration of all land sales was ever established in England, such as makes possible in principle a firm statistical basis for the study of land turnover in Scotland, France, Belgium, and most other civilized countries. In its absence we can only attempt to reconstruct a picture of the volume of land transfers from less direct evidence. Apart from such literary evidence as is readily applicable, use is here made of two statistical series, the yield from the auction duty and the figures

[1] Nathaniel Kent, *Hints to Gentlemen of Landed Property* (1793 ed.), p. 267; David Low, *On Landed Property and the Economy of Estates* (1844), p. 29; Francis Cross, *Landed Property: its Sale, Purchase, Improvement and General Management* (1857), p. 68; *Transactions of the Institution of Surveyors*, xxii, 1889/90, pp. 5–7.

[2] Sir J. H. Clapham, *An Economic History of Modern Britain, 1850–1886*, ii, p. 254. The paradoxical statement that 'land came rather freely into the market' is however contained in the same paragraph.

compiled by the Estate Exchange. Both are a good deal less than satisfactory, but they can be made to serve as indicators of the movements in land transfers, albeit rough ones, which are adequate for the purpose of establishing trends and for suggesting the order of magnitude of total sales.

The duty on sales by auction was imposed by Lord North in 1777, and continued until repealed by Peel in 1845. Throughout its life two rates of duty were levied: a lower rate on sales of land, tenements, houses, shares, annuities, reversionary interests in the public funds, ships, plate, and jewels; and a higher rate on sales of furniture, fixtures, pictures, books, horses, carriages, and all other goods and chattels. The introduction, from 1815 and 1817, of separate rates for auctions of home-grown wool and of imported foreign produce on its first sale, does not concern us. The Excise Inquiry in 1835 produced figures of the yield of the duty in every year from 1778 to 1833, broken down by countries and by categories, so that it is possible to reconstruct the total value of property in England paying the lower rate of auction duty.[1] Unfortunately it is not possible to continue the series up to 1845, since subsequent figures from the annual finance accounts, though broken down by countries, show only the total yield of auction duty from all classes of property and goods. It is abundantly clear from the 1835 analysis that there was no remotely constant relationship between the yields of the two main classes, and year-to-year variations in total amount sometimes even concealed opposite movements. Only an isolated and highly detailed analysis of auction duty receipts for 1840 is available to extend the series.[2] The figures are in Table I.

As this class of auction duty covered property other than land, it is necessary to estimate the amount of auction sales of shares, annuities, reversionary interests in the public funds, ships, and plate and jewels, which is included in the above totals. The excise authorities were unable to make this distinction, as they were entirely dependent in the collection of the duty on the aggregated accounts rendered to them by individual auctioneers. The Inquiry Commissioners in 1835, and all the witnesses examined, in fact assumed that this class was in practice almost exclusively concerned with auctions of real property. Some confirmation of this can be derived from the 1840 analysis, which showed both amounts on which duty was charged and amounts which were exempt because they were bought in and no sale was effected at the auction. Of the total bought in, plate and jewels formed 0·2 per cent., ships 1·5 per cent., and real property 98·3 per cent.: there is no reason why the ratios in actual sales should not have been roughly similar.[3] Corroboration of the

[1] *Twelfth Report from the Commissioners of Excise Inquiry (Auctions)*, P.P. 1835: xxx.
[2] *Accounts and Papers*, P.P. 1845: xxviii.   [3] Loc. cit., pp. 240–3.

Table I

Purchase money of lands, &c., on which auction duty was charged, by calendar years

	£'000		£'000		£'000
1778	503	1798	1,900	1818	3,748
79	737	99	2,198	19	3,771
80	861	1800	3,027	20	3,278
81	806	01	4,002	21	2,551
82	941	02	4,513	22	2,660
83	1,020	03	4,884	23	3,252
84	1,409	04	3,369	24	5,062
85	1,288	05	3,722	25	5,768
86	1,306	06	3,882	26	3,027
87	1,615	07	4,052	27	3,740
88	1,664	08	4,162	28	3,433
89	1,555	09	5,011	29	3,126
90	1,459	10	6,096	30	2,480
91	1,993	11	6,510	31	2,611
92	2,538	12	5,673	32	2,716
93	2,817	13	5,843	33	2,893
94	1,963	14	4,948	1840	4,229
95	2,318	15	3,727		
96	2,778	16	2,456		
97	2,341	17	3,201		

Quinquennial averages

	£		£
1780–4	1,007,890 p.a.	1810–14	5,814,230 p.a.
1785–9	1,485,910 p.a.	1815–19	3,380,957 p.a.
1790–4	2,154,293 p.a.	1820–4	3,361,353 p.a.
1795–9	2,307,565 p.a.	1825–9	3,819,150 p.a.
1800–4	3,959,504 p.a.	1830–3	2,675,364 p.a.
1805–9	4,166,193 p.a.		4 years only

relatively small amounts of shares, annuities, and reversions passing by auction is more conjectural. Analysis of auctioneers' advertisements in *The Times* in 1839 shows these to have formed about 5 per cent. of the total number. An analysis in the *Estates Gazette* in 1859 showed that all the non-landed items advertised by auctioneers formed between 7 and 10 per cent. of the total.[1] In the 4 years 1889–92 auction sales of shares, annuities, and reversions formed on average 4 per cent. by value of the total auction business recorded by the Estate Exchange.[2] To argue back from this evidence to the years of the auction duty, and to assume constancy of auction habits over such a long period, is risky. But until

[1] *Estates Gazette*, 1 Mar. 1859, p. 75.
[2] Ibid., 11 Jan. 1890, p. 31; 3 Jan. 1891, p. 7; 8 Jan. 1892, p. 35; 7 Jan. 1893, p. 13.

further evidence is forthcoming on the amount of auction sales of these goods and interests it seems reasonable to assume that at least 90 per cent. of the amounts in Table I represent sales of real estate. This 90 per cent. is of course made up of sales of land and sales of houses, and between these two it is impossible to distinguish.

However, before accepting the auction figures as a chart of activity in the real estate market, there are two further vital but elusive factors to consider. First, what was the relation between figures of purchase money and actual quantities of property sold? Secondly, what was the relation between auction sales and total sales, and did it remain constant? The answer to the first question depends on movements in rents and in number of years' purchase; rises or falls in the totals of purchase money could be caused entirely by changes in these elements, with the number of houses and acreage of land passing remaining unchanged. For house rents and house prices no usable evidence is available for the period 1778–1833. For land values we are in somewhat better case. Between 1778 and 1815 agricultural rents perhaps doubled: this was the experience in Norfolk; the increase was rather smaller in Northumberland, about the same in Yorkshire, and rather greater in Durham and Shropshire.[1] Between 1816 and 1833 rents fell, perhaps by 10 per cent. on average, with a low point in the first 2 or 3 years of the 1820's, and with some areas showing no overall decline at all.[2]

Tentative as must be any reliance on these measurements of the magnitude of rent movements, in the case of variations in the number of years' purchase commonly given we cannot do much more than indicate the directions of the movements. Arthur Young in 1812 produced a table of land prices with precise figures of years' purchase: 1768–73, 32 years' purchase; 1778–89, $23\frac{1}{4}$; 1792–9, 27; 1805–11, 28.[3] He does not specify his sources, nor tell us what steps, if any, were taken to eliminate the exceptionally high or low figures which could be produced by under-renting—an unusual residential or estate element in value—or over-renting, in any particular sale. Nevertheless this is probably a reliable picture of the direction of movement, though not of its amplitude: the fall in the American War and the following decade was probably smaller, the rise in

[1] For Norfolk, R. A. C. Parker, 'Coke of Norfolk and the Agrarian Revolution', *Econ. Hist. Rev.*, 2nd ser. viii, p. 157. For Northumberland, *Alnwick MSS.*, Audit Accounts. I am indebted to His Grace the Duke of Northumberland for permission to work at Alnwick on many occasions. For Durham and Shropshire, *Raby MSS.*, Estate Accounts. I am indebted to Lord Barnard for permission to consult these records. For Yorkshire, *Fitzwilliam MSS.*, Estate Accounts. I am indebted to Earl Fitzwilliam and the Trustees of the Fitzwilliam Settled Estates for permission to use these records.

[2] R. J. Thompson, 'An Inquiry into the Rent of Agricultural Land in England and Wales in the 19th century', *J.R. Stat. Soc.* lxx. 1907; and MSS. sources as in previous footnote.

[3] Arthur Young, *An Enquiry into the Progressive Value of Money in England* (1812), p. 99. Dr. L. S. Pressnell drew my attention to this work.

the Revolutionary and Napoleonic Wars probably greater. Other sources at any rate indicate a higher rate as usual during the Napoleonic Wars, up to 35 years' purchase of existing rents. This is what we would expect, when rents were expected to go on rising and when small farmers were anxious to purchase their holdings as opportunities offered. After 1815 there was a decline, so that by the early thirties 26 to 28 years' purchase seems to have been normal.[1]

This information is not sufficiently clear, detailed, or reliable to warrant any attempt at refined statistical manipulation of the auction duty figures to convert totals of purchase money into numbers of acres sold. It is apparent that the increase in average annual purchase money between 1780–4 and 1810–14 exaggerates the increase in acreage sold, and that the decrease in purchase money after 1815 exaggerates the decrease in acreage sold. If we were to assume that the ratio between house property sold by auction and total sales of real estate by auction did not vary much in the period 1780–1833, then it would seem roughly true that the number of acres of land sold by auction doubled between 1780–9 and 1810–14, the increase in activity being steady after 1790 and rapid after 1800. After 1815 there was a sudden and marked drop in the area of land sold in the period 1815–19, but there was perhaps a recovery between 1820 and 1829 with the acreage being sold by auction little below the level of the last years of the war, a decisive decline to about two-thirds of that level coming only after 1830. Even the war-time peak represented a very modest volume of land transfers by auction; at the outside, making no allowance at all for sales of house property, not more than 170,000 acres a year were sold between 1810 and 1814; the actual amount might have been as little as half this.[2]

The relation between auction sales and total sales cannot be established with any confidence. If the estimate of a leading conveyancer, James Humphreys, was to be believed, that in 1825 the yield of stamp duties on land transfers was £440,000 at an average rate of 1¼ per cent. *ad valorem*, giving a total purchase money for the year of £35 million,[3] it would make auction sales form about one-tenth of all sales. If on the other hand, the estimate of the Stamp Office is accepted, from its 'account of stamps for

---

[1] *S.C. on the State of Agriculture*, P.P. 1833: v, current land values contrasted with war-time values, pp. 51, 70, 82, 94, 107, 109, 167, 278, 437. *Alnwick MSS.* contains some evidence on land values, especially post-1815. Norton, Trist, and Gilbert's letter 'A Century of Land Values', *The Times*, 20 Apr. 1889, p. 11, shows, when averaged over 5-year periods, a decline from 32 years' purchase 1800–14, to a low point of 23 years' purchase 1830–9: it does not however show any rise between 1781 and 1800.

[2] Taking £35 per acre as a modest price for 1810–14; cf. 'A Century of Land Values'. In a later period of peak auction sales, that of the 1870's, land sales formed about 50 per cent. of total sales, by value: Estate Exchange reports, *v. infra*, Table III.

[3] James Humphreys, *Observations on the Actual State of the English Laws of Real Property* (1826), p. 204.

conveyances issued . . . so far as the same can be made up' for the years 1816–24, the picture is radically altered. These figures of stamp receipts, converted at the same rate of a 1¼ per cent. average duty, show total annual purchase moneys of between £4,314,720 in 1816 and £6,080,640 in 1824.[1] This would make auction sales more than one-half of all sales. These were the lower and upper limits. The first was too low, since Humphreys was almost certainly inflating the amount of land transfers by taking an estimate of the duty on all transactions relating to land, including mortgages and leases, as though it related to sales alone. The second was too high, since in view of the large amount of property which went to auction, was bought in, and subsequently sold privately, it implies that nearly all land eventually sold was in the first instance offered at auction, a palpable absurdity. Further than this we cannot go.

It is, however, clear that the relation between auction sales and total sales varied. The witnesses heard by the Excise Commissioners agreed not only that 1810–13 and 1824–5 had been high times for land sales, but also that the number of actual sales of land by auction had been decreasing since the war. That is, of the total advertised and put up for auction, a smaller proportion than formerly was actually sold, and a larger proportion was bought in. The reason was held to be a desire to avoid payment of auction duty: an estate would be put up to auction in order to find out its market value, it would be bought in just above the final bid, and would then be sold by private contract. This check on successful auctions had not operated in war-time because competition for land was then such that bidders at auctions were not willing to run the risk of failing to be the purchasers simply for the sake of avoiding duty.[2]

In 1840 less than one-third of the real estate offered by auction was actually sold, and if this was typical of the situation in the auction duty period it contrasted quite strongly with the half which the *Estates Gazette* persuaded itself was the normal proportion between sales and offerings 20 years later.[3] We may accept that the witnesses in 1834 stated the facts correctly: their explanation of them was probably astray. A similar marked increase in the number of abortive auctions was noticed in the 1890's, when there was no auction duty to account for it, and in 1892 less than a quarter of the acreage offered at auction was sold.[4] This seems in other words to have been a characteristic of periods in which

---

[1] *Accounts and Papers*, P.P. 1825: xxi, p. 325. The Stamp Office never again ventured on such an apparently precise return of conveyancing stamps, not surprisingly since it possessed no means of distinguishing between the variety of purposes for which stamps of similar denominations were required.
[2] *Twelfth Report from the Commissioners of Excise Inquiry*, app.'s 16, 24, 26, and 27.
[3] *Accounts and Papers*, P.P. 1845: xxviii; *Estates Gazette*, 15 Feb. 1860, p. 58; 15 Mar. 1861, p. 101.
[4] *Estates Gazette*, 7 Jan. 1893, p. 12; 6 Jan. 1894, pp. 9, 13; 12 Sept. 1896, p. 387.

the outlook for agriculture and agricultural land values was depressed and uncertain. A seller would go to auction with a reserve price based on a more or less conventional idea of the value of his estate. In buoyant times an optimistic view of the prospects of rent increases and capital appreciation could easily carry biddings beyond the reserve. In uncertain times, however, the reserve was not readily adjusted to prevailing lack of confidence in the future, since no seller would be inclined to accept great sacrifices in advance of their being proved necessary, with the result that prospective purchasers found property overvalued. An abortive auction gave both the owner who was prepared to go on with a sale, and prospective purchasers, an idea of the price on which realistic negotiations could be conducted, and helped to establish contact between them. In times of depression the auction machinery became a means of testing the state of the market as much as a means of effecting actual bargains.

If after 1815 the share of auction sales in total land sales fell, and that of private treaty sales rose, it follows that the volume of land transfers in the 1820's must have been well above the war-time peak. This is what one would expect as deflationary pressure forced those with high fixed charges based on war-time values to unload their property on to the market, and it is consistent with such printed and documentary evidence as is available.[1] Such a spate of land sales, if it existed, did not however show in the stamp duty receipts. Although it is highly probable that falls in the stamp yields of other components in the mixed bag of 'deeds and other instruments' could mask a rise in the yield on conveyances, the fact that the total yield of the category shows a steady annual decline from a peak in 1809 to a trough in 1832 must mean that any such masked rise could not have been very substantial.[2] Indeed the outside estimate of the yield of stamp duties on conveyances, by James Humphreys, assuming the average fee simple value to be as low as £35 an acre, means that not more than one million acres of land were passing by sale in a year; that was a flood of land transfers only in a relative sense, since it represented a rate of turnover of the land of England below the level of once per generation which many regarded as the theoretically desirable minimum.[3]

---

[1] *S.C. on State of Agriculture*, 1833: v, p. x; *Alnwick MSS., Fitzwilliam MSS., Ridley MSS.*; and the *Ashburton MSS.* in the Hampshire Record Office, Winchester, all show considerable purchasing activity in this period. I am indebted to Viscount Ridley for permission to use his records at Blagdon Hall, Seatonburn, Northumberland. Curiously enough a prominent auctioneer, Alexander Rainy, expected a flood of land sales 'owing to the incumbrances and charges which were created during the period of agricultural prosperity and an extended currency and credit' to occur in the few years after 1834, whereas it is likely that this flood was by then over. He was, however, concerned to marshal arguments against the auction duty: *Twelfth Report from the Commissioners of Excise Inquiry*, app. 26.

[2] *13th Report of the Commissioners of Inland Revenue*, with some retrospective history, P.P. 1870: xx, p. 121.

[3] James Stewart, *On the Means of Facilitating the Transfer of Land* (1848), pp. 82–84.

The auction duty figures suggest that the volume of land transfers turned downward in the early 1830's, and there is some suggestion that from then until the end of the 1840's the land market was generally slack and dull, with one bright interval of revived business in 1838–41. Witnesses in 1846 spoke of land, in this period, being 'rather an unsaleable article', of a particular depression in values in 1835–7, and of the small quantity of land which came into the market. Certainly purchasing activity on the Duke of Northumberland's estate declined markedly.[1]

Some contemporaries argued that the stamp duty figures showed that the traffic in land was decreasing. In fact the figures for receipts of duties on deeds and other instruments included the duties on transfers of stocks and shares (though Bank of England, South Sea, and government stocks were exempt), the duties on patents until 1854, and the duties on bonds, bills of lading, and articles of clerkship and solicitors' admissions, among the more important revenue-yielding, non-landed items. Among the instruments relating to real property which were subject to stamp duties, leases, mortgages, and settlements of capital sums though not of land itself, were included alongside conveyances. Movements in the total yield of this heterogeneous category are therefore impossible to interpret, and cannot be made to show anything. The best-informed contemporary, the secretary to the Board of Stamps and Taxes, confessed himself quite unable to tell how many stamps were used for conveyances, and would only venture the opinion that out of a total yield of £1,646,000 for deeds and other instruments in 1844 'it appears true that the sum paid for stamps on conveyances of real property are a very small proportion'.[2]

The most that can be said is that the stamp duty figures, falling until 1832, fluctuating around this low level until 1837, rising somewhat in 1838–40, falling back again, rising sharply in 1844–5 and then falling fairly slowly back to the low level of the 1830's by 1850, are consistent with the idea that this 20-year period was one of relative stagnation in land transfers. The number of dutiable transfers of stocks and shares must have been increasing in this period, in view of railway activity, and the generally static to declining total stamp yields of the period can only have accommodated this increase by showing decreases in other components.

In explanation of this apparent stagnation, one can argue that on the supply side the flood of forced sales of the post-war years had dried up, and on the demand side that agricultural depression followed by uncertainty

---

[1] *S.C. of H. of L. on Burdens on Real Property*, P.P. 1846: vi, part i; Baker Q 504, 511; Clutton Q 5619; Davy Q 7428–9. See my unpublished thesis, 'The Economic and Social Background of the English Landed Interest, 1840–70', Bodleian Library Oxford, 1956, ch. iii.

[2] Stewart, op. cit., p. 89, and *The Spectator*, 26 Feb. 1848. *S.C. on Burdens on Real Property*, Pressly Q 7022.

over the future course of rents engendered by the corn law controversy discouraged purchasers. Confidence returned after 1850 as agricultural rents began to rise, from 1853 at least; expectations of further rises and competition to purchase land, mainly from the new rich, combined to push up land prices from the 23 to 27 years' purchase of the 1830's and 1840's to the 35 to 40 years' purchase of the late 1860's and early 1870's;[1] it became attractive to sell land, and there are several signs that the volume of land transfers began to move upwards, reaching a peak in the early 1870's, which was possibly the highest in the century.

The 1850's saw the establishment of several journals dealing exclusively or in large part with the property market. To some extent this was undoubtedly a response to the progressive abolition of press taxation. For instance the expansion of a column in the *Law Times* into an independent weekly, the *Journal of Auctions*, in 1853, was specifically attributed to the repeal of the advertisement and supplement duties.[2] Another, the *Freeholder*, was founded in 1850 for political rather than fiscal reasons, to support the freehold land society movement. In the case of the *Freehold Land Times*, established in 1854, and the *Estates Gazette*, established in 1858, the fiscal impulse seems from the dating to have been muted. On the whole there seems to have been a fairly widespread feeling that there was a need for a specialized advertising medium for real estate, and for some attempt to provide regular property market reports. That this feeling arose when it did seems to imply that there was heightened activity in the land market, calling for alterations and improvement in its machinery.

The most notable departure in land market organization, however, and one that was definitely an attempt to replace the characteristic personal relationships and informal arrangements of land marketing by an impersonal institution more suited to an expanding traffic, was the establishment of the Estate Exchange in 1857. This was formed by a group of London auctioneers with the dual object of providing an institution to regulate the affairs of the profession, safeguard its legal and fiscal interests, and enhance its standing, and of providing a medium for bringing buyers and sellers together. The initial step was to set up registers of property for sale, and of property sold, so that agents from all over the country could find information on what was in the market, and on the state of the market, assembled in one office. The further intention was to develop the exchange on stock exchange lines so that it should become an actual market, the place in which the bulk of the country's real estate business was concentrated, run by brokers and jobbers who would be the obvious

---

[1] See my unpublished thesis, ch. iv; *The Economist*, xxviii, 16 July 1870, pp. 880–1; Norton, Trist, and Gilbert, 'A Century of Land Values', 1889.

[2] *Journal of Auctions*, 6 Aug. 1853, p. 1. It survived until 1856.

resort of buyers and sellers of property in preference to advertisements in the press, and who would specialize out into separate sub-markets for home lands, home houses, Irish lands, colonial lands, and mortgages, as business expanded.[1]

The idea of such an exchange, with a register of all properties which were for sale and a monthly publication carrying their particulars, had first been suggested by Rainy, one of the leading London auctioneers, in 1838.[2] That the idea was not realized until 1857 again suggests a contrast between the land market conditions of the two periods, and an upsurge of activity in the fifties. The further development of the Estate Exchange, from an office keeping a register into a market more akin to its title, never took place, because the size of the business and its inherent character did not justify it. But the registers were established and maintained, recording reports from a fairly wide range of auctioneers and estate agents, both members and non-members of the institution, and they were held to provide the profession with a valuable service, particularly in assisting accurate valuation.[3]

Unfortunately for the historian these new departures of the fifties did not leave behind them such informative evidence as might have been expected. Of the land market journals the *Freeholder* survived for two years only, the *Journal of Auctions* for three. The *Freehold Land Times* was long-lived, becoming in turn the *Land and Building News* and the *Building News*, but it retained an active interest in the land market for only three years, after which it settled down as a paper devoted to architecture, building, and civil engineering. During those 3 years a diary of forthcoming sales and a report of the results of auctions were regular features, but nothing much is to be learnt from the stray facts that some 118,000 acres were announced for sale in 1854 and some 190,000 acres in 1856, or that details of the actual sale of some 38,000 acres were reported during 1854.[4]

The *Estates Gazette* alone survived, and survives, with its original purpose unbroken. In its early years it carried intermittent editorials discussing the previous year's experience in the land market, but these ceased after 1864, and for the remainder of the career of its first proprietor, Henry Allnutt, it was essentially a paper of advertisements, carrying a slender load of

---

[1] The Estate Exchange, 155 Queen Victoria Street, E.C.4, possesses some useful printed material, including the weekly *Index to the Estate Exchange Registers*, published from 1868, which is not in the British Museum; it has no documentary material beyond the manuscript property registers. *Building News*, iii, 27 Feb. 1857, pp. 207–8; *The Times*, 6 Feb. 1857, p. 8; *The Economist*, xv, 10 Jan. 1857, p. 35.

[2] Alexander Rainy, 'Transfer of Real Property', 1828, *University College London, Hume Tracts*, 2nd ser., cxlviii.

[3] *Estates Gazette*, 1 Feb. 1859, p. 41; 8 Aug. 1866, p. 389; 28 June 1871, p. 295.

[4] Information supplied to the *Freehold Land Times* in 1854 and to the *Land and Building News* in 1856 by some 350 auctioneers, and totalled from the fortnightly reports.

articles reprinted from the daily and weekly press, but without a voice of its own. In 1879, under the pressure of 'a very gloomy view of the state of the land market', editorial comment was revived,[1] and from 1885 an analysis of the year's operations became a regular annual feature, providing a continuous series for the literary, though not statistical, assessment of the market.

The Estate Exchange similarly began life with a burst of activity followed by an interval of quiescence. For its first three years it produced figures of the amount of business reported to it from the London auction rooms, distinguishing the total value of property sold and bought in, but not distinguishing between the types of property involved:

	Offered	Sold	Bought in
	£	£	£
1858	8,478,297	3,440,665	5,037,632
59	6,115,492	2,860,509	3,254,983
60	6,475,273	3,062,453	3,412,820[2]

This service ceased with the production of figures for June 1861, the first half of 1861 showing business slightly less than in the first half of 1860, and was not resumed until 1871. From 1871 a continuous series of figures is available, representing the total value of property sold at the London Auction Mart and a small amount of private contract sales which auctioneers reported to the exchange. From 1896 a wider cover of sales was instituted, and the results tabulated under London sales, provincial sales, and private treaty sales. For eleven of the years between 1871 and 1896 a breakdown of these totals is available, showing the total proceeds of land sales and the acreage sold. For the remainder of that period, and for all years after 1896, only the annual grand totals are available, made up of sales of houses, ground rents, building sites, and miscellaneous properties such as public houses, reversions, shares, annuities, and boxes in the Albert Hall, as well as land sales. The series cannot, therefore, do more than provide a rough guide to probable trends in land transfers.

What proportion these figures formed of the business of the country as a whole it is extremely difficult to say. At the end of the fifties the *Estates Gazette* thought that the London sales recorded by the Estate Exchange amounted to half the total property sales in England and Wales, but this was only a guess not based on a great deal of information.[3] As late as 1891 the *Estates Gazette* still held to the view, a more experienced view than that of 1859, that London sales were not far short of half the total

---

[1] *Estates Gazette*, 1 Dec. 1879, p. 579.
[2] Ibid., 15 Feb. 1860, p. 58; 15 Mar. 1861, p. 101.
[3] Ibid., 1 Nov. 1859, p. 330.

Table II

Estate Exchange reports of real estate business

(i) 1871–95, annual totals of sales at the London Mart

	£'000		£'000
1871	5,769	1884	5,976
72	9,901	85	4,453
73	8,948	86	4,120
74	11,160	87	3,989
75	11,466	88	4,447
76	10,495	89	4,304
77	11,738	90	4,287
78	9,839	91	4,174
79	7,693	92	4,597
80	7,354	93	4,230
81	7,052	94	4,125
82	6,163	95	4,930
83	5,147		

(ii) 1896–1913, annual totals of sales at the London Mart and country and private treaty sales

	London mart £'000	Country £'000	Private treaty £'000	Total £'000
1896	4,476	3,972	2,105	10,554
97	5,257	5,598	1,349	12,205
98	6,674	5,372	1,316	13,363
99	6,290	4,385	1,677	12,353
1900	4,934	2,757	1,310	9,002
01	5,553	3,109	1,408	10,071
02	5,748	2,705	1,561	10,015
03	5,767	2,654	1,676	10,097
04	4,896	1,990	650	7,537
05	4,781	2,271	1,365	8,418
06	4,335	2,100	1,552	7,988
07	3,343	1,708	512	5,564
08	2,733	1,829	1,056	5,620
09	2,782	2,230	1,331	6,344
10	2,279	2,547	867	5,694
11	2,623	4,508	1,265	8,397
12	2,554	4,698	1,836	9,089
13	2,345	4,039	2,188	8,574

Sources: *Index to the Estate Exchange Register*; *The Times*; *Estates Gazette*; *Land*.

sales. 'The total of sales recorded at the Estate Exchange is merely an index to, not a record of, business done in the land market.... The offices of solicitors having important conveyancing practice are in themselves a

Table III

Estate Exchange reports of sales of land other than building sites

	Total sales reported £'000	Land sales reported £'000	Acreage sold
1871	5,769	3,225	76,356
72	9,901	6,596	119,054
75	11,466	4,969	95,894
85	4,453	986	31,070
89	4,304	1,172	22,863
90	4,287	1,231	29,939
91	4,174	739	17,518
92	4,597	755	15,518
94	4,125	283	11,518
95	4,930	683	36,291
96	10,554	2,327	77,696

Sources: *The Times*; *Estates Gazette*; *Transactions of the Institution of Surveyors*.

medium of transfer at figures probably in excess of all the public business recorded at the Auction Mart.'[1] Two years later it noted that London sales were a smaller proportion than usual of the total turnover of the property market, owing to a rise in private treaty business, without however guessing what this lower proportion might be.[2]

For the early 1890's the *Estates Gazette* itself contained the evidence that London's share of total land sales was definitely less than a half. For 1890–2 an addition was made of all the land sales, whether by auction or by private treaty, which had been reported in the paper during the year. The results for England were:

	Value of land sales £'000	Acreage sold
1890	3,338	74,591
91	2,106	49,592
92	2,556	53,254[3]

This appears to show that sales at the London Mart were an annually diminishing proportion of all land sales, a development which the trend visible between 1911 and 1913 in the second part of Table II also suggests as a possibility for that period. This could have been due to a redistribution of business within London, a diversion of auctions from the public rooms of the Mart to the private, mainly West End, sale rooms of the larger firms; but this seems to have been a later development. On the whole it

---

[1] *Estates Gazette*, 2 Jan. 1892, p. 5.   [2] Ibid., 6 Jan. 1894, p. 13.
[3] Ibid., 17 Jan. 1891, p. 49; 30 Jan. 1892, p. 97; 28 Jan. 1893, p. 74.

seems that with the break in land values after 1878 a more pronounced change came over the structure of the land market. The outside buyers, who had dealt through London, investing in social position through large estate purchase, became less prominent; the local buyers, farmers, landowners, local business and professional men, to whom it was natural to deal in the local market, relatively more prominent. To the seller the conditions of strong competition to purchase land in the late sixties and early seventies had made it worth while going to London to get the best prices; the collapse of this competition diminished the advantages of London as a market, and the seller tended to revert to selling on his own door-step. The *Estates Gazette* saw in the experience of 1905 indications of a 'slow tendency towards greater diffusion of sales' away from London.[1] In 1913 well over £6,000,000 worth of land was reported as sold, and London's share of this was at most one-third, and in view of the importance of house property sales at the Mart, was almost certainly not more than one-sixth.[2]

The figures for 1890–2 suggest that the decline in London's control of the land market was then already under way. That such a decline is not apparent in the wider Estate Exchange coverage after 1896, which shows London doing a steady half of the business of the prosperous years 1896–1903, seems to be due to the varying proportion which land sales bore to the total sales covered by the Estate Exchange reports. Thus in the 3 years 1911–13 land sales accounted for 58 per cent. of the total property sales recorded, while in 1896 they formed only 22 per cent. of the total. While houses, ground rents, and other types of real property in which London retained its place formed the major part of the year's business, any decline in London's share in land dealings was masked.

In 1890–2 sales of land at the London Mart formed a third or rather more than a third both by value and by acreage of the total land sales reported in the *Estates Gazette*. There is of course no means of telling what percentage of the land sales that actually took place in England managed to get reported in the *Estates Gazette*. One is groping in the dark, but if it is assumed that the *Estates Gazette* was reasonably well served with reports of land sales in the home counties, it is possible to gauge very roughly the bias its reports may have shown in omitting a proportion of provincial sales. Sales reported in Berkshire, Buckinghamshire, Essex, Hertfordshire, Kent, Middlesex, and Surrey formed some 28 per cent. of the total area reported as sold, and a rather higher percentage of the total value owing to the high prices given, particularly for land in Surrey. These same counties constitute about 13 per cent. of the total land area of England.

---

[1] Ibid., 6 Jan. 1906, pp. 20–21.
[2] Ibid., 4 Jan. 1913, p. 14, compared with 3 Jan. 1914, p. 14.

One would expect a higher rate of turnover of land in the home counties than in the rest of England, though not perhaps so much as double the rate, which is what these percentages imply. The omission of provincial sales would not therefore appear to have been of overwhelming proportions, and if one assumes that as much land again escaped the net of the *Estates Gazette* as was caught by it, any error is probably on the generous side.

Doubling the *Estates Gazette* figures for 1890–2 means that land sales at the London Mart were then about one-sixth of total English land sales. The preceding argument suggests that this proportion had been greater before 1878, perhaps one-fifth. In that case the volume of land transfers in the peak period for which there are figures, the early 1870's, was perhaps at the rate of 500,000 to 600,000 acres a year. At the low point in the series, 1894, it seems that well under 100,000 acres changed hands; and in any year between 1885 and 1896, indeed as far as one can tell in any year between 1885 and 1911, it is unlikely that as much as 200,000 acres was sold.

This peak rate indicates a low velocity of land circulation. It is, however, consistent with Norton, Trist, and Gilbert's estimate that there were '18 million acres of what may be called marketable land . . . which once a generation, or at the most in every two generations, comes into the market and changes hands.'[1] An annual turnover in the range of 300,000 acres to 600,000 acres was what experienced auctioneers regarded as normal for the period before 1880 to which their figures referred.

If Norton's belief was correct, that if the figures of the firm's business were averaged over 5-year periods they would provide a fairly accurate index to the behaviour of the land market as a whole, it is possible that this peak of the early 1870's was not the summit of the entire period, 1778–1914, which is under review. Such averages show that the average annual proceeds of land sales in 1870–4 were the highest in the 100 years (1781–1880) covered by the firm's statistics. But the average annual acreage sold in 1870–4 was exceeded in the decades 1820–9 and 1855–64, even if one disregards what was obviously a single very large sale of inferior land in 1827. In the intervening years the acreage sold was down to half the 1870–4 level in 1830–4 and 1840–4, three-quarters in 1850–4, and nine-tenths in 1835–9 and 1845–9.[2] Since the business of this single firm, though it was large by comparison with that of other firms, probably did not constitute more than 2 per cent. of the total business of the country, no more should be read into these results than some confirmation of the existence of a boom in land transfers in the 1820's, a decline from 1830, and an upward movement from the middle 1850's.

[1] 'A Century of Land Values', *The Times*, 20 Apr. 1889, p. 11.
[2] Loc. cit.

Whatever proportion the Estate Exchange figures formed of the business of the country as a whole, informed contemporaries were satisfied that those figures were a reliable index to the state of the property market.[1] The figures were compiled on a consistent year-to-year basis, with a break in 1896. Though over long periods, in so far as the efficiency of the Estate Exchange was increasing, and its net was being spread wider, its figures would exaggerate upward and minimize downward movements. Treated as such, the trends shown in Table II indicate a fairly close correspondence between movements in the real estate market and what is known of the building cycle.[2] A boom getting under way in the early 1870's, attaining a sustained high level of activity between 1874 and 1877, breaking during 1878 and ushering in a prolonged depression; beginning to revive about 1895, reaching a peak in 1898 but maintaining a fairly high turnover until a sharp break after the end of 1903; then falling and remaining low until a revival began to show in 1911. This picture shows a closer correlation with the Glasgow than with the London building cycle, except that there is no sign of a revival beginning in the early 1890's. It is perhaps significant that the figures for business done in London, though conforming to the rest of the pattern, do not show the revival from 1911. In the decade before 1914 the business done in London was increasingly composed of sales of London properties, houses, ground rents, and gas and water company stocks;[3] earlier it had contained a fair share of sales of provincial properties, principally land, and its movements had then conformed to the national trends.

The suggestion is that transfers of existing capital in the form of real estate kept pace with creations of fresh capital in the form of new houses. The connexion between transfers of existing houses and new construction was obviously mechanical as well as economic. Many purchasers of new houses were not taking their first step in house-ownership, but were improving their housing conditions by quitting older houses, which were thus thrown on the market. However, this process by itself would increase the quantity of existing houses in the market, without creating a demand for them. The evidence indicates that the periods in which the greatest quantities changed hands were the periods of highest prices.[4] In the case of land transfers no shuffling of owners caused by vacancies higher up the scale could produce the appearance of activity. In general, active transfers

[1] *Transactions of the Institution of Surveyors*, xxiii, 1890/1, presidential address by R. C. Driver, p. 2; *Estates Gazette*, 3 Jan. 1891, p. 12; 31 Dec. 1898, pp. 1132–3.
[2] A. K. Cairncross, *Home and Foreign Investment*, 1870–1913, ch. ii, pp. 12–36; E. W. Cooney, 'Capital Exports and Investment in Building in Britain and U.S.A. 1856–1914', *Economica*, n.s. xvi, 1949, pp. 347–54.
[3] *The Times*, 1 Jan. 1910, p. 12; 31 Dec. 1910, p. 4.
[4] *Estates Gazette*, 1 Jan. 1898, p. 19; 31 Dec. 1898, p. 1133; 30 Dec. 1899, p. 1124; 5 Jan. 1901, pp. 20–21.

of houses and land were not the result of active housing construction, but all three were responses to the same causes.

Doubtless the most acceptable explanation would be to see expansion of building, house and land transfers all as the reverse side of a capital exports cycle. But if the land transfer boom of the 1820's is to be fitted into a single analysis there is need for a more general explanation than this. Essentially the oscillation seems to have been between speculative investments offering prospects of high returns and safe investments with low but secure yields. Or, since falling agricultural rents from the 1880's somewhat impaired the security of the yield on land, we should restate the swing as being simply between more risky and less risky investments.

Contemporaries were aware of this process, though as an aberration rather than as a rhythm. 'To those who have been watching the falling market for the last eight or nine years', wrote an estate agent in 1889, 'and wondering how the British investor could turn aside, even temporarily, from the most stable of investments, and be lured, by the fallacious expectations of high profits and percentages, into putting his money into risky and unsound companies, the increase during the past year will come in fulfilment of an oft-disappointed expectation instead of a surprise.'[1] The *Estates Gazette*, searching for the symptoms of a revival in the land market in 1885, scented 'a readier disposition on the part of the investing public to deal in home securities, of which land is, and necessarily must be, the most important'. The revival did not come, and at the end of 1892 it was encouraging itself with the thought that the small investor was learning the superior security of bricks and mortar over wild-cat schemes. A year later it was still hoping that 'disenchantment with bubble schemes —and the experience of the Balfour swindle—will swing investors back to real property, at lower rates of return but higher security'.[2] In the second half of the nineteenth century it happened, of course, that most of the more risky investments were foreign stocks and ventures. However, it seems probable that the property market was moved not by changes in the geographical direction of investment as such, but by changes in security preferences.

The market in land itself was of course subject to its own special influences as well as to those which swayed the investment market in general. Among these the condition and prospects of agriculture were of greatest importance, legislation and fears of legislation affecting the political and fiscal position of landlords a secondary but well-publicized factor. Their effective operation seems to have been more through the demand for land than through the supply of land for sale.

---

[1] W. H. Daw to *The Times*, 5 Jan. 1889, p. 11.
[2] *Estates Gazette*, 9 May 1885, p. 160; 7 Jan. 1893, p. 12; 6 Jan. 1894, p. 13.

The peak in volume and value of land transfers was reached in the years just before the agricultural depression. This led to a dramatic and prolonged contraction in land sales. The recovery in the property market of 1896–9 was certainly felt in the land section, but continued uncertainty as to the future of agricultural land values made the revival in land transfers moderate, satisfactory only by comparison with the 20 lean years which preceded it.[1] Not until the 1900's was agriculture felt to have adjusted itself to its changed situation, and not until 1911–13, under what were regarded as exceptional circumstances, was it felt that the volume of land sales again approached the level of the seventies.

Other things being equal, we would expect the depression, with the falling rents and falling number of years' purchase which it brought, to have caused a decline in the value of land transfers. In addition the evidence of the figures and of the annual reports points unmistakably to a great drop in the amount of land sold: land was a drug in the market, unsaleable, the market was flat and dull and little business was done, the wording of the reports in the eighties and early nineties was monotonously regular.[2] This was in marked contrast to the experience of the post-1815 agricultural depression. We might expect similar causes, mortgagees becoming nervous over their security, and the scissors of fixed charges and falling incomes from land, to produce similar effects, a spate of forced sales and a flood of land transfers. That they did not do so calls for explanation.

There was an important difference in the supply of land in the two periods, and this was part of the explanation. After 1815 it was the small owners, particularly those who had purchased during the war, who were vulnerable and were forced to sell out. After 1878 there was no large body of recently established small owners to feel the squeeze; on the whole the land was in the hands of larger owners, less liable to distress sales, more capable of riding adversity. But this was only a small part of the answer. Everyone agreed that after 1878 there was an abundant supply of land for sale, as falling rents, mounting arrears, and accumulations of unlettable farms made it necessary or urgent for many owners to try to unload not entire estates, but parts of estates, on to the market. Moreover the potential supply of land was simultaneously increased by the passing of the 1882 Settled Land Act; under it, wrote the Duke of Marlborough in 1885, 'were there any effective demand for the purchase of land, half the land

---

[1] Ibid., 2 Jan. 1897, p. 19; 1 Jan. 1898, p. 19; 31 Dec. 1898, pp. 1132–3; 30 Dec. 1899, p. 1124.
[2] Ibid., 1 Dec. 1879, p. 579; 1 Jan. 1880, p. 5; 8 Jan. 1881, p. 5; 6 Jan. 1883, p. 5; 1 Jan. 1887, pp. 6–7; 5 Jan. 1889, p. 4; 17 Jan. 1891, p. 56; 7 Jan. 1893, p. 12; 6 Jan. 1894, p. 9; 5 Jan. 1895, p. 16; *The Times*, 3 Oct. 1885, p. 10; 14 Oct. 1887, p. 9; *The Estates Roll*, June 1881, p. 1; *Trans. Inst. of Surveyors*, xiii, 1880/1, pp. 7–8; xvi, 1883/4, pp. 8–9; xxii, 1889/90, pp. 5–7.

of England would be in the market tomorrow'.¹ Reduced land sales were the result of a failure in demand, not supply.

The collapse in the demand for land, and the great difficulties experienced in selling it, were caused by alarm and despondency over the future of agriculture. 'Scarcely anyone will venture on purchasing land, for it is impossible to know what is looming in the future; buyers at present are afraid of agricultural land; how can it be expected that land will be bought for an investment when it appears almost impossible to let farms; capitalists . . . mistrust the security which land offers in present circumstances in England.'² Presidential addresses to the Surveyors' Institution told the same tale. The Settled Land Act might be expected to produce a stir in the land market 'as soon as the future conditions of agriculture can be more clearly foreseen, and capitalists are in a position to judge what returns may confidently be reckoned upon from investments in land. Until that is more accurately determined, we shall probably look in vain for any great increase in the demand for land, and the market will be filled, as at present, with anxious owners, of whose offers to sell no heed is taken by capitalists.' 'Capitalists will change their resolution not to purchase land as soon as they may safely reckon on a given income from land.' 'The foremost cause' of indisposition to purchase land 'is doubt whether present rents have touched bottom.'³

After 1815 the demand for land had been maintained: after 1878 it was not. The purchasers of the twenties had been mainly the established large landowners and new men intent on founding landed families, men who took a long view of and placed a high value on family territorial ambition, social position, and political influence. They found few imitators in the eighties, though the Earl of Derby and others tried to incite people to seize the opportunity of amassing large estates on the cheap.⁴ In explanation it was argued, without much force, that legislation like the Ground Game Act of 1881 and the Agricultural Holdings Act of 1883, and fears of anti-landlord legislation engendered by political agitation, had seriously weakened the attractions of landownership.⁵ More plausibly it could have been argued that the second and third Reform Acts, and the Ballot Act, had between them all but removed one of the elements in the demand for land, the desire to acquire or consolidate political influence;

---

¹ *The Times*, 3 Oct. 1885, p. 10.
² *Estates Gazette*, 1 Jan. 1880, p. 5; 13 Aug. 1881, p. 420; 6 Jan. 1883, p. 5. *The Times*, 14 Oct. 1887, p. 9.
³ *Trans. Inst. of Surveyors*, xvi, 1883/4, pp. 8–9; xvii, 1884/5, p. 14; xxii, 1889/90, pp. 5–7.
⁴ *Land*, 13 Jan. 1883, p. 374; *The Estates Roll*, Nov. 1881, p. 1; *Estates Gazette*, 23 Aug. 1884, p. 342; 7 Jan. 1888, pp. 6–7; 3 Jan. 1891, p. 11. S. Cunliffe Lister was one of the industrialists who acquired a vast landed estate in the depression. Norton, Trist, and Gilbert to *The Times*, 15 Oct. 1887, p. 10.
⁵ *Trans. Inst. of Surveyors*, xiii, 1880/1, pp. 7–8; xvi, 1883/4, pp. 8–9; 1889/90, pp. 5–7.

and that, after 1888, the establishment of county councils had tarnished another of the delights of landownership, the exercise of local power. Nevertheless, one would have thought that the place of landowners in society remained up to 1914 such as to make the position of a country gentleman attractive and desirable, even though it was no longer the almost exclusive road to social acceptance it had been in the twenties.

Some weight must be given to a decline in the political and social advantages of landownership in accounting for the weakness of demand for land in the eighties and nineties at a time when prices were low compared to the level of the previous decades. As much perhaps should be given to the possibility that one class who had been purchasers in the earlier depression, the established large landowners, were now largely absent from the market because they had already reached territorial saturation point before 1878. But the chief reason for the contrast in the behaviour of demand between the two depressions must be found in the contrast between the nature of the depressions themselves. The first depression was selective, moderate, accompanied by continuous expansion of output in many areas, and hopes for recovery were always reasonable; the later depression was general, severe, and even catastrophic in its effects, accompanied by continuous contraction of cultivation, and any reasonable grounds for expecting a recovery or even a halt in the decline were hard to discover. In other words potential purchasers after 1878 were not readily convinced that land was really cheap, since subsequent falls in rent could easily make low prices into dear prices.

In time, of course, supply became more or less adjusted to demand, as those who would have liked to sell but were not compelled to accept great sacrifices ceased to make what were inevitably fruitless offers. In some of the later slack seasons it was noted that exceptionally little agricultural land was on offer, for this reason.[1] But when the first modest revival in business came, towards the end of the nineties, there was no doubt that it was due to an alteration in the conditions of demand, not supply. After plunging until the early nineties, rents and prices seemed to have levelled out or even recovered slightly, and buyers of land no longer faced the risk of making a loss on their purchases.[2] With the really considerable revival in business, however, in the years just before 1914, observers were confident that an artificial increase in the supply of land for sale was responsible.

The 1909 budget, it was argued, while it paralysed all other sections of the real estate market by destroying confidence, stimulated the sale of land by inducing many large landowners to sell out while the going was good. The budget proposals did not impose any new taxation on agricultural

[1] *Estates Gazette*, 4 Jan. 1890, p. 10; 3 Jan. 1891, p. 12.
[2] Ibid., 2 Jan. 1897, p. 19; 1 Jan. 1898, p. 19.

land, but they created an apprehension of future impositions, particularly on large landowners, and through the consequential inquiry into land values and ownership created the basis for their collection. Moreover, the increasingly radical tone of government policy generally brought fears of land nationalization to the fore.[1] Walter Long said as much, explicitly and publicly, when he announced the forthcoming sale of the bulk of his Wiltshire estate in 1910; but he was a prominent Conservative politician with an interest in showing the, to him, undesirable effects of his opponents' policies.[2]

The report of a departmental committee appointed by the Board of Agriculture in March 1911, to inquire into the position of tenant farmers on changes of ownership, confirmed these opinions to some extent. The committee was satisfied that an abnormal number of estates were being broken up and sold, and it was said that this was 'partly due to a feeling of apprehension among owners as to the probable course of legislation and taxation in regard to land'. At the same time the committee reported that there were many other inducements to sell. Many owners found their farms were now under-rented, and found it preferable to sell rather than to raise rents. Others found that at the prices land was now fetching it was advantageous to sell, pay off mortgages, and invest the balance of the capital so that their net income was increased. In other cases mortgagees who had long been apprehensive that their securities were inadequate and unrealizable were taking the first favourable opportunity for realization.[3] In all these motives for selling the attraction of the good price for which land could be sold as compared with previous years was the operative factor: strong demand, in other words, was bringing forth the supply.

After 1910, for the first time there was talk of the break-up of estates. 'Not for many generations has there been so enormous a dispersal piecemeal of landed estate as in 1911 and 1912', it was reported, 'and the supply of ancestral acres in the provinces is apparently unlimited.' Long rolls of aristocratic sellers were published, and the effects of the dissolution of great estates on agriculture were canvassed.[4] The phraseology might with some justice have been used of several seasons in the eighties and nineties, when the lists of aristocratic owners endeavouring to sell portions of their estates were impressive,[5] that it was adopted when it was undoubtedly owed much to political inspiration. Nevertheless there was a new pheno-

---

[1] *Estates Gazette*, 25 Dec. 1909, p. 1031; 17 Dec. 1910, p. 995; 14 Jan. 1911, pp. 60–61; 16 Dec. 1911, p. 953. *The Times*, 31 Dec. 1910, p. 4; 30 Dec. 1911, p. 13.
[2] Ibid., 24 Sept. 1910, p. 8.
[3] Cd. 6030 of 1912; extracts in *The Times*, 25 Jan. 1912, p. 4.
[4] *Estates Gazette*, 4 Jan. 1913, pp. 14, 20; 3 Jan. 1914, p. 14; 7 Jan. 1911, pp. 12–13. *The Times*, 15 Apr. 1911, p. 10; 25 Jan. 1912, p. 4.
[5] *Estates Gazette*, 1 Jan. 1887, p. 7; 7 Jan. 1888, pp. 6–7; 4 Jan. 1890, pp. 10–12.

menon in the years 1910–14. Howard Frank, of Knight, Frank and Rutley, which had become one of the leading firms in the business, could see no boom in the land market, only the melancholy and disquieting prospect of a large number of the landed aristocracy and gentry feeling obliged to part with portions of their ancient possessions.[1] The outstanding feature, however, was that these sellers found someone to sell to; this would not have been so earlier.

The great unloading of landed estates did not glut the market, did not force prices down, did not lengthen the lists of unsold properties remaining on agents' hands. Prices remained steady or even rose; Howard Frank reported of 1911 that 'very little land offered remains unsold'.[2] The type of demand on which most attention was focused was that of tenant farmers, and they clearly purchased their holdings extensively in these years. They purchased, some said reluctantly, more truly perhaps against what ought to have been their better economic judgement, because competition to occupy farms had revived, empty farms were increasingly hard to come by, and they feared eviction by new owners. Before about 1908, when many owners still had unlet farms involuntarily on their hands, this pressure to purchase did not exist.[3] Another new type of demand referred to was that of county councils, purchasing to fulfil their responsibilities under the Small Holdings Act of 1908, though this cannot have been large enough to produce any great effect. Tenant farmers, however, were by no means the only purchasers on a large scale; land companies were mentioned, and also not a few individuals of the aristocratic and business world who were clearly not buying for personal occupation.[4] It seems likely that the same circumstances which brought the tenants into the field, an end to difficulties in letting farms, a tendency to rising rents, an agricultural revival, also brought out the other categories of purchasers for social, residential, or investment purposes.

Confidence in the prospects of landownership was rising on economic grounds just as some landowners lost confidence on political grounds. The convenience of thus striking a buoyant market for these reluctant, politically induced sales was remarkable. On the whole it seems more plausible to suppose that these sellers had long been disposed to sell when the moment should be favourable, and that the political developments figured in their decisions to sell, if at all, mainly as self-justification for a

[1] Ibid., 17 Dec. 1910, p. 995.
[2] Ibid., 16 Dec. 1911, p. 953; 4 Jan. 1913, p. 14; 3 Jan. 1914, p. 14. *The Times*, 30 Dec. 1911, p. 13; 4 Jan. 1913, p. 4.
[3] *Estates Gazette*, 2 Jan. 1909, p. 24; 17 Dec. 1910, p. 995; 16 Dec. 1911, p. 953. And see S. G. Sturmey, 'Owner-Farming in England and Wales, 1900–50', *Manchester School of Economic and Social Studies*, xxiii, 1955.
[4] *Estates Gazette*, 4 Jan. 1913, p. 14.

course which after all involved a break with deeply held traditions of the inviolability of family estates.

Because demand appears to have been the determining factor in the behaviour of the land market in the later nineteenth century it does not follow that this had always been so. The years 1874–8, the onset of the depression, might well be regarded as the hinge on which a change in the form of the land market turned, limited demand replacing limited supply as the critical factor. The very high prices of 1865–75 indicate that land was then extremely scarce, and it was indeed a sellers' market. Yet even then it seems that more land actually changed hands at these high prices than had done at earlier lower prices. So that the insistent demand shown by the prices which purchasers were prepared to give did call forth some extra supply; only the supply was less elastic than the demand. Before this it seems fairly certain that it was a good demand, meeting the post-war supply, which sustained the market in the twenties, and a collapse of demand which failed to sustain it in the thirties and forties.

If the emphasis placed on the demand for land is warranted, certain general consequences follow. The foregoing analysis suggests that the volume of land transfers fluctuated over fairly long periods around a rather low level, that peaks of activity were likely to coincide with peaks of activity in building new houses and selling old ones, that they were more likely to come in times of agricultural prosperity than in times of agricultural depression. If on the whole it was demand which called the tune, and that demand fluctuated broadly with economic conditions and expectations, then investment in land occurred as opportunities for it seemed attractive, and land changed hands as freely as was consistent with the relatively high value put upon it. Whether land might have been more effectively mobilized than that is not for the historians to say.

AN ENQUIRY INTO THE RENT OF AGRICULTURAL LAND IN ENGLAND AND WALES DURING THE NINETEENTH CENTURY

R. J. Thompson

An INQUIRY *into the* RENT *of* AGRICULTURAL LAND *in* ENGLAND *and* WALES *during the* NINETEENTH CENTURY.

By ROBERT J. THOMPSON.

[Read before the Royal Statistical Society, 17th December, 1907. Major P. G. CRAIGIE, C.B., Hon. Vice-President, in the Chair.]

THE share of the produce taken by the landlord for the use of the soil and for the equipment of the farm, which we call rent, has formed the subject of much economic argument, but comparatively few statistics exist to enable us to take a larger view of the general rise and fall in agricultural rents than is afforded by the casual records of individual estates. There is, in fact, but one general statement referring to the country at large, viz., the Inland Revenue return of the gross income derived from the ownership of "lands." This dates from the year 1842-43, though there are the earlier figures of the assessments under the Property and Income Tax Acts for the years 1810-11 and 1814-15.

Besides these general statements, the reports of numerous Committees and Commissions which at various times inquired into the "State of Agriculture," contain many scattered references to the subject of rent, though until we come to the Royal Commission on Agriculture of 1893-96 very little effort seems to have been made to obtain actual records over a series of years. This Commission, however, applied to a number of the principal landowners, and was successful in obtaining detailed statements of rent and expenditure, which form a valuable mine of information for the comparatively short period which they cover. The Committee on Tithe Rent Charge in 1890 also made inquiries, but the results were embodied in general statements of the fall in rents in different counties. Another official body which took evidence on the point was the Royal Commission on the Depression in Trade in 1886. Sir James Caird seems to have been the principal witness, and he based his conclusions chiefly on the income tax figures. Apart from these official statements, mention may be made of the estimate made by Sir James Caird in his "English Agriculture in 1850-51," and of his later statement in 1878. There is also the valuable record of two of the Bedford estates given by the Duke of Bedford in his book, "The Story of a Great Agricultural Estate," while the rents received by certain Oxford Colleges have been given in several interesting papers read before this Society by Mr. L. L. Price. On the whole, however, the statistical evidence of the general trend of rents in the past century is very meagre.

The deficiency of information no doubt largely arises from the nature of the subject. The great diversity of soil and situation, of size of farms, of buildings, and of methods of cultivation causes wide variations in the rent paid per acre, and makes it difficult to arrive at an average which can be regarded as typical of the $27\frac{1}{2}$ million acres of cultivated land in England and Wales. Rents, however, necessarily tend to adjust themselves to prices, so that continuous returns from the same area ought to afford an approximately accurate indication of the average rise and fall of rents in the country as a whole.

It will easily be understood that the difficulty of obtaining returns covering any long period is considerable. Old account books may have been lost or destroyed, or may be practically inaccessible, or they may have been kept in such a way that the labour of extraction is prohibitive. Frequently estate accounts only deal with the estate as a whole, and it is practically impossible to separate the agricultural land from the villages, woods, moors, parks, and residential houses, which are included in it. It is difficult again to get returns which synchronize sufficiently with one another to be of much use.

I have been fortunate enough, however, to obtain more or less detailed statements from 16 estates, and in addition I have made use of the information given in the publications of the Royal Commission on Agriculture and in the Duke of Bedford's book. From these sources tables have been constructed showing the rent actually received for—

(1.) 70,000 acres from 1801 to 1900.
(2.) 120,000 ,, '16 ,, '00.
(3.) 400,000 ,, '72 ,, '00.

The information has been supplied on the understanding that the particulars should not be published in such a way as to enable any particular estate to be identified. The tables, therefore, represent in every case a number of estates and are given without identification.

My sincere thanks are due to the following landowners who were good enough to allow certain particulars of their estates to be supplied to me: the Duke of Bedford, the Duke of Newcastle, the Marquess of Ripon, the Marquess of Northampton, the Earl of Jersey, Lord Carrington, Lord Onslow, Mr. Christopher Turnor, the Ecclesiastical Commissioners (through Sir Alfred de Bock Porter), and the Trustees of Guy's Hospital (through Mr. Cosmo H. Bonsor). I have also to express my thanks to the following gentlemen for the trouble they have taken in furnishing me with statements and other information: Mr. R. H. Inglis Palgrave, F.R.S.; Mr. L. L. Price, M.A.; Mr. Alex. Goddard, Mr. H. Herbert Smith, Mr. D. T. Thring, Sir Francis Walker, Mr. W. Forrester Addie, Mr. Oswald H. Wade, Mr. Frank H. M. Savile, Mr. J. J. Done, Mr. Arthur E. Elliott, Mr. H. M. Jonas, Mr. Arthur H. Bowles, Mr. R. E. Prothero, Mr. C. P. Hall, Mr. W. D. Little, and to many other gentlemen who have assisted me in one way or another.

The information covers but a very small part of the actual agricultural area of England, and is open to the criticism that there is no guarantee of its representative character, but in so far as a general agreement is shown, the returns may, I think, be regarded as typical of the rise and fall in rents in England generally, though they cannot always be taken as an absolute indication of the average rent over the whole country.

Naturally, the main interest to us lies in the trend of rents in comparatively recent times, but it may be of some value if I give first of all the particulars available for earlier years, and so trace by gradual stages the various changes in agricultural rents during the past century.

Changes in Rent (a) 1801-20.

In the early years of the century many factors combined to favour a rise in rent: there was, first, the growth in the population and the increased demand for produce; secondly, the high prices, resulting from bad crops, war taxes and a depreciated currency; thirdly, the improved knowledge of agriculture, which enabled more produce to be obtained from the land; and, finally, the enclosure of common-fields. In the case of farms already enclosed, high prices and the consequent large profits of the farmers were alone sufficient to cause an increase in rent, while in the case of the enclosures the considerable outlay of capital required in buildings, drainage, fencing, and in legal expenses necessitated the promise of a substantial return. The rise in rent on newly enclosed land was estimated by Sir John Sinclair to average 9s. per acre.[1]

The only early statement of a general character is based on an inquiry made by the Board of Agriculture through their correspondents in 1804.[2] The result of this inquiry showed that the average increase in rent over the whole of England between 1790

[1] "Communications to the Board of Agriculture," 1797, vol. i, p. lviii.
[2] *Ibid.*, 1806, vol. v, p. 21.

and 1804 was $39\frac{6}{7}$ per cent. On the average of twenty-five counties, the rent per 100 acres in 1790 is put at 88*l*. 6*s*. (17*s*. 8*d*. per acre), and in 1803 at 121*l*. 2*s*. 7*d*. (24*s*. 3*d*. per acre). From an examination of publications of the time, however, I cannot but think that these figures (which merely represent the opinions of certain individuals) are unduly high if taken as an average. There is probably little doubt that insufficient allowance was made for the large areas of poor, low-rented land.

The figures which I have been able to obtain for the period 1801-20 (see Appendix A) represent the rental actually received from some 65,000 acres situated in Lincoln, Essex, Hereford, and North Wales. They are shown in the following table in five-year periods, but the area is too small and not sufficiently distributed to be really representative :—

TABLE I.

Years.	Acreage.	Average Rent per Acre.		Years.	Acreage.	Average Rent per Acre.	
		s.	*d.*			*s.*	*d.*
1801–05	62,655	11	2	1811–15	65,920	14	7
'06–10	63,981	11	7	'16–20	67,143	15	2

This table shows an increase from 11*s*. 2*d*. per acre in 1801-05 to 15*s*. 2*d*. per acre in 1816-20, or about 36 per cent. The extreme rise, however, was from 10*s*. 10*d*. in 1802 to 15*s*. 11*d*. in 1818, or about 47 per cent.

I have no means of estimating to what extent these figures represent the average tendency of rents in England during these years, but it seems certain that some such general rise actually took place. Contemporary records contain many references to the great increases which occurred in individual farms, and I give in Appendix E several cases showing the rent of separate farms over long periods. The only figures which can be quoted for comparison are those given by McCulloch,[3] which are based on the property tax. According to these estimates the average rent in England and Wales was 15*s*. $9\frac{1}{2}d$. per acre in 1810-11, and 18*s*. $4\frac{1}{2}d$. per acre in 1814-15: a rise of 16 per cent. in four years. It will be seen that McCulloch's average for England and Wales is higher than that given in Appendix A. This is chiefly owing to the fact that the area included in the latter contains a large proportion of Welsh land which unduly depresses the average. In Appendix B, however, the proportion of English land is increased by the inclusion of additional areas from the year 1816, and it is interesting to notice that in that year the average is 18*s*. per acre or within $4\frac{1}{2}d$. of the amount given by McCulloch for the preceding year.

[3] "Account of British Empire, 1854," vol. i. p. 551.

An important fact which should be borne in mind in speaking of this period is the suspension of specie payments,[4] owing to which the currency was depreciated above 18 per cent. during the five years ending 1815, though, as McCulloch points out, rents might not be raised in consequence by more than 10 per cent. because many long leases would not fall to be renewed.

(b) 1820-45.

Throughout the foregoing period prices kept at a high level, and farmers found consolation for bad seasons and deficient harvests in the enormous returns obtained for their produce. In the next twenty-five years, however, prices were comparatively low, and farmers, accustomed to the high war prices, made loud complaints of the unremunerative character of their business. Much of the distress was undoubtedly due to the disorganisation in values resulting from the currency being placed on a gold basis in 1819, while losses from sheep-rot and indifferent crops contributed to the distress in certain years. That agriculture had ceased to flourish may be gathered from the Parliamentary inquiries of 1821, 1833, 1836 and 1837 into the depressed state of the industry and into "the Burdens on Land" in 1844, but the bulk of the distress after the country had begun to recover from the dislocation of prices caused by the resumption of cash payments was confined to the heavy clay lands, which at current prices would not bear the cost of growing grain, and were, it is stated, "allowed to run down and in many cases abandoned."[5] The history of the lighter soils and grazing counties seems to have been less eventful, and it must not be forgotten that these represent the major part of the country.

The position in the earlier years of the period is probably well reflected in the observations of the Select Committee on the State of Agriculture of 1833, who state that "the landlords in every part "of the United Kingdom, though in different degrees, have met "the fall of price (since 1820) by a reduction of rent, except where "during the war the rents on their estates had not been raised, or "where, by a large expenditure of capital, permanent improvements "have enriched the nature of the soil itself. The spread of the drill "system of husbandry, a better rotation of cropping, a more judi- "cious use of manures, especially of bones, improvement in the

[4] Porter notes that "owing to the depreciated state of our currency" the average price of wheat in 1810, viz., 103s. 3d., was not equal to more than about 90s. in gold. He estimates 122s. as equal to 100s. in 1812, and 72s. 1d. as equal to 54s. in 1814. ("Progress of the Nation," vol. i, 1836.)

[5] Committee of 1833.

"breed both of cattle and sheep, have all contributed to counter-
"balance the fall in price, and to sustain that surplus profit in the
"culture of the soil on which rent depends."

The later years of the period showed signs of a revival. The
Tithe Commutation Act was passed in 1836, and removed a source
of annoyance, as well as a hindrance to improvements, while the
value of drainage, of artificial manures, and of the application of
science to agricultural practice began to be more generally recognised.

Table II gives in quinquennial periods the rent of about
110,000 acres, from 1816 to 1845. The figures for each year
are given in Appendix B.

TABLE II.

Years.	Acreage.*	Average Rent per Acre.		Years.	Acreage.*	Average Rent per Acre.	
		s.	d.			s.	d.
1816–20....	110,476	18	8	1831–35....	113,945	18	5
'21–25 ...	111,255	17	11	'36–40....	114,894	18	8
'26–30....	112,483	17	9	'41–45....	118,371	20	1

* In Lincoln, Hereford, Bucks, Beds, Cambridge, Essex, and North Wales.

It will be seen that there was a downward tendency in the first
half of this period, followed by a recovery after 1830. The figures
for the individual years (Appendix B) show a decline from 19s. 5d.
in 1818 to 17s. 2d. in 1822, or 11½ per cent., corresponding to the
initial period of depression, followed by a number of fluctuations
up to 1830. There was little variation between 1830 and 1839,
from which date a steady upward movement is recorded. Over
the whole period the increase is only 7½ per. cent., but the extreme
variation was from 17s. 2d. per acre in 1822 to 20s. 6d. in 1845, or
nearly 20 per cent.

On the whole, these years represent, first, a decline, then a
period of adjustment and recovery, and then the beginning of an
upward tendency, which continued with little intermission until
1878.

McCulloch, by a calculation based on the Income Tax Returns,
puts the average rent in England and Wales in 1842-43 at 21s. 6¼d. per
acre. From this it would seem that the figures given in Appendix B
are still somewhat low, and comparing them with those for later years
I believe this to be the case, though they probably represent fairly
well the general trend of rents during the period. McCulloch's
figures, however, have no special significance, as they are arrived at
simply by dividing the total area of England and Wales into the
total value of the assessment.

(c) 1845-72.

This period is distinguished by the general advancement of the standard of farming throughout the country. The agricultural practices, which in 1845 were known and adopted here and there, came into general use. An indication of awakened interest may be found in the establishment of the Royal Agricultural Society in 1839, and the spirit in which that great Society was founded well reflects the new attitude taken up by farmers in this country. In the letter to Earl Spencer, which led to the formation of the Society, Mr. H. Handley, M.P., observes: " Farmers are at length convinced " that it is not in parliamentary interference that they must seek a " remedy (for low prices). Repeated inquiries have terminated in " repeated disappointments. It is to their own energies and their " own resources they must look, and by cheapening the cost and " increasing the amount of production pave the way to future " prosperity." [6]

The introduction of free trade in 1846 gave an emphasis to these words, although it did not for many years produce any effect on the price of corn. In fact throughout this period prices generally showed a steady tendency to rise, though not to any very marked degree until towards 1870. Sauerbeck's index-number for the two groups, "animal and vegetable food," averaged 87 for the five years 1846-50, 89 for 1851-55, 92 for 1856-60, 90 for 1861-65, 97 for 1866-70, and 99 for 1871-72.

There were two other factors which also operated to increase rents. The first was the outlay of capital in drainage and other improvements, and the second the development of the means of transit by railway.

The advantages of soil drainage were hardly recognised before 1840. In that year Philip Pusey, one of the foremost agriculturists of the day, says "its introduction is too new to be placed altogether " beyond the risk of disappointment," [7] but so rapidly did it advance in public favour that in 1846 the Government set aside a sum of 2,000,000*l.* to promote the improvement of land in Great Britain by drainage through the medium of loans to landowners, because, as the preamble to the Act states: " the productiveness and value " of much of the land in Great Britain and Ireland are capable of " being greatly increased by drainage." [8] In 1850 a further two millions were granted, the money being also applicable to other improvements. Under these and other Acts no less than 7,381,000*l.*

---

[6] A letter to Earl Spencer on the formation of a National Agricultural Institution, by Henry Handley, M.P., 1838.

[7] "Journal of the Royal Agricultural Society," vol. i, p. 6, 1840.

[8] 9 and 10 Vict., c. 101.

was expended on drainage between 1846 and 1872, and 2,797,000*l*. on other works, or in all 10,178,000*l*., and up to 1906 the total outlay under these Acts was 18,000,000*l*. No record exists of the outlays out of private capital, apart from that mentioned under the Improvement of Lands Acts, but with the increasing recognition of the utility of drainage, the expenditure from this source must have been very large, and it may fairly be assumed that an important factor in the rise in rents in this period is to be found in the improvement in the soil by drainage, and of the farm by better buildings.

The third factor, to which I am inclined to attribute a greater influence than has been usually ascribed to it, was the development of railway communication. The network of railways which spread over the country after 1840 brought remote and inaccessible districts into touch with the Metropolis and the large towns, opened up new markets, and enabled farmers to send their produce distances which would have been impossible by road. The cost of production was cheapened, farming became more profitable, and the rent which farmers could afford to pay consequently increased.

In the next table I have included, in addition to the figures given in Appendix B, some 12,000 acres for which particulars have been supplied at five-year intervals only, but the average rent is practically unaffected.

TABLE III.

Years.	Acreage.*	Average Rent per Acre.		Years.	Acreage.*	Average Rent per Acre.	
		s.	d.			s.	d.
1846–50....	131,347	21	–	1861–65....	134,020	23	7
'51–55..	132,885	20	9	'66–71†	134,719	24	8
'56–60....	133,785	23	1				

* In Lincoln, Hereford, Bucks, Beds, Cambridge, Essex, Northampton, Warwick, and North Wales.

† Six years.

The increase shown in this table from 21*s*. in 1846-50 to 24*s*. 8*d*. in 1866-71 is equal to 17 per cent., but the extreme range was from 19*s*. 10*d*. in 1851, a year of great depression, to 24*s*. 10*d*. in 1869, or about 25 per cent. A comparison of prices with rents in this period will be made later.

There are two general estimates of rent at the beginning of this period with which the above figures may be compared. McCulloch, on the same basis as before, estimated the average rent of land in 1851-52 in England and Wales at 22*s*. per acre. Caird, on the other hand, as the result of his enquiry in 1850,[9] put the rent of " cultivated land " in England alone (32 counties) at 27*s*. 2*d*. per acre.

[9] English Agriculture in 1850-51.

It is probable, however, that he subsequently thought this figure too high, as in 1878 he put the average rent at 30s., an increase of only about 10 per cent. From the figures given in Appendix C, showing the rent of 400,000 acres from 1872, it would seem that the average rent given in the table above is still too low. The true average would probably be 2s. or 3s. higher.

(d) 1872-1900.

About midway between the seventies and the eighties, the country entered upon a remarkable and long-sustained period of agricultural depression. To sum it up briefly, it may be said to have had two distinct and separate causes: Unfavourable seasons and low prices. The witnesses before the Royal Commission on Agriculture of 1879-82 agreed in ascribing the depression at that time " mainly to a succession of unfavourable seasons," while the subsequent Commission of 1892-96 found a " concensus of opinion " that the chief cause of the existing depression is the progressive " and serious decline in the prices of farm produce."

It is interesting to notice that a new influence was at work. Hitherto, bad harvests and unfavourable seasons had always in the history of agriculture offered some compensation in the fact that owing to the scarcity the farmer obtained a higher price for his produce, though the quantity for disposal may have been small.[10] From this time, however, the harvests of distant climes began to be brought to our markets at little extra cost, and the English crops ceased to influence the market, which was controlled by the combined production of the world. The following table, based on Appendix C, shows the average rent in 1872-92 for the whole area for which I have particulars, but unfortunately I have not been able to continue it up to 1900.

TABLE IV.

Years.	Acreage.*	Average Rent per Acre. s. d.	Years.	Acreage.*	Average Rent per Acre. s. d.
1872–74....	416,801	28 10	1884–86....	406,545	24 11
'75–77....	419,793	29 4	'87–89....	405,149	22 11
'78–80....	421,201	27 6	'90–92....	403,237	22 10
'81–83....	413,036	26 9			

* In Lincoln, Essex, Hereford, Beds, Bucks, Cambridge, Montgomery, Rutland, Norfolk, Suffolk, Gloucester, Northumberland, Devon, Sussex, Westmorland, Yorks, Cheshire, Oxford, Derby, Nottingham, Northampton, Kent, Worcester, Wilts, Somerset, and other counties.

Rents continued to rise until 1878, when a sharp fall occurred followed by a progressive decline which continued until the close of

[10] Address to Statistical Section of the British Association, by Mr. G. Shaw-Lefevre, M.P., 1879.

the century. For the twenty years shown in the above table, the fall from 29s. 4d. in 1875-77 to 22s. 10d. in 1890-92 represents 22 per cent., while the fall between 1877 and 1892 is equal to 25 per cent.

Although the figures on which the above table is based cannot be given beyond 1892 as regards some 300,000 acres, I have obtained another collection of returns representative of a very similar area and equally distributed over England, the figures in regard to which approximate so closely to the first series that no great error is likely to arise, if the two tables are regarded as continuous.

TABLE V.

Years.	Acreage.	Average Rent per Acre.		Years.	Acreage.	Average Rent per Acre.	
		s.	d.			s.	d.
1893–94....	377,234	21	8	1897–98....	390,263	20	6
'95–96....	385,750	21	1	'99–1900	399,043	20	–

On this assumption, which is obviously sufficiently accurate for the purposes of a broad statement, the average fall in rents between the early seventies and the end of the century was approximately 30 per cent. The average rental in 1900 was, roughly, about 20s. per acre. On the whole area of 482,000 acres for which I have particulars for that year, the average rent works out to 20s. 2d. per acre.

The majority report of the Royal Commission of Agriculture (1893-96) does not make any definite estimate of the average reduction in rent, apart from estimates based on the income-tax figures, but observes that rents in the most depressed parts of England have fallen by 50 per cent. ; in less depressed districts the fall ranged from 20 to 30 per cent., and in some dairying and grazing districts it was not more than 15 per cent. Mr. G. Lambert, however, in his supplementary report, puts the average decrease between 1878 and 1892 in England alone at 18·7 per cent.

Comparison of Figures of Rent with Income Tax Returns and with Prices of Agricultural Produce, 1845-1900.

The second half of the nineteenth century covers a period of great agricultural interest, and it is worth while to examine it rather more closely than I have done in the foregoing general survey.

Four sets of figures are available for comparison :—

(1.) Returns of the net rent received for some 120,000 acres in Lincoln, Hereford, Bedford, Bucks, Essex, Cambridge, and North Wales for fifty-five years, 1845-1900. These furnish a continuous record over practically the whole period of the prosperity of British agriculture up to about 1878 and of the subsequent depression.

(2.) Returns of the net rent received from approximately 400,000 acres distributed over the whole of England and Wales from 1872 to 1900. As I have explained, there is a break in these figures between 1892 and 1893, but, for all practical purposes, I think they may be regarded as continuous.

(3.) The only official or other statements which afford any means of testing the accuracy of the two preceding sets of figures are the Inland Revenue Returns of the gross annual value of the property assessed for income tax (Schedule A), under the heading, " Lands, including tithes commuted under the Tithe Commutation " Acts."

The income tax figures have been relied upon by various writers and Royal Commissions as affording an indication of the rise and fall of rents, but they are subject to several qualifications, which it is well to bear in mind. In the first place, the figures refer to "lands" whether cultivated or uncultivated, including ornamental grounds, gardens attached to houses when exceeding one acre in extent, tithe rent charge, and farm-houses and farm-buildings. Secondly, the amount returned is to be the gross rent payable under the lease or agreement, and not the rent paid after deducting any temporary abatement or remission of rent allowed by the landlord. Thirdly, the valuation is only made every five years (formerly every three years), so that changes between each valuation are only made on appeal to the District Commissioners. Fourthly, the valuation of "lands" built on or appropriated to other uses is transferred to "houses."

It will be seen that the inclusion of ornamental gardens and grounds, and the non-deduction of abatements, would tend to keep the total valuation up; the triennial or quinquennial valuation tends to refer the bulk of the changes to years not necessarily those in which they were made, while the transfer of building land produces, as far as it operates, an artificial decline in the total, which is not attributable to any fall in "rents." It may be noted also that a rise in 1864-65 was stated to be due to improved administrative control.[11]

---

[11] The question of the validity of these figures is discussed at great length in the "Report of the Royal Commission on Land in Wales," p. 361. The "Final Report of the Royal Commission on Agriculture, 1896" also deals with the subject. In this Report (p. 26) some importance is attached to the transfer to Schedule A, since 1842 of the uncommuted tithe amounting to 1,964,000*l*. So far as this has taken place, it would tend to keep up the assessment.

(4.) For the purpose of comparing these three sets of figures with the prices of agricultural produce, I have taken Mr. Sauerbeck's index number for the articles included by him under the headings "animal and vegetable food" (groups I and II), viz., wheat, flour, barley, oats, maize, potatoes and rice; beef, mutton, pork, bacon and butter. This list includes rice which does not affect the farmer and omits wool which does, but broadly it may be accepted as a fair indication of the course of agricultural prices. In the following table these four sets of figure are expressed as percentages. For the purpose of comparison with Sauerbeck's index number, the period 1867-77 has been taken as a base, except in the case of column 2, where the year 1872 has been chosen as the mean of 1867-77.

TABLE VI.—*Comparison of the Figures of Rent, Income Tax Returns, and Prices expressed as Percentages.*

Year.	1 Rent of 120,000 Acres. 1867-77 =100.	2 Rent of 400,000 Acres. 1872 =100.	3 Income Tax Returns. 1867-77 =100.	4 Sauerbeck's Index Number. 1867-77 =100.	Notes as to Seasons.
1846....	83	—	84	93½	
'47....	82	—	84	108½	
'48....	85	—	86	87½	
'49....	81	—	86	75	
1850....	82	—	86	70½	Bad season; great agricultural distress.
'51....	79	—	84	70½	
'52....	81	—	84	74½	
'53....	81	—	84	91	
'54....	82	—	84	103½	
'55....	84	—	84	103½	
'56....	88	—	84	98½	
'57....	92	—	87	97	
'58....	93	—	87	85	
'59....	93	—	88	85	
1860....	92	—	88	95	Wet and cold; crops deficient.
'61....	94	—	91	96½	
'62....	94	—	91	92	
'63....	94	—	91	86	
'64....	94	—	95	84	
'65....	93	—	95	90½	
'66....	94	—	95	95½	Cattle plague.
'67....	95	—	97	102	
'68....	99	—	97	100½	
'69....	100	—	98	93½	

TABLE VI.—*Comparison of Figures expressed as Percentages—Contd.*

Year.	1 Rent of 120,000 Acres. 1867-77 = 100.	2 Rent of 400,000 Acres. 1872 = 100.	3 Income Tax Returns. 1867-77 = 100.	4 Sauerbeck's Index Number. 1867-77 = 100.	Notes as to Seasons.
1870....	96	—	100	93	
'71....	98	—	100	97	
'72....	100	100	100	101	
'73....	101	101	102	107½	
'74....	102	102	102	104	Crops generally below the average.
'75....	102	102	103	100½	
'76....	102	102	106	100	
'77....	105	104	106	100½	
'78....	106	103	105	98	
'79....	79	93	106	80½	"The most disastrous season this century."
1880....	86	92	105	95	
'81....	82	91	104	92½	
'82....	94	95	99	94	
'83....	93	96	98	92½	
'84....	90	93	97	84	
'85....	72	84	94	78	
'86....	84	85	93	76	
'87....	68	79	91	71½	
'88....	78	81	86	74½	
'89....	80	82	85	75½	
1890....	78	81	84	73½	
'91....	78	81	84	78	
'92....	74	79	83	74½	
'93....	68	77	82	72	Prolonged drought; heavy losses.
'94....	64	75	81	67½	
'95....	65	75	80	66	
'96....	68	73	79	63	
'97....	68	72	78	69¼	
'98....	68	72	76	72	
'99....	69	70	76	69½	
1900....	69	70	75	73½	

Note.—Column 1 is based on Appendix B; column 2 on Appendix C; column 3 on Appendix D; column 4 is the mean of the two groups—vegetable food (corn, &c.) and animal food (meat, &c.)—in Mr. Sauerbeck's tables.

Looking at this table (Table VI) and the diagram, it will be seen that the income-tax figures in column 3 start at practically the same level as the rent figures in column 1, and in 1851 showed a decline corresponding to the fall in column 1, which was the result of the short period of depression in prices which occurred in 1849-52. The influence of the decline in rents operated in the case of the income-tax returns until 1856, from which date a steady rise set in

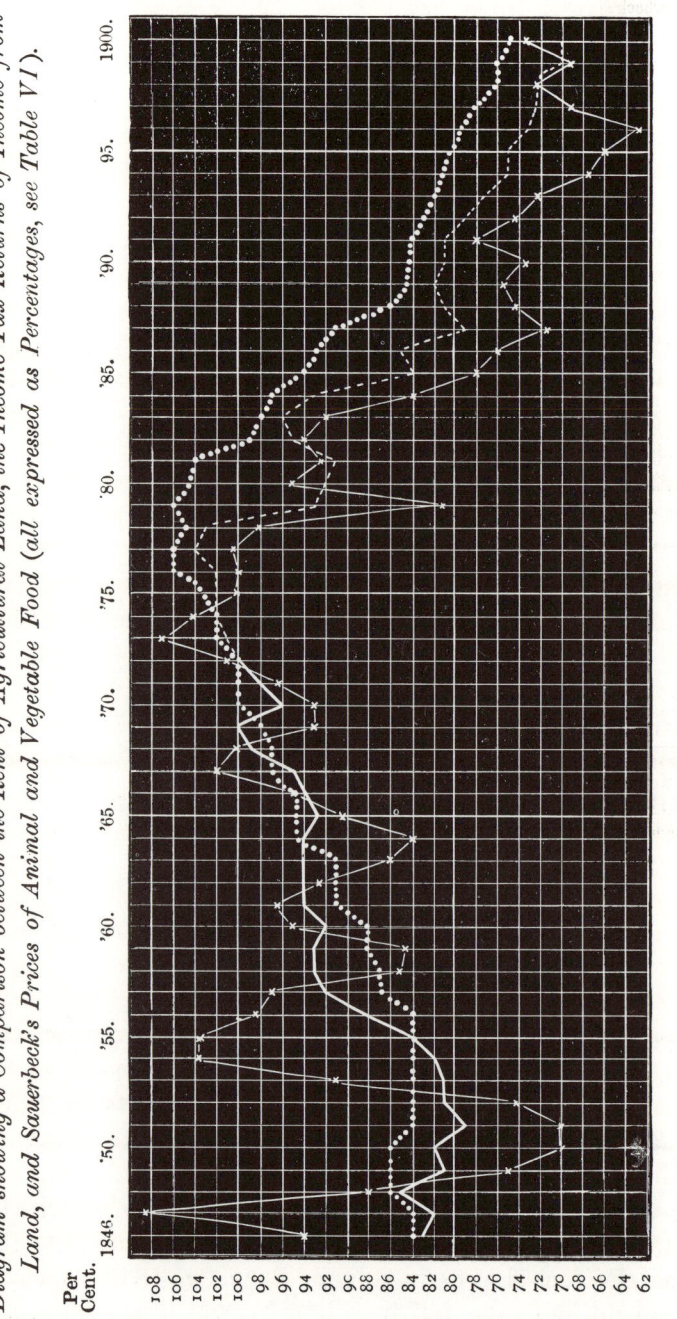

Diagram showing a Comparison between the Rent of Agricultural Land, the Income Tax Returns of Income from Land, and Sauerbeck's Prices of Animal and Vegetable Food (all expressed as Percentages, see Table VI).

and continued until 1879, though the influence of the triennial valuation is very well marked.

The income-tax figures moved much more slowly than the rent figures. It is interesting to notice that they stood several points above the figures for rent in each of the periods of depression, for instance in 1849-53, 1864-67, 1870-72, and 1879-1900, whereas, in prosperous times of rising rents they are usually a few points lower. This is only natural, as their adjustment must come subsequent to alterations in rent, but there is, I think, another reason why they should remain higher than a falling rent, viz., that, as explained above, abatements and deductions are not shown in the income-tax figures, which represent the gross rent payable under agreement. The rent-curve, on the other hand, shows only the rent actually received, and it must be remembered that the decline in the rent is very largely caused by abatements, which are called "temporary" for several years (and sometimes for long periods) before they are made permanent. It is natural, therefore, that the rent-curves should reach a lower point and reach it earlier than do the income-tax figures. The latter attained their lowest point in 1900, when they stood nine points below what they were fifty-four years earlier.

The figures in column 1 show the same general movement, though with more fluctuations and with a marked tendency to respond to changes in price. In 1872 the figures in columns 1, 2 and 3 are identical, and continue very close together up to 1878, when column 2 shows a fall of one point, followed in 1879 by a decline of 10 points. A much greater fall is shown in column 1, and from this year the fluctuations in this column are considerable, though they agree substantially with those of column 2, where the larger area tends to smooth out the curve. In the diagram the figures for column 1 are given up to 1872, and for column 2 subsequent to that date. The diagram also enables the rent curve to be compared with Sauerbeck's index number for food products, and shows fairly well the dependence of rent on prices. It will be seen that each of the periods of low prices, viz., 1848-52, 1858-9, 1863-64, 1869-71 found a corresponding check in rents a year or two later. Prices reached their maximum point in 1873, but rents continued to rise until 1877, four years after prices began to fall. This fact seems to lend some support to a contention which was strongly brought to the notice of the Royal Commission on Agriculture of 1882, to the effect that rents had not been reduced in time. I attribute this principally to the fact that prices, though falling, still remained very high, the depression in agriculture which was felt in 1879 being chiefly due to bad seasons, and not to exceptional prices. Another factor tending to keep up rents was that agriculture had, on the whole, been flourishing for nearly thirty years. Consequently, there was a very good demand for farms, and a succession of bad seasons, though disastrous for the sitting tenants, did not act as a deterrent to those who wished to take up land.

After 1879 every successive year saw prices fall lower and lower, a movement which it will be seen was closely followed by rents.

On the whole, the general agreement of all these figures constitutes a strong argument in favour of the substantial accuracy of the particulars as to rent given in columns 1 and 2. They show that the average rent of agricultural land in England and Wales in 1900 was 30 per cent. below the figure of 1872, 34 per cent. below the maximum of 1877, and 13 per cent. below the figure of 1846.

Estimate of the Proportion of the Gross Rent Expended in Repairs, Improvements, and other Out-goings.

Up to now we have been considering the gross rent paid for land in this country, but it has to be remembered that the gross rent is in part interest on capital expended in equipping the estate, and as such is subject to a number of deductions for repairs, insurance and expenses of management, as well as for the works executed from time to time under the heading of permanent improvements. These expenses amount in the aggregate to a substantial proportion of the gross rent, and, as this fact is not perhaps always borne in mind in discussions about rent, I have thought it worth while to tabulate the figures relating to certain estates, with a view to showing what may reasonably be regarded as the average deductions to which rent is subject in England.

The main outlay is naturally on repairs, fencing, gates, new buildings, drainage, and other so-called permanent improvements. I have not attempted to distinguish between "repairs" and "permanent improvements," because in many accounts the distinction is not made, and in any case it seems to me to be a purely artificial one. Repairs are intended to maintain the letting value of the farm, while new buildings and other permanent improvements are intended either to maintain or increase the letting value, and as such are reflected in the rent. It would not, of course, be justifiable to burden one year's rent with the whole cost of improvements, which may last for many years, but, taking the average of a number of estates and of a number of years, they may fairly be charged against income, as they are when money is borrowed under the Improvement of Land Acts, to be repaid, capital and interest, over a number of years.

The other outgoings include tithe (where payable), land tax, drainage and local rates paid by owner, expenses of management, and miscellaneous payments.

The figures given in the table below are compiled from certain estates of which particulars were furnished to the Royal Commission on Agriculture,[12] excluding, I may observe, those which, from any special circumstances, appear exceptional, or for which particulars are given for less than twenty years. It is for this reason that they do not agree with certain calculations put forward by the Commission itself, which were based on a somewhat larger number of estates, but which extended over only seven years, from 1886 to 1892. The Commission observes: " if we take the average " of these seven years, we find from these accounts, which include " estates in some of the most favoured parts of the country, that " for every 100l. received during the seven years, 1886-92, by the " owners in England and Wales, 39l. 4s. was absorbed by ordinary " outgoings, and an additional sum of 15l. 12s. was spent upon " improvements, leaving the owner 45l. 4s. out of 100l.," that is to say, that 55 per cent. of the gross rent disappeared in outgoings. Such information as I have been able to obtain leads me to believe that these figures are too high for use as applicable to ordinary conditions in this country. For one thing it must be remembered that they refer to a period of exceptional depression, and include a number of estates where the rents on the one hand were reduced and the expenditure on repairs well maintained, with the result that the percentage of outgoings was abnormally increased, whereas I think it is more generally true that the outgoings at the time of the depression were reduced to some extent to compensate for the reduced net income.

TABLE VII.

Year.	Gross Rental Received.	Cost of Repairs and Permanent Improvements.	Per Cent. of Gross Rent.	Net Income.*	Per Cent. of Gross Rent.
	£	£		£	
1872–76	357,487	96,404	27	204,209	57
'77–81	348,583	95,401	27	192,562	55
'82–86	322,413	89,227	27¾	171,698	53
'87–91	288,756	63,998	22	171,270	60
Total	1,317,239	345,030	26	740,359	56

* This is the balance of the gross rent received, after deducting all outgoings, including permanent improvements.

[12] " Particulars of Expenditures and Outgoings on certain Estates in " Great Britain," Cd-8125, 1896.

For the fifteen years 1872-86 the cost for repairs and permanent improvements amounted to about 27 per cent., while in 1887-91 it fell to 22 per cent. The net income in the first fifteen years was about 55 per cent., but when rents were so largely reduced an effort was naturally made to reduce the outgoings, with the result that the net income was maintained at the same amount as before, but represented 60 per cent. of the gross. Over the twenty years, the repairs represent 26 per cent. of the rental, and the net income 56 per cent. of the gross.

On the large estates of the Ecclesiastical Commission, the repairs appear to fall only in part on the landlord, but with permanent improvements the cost amounted in thirteen years (1880-92)[13] to about 21·3 per cent., while the net income represented 62·7 of the gross. On certain of the Crown estates, where the conditions are approximately the same, the repairs and improvements in six years (1888-93) represented 21·5 per cent. and the net income 64·7 per cent. On one large estate of over 150,000 acres the expenditure on repairs and improvements has averaged $25\frac{1}{3}$ per cent. during the last five years, but a similar calculation about the year 1852 showed the expenditure at that time to be 40 per cent. of the rent. On another estate of 45,000 acres, the outlay over forty years has averaged 23 per cent.

From these figures and from a number of enquiries I have made, I suggest 25 per cent. as a fair average figure for the cost of repairs and improvements in this country. No doubt in very many instances this figure is exceeded. One large landowner writes to me as follows: "Speaking roughly, there has never been less than 40 and often 50 per cent. of the rental value returned to the estate in improvements for the benefit of tenants; creation of farms and farm-buildings to meet increased demands for stock consequent upon the improvement of land. During the last forty years the property has all been drained, and the drains constantly require re-laying." Many similar instances are to be found in the publications of the Royal Commission.[14]

With regard to the balance of the gross rent left after paying all charges, the estates given in the table above show an average net income of 56 per cent. of the gross over twenty years, or 60 per cent. during the last five years, the estates of the Ecclesiastical Commissioners showed $62\frac{3}{4}$ per cent. and the Crown estates about $64\frac{3}{4}$ per cent. It would seem, therefore, that the net income ranges from 60 to 65 per cent. of the gross receipts. For the purposes of an average estimate applicable to England

[13] "Royal Commission on Agriculture, 1893," Evidence, vol. i, p. 420.
[14] Final Report, p. 287.

and Wales generally, it will I think be safer to take the higher figure; we may probably assume that most of these estates are dealt with somewhat liberally and it is almost certain that with reduced rents there has been a tendency to reduce expenses. I suggest, therefore, on the basis of these figures that the net income derived on the average from agricultural land in this country represents 65 per cent. of the gross rent, the difference being made up of 25 per cent. for repairs and permanent improvements and 10 per cent. for management, tithe and land tax, local and drainage rates, and other miscellaneous outgoings.

Estimate of the " Landlord's Capital" Invested in Buildings, Drainage, Fencing, &c.

John Stuart Mill drew a distinction between the rent defined by Ricardo as a payment for the use of " the natural and indestructible " powers of the soil," and that part of rent which is a payment for the landlords' improvements. "Under the name of rent," he says, " many payments are commonly included which are not a remunera- " tion for the original powers of the land itself, but for capital " expended on it," and the question which I now propose to consider is what is the amount of capital sunk in the land and what return the rent represents. Mill distinguished between " capital actually " sunk in improvements and not requiring periodical renewals, " but spent once for all in giving the land a permanent increase " in productiveness" (as in the case of the Bedford Level), the improvement of which, as he observes, cannot, after it is once done, be separated from the land itself, and capital represented by buildings, fences, &c., requiring renewal. The distinction is not one which it is always very easy to draw, and for my purpose I propose to consider what may roughly be assumed to be the cost of " making a farm," charging against it those obvious improvements which having involved an outlay of capital may fairly be expected to yield interest.

This is a question which was discussed in a very interesting paper, written by the late Mr. Albert Pell, on "The Making of the " Land in England,"[15] with the object of showing that the land as such was worth nothing, and that the rent represented a very small return on the capital expended in developing it.

In drawing attention to the considerable outlays which had been incurred in bringing the land from a state of nature, Mr. Pell included not only grubbing and clearing the land, but also the making of parish roads, as well as a charge for the provision of public worship; he also stated that the whole area with which he

[15] "Journal of the Royal Agricultural Society," 1887, p. 355.

was dealing was drained. In attempting to arrive at an average figure we cannot, however, charge drainage on the whole, as drainage is not necessary on every class of land. Moreover, for the purpose of considering the relation of rent to the capital invested in the land, we can only take, as Mill says, the cost of those improvements requiring periodical renewal. The provision of public roads must be put with other facilities for transit and advantages of position, which give land an economic value, and for which rent, as distinct from interest on capital is paid.

The sum arrived at by Mr. Pell was made up as follows:—

	Per Acre. £
Grubbing and preparing the land	5
Roads, fences, gates, drainage and various miscellaneous expenses	12
Buildings	9
	26

"For some such outlay [16] as this," Mr. Pell observes, "or its equivalent, at the time when the several operations were carried out, the open wild waste, denuded of its saleable timber, mere rough naked land, in fact, has been converted into cleared and levelled enclosures, ready for the occupancy of the cultivating farmer and his staff."

Another estimate of the landlord's capital was made by Mr. Elias P. Squarey,[17] and this includes four different kinds of farms, as follows:—

Cost of Buildings, Cottages, Water Supply, Drainage (where necessary), Roads, and Fencing.

	£	Per Acre. £ s. d.
On a dairy farm of 200 acres mostly pasture	4,050 =	20 5 –
On a mixed arable and pasture farm of 500 acres	5,000 =	10 – –
On a mixed upland, arable, and pasture farm of 1,000 acres	7,350 =	7 7 –
On a grazing farm of 300 acres (without drainage)	2,600 =	7 10 –

The mean of these estimates is about 11*l*. 6*s*. per acre.

As the size of a holding diminishes, the average cost has usually a tendency to increase. An example of this occurs in the recent Report of the Small Holdings Committee. The cost of buildings on 30 acres is put by the Committee at 360*l*., or 12*l*. per acre, while

---

[16] The 12*l*. per acre includes 700*l*. per mile for parish roads, 200*l*. per mile for two boundary fences, 550*l*. for one mile of occupation road and its fences, 36 miles of quick fences at 112*l*. per mile, 200 gates at 40*s*. each, and 1,600 acres drained at 6*l*. 6*s*. per acre.

[17] "Journal of the Royal Agricultural Society," 1878, p. 431.

very similar buildings costing 400*l.* would serve for 50 acres; no proportionate reduction could, however, be secured for a 12-acre holding where the cost might run up to 20*l.* or 25*l.* per acre.

The very substantial difference between Mr. Pell's figures and those of Mr. Squarey is partly due to the inclusion by Mr. Pell of several items which cannot correctly be regarded as "capital "expenditure." A more accurate idea of the landlord's capital can perhaps be arrived at by taking some particulars which are available of the actual cost incurred in converting some mixed forest land on the Crown estates into cultivated land. These figures were supplied by Mr. John Clutton in a paper read by him before the Surveyors' Institution[18] in 1871, and are not estimates but actual results obtained by the disafforestation of portions of the Royal Forests of Hainault in Essex, Whichwood in Oxford, Whittlebury in Northampton, and Delamere in Cheshire between 1850 and 1860. The land was more or less heavily timbered, and the receipts from the sale of wood represented a substantial contribution towards the cost of the conversion, and also paid for the cost of public highways, legal expenses and some fencing.

The figures are as follows :—

	Hainault, 2,255 Acres. £	Whichwood, 3,016 Acres.* £	Whittlebury, 300 Acres. £	Delamere, 1,554 Acres. £
Clearing and grubbing	13,730	6,233	1,714	9,214
Marling	—	—	—	19,451
Draining	22,618	520	1,602	1,417
Fencing	Included with draining	1,506	220	1,397
Farm roads	1,123	811	—	894
Farm-buildings and cottages	15,070	14,337	2,014	14,377
Miscellaneous	836	—	—	—
	58,377	23,407	5,550	46,750
Receipts from timber	55,000	14,080	5,800	17,815

* Part of this area was already cultivated and provided with buildings.

The total cost of the conversion, therefore, was 134,084*l.*, towards which the timber contributed 92,695*l.* Where, however, land is covered with inferior timber or brushwood or is merely common or waste, the cost of preparing the land for cultivation, *i.e.*, grubbing or clearing, may easily involve a loss.

To arrive at an estimate on the principle explained above, I have excluded all charges for felling, clearing and grubbing the

[18] "Surveyors' Institution, Transactions," vol. iv, p. 17, 1871-72.

land and also marling,[19] confining the outlay entirely to draining, fencing, buildings, and farm-road making. The total area affected was about 6,679 acres, and the sum expended was:—

	£	Per Acre. £ s. d.
Drainage and fencing	29,280	= 4 8 –
Farm buildings	45,798	= 6 17 –
Roads and other expenses	3,664	= – 11 –
	78,742	= 11 16 –

There were about 13 farms and some small holdings. The farms were mostly arable, and varied a good deal in size.

Only a little over one-third of the land required draining, while the cost of fencing was partly charged against the timber. Owing to the character of the land, the cost of draining, however, so far as it was done, was above the average. The farms were well provided with buildings and cottages, and Mr. Clutton observes that the cost of building from various causes was somewhat high. The charge for roads, on the other hand, is low, as they are exclusively occupation roads, the expense of making public roads to serve the estates being put against the timber. It may be noted that the farms were all let at very low rents for the first two or three years.

For purposes of comparison, some particulars of the cost of the various operations in general is given below:—

Draining.—Pipe drainage costs from 5*l.* to 7*l.* per acre. The actual cost over 15,000 acres, including every variety of soil, was stated by Mr. Grantham to average 6*l.* per acre, while another surveyor gave as his experience in draining upwards of 90,000 acres the average cost as 5*l.* 15*s.* per acre.[20] As only a proportion of the land is drained, any estimate of the average outlay would have to be put much lower.

Fencing.—On fencing, the sum spent in the estates given above was 17*s.* per acre, but this was exclusive of outside fences round the estates. A hedge-and-ditch fence would cost a 1*s.* a yard or 88*l.* per mile.

Buildings.—The cost of erecting farm-houses and buildings was given by Mr. Bailey-Denton in about 1860 as averaging about 4*l.* 10*s.* per acre on 1,000-acre farms and upwards, 6*l.* per acre on mixed farms of 500 to 1,000 acres, and 7*l.* per acre on farms of 200 to 500 acres; but Mr. Tom Bright[21] says that under the more

---

[19] Marling is excluded as being an operation which improves the natural fertility of the soil.

[20] "Surveyors Institution, Transactions," 1871-72, pp. 66 and 102.

[21] "Agricultural Surveyor and Estate Agents Handbook," 1899.

economical systems of farm management of the present day the cost may be as follows :—

Approximate Size of Holding.	Approximate Cost of Buildings.				Approximate Size of Holding.	Approximate Cost of Buildings.			
Acres.	Per Acre.				Acres.	Per Acre.			
	£	s.	£	s.		£	s.	£	s.
40	8	–	to 11	10	375	3	–	to 3	10
100	5	10	„ 6	10	500	3	–	„ 3	15
150	4	15	„ 5	15	650	3	–	„ 3	15
220	4	–	„ 5	–					

This is exclusive of cottages, of which one or more must be allowed per 100 acres, or an additional cost of, say, 2*l.* or 2*l.* 10*s.* per acre.

Roads.—The cost of making a farm road may be put at 1*s.* a square yard or about 350*l.* a mile, or say about 10*s.* per acre.

Another charge which has to be included is that for providing a water supply.

It would seem from the foregoing that there is nothing exceptional in the outlay incurred on the Crown lands quoted by Mr. Clutton, and on that general basis I suggest the following estimate of landlord's capital as one which may be regarded as broadly applicable to agricultural land in England and Wales generally.

	£	s.	d.
Drainage and fencing	4	10	–
Roads...	–	10	–
Buildings, including cottages and water supply	7	–	–
	12	–	–

It is perhaps a matter for consideration whether in view of the number of small farms the estimate for buildings ought not to have been put somewhat higher, but on the whole, I think 12*l.* per acre may be taken as a reasonable average figure of the capital outlay incurred by landowners throughout England in the equipment of agricultural holdings.

Estimate of the "Economic Rent" of Agricultural Land.

If, then, we assume that the capital invested in the land in improvements requiring renewal and repairs, such as buildings, fences, gates, drainage, roads, &c., amounts on the average to 12*l.* per acre, and that the average gross rent at the present time is 1*l.* per acre (see Appendix C) the gross return is $8\frac{1}{3}$ per cent. Deducting 35 per cent. from the gross rent for repairs and upkeep, the net return on the capital invested in buildings, &c., is 5*l.* 8*s.* 4*d.* per cent. Or it may be put in this way :—

	Per Acre.		
	£	s.	d.
Gross rent	1	–	–
Repairs, management and outgoings of all kinds, and sinking fund for new buildings, drainage, fencing, at 35 per cent. of the gross rent	–	7	–
Interest on 12*l.* capital invested in permanent improvements at 3½ per cent.	–	8	5
Balance representing rent of the land itself, *i.e.*, the economic rent	–	4	7

It will, of course, be understood that in speaking of the capital invested in the land I am referring solely to the average sum which the provision of drainage, fencing, gates, roads and buildings would cost to supply. The capital invested in land when purchasing it represents all this, and also a payment for the "economic rent" which it may be expected to produce, as well as in many cases a payment for amenities appertaining to its possession.

If the above figures are accepted as of approximate accuracy, they would seem to show that the average rent of land in England and Wales, after deducting interest on capital, is about 4*s.* 6*d.* an acre, that is to say, that the net surplus remaining above the whole cost of production on 27,400,000 acres is about 6,300,000*l.*

This economic rent may be regarded as the net return which accrued to the nation at the end of the nineteenth century from the cultivation of the soil through its individual owners, and it is questionable whether it was not a lower figure than at any time in the previous hundred years, as the gross rent in 1815-30, which probably averaged about 20*s.* per acre, would undoubtedly have been subject to smaller deductions for repairs and interest than is the case with the gross rent in 1900. In short, the progress of agricultural knowledge, the advance of science, the development of the country by road and rail, the increase in the population, the proximity of markets and the better equipment of farms, have not resulted, in the face of reduced prices, in obtaining as great a surplus as was got some seventy or eighty years earlier.

As a nation, the smaller return from the soil is compensated for by the cheapness of some of the principal articles of food, but the fact that the progress and improvement of agriculture in the past century have failed to increase the economic value of land cannot be regarded as satisfactory. It suggests that those changes which are no doubt slowly taking place in our agricultural system must go much further before the full return to be expected from land so favourably situated as that of England can be obtained.

At the beginning of the nineteenth century, when "the agri-"culture of the kingdom was the first of all its concerns, the "foundation of all its prosperity," the growth in the population demanded the increased cultivation of corn to feed the people, and the formation of large farms was wisely urged as enabling a maximum of production at a minimum cost.

The opening of the twentieth century, however, finds an enormously increased population dependent for the greater proportion of its corn and meat on regions beyond the seas, and the arguments which encouraged the large farm to the disadvantage of the medium and small holding have no longer the same weight.

To split up a large farm is not, however, a change which a landowner can lightly undertake. New buildings, fences, and roads may be necessary, and without the prospect of a good return the necessary money is not likely to be forthcoming.

But it is in a return to the conditions of earlier times, to a more even distribution of the land in a larger number of holdings, that we may perhaps anticipate more profitable results from the utilisation of the soil. The medium farm, with a reasonable proportion of still smaller holdings, favours and encourages the growth of those products which can be produced as cheaply and as well in this country as abroad. In milk, dairy produce, eggs, pigs, calves, poultry, vegetables, and fruit, the farmers of this country are at no disadvantage as regards climate or soil compared with their principal competitors, while they have the advantage of nearness to markets; and it is probably true that a greater proportion of the soil of Great Britain could be advantageously devoted to these products than is the case at present, without interfering with large farms which, from soil or situation, are especially suitable to the growth of grain, beef, mutton, or wool.

APPENDIX.

A.—*Average Rent per Acre of Agricultural Land on certain Estates in Lincoln, Essex, Hereford, and North Wales from* 1800-1900.

Year.	Acreage.	Average Rent per Acre.		Year.	Acreage.	Average Rent per Acre.	
		s.	d.			s.	d.
1801	62,655	11	8	1850	72,585	16	3
'02	62,655	10	10	'51	72,603	16	–
'03	62,655	10	11	'52	72,602	16	6
'04	62,655	11	2	'53	72,805	16	7
'05	62,655	11	2	'54	72,784	16	8
'06	63,325	11	2	'55	72,799	16	9
'07	63,620	11	3	'56	72,799	17	1
'08	64,320	11	8	'57	72,802	17	6
'09	64,320	11	8	'58	72,812	17	9
				'59	72,814	17	9
1810	64,320	12	3	1860	72,353	18	–
'11	65,320	13	6	'61	71,900	18	2
'12	65,320	14	6	'62	72,177	18	1
'13	66,320	14	11	'63	72,222	18	2
'14	66,320	15	–	'64	72,234	18	2
'15	66,320	15	2	'65	72,246	18	5
'16	66,320	14	7	'66	72,185	18	6
'17	67,348	14	5	'67	72,251	18	7
'18	67,348	15	11	'68	72,423	18	9
'19	67,349	15	5	'69	72,411	18	11
1820	67,349	15	5	1870	72,804	18	9
'21	67,349	14	10	'71	72,811	19	2
'22	67,549	13	7	'72	73,237	19	5
'23	67,750	14	10	'73	73,242	19	9
'24	67,950	16	1	'74	73,240	20	–
'25	68,150	16	9	'75	73,240	20	1
'26	68,350	14	11	'76	73,251	20	1
'27	68,550	15	–	'77	73,249	20	3
'28	68,750	15	5	'78	73,203	20	6
'29	68,950	14	10	'79	73,201	20	2
				1880	73,172	18	5
1830	69,150	15	3	'81	71,172	18	7
'31	69,251	15	10	'82	71,179	18	2
'32	69,376	15	2	'83	71,177	17	6
'33	69,595	15	3	'84	71,165	16	11
'34	69,832	15	2	'85	71,165	16	8
'35	70,025	15	6	'86	71,165	16	4
'36	70,225	15	3	'87	71,165	15	10
'37	70,365	15	9	'88	71,160	15	6
'38	70,465	15	9	'89	71,656	15	6
'39	70,678	15	4	1890	71,656	15	7
				'91	71,656	15	2
1840	70,878	15	7	'92	71,656	15	7
'41	71,261	16	6	'93	71,656	14	8
'42	71,472	16	3	'94	71,601	15	–
'43	71,568	16	5	'95	71,147	14	6
'44	71,667	16	8	'96	71,323	14	7
'45	71,911	16	8	'97	71,346	14	2
'46	72,019	17	1	'98	71,338	14	5
'47	72,168	16	8	'99	71,469	14	7
'48	72,414	17	3	1900	71,469	14	7
'49	72,538	16	1				

B.—*Average Rent per Acre of Agricultural Land on certain Estates in Lincoln, Hereford, Bucks, Beds, Cambridge, Essex, and North Wales from 1816-1900.*

Year.	Acreage.	Rent per Acre. s. d.	Year.	Acreage.	Rent per Acre. s. d.
1816	109,421	18 –	1860	121,949	23 –
'17	110,500	18 9	'61	121,545	23 5
'18	110,500	19 4	'62	121,784	23 4
'19	110,876	18 9	'63	121,126	23 6
			'64	122,145	23 4
			'65	122,222	23 2
1820	111,082	18 8	'66	122,140	23 4
'21	111,081	18 3	'67	122,258	23 9
'22	111,239	17 2	'68	122,463	24 7
'23	111,240	17 6	'69	122,340	24 10
'24	111,348	18 2			
'25	111,375	18 6			
'26	112,377	17 2			
'27	112,399	17 3	1870	122,805	24 –
'28	112,502	18 4	'71	122,889	24 4
'29	112,568	17 10	'72	123,419	24 10
			'73	124,776	25 3
1830	112,568	18 4	'74	125,000	25 6
'31	112,799	18 8	'75	125,014	25 6
'32	113,824	18 4	'76	125,323	25 5
'33	114,320	18 5	'77	125,463	26 1
'34	114,349	18 4	'78	125,351	26 5
'35	114,434	18 6	'79	125,368	19 9
'36	114,434	18 8			
'37	114,181	18 6			
'38	115,190	18 5			
'39	115,153	18 5	1880	125,337	21 4
			'81	121,424	20 6
			'82	119,423	23 6
1840	115,514	19 1	'83	117,158	23 3
'41	115,597	19 9	'84	116,204	22 4
'42	119,272	19 10	'85	116,405	18 –
'43	119,330	20 1	'86	116,405	20 11
'44	118,814	20 4	'87	116,418	17 –
'45	118,762	20 6	'88	116,332	19 6
'46	118,759	20 9	'89	116,821	20 1
'47	118,847	20 6			
'48	119,042	21 1			
'49	119,222	20 3			
			1890	116,868	19 6
1850	119,484	20 6	'91	116,868	19 6
'51	119,983	19 10	'92	119,068	18 6
'52	120,453	20 3	'93	118,823	17 –
'53	120,758	20 1	'94	119,149	15 11
'54	121,014	20 4	'95	118,790	16 1
'55	121,092	20 10	'96	119,299	17 0
'56	121,151	21 10	'97	119,022	16 11
'57	121,750	22 11	'98	118,990	17 0
'58	121,759	23 3	'99	119,144	17 1
'59	122,145	23 1	1900	119,178	17 2

C.—*Average Rent per Acre of Agricultural Land on certain Estates distributed throughout England and Wales from 1872-1900.*

Year.	Acreage.	Rent per Acre. s. d.	Year.	Acreage.	Rent per Acre. s. d.
1872	415,003	28 6	1887	405,946	22 5
'73	416,749	28 10	'88	405,058	23 –
'74	418,650	29 –	'89	404,444	23 4
'75	418,852	29 1			
'76	419,936	29 3	1890	405,248	23 1
'77	420,591	29 9	'91	402,310	23 –
'78	421,903	29 6	'92	402,152	22 5
'79	421,654	26 8	'93	373,895	22 –
1880	420,045	26 4	'94	380,574	21 5
'81	416,941	25 11	'95	381,479	21 4
'82	413,258	27 1	'96	390,021	20 10
'83	408,910	27 4	'97	390,482	20 6
'84	406,096	26 6	'98	390,044	20 6
'85	406,239	24 1	'99	398,920	20 0
'86	407,299	24 4	1900	399,167	20 1

D.—*Income Tax (Schedule A). Gross Income derived from the Ownership of Lands in England and Wales for the years 1843-1905.*

Year ending April	Amount in Thousands. £	Percentage. 1867-77 = 100	Year ending April	Amount in Thousands. £	Percentage. 1867-77 = 100
1843	40,167	82	1874	49,906	102
'44	—	—	'75	50,125	102
'45	—	—	'76	50,218	103
'46	41,227	84	'77	51,811	106
'47	41,215	84	'78	51,722	106
'48	41,180	84	'79	51,658	105
'49	42,348	86	1880	51,799	106
1850	42,329	86	'81	51,599	105
'51	42,290	86	'82	51,182	104
'52	41,118	84	'83	48,403	99
'53	41,086	84	'84	47,955	98
'54	41,085	84	'85	47,594	97
'55	41,237	84	'86	45,994	94
'56	41,118	84	'87	45,376	93
'57	41,177	84	'88	44,472	91
'58	42,685	87	'89	42,274	86
'59	42,702	87	1890	41,796	85
1860	42,940	88	'91	41,379	84
'61	42,976	88	'92	41,130	84
'62	44,639	91	'93	40,805	83
'63	44,611	91	'94	40,066	82
'64	44,672	91	'95	39,680	81
'65	46,403	95	'96	39,366	80
'66	46,422	95	'97	38,806	79
'67	46,492	95	'98	38,143	78
'68	47,711	97	'99	37,296	76
'69	47,744	97	1900	37,111	76
1870	47,803	98	'01	36,942	75
'71	48,938	100	'02	36,804	75
'72	48,964	100	'03	36,624	75
'73	49,009	100	'04	36,923	75

E.—*Rent of certain Individual Farms.*
Farm of 204 Acres in Wilts.

Year.	Rent, less Abatements.			Remarks.
	£	s.	d.	
1809	255	–	–	Held on lease expiring in 1816.
'16	370	–	–	The rent was much below the average of rents during the war, and on the expiration of the lease, the farm was re-let on a yearly tenancy.
'17	325	–	–	Rent reduced in consequence of fall of prices on conclusion of peace.
'22	288	–	–	Reduction 10 per cent. and allowance for damage by quarry.
'30	273	10	–	Abatement 10 per cent.
'31	267	5	–	,, 15 per cent.
'31–49	288	–	–	
'50–53	259	–	–	,, 10 per cent.
'54	288	–	–	
'56	289	10	–	}Interest on draining added.
'62	291	2	–	
'63	295	–	–	
'64	333	10	–	Farm re-let at an additional rent of 38*l*. 10*s*. the first year and a further 25*l*. in subsequent years, less 16*s*. for land taken for cottages.
'65–80	357	14	–	
'80–81	304	1	–	Abatement 15 per cent.
'81–86	307	14	–	,, of 50*l*. each year.
'86–1907	250	–	–	

Note.—During the last forty-five years the landlord (besides paying half the labour and providing the materials for ordinary repairs) has expended on the buildings 535*l*. 16*s*. 9*d*., and in draining (for which no interest was charged) since 1863 259*l*. 14*s*. 11*d*.

A Farm of 225 Acres in Norfolk.

Year.	Rent.	Year.	Rent.	Year.	Rent.
	£		£		£
1712–22	80	1799–1806	210	1876–80	450
'22–28	84	1806–14	200	'80–83	380
'28–57	100	'14–20	700	'83–90	300
'57–70	120	'20–27	585	'90–93	250
'70–86	130	'27–34	375	'93–94	225
'86–92	170	'34–41	261	'94–97	210*
'92–99	190	'41–76	500	'97–1906	225*

* The landlord has paid the tithe since 1894. In 1905 this amounted to 64*l*. 3*s*. 8*d*., so that if this is deducted from the rent of 225*l*., the net rent in that year was 160*l*. 16*s*. 4*d*.

Note.—According to the agreement for this farm, the tenant pays the drainage rate and all other outgoings except land tax and property tax, and keeps in repair the windows, fixtures, gates, fences, &c., the house and buildings being repaired by the landlord. In 1822 a new bullock shed was erected and since that time the farm-house, barns, and other portions of the out-buildings have been re-built. The tenant paid the tithe up to 1894.

E.—*Rent of certain Individual Farms—Contd.*

Four Typical Farms in the South Midlands.

Year.	Farm C.		Farm D.		Farm E.		Farm F.	
	Acreage.	Rent.	Acreage.	Rent.	Acreage.	Rent.	Acreage.	Rent.
		£		£		£		£
1807	352	399	122	103	—	—	454	524
'17	352	500	122	147	—	—	443	606
'27	356	434	121	127	—	—	448	494
'32	—	—	—	—	393	422	—	—
'37	360	390	121	110	—	—	472	500
'42	—	—	—	—	396	492	—	—
'47	356	442	120	122	396	492	478	526
'57	356	410	122	134	424	603*	475	739*
'67	357	460*	122	152*	424	492*	475	626*
'77	354	473*	122	198	416	570	500	800
'87†	354	225	122	79	416	285	487	350
'97	354	302	122	100	417	330	468	425
1907	359	302	122	100	417	330	467	420

* In these years the rent was partly a corn rent.

† In 1887 50 per cent. of the rent was remitted. The figure given is the sum actually paid.

Note.—Farm C is a grass farm; farm D is a heavy land arable farm; farm E is a mixed heavy and light land farm, half arable and half grass; farm F is a light limestone "turnip and barley" farm.

THE COMMISSIONERS
OF ENCLOSURE

M. W. Beresford

COMMISSIONERS OF ENCLOSURE

By M. W. BERESFORD

THIS essay is concerned with those men who were given by Statute an all-but-absolute authority to enclose and redistribute common and open fields between about 1745 and the General Act of 1845. It deals with Commissioners as professional men tackling problems which were novel in the first generation, and only slowly evolving standards of procedure. Criticism of the partiality (as apart from the cost) of a Commission was rare, so that the questions of proper or improper motive which surround the discussion of many enclosure problems will not arise here. The materials for this investigation are the minutes, accounts, letters and working papers of Commissioners in several Midland counties,[1] and a study of the Commissioners named in all the Acts for Warwickshire, Worcestershire and Staffordshire. The private diary of one Commissioner[2] and the personal account book of another[3] have survived to yield details of work before and after the meetings recorded in the Minutes. The scarcity of these minutes has been frequently commented upon.[4]

The earliest Commissions (1730–60) were very large, and often local, giving something of the appearance of a grand jury of umpires seeing fair treatment of their fellow landowners. When the pace of enclosure quickened, and anxious eyes were cast on the expense of a Commission, a smaller appointment became the rule and the paid professional Commissioner appeared. If landowners could have agreed, an Act and a Commission would have been superfluous. The multiplicity of Acts may be read not only as evidence of dissension on the issue of enclosure[5] among the gentry who flew to Parliament as an arbiter, but perhaps as showing that many who agreed that enclosure was necessary could not agree on the details of property redistribution. A Commissioner disinterested in the lands to be enclosed, but trusted by the owners who had nominated him, might produce an Award about which there might be individual complaints, but which could be accepted as being at the worst equally unfair to everyone.

A Commissioner described his powers in 1766 in these terms:

A Commissioner is appointed by Act of Parliament for dividing and allotting common fields and is directed to do it according to the respective interests of proprietors... without undue preference to any, but paying regard to situation,

---

[1] Cambridgeshire: in University Library, Cambridge, Class ADD 6013–88 and 6955–6; Class DOC 624 et seq. A complete list of these parishes (45 out of the 115 statutory enclosures in the county) is given in *Trans. Cambs. Antiq. Soc.* XL, 78.
Bedfordshire: County Records, Shire Hall, Bedford.
Leicestershire: Muniment Room, The Museum, Leicester.
Yorkshire: Sheffield City Library.
Northamptonshire: Northampton Borough Library.
Staffordshire and Worcestershire: Birmingham Reference Library.
Warwickshire: Birmingham Reference Library; County Records, Shire Hall, Warwick; Birthplace Library, Stratford on Avon.
Buckinghamshire: Drayton Parslow Minutes summarized in *Records of Buckinghamshire*, XI, 256. Buckingham, 1926.
[2] Sheffield, WC/2219.
[3] Warwick, HR/5.
[4] A list is given in *E.H.R.* LVII, 250–63 by W. E. Tate, but is incomplete.
[5] As Paul Mantoux argues, *The Industrial Revolution in the Eighteenth Century*, 1928, p. 170.

quality and convenience. The method of ascertainment is left to the major part of the Commission...and this without any fetter or check upon them beside their own honour confidence (and late indeed) awed by the solemnity of an oath. This is perhaps one of the greatest trusts ever reposed in one set of men; and merits all the return of caution attention and integrity which can result from an honest impartial and ingenuous mind.[1]

The author, the Rev. William Homer of Birdingbury, was a prolific pamphleteer and himself known to have been Commissioner in all the Midland counties. His name appears in Acts for at least twenty enclosures in surrounding counties alone, and the tone of these words from his preface is exactly that of a man self-consciously surveying the importance of his new profession, anxious to set its standards high and to offer guidance to others who would succeed to these duties:[2]

In this age abounding with Inclosures it cannot be an uninteresting subject to canvass the Principles upon which the determination of Commissioners are usually founded. This is now a Science, which in its infancy was confessedly understood very imperfectly. What is here offered is drawn upon a Plan.

And again:[3]

It is the principal design of the writer of this Essay to establish all determinations about Property as much as possible upon certain and invariable Principles.

Eighty years later, the 1844 Commons Committee on Inclosures printed its evidence covering some seven thousand questions to witnesses.[4] Except for minor criticisms of certain Commissioners, there is no evidence of widespread dissatisfaction with the work of the Commissioners.

A contemporary account of the enclosure of Charnwood Forest (c. 1840) puts the position fairly:[5]

They executed their very onerous duties with fairness and fidelity although it must not be concealed that a considerable degree of dissatisfaction prevailed at the unparalleled expenditure. A leaning in favour of the principal proprietors has also been imputed to the Commissioners...chiefly in their endeavours to accommodate the Lords by fixing their allotments as near as possible to their respective parks. The reader may satisfy himself as to the general impartiality of the Commissioners by studying the list of claims with reasons for their rejection. The claims of the most influential persons were disallowed: while those possessed of no influence whatever were admitted.

Homer speaks of an age 'abounding with Inclosures', and the world must have seemed like this to a busy Commissioner. It will emphasize the professional pride which we have seen in Homer if we examine the number of enclosures which a Commissioner might undertake.

In 1844, when the main flood of enclosure was almost spent, the Select Committee of the Commons on Inclosure heard witnesses who had been engaged in Commissions. One from Lincolnshire had been fourteen times Commissioner,[6] another, Commissioner, Agent or Solicitor in twenty parishes,[7] and George

---

[1] William Homer, *An Essay on the Nature and Method [of] the Inclosure of Common Fields*, p. 61. Oxford, 1766. This is the author called 'Horner' by E. C. K. Gonner, *Common Land and Inclosure*, 1912.
[2] Ibid. p. 1.   [3] Ibid. p. 2.
[4] Parliamentary Papers (hereafter called P.P.) 1844, v, Q 3005/6.
[5] T. R. Potter, *Charnwood Forest*, 1842, p. 30.   [6] P.P. 1844, v, Q 1328.
[7] *House of Commons Committee Reports*, 1800, IX, 227.

Maxwell told an earlier Committee that from 1773 to 1800 he had been over a hundred times a Commissioner.[1] Christopher Pemberton was Clerk to 45 Cambridgeshire enclosures and his firm's collection of Minutes is now in the University Library.

That these are not boasting or spectacular exceptions to a more moderate rule is shown by the following table:

Table 1

328 Commissioners in 400 Warwickshire, Worcestershire and Staffordshire Enclosures[2]

194 acted in	1 enclosure	49 acted in	2 enclosures
22	3 enclosures	12	4 ,,
13	5 ,,	8	6 ,,
3	7 ,,	3	8 ,,
1	9 ,,	4	10 ,,
2	12 ,,	3	13 ,,
1	14 ,,	1	15 ,,
2	16 ,,	1	17 ,,
2	18 ,,	1	20 ,,
1	21 ,,	1	22 ,,
1	23 ,,	2	29 ,,
1	32 ,,		

966 Commissioners are named in 400 Acts: an average of over two Commissioners per enclosure. Somewhat similar results could be shown by the tabulation of the 80 Cambridgeshire Commissioners named in 36 Cambridgeshire Enclosures.

Many of these Commissioners are to be found working in other parishes. John Chamberlain was twelve times Commissioner in Warws, Worcs, and Staffs, eighteen times in Oxon,[3] and at least once in Bucks.[4] It was only natural for a landowner looking for a suitable Commissioner to think of those already experienced. The same is true of surveyors, many of whom appear in minute book after minute book. In some cases Commissioners seem to have worked in groups, undertaking as a team[5] (although of course engaged as individuals) work in many parishes. We have families like the Nockolds, three generations of whom were Commissioners; or the Bloodworths of Kimbolton; or such indications of continuity as those seen in the Chesterton (Cambs) papers in 1838 where the MSS. pencil notes[6] make it clear that they were used as a basis for the proceedings *mutatis mutandis* in the Willingham enclosure of 1846, just as Stow-cum-Quy[7] was utilized for Cottenham in 1842.

The Commissioner was usually named in the Act, but the choice lay, not with the Parliamentary Committees who examined the Bill, but with the landowners concerned. This arrangement was given implicit statutory recognition in such a clause as that in the Bottisham (Cambs) Act (1801) which names three persons as Commissioners, and then continues that, if any die, the three principal proprietors are to make the reappointment. At Abberley (1814), if the Commissioner dies the majority in value of the proprietors are to choose a Commissioner.

[1] *House of Commons Committee Reports*, p. 223.
[2] From the collection of Acts at Birmingham, 17240.
[3] Ex inf. W. E. Tate, unpublished thesis. [4] Buckinghamshire, op. cit.
[5] In Cambridgeshire Hare and Maxwell worked together on three enclosures; Truslove and Custance on eight; Wedge and Custance on five; Thorpe and Custance on three.
[6] Cambridge, ADD 6028. [7] Ibid. 6032.

At Abbots Morton (1770) the surviving Commissioners are to replace a dead member. At Kingswinford (Staffs) four Commissioners are named, and these four are to choose a fifth themselves.[1] It was common enough for the proprietor of great importance to regard it as his right to nominate a Commissioner: thus the Hathersage Bill states that if the Commissioner John Dowland dies, his successor shall be nominated by the Duke of Devonshire;[2] on 19 January 1824 this provision fell to be carried out.[3] On the other hand, we know from the case of Barton[4] (where some proprietors unsuccessfully tried to have Nockolds as Commissioner) that meetings would reject some suggested Commissioner.

The extant MSS. notes of evidence given to a Parliamentary Committee on the Barton (Cambs) Bill show an agent of one of the parties concerned describing the proprietors' meeting earlier in 1839. It is a great loss that so little other verbatim reporting of evidence before Lords' or Commons' Committees has survived.[5] This note was found among the Pemberton papers.[6]

Mr Adcock called and examined 6th June 1839. He is agent for the Incorporated Society of the Governors of the Sons of the Clergy. He was present at a tithe and enclosure meeting of the proprietors of Barton in Cambridge in February. He had no official instructions, but there stated that he thought the Governors would oppose the project, if it ignored their claims. This later proved to be true. Mr Jackson was appointed Commissioner by the Lords of the Manor, Mr Utton the other. He was not called to another meeting. He did not make any formal objection to the appointments, or vote for or against the Commissioners. At the meeting there were the Lords of the Manor and some proprietors who said very little. There was very little discussion except over the size of the assignments to the Lords, i.e. 1/20th or 1/16th or 1/25th. Mr Pemberton conducted most of the business. There was some discussion of the amount to be paid to the Commissioners and Surveyor.

Professional Commissioners were consulted before Bills went to the Commons, and this tended to give uniformity to the many Private Acts which preceded the General Acts of 1801 and 1845. From the papers of the Yorkshire Commissioner, Fairbank, we know that he was consulted by Sir John Sinclair, President of the Board of Agriculture, who was vainly attempting in 1796 to obtain the third reading of a General Bill.[7]

Proprietors' consultation of Fairbank included an examination of the draft,[8] dining out and spending an evening with some of the promoters[9] and being present at the meetings of proprietors called to discuss the promotion of the Bill.[10] It is clear that a great deal of contentious matter was eliminated and the major proprietors' interests satisfied *before* the Bill went to Westminster.

The Duke of Kingston wrote to the attorney of one proprietor in 1786:[11]

> The Duke and several owners desire you will please meet them...in order to consult proper measures for the bringing in a Bill in the next session for inclosing the open field and Commons.

---

[1] Birmingham, 529363.
[2] Sheffield, Fairbank MB/237, i.
[3] The implicit right of the great proprietors to reappoint their nominees is shown every time a death occurs while a Commission is in progress. Cf. Cambridge, ADD 6053, f. 48.
[4] Ibid. DOC 622, f. 56.
[5] The accounts in W. E. Tate, art. cit. and in his *Parliamentary Land Enclosures*, Nottingham, 1935, show how useful and at the same time how limited is the information of the Lords' and Commons' Journals. No Committee minutes have survived in the Lords' or Commons' MSS. records and none were printed.
[6] Cambridge, ADD 6022.
[7] Sheffield, WC/2219.
[8] Ibid. sub 23 November 1795.
[9] Ibid. 28 December 1795.
[10] Ibid. 30 December 1795.
[11] Ibid. WC/2240, f. 5.

The attorney's reply is significant:[1]

It is unnecessary for Mrs S. to see a draft. She only desires that Mr J. Brettle be appointed a Commissioner.

The correspondence which ensued between the Duke's steward and Mrs S.'s attorney is also significant. It shows how the Commissioners were considered as nominees; it moves over to a reminder of the impartiality which the Oath enjoined upon the Commission; and it touches upon the vexed point that Commissioners cost money:[2]

All the proprietors, being aprized of the great expense and delays that would consequently arise by having too great a number of Commissioners did agree that Mr Oldknow should stand as Commissioner for all the parties, and, to prevent an undue preference to be given to any of the parties, Mr Oldknow should name two other Commissioners who had no other connection with any of the parties: viz. Mr Ayre and Mr Stone. Therefore it makes it impracticable for Mrs S. to propose any alteration...and were it not so that, if Mrs S. names her Commissioner, no doubt but the Duke, Mr Broughton, Mr Edge, Mr Saltmarsh, the Vicar and several others would expect to do the same, so that... instead of three Commissioners we should have a dozen? You know too that you told Mr Shering that if the Vicar named a Commissioner you would do so too, but that if he gave up that point you would do likewise. Are not the three Commissioners persons of Honour, Worth and Probity and are not they obliged by the intended oath to make the allotments to the proprietors without favour?

At another meeting of Yorkshire proprietors the draft Bill is approved with the addition,[3] 'that the greatest economy in expenses are to be observed, as otherwise the expenses of the enclosure are likely to be greater than the advantages', and many other proprietors expressed publicly and privately their anxiety to reconcile adequate representation of interests with decent economy in number (and costs) of Commissioners. Sir John Beckett spoke of 'that necessity of representing all interests—which *drives* you to three Commissioners' in his evidence to the 1844 Commons Committee.[4]

Sometimes, a witness told the same Committee,[5] a Commissioner would be chosen from a distance if local feeling was running high. The distance added to the expenses, since three guineas a day was paid for travelling expenses. The letter inviting him to be Commissioner came, said this witness, as a complete surprise: it was from Radnor and he was in Bedford.

An unsuccessful petition meant that the petitioning landowners would have to bear the cost of the application: some idea of this cost is given by the solicitor's bill[6] for obtaining the Badsey (Worcs) Act. Even excluding £225 legal fees, expenses totalled £562 between September 1811 and May 1812. Another £58 went in travelling expenses to meetings of proprietors to obtain their signature of consent, and to London to watch over the Bill in the House. Pemberton's bill for Long Stow[7] totalled £225, including an amount for 'attendances on the members for the County of Cambridge while the Bill was before the Commons and on Earl Hardwick while it was before the Lords...5 guineas' with a note signed by Pemberton: 'many attendances not charged for.'

Pemberton's Bills for soliciting twenty-five enclosures totalled £6215—an average of £248. A Board of Agriculture estimate put the solicitor's cost for an

---

[1] Sheffield, WC/2240, f. 5.
[2] Ibid.
[3] Ibid. WC/2251, f. 29.
[4] P.P. 1844, v, Q 3631.
[5] Ibid. Q 3697.
[6] Birmingham, 377180.
[7] Cambridge, DOC 645, ff. iv and v.

average bill at £497,[1] but this probably included the usual £200 or more for Parliamentary fees.

The impartiality of Commissioners in their task of reallocation and assessment was essential. The oath inserted in the Acts after 1760 was an attempt to ensure this. There were other attempts to exclude Commissioners with direct interest in the parish. A resolution of the Commons' 'Committee to consider Persons to be appointed Commissioner' ran:[2]

Resolved: there be inserted an oath that the Commissioner is not to be interested in lands so intended to be enclosed or to be steward, bailiff or agent of any person so intending.

Resolved: that the words 'and has not been steward for the last three years' be added.

This was not always observed: the obituary of the first Commissioner for the enclosure of Erdington and Witton[3] described him as: 'Steward of Heneas Legge, of Aston Hall, lord of the Manor of Erdington and Witton.'[4]

We have seen that the expense of a Commission loomed large in the proprietors' eyes, for that sum would be found by an assessed rate on their property. What were those expenses?

There was the cost of promotion, whether successful or unsuccessful. There were the fees of the officers—clerk, surveyor—and the cost of the fencing, hedging and ditching consequent upon the new lay-out of the fields. And there was the Commission's fee. 'There were usually three Commissioners with a fee of three guineas a day each', reports a witness before the Commons' Committee of 1844.[5] In 1800, Maxwell, an experienced Commissioner, said that two sufficed.[6] John Iveson, another witness[7] in 1844, was one of six Commissioners for Charnwood, and often all were present. We have seen that the average number of Commissioners for the 450 enclosures which have been examined was just over two.[8]

The Commissioners' fees were sometimes mentioned in the Act, as was the two guineas for Hathersage,[9] but by no means always. The Board of Agriculture Reports give £344 as the average cost of a Commissioner. The Stow (Cambs)[10] Act laid down three guineas a day, but for fifteen meetings the Commissioner was actually paid £189.[11]

Homer says that:[12]

Commissioners ought themselves particularly to set examples of moderation both in their demands and their expenses, neither to desire to be paid for Commission Days upon which they cannot give attendance on the business, nor to live, when they do attend, beyond their station, nor to make meetings of this kind seasons of jollity for themselves at the expense of the proprietors.

These strictures are echoed by the House of Commons Committee of 1795:[13] 'many complaints have been made of the remissness with which Commissioners

[1] Quoted by E. C. K. Gonner, op. cit.
[2] *House of Commons Committee Reports*, 1801, III, 20.
[3] Birmingham, 326709.
[4] *Aris, Birmingham Gazette*, 7 December 1801.
[5] P.P. 1844, V, Q 2342.
[6] *House of Commons Committee Reports*, 1800, IX, 233.
[7] P.P. 1844, V, Q 3696. But this was a vast enclosure.
[8] Table 1, p. 132 supra.
[9] Sheffield, Fairbank MB 237.
[10] 1839.
[11] Cambridge, ADD 6063.
[12] Op. cit. 108.
[13] *House of Commons Committee Reports*, 1795.

proceed and the exorbitant charges which they sometimes make or expenses which they occasion.' Five years later another Committee reported:[1] 'We have been able to discover no flagrant instance of misbehaviour of a Commissioner' and recommended a fee of two guineas a day, exclusive of travelling day, since Commissioners come 'sometimes from considerable distances where their avocation has carried them'.

One witness spoke of coming fifty miles for an enclosure and protested against the type of contract wherein Commissioners were paid a fixed lump sum: in this case, of two hundred guineas.[2] His colleague had received the same sum, but had travelled only half a mile! To the Committee of 1844 no witness could relate such an agreement within his personal experience,[3] although it had in fact been a recommendation of the Commons Committee of 1801 that a total sum should be named in all Enclosure Acts as a Commissioner's fee.[4]

Even after the General Act there was considerable variety in the fee-clauses, which in some Acts did not even appear at all. Concern for economy in fees moved some petitioners to insert detailed directions into the Act, as at Alstonefield (1834)[5] or Colmworth (Beds) where a detailed Time Book has survived, giving exact times spent on the journey and in the fields.[6]

What were the Commissioners' expenses? One Commissioner spoke of six guineas expenses for a single day; and another that the chief proprietor had made an agreement with him before the Bill for one payment only of £200 and eleven guineas expenses which proved to be insufficient.[7] At Aspley Guise, Beds, the Commissioners' inn-charges of 5s. 3d. a day were met by the proprietors, although the fee was there only 10s. a meeting.[8]

The survival of the private accounts of the Commissioner for Bickenhill, Warws,[9] shows that it cost him about 10s. a meeting for inn-charges for himself and servant. These are not charged in the printed accounts but covered by three guineas allowance 'for each travelling day'. The Commissioner received 183 times three guineas, in fact: that is, three guineas fee for each of the 68 meetings and three guineas for a day's journey to the enclosure and three guineas for the day after the meeting. In many instances the business lasted for more than one day, and the Commissioner's inn at Coleshill was less than five miles from the enclosed fields!

Table 2 takes three busy Cambridgeshire Commissioners and analyses their income and what they did to earn it.

Table 2

Commissioner:	Dugmore	Custance	Hare
Number of meetings	88 [12 years]	443 [22 years]	186 [14 years]
Total remuneration	£1018	£4556	£979
Average fee per day	£12	£10	£5
Average income per annum	£85	£207	£70

These fees are well above the statutory three guineas and probably include travel and subsistence allowances. The total sum was paid to the Commissioners usually not in a lump sum, but in instalments.

[1] *House of Commons Committee Reports*, 1800, IX, p. 1.
[2] Ibid. loc. cit.
[3] P.P. 1844, Q 202.
[4] *House of Commons Committee Reports*, 1801, III, 209.
[5] 4 Geo. IV, c. 15.
[6] Bedford DD/WG/9.
[7] *House of Commons Committee Reports*, 1800, IX, 223–7.
[8] T. Batchelor, *General View of...Bedfordshire*, 1808, p. 221.
[9] Warwick, HR/5.

Each of the recorded meetings in any set of minutes details the business which the Commissioner undertook. Broadly, these vary very little from Cambridgeshire to Warwickshire, although there was no rule of thumb which could indicate how long each detail of the enclosure would take in any one parish.

An enclosure was not to be concluded in one autumn. To survey; or to check an old survey; to value and reallocate; to settle claims and disputes: these were long and arduous labours. Early work of receiving claims took many meetings but could be done rapidly. The later work of valuing and redistributing (with accompanying disputes) was a long task. Many proprietors found that it might be a matter of years, although few offered the Alstonefield incentive to speed by diminishing fees as time passed. Sometimes a forfeit was exacted if the Commissioner was late in the completion of the enclosure. Harwood could not attend a Committee of the House of Commons on the Barton (Cambs)[1] Bill because he had to finish an enclosure engagement by the first of May.

How long did those enclosures take which were not hampered by some such local impediments as the litigation which made the Rhyddlan enclosure last over 40 years[2] or the bankers' bankruptcy at Clun Forest?[3]

Table 3 gives time tables of 53 enclosures whose minutes have been examined.

Table 3

Summary of 53 enclosures[4]

Number of enclosures complete in	1 year	2
,,	,,	2 years	8
,,	,,	3 ,,	8
,,	,,	4 ,,	8
,,	,,	5 ,,	6
,,	,,	6 ,,	2
,,	,,	7 ,,	6
,,	,,	8 ,,	1
,,	,,	9 ,,	—
,,	,,	10 ,,	2
,,	,,	11 ,,	2
,,	,,	12 years or more	8

Commissioners did not have to hold meetings at regular intervals. The adjournments display no regular pattern, and there was no statutory guidance. Enclosures usually began in June, July, August or September (probably to begin after harvest). Of forty-five sets of minutes examined, only eleven began in other months. Good weather and long daylight hours favoured summer meetings, and the cold months were unpopular for journeys to distant parishes. We have seen that the meetings in an enclosure were most frequent at the beginning, when much formal receipt of claims had to be undertaken, so that it is not surprising that Table 5 analysing 659 meetings,[5] shows a significant grouping, with few meetings in the early summer with its growing crops, and many in the autumn.

---

[1] Cambridge, ADD 6022.
[2] P.P. 1844, v, Q 2248.
[3] Ibid. Q 2493.
[4] Collected from the sources named in n. 1, p. 130 supra.
[5] Ibid.

Table 4

Length of time taken over enclosure and frequency of meetings

Cambridgeshire enclosures		Summary of all known enclosure meetings	
Parish	Dates covered	Total meetings	Average per year
Rampton	1839–1843	29	6
Harston	1798–1801	35	8
Barnwell	1807–1811	37	7
Barton	1839–1840	18	9
Bassingbourn	1801–1814	40	3
Bottisham	1801–1808	31	4
Chesterton	1838–1840	31	10
Comberton	1839–1841	19	6
Connington	1800–1801	5	3
Cottenham	1842–1847	30	5
Eversden	1811–1814	21	5
Fulbourn	1806–1830	37	2
Girton	1808–1814	16	2
Gransden	1813–1826	28	2
Guilden Morden	1800–1814	40	3
Hardwick	1836–1838	40	13
Kingston	1810–1815	24	4
Landbeach	1807–1813	33	5
Longstanton A.S.	1811–1816	32	5
Longstanton St.M.	1813–1816	15	4
Long Stow	1798–1800	16	5
Oakington	1833–1835	36	12
Stow-cum-Quy	1839–1841	15	5
Sawston	1802–1811	33	3
Stapleford	1812–1814	24	8
Steeple Morden	1807–1817	40	4
Stetchworth	1814–1820	26	4
Swaffham	1805–1814	23	2
Swavesey	1838–1839	7	3
Teversham	1810–1818	27	3
West Wickham	1812–1822	44	4
Whaddon	1840–1841	4	2
Willingham	1846–1853	24	3
Waresley	1808–1822	48	4

Table 5

Meetings held in each month

Jan.	Feb.	Mar.	Apr.	May	June	July	Aug.	Sept.	Oct.	Nov.	Dec.
56	54	51	35	38	50	51	66	56	76	68	58

With all the possibilities of delay, proprietors sometimes expressed natural impatience. One wrote:[1]

I must express my wish that the enclosure might not stand over another season. I am afraid that this will be the case unless you take the trouble to remind the Commissioner that he has now been indulged with every reasonable time, and that after such indulgence every delay increases the expense.

[1] Sheffield, F/CP/31/8.

Not all were as lucky as Whaddon,[1] enclosed in three meetings. One optimistic forecast is to be found among the MSS. notes on a proposal to enclose Atherstone (Warws) where the solicitor wrote in pencil:[2]

> Act passed ann 1731 then
> to be surveyed by 2 ffebry 1731
> to be aloted by 2 ffebry 1732
> and to be finished by 24 March 1733

Sometimes Commissioners attributed the delay to proprietors who had not paid their share of the levy. At Leighton Buzzard one Commissioner wrote to the Clerk:[3]

I quite think with you that it is time the Business was brought to a close and I considered we had so settled at our last meeting...'that those proprietors who had neglected to have paid their Rate by a stated time should be proceded against', and as you have since then made several applications...I would take the necessary steps which I consider there is no necessity of our holding a meeting expressly for.

Sometimes the Commissioners themselves were reproached. A solicitor wrote to the Commissioner for Attercliffe (Yorks):[4]

We hope that the enclosure has not encroached too much on your other engagements, but we think it is high time that the business should be closed.

Commissioners were busy men. Apart from the pressure of other enclosure meetings, some Commissioners were clergymen, some land-agents, some surveyors, some stewards. Men who can be called 'professional Commissioners' include Arthur Elliot, whose private diary[5] shows that in the year 1797/8 he spent 105 days holding formal enclosure meetings, and fourteen on consultative work. In eight weeks in 1795 he was engaged in negotiations for the enclosure of eight parishes, and in the next year held 117 meetings for twelve parishes.

To save time, Commissioners held meetings for different enclosures on the same day, usually at the same Inn. To the Commissioner this might seem to save time, but to any one parish it might seem a hindrance, since the meeting would always be outside one of the parishes concerned, and if it were at some central point (such as the Eagle Inn at Cambridge) it would be outside all the parishes concerned. On the other hand if all the meetings were in the parishes concerned, then a Commissioner would spend his time (and the proprietors' money) on the road. Many Acts contained a clause prohibiting meetings more than 6 or 10 miles from the parish.

'It would be a good thing to prohibit Commissioners working more than one enclosure on one day', said Thomas Harrison, himself twenty times a Commissioner, to the Committee of 1800,[6] and to the 1844 Committee another witness said:[7]

Commissioners often find it difficult to give time continuously to one enclosure because of their other commitments.

The Cambridgeshire minutes when examined for simultaneous enclosures, often with the same Commissioners, yield many examples of coincident meetings: the Commissions for Barton and Comberton opened on the same day, and held seven coincident meetings in 1842. Twice in 1814, Thorpe, Commissioner for

[1] Cambridge, ADD 6084. [2] Warwick, HR/35.
[3] Bedford. Uncatalogued MSS., shelf BO.
[4] Sheffield, CP/35/75. [5] Ibid. WC/2219.
[6] *House of Commons Committee Reports*, 1800, IX, 232.
[7] P.P. 1844, V, Q 199. Elmhirst, the author of *A View of the Agriculture of...Lincolnshire*, 1794, says on p. 84 that he was once engaged simultaneously on nine enclosures.

Kingston, Longstanton and Teversham held meetings for all three parishes on the same day. An inn was a convenient rendezvous, and neutral ground. There is only one meeting at a private house recorded in these 45 sets of minutes.[1]

Did all the Commission attend? There are many cases when the Commission is incomplete. This is usually acknowledged in the minutes: at Whitwick there were three adjournments because only one Commissioner was present, and on three other occasions there is a blank page when no Commissioner came. It must be remembered that the earliest Acts (1730–60) appointed a large Commission. A small quorum was usually designated. At Rothley only four of the five Commissioners were present for over 50% of the meetings. Alderminster (1726) was enclosed by ten Commissioners, with a quorum of five. Later Acts presupposed a small Commission of professionals, and the Astley Act (1811) rules 'if any Commissioner is absent from the first and second or any two subsequent meetings then he shall be deemed to refuse to act'. I know of no Commissioner who was removed from office: but there were at least one resignation,[2] two refusals to stand,[3] and several Commissioners died in harness.[4]

Proprietors were not compelled to attend meetings. Attendance usually depended on interest. Claims could be delivered by post or proxy.[5] Rampton had twenty-three meetings: at six no proprietors were present; at five over fifteen attended. At these five meetings the business included voting the Commissioners' fees; auditing the accounts; objecting to claims; and considering the result of a lawsuit against one of their number. At Erdington three proprietors heard the award read, although twenty-seven had attended a meeting concerned with a disputed common. The usual formula in the minutes was that 'the award was executed in the presence of such proprietors as attended'.

The reading of the award and its formal enrolment were the Commissioner's last acts. In no set of minutes is there any formal dissolution. It is quite common for the minutes to stop in the middle of a page, or to adjourn to a given date, for which there is no entry. An adjournment *sine die* only appears once, at Salford (Beds). In the Newbold Vernon (Leics) minutes the last three entries are in pencil instead of ink, and then there is a blank.

Since the minutes are in large folio volumes, many pages are left blank. There was no legal compulsion to deposit minutes with the Clerk of the Peace and they seem to have passed into the hands of the Clerk to the Enclosure. Those which survive derive generally from solicitors' offices, where the Clerk had bound them up with a copy of the relevant Private Act, embossed them with the name of the parish and then added them to the office files. There they remained until they passed to the County Records Office or to the Library where they now lie.[6]

---

[1] References to these meetings will be found in the minutes of the parishes named among the Cambridge enclosure papers cited in n. 1, p. 130 supra.

[2] Cambridge, ADD 6023, 16 November 1801.

[3] Cardington and Wilshamstead enclosure papers, Bedford, DD/HA/16.

[4] Alexander Watford (Rampton), Jacob Nockolds (Oakington), Martin Nockolds (Chesterton) are some of these.

[5] Leicester, 4D/31/242, is a bundle of proxy claims.

[6] I am grateful to the various archivists and librarians who have helped to track down minutes; to Mr W. E. Tate for answering queries; and to Mr E. Welbourne who first aroused my curiosity unwittingly by stating baldly: 'the only people who gained by enclosures were the Liberals who won a political grievance; the lawyers who gained by the legalism of the procedure; and the Surveyor-turned-Commissioner who lived in the new house overlooking the fields where he made his fortune.'

BIBLIOGRAPHICAL NOTE, 1966

M. W. Beresford, 'Minutes of enclosure commissioners', *Bull. Inst. Hist. Res.* (1947), 59–69, was an attempt to survey the minutes and working papers that I had encountered in archives. Since that date the expansion of county Record Offices has much increased the availability of this type of document, gathered in from parish chests, estate offices and solicitors' offices. Reference should be made to the accession lists and guides published by the C.R.O.s.

M. W. Beresford, 'The minute book of a Leicestershire enclosure', *Trans. Leics. Arch. Soc.*, xxiii (1947), 3–23, was a transcript, with notes, of the minutes for the enclosure of Newbold Verdon.

W. E. Tate, 'The cost of Parliamentary enclosure in England', *Econ. Hist. Rev.*, 2nd ser., v (1953), 258–65, gives figures from the papers of Lincolnshire, Oxfordshire and Cambridgeshire commissioners. H. G. Hunt, 'The chronology of Parliamentary enclosure in Leicestershire', *Econ. Hist. Rev.*, 2nd ser., x (1957), 265–272, also has data on costs.

AGRICULTURAL RETURNS AND THE GOVERNMENT DURING THF NAPOLEONIC WARS

W. E. Minchinton

Agricultural Returns and the Government during the Napoleonic Wars

By W. E. MINCHINTON

IN the course of the second half of the eighteenth century Great Britain virtually ceased to be self-sufficient in grain, and imports were required to supplement home production. The situation in agriculture became more acute in the last twelve years of the century and there was much discussion of the problem of food supplies. Already, with the rapid growth of population, the demands of the home market had become more pressing, and the stage was set for the Malthusian dragon to make his appearance. The scanty crop of 1789 and the poor harvest of 1790 evoked an outburst of pamphleteering and an agitation for greater protection for agriculture. Although these demands were opposed by the commercial and industrial centres, the agricultural interests had their way and a new corn law in 1791 increased the price at which the free import of grain was permitted. This was the immediate reaction to the problem. But the decade which followed was distinguished by an unusual number of bad harvests and it saw Great Britain involved in war. As a result, the clause which enabled the act of 1791 to be modified in case of need was employed every year from 1793 to 1801.

The poor harvest of 1792 forced the government to prohibit the export of grain. Two years later the harvest failed again, the following winter was wet and cold and the crop of 1795 was meagre in consequence. Wheat, which had averaged 43s. a quarter in 1792, 49s. 3d. in 1793, and 52s. 3d. in 1794, rose to 108s. 4d. in August 1795, an increase of 50s. in eight months. As prices rose, unrest spread through the country. In May, for example, "an unlawful assembly of colliers met on Rodway Hill (near Bristol) on account of the dearness of provisions" and had to be dispersed by troops.[1] And similar meetings, some of which led to rioting, took place in other parts of England and Wales.[2] In the same month, the magistrates of Speenhamland in Berkshire drew up a scale of assistance for agricultural workers, based on the price of bread and the size of the family, which came to be widely adopted. At the same time the government was besieged with appeals for assistance,

[1] PRO H.O. 42, 34, f. 136.
[2] See J. L. and B. Hammond, *The Village Labourer*, pp. 96–8.

whose general burden was "an immediate supply of wheat is absolutely necessary."[1] It endeavoured to meet these demands "by sending supplies of foreign corn... to the different ports of this kingdom where the need is most felt."[2] In July, a ship laden with 500 quarters of wheat was ordered to proceed to Chepstow to supply the Forest of Dean. And similar cargoes were sent to other ports.

But though such action might mitigate, it could not entirely counteract, the effect of the bad harvest. Prices continued to rise and disaffection to spread. In October the carriage of the king was attacked as he was on his way to open parliament. Immediately the government provided time for a debate on the high cost of provisions. In the course of it, on the 3rd of November, William Pitt announced that "he wanted to lay the foundation of a permanent enquiry ... (and) he hoped that the measure to be proceeded with on this occasion would be facilitated by the steps which the government had already taken."[3] The House then set up a select committee "to enquire into the circumstance of the present scarcity and the best means of remedying it," a move opposed by Arthur Young, who argued "whatever the price of corn, they will have a tendency to raise it."[4] But he would have approved of "the steps which the government had already taken" to set in train a nation-wide enquiry into the state of the harvest.

I

There had long been a demand for the collection and publication of accurate, statistical information about agricultural matters, about crops and yields and prices.[5] As early as 1676 John Graunt had urged that details about arable crops and livestock should be obtained so that measures could be taken to supply any want if crops failed.[6] But apart from estimates like those of Gregory King[7] and the prices published in Houghton's *Collection*

[1] See H.O. 42, 34–6 and 43, 6 *passim*. [2] H.O. 42, 37, ff. 1–3.

[3] *Cobbett's Parliamentary History*, XXXII, 1795–7; *House of Commons Journal*, LI, 1798, pp. 19, 58. I owe these references to Dr Joan Thirsk.

[4] *Annals of Agriculture*, XXV, 1795, p. 450.

[5] For the history of English agricultural statistics see P. G. Craigie, 'Statistics of English agricultural production', *J. R. Statist. Soc.*, XLVI, 1883; 'Early estimates of grain growing in Great Britain', *J. Min. Agric.*, XXX, 1924; J. A. Venn, *The Foundations of Agricultural Economics*; J. M. Ramsay, 'The development of agricultural statistics', *J. Proc. Agric. Econ. Soc.*, VI, 1940; and G. E. Fussell, 'The collection of agricultural statistics in Great Britain', *Agricultural History*, XVIII, 1944.

[6] 'Natural Political Observations Mentioned in a Following Index' in *The Economic Writings of Sir William Petty*, ed. Charles H. Hull, II, p. 396.

[7] *Natural and Political Observations and Conclusions upon the State and Condition of England*, (1696), Section VII.

of Letters for the Improvement of Husbandry and Trade (1692–1703), little was done till the growing interest in agriculture in the middle of the eighteenth century led to a renewal of demands for information. Both Pennington (1769) and Donaldson (1775) suggested that some organization should be established to maintain a permanent enquiry into the condition of agriculture.[1]

The want of information was gradually met by the work of commentators, of whom William Marshall and Arthur Young were the chief, and by the *Annals of Agriculture*, which began publication in 1784. Nine years later, when a Board of Agriculture and Internal Improvement was set up with government support, almost its first action was to arrange for a series of county agricultural reports. Originally Sir John Sinclair proposed to collect the required information by circulating questionnaires to the clergy,[2] as he had done for his *Statistical Account of Scotland*, but this plan had to be abandoned because of the opposition of the archbishop of Canterbury. Fearing such an investigation would lead to action on the tithe question, he threatened to withdraw the support of the Church from Pitt's government.[3] Itinerant surveyors, of varying capability, were appointed instead to carry out the survey.

But it was harvest failure which gave real point to enquiries into agriculture. The bad harvests of 1756 and 1757 led Charles Smith to make his investigation,[4] and later harvest failures roused the interest of Arthur Young. In 1788 he called for reports from his correspondents about conditions in their neighbourhoods, and the bad harvest of the following year led him to repeat his request. These reports he published in the *Annals of Agriculture*. Then, when "apprehensions of a scarcity of provisions" were expressed in the House of Commons early in 1795, Arthur Young sent out the following list of questions which he asked his correspondents to answer.[5]

I. What is supposed to be the stock of wheat and rye in hand relative to the consumption of the remainder of the year, previous to the next crop coming to market?

II. What are the expectations of the next year's supply, relative to any deficiency which it is supposed may result from the autumnal rains and the present severe frost?

[1] W. Pennington, *Reflections on the Various Advantages Resulting from the Draining, Inclosing, and Allotting of Large Commons and Common Fields*, p. 47; W. Donaldson, *Agriculture Considered as a Moral and Political Duty*, p. 172.
[2] The suggested form is to be found in *Communications to the Board of Agriculture*, I, 1797, p. xli.
[3] *Lords' Journal*, XLII, p. 402. [4] *Tracts on the Corn Trade* (1766).
[5] *Annals of Agriculture*, XXIV, 1795, pp. 42–3.

III. What have been the most successful methods adopted for the relief of the poor?

IV. What has been the rise (if any) in the pay of agricultural labour, on comparison with preceding periods?

V. Has any article of food, as a substitute for wheaten bread, been successfully used?

VI. What is the present price per pound of mutton, beef, pork, butter, cheese, and potatoes, regard being paid to such joints of meat as come within the consumption of the poor?

VII. What is the present and ordinary price of coals?

VIII. What has been the effect of the frost on turnips, cabbages, and other articles of green winter-food for cattle and sheep, also on the young wheat?

IX. What is the present price of hay and straw per ton?

X. What is the present or late price of the wool of your country?

An exhaustive enquiry for an individual to carry out. The replies were printed in the *Annals of Agriculture*.[1]

The worsening conditions of 1795 produced a spate of investigation. In June the Board of Agriculture proposed the issue of a questionnaire asking "the landed interest": (i) What number of acres are, by estimation, or from regular survey, contained in your parish, constablewick, tithing, division, or district? and (ii) How many of such acres are arable, how many generally kept under each species of crop, how many in fallow, and how many in grass?[2] A month later it sent out a statement "on the present scarcity of provision" suggesting "measures to prevent any risk of real want previous to the ensuing harvest." The Board clearly stated that "the collecting of information respecting the agricultural state of the country" was necessary before measures could be recommended to parliament.[3] "The result of the new crops being uncertain" in October, Arthur Young again circularized his correspondents in terms similar to those of January 1795, with the significant addition of the following question.[4] "It having been recommended by various quarter-sessions, that the price of labour should be regulated by that of bread corn, have the goodness to state what you conceive to be the advantages or disadvantages of such a system." Speenhamland was already under scrutiny.

Other enquiries were also on foot. The Rev. David Davies was gathering material for his statement of *The Case of Labourers in Husbandry*, Sir Frederic Eden was stimulated by these conditions to begin his examination

[1] *Ibid.*, XXIV.   [2] *Ibid.*, XXIV, p. 567.   [3] *Ibid.*, XXIV, pp. 579–81.
[4] *Ibid.*, XXV, 1795, pp. 344–5.

of *The State of the Poor*, and Malthus was turning his mind to a different aspect of the same problem, the pressure of a growing population on food resources. Already the last decade of the eighteenth century was dimly perceiving, what the nineteenth had to learn through painful experience, that effective remedial measures for social problems can only be taken when enquiry has revealed, preferably in statistical form, the dimensions of the question. And war provided, as it has continued to do, the opportunity for the government to embark on a statistical investigation. The ground had been prepared by the work of individuals, the failure of the harvest in 1795 provided the occasion for a government enquiry.

II

Late in October, the Secretary of State for Home Affairs, the duke of Portland, sent a letter to the lords lieutenant of the counties asking them "to procure an account of the produce of the several articles of grain ... comparing the same with the produce of a fair crop of every such article of grain in common years and with the produce of the crop of 1794 of every such article of grain ... and to report such account as early as possible."[1] Within the counties, the information was to be collected by the justices of the peace and the high constables of the hundreds. The government was now to learn by experience of the problems involved in carrying out such an enterprise.

First, this task was not universally welcomed. The lord lieutenant of Berkshire, the earl of Radnor, voiced the scepticism of some. Writing to the duke of Portland, he confessed himself "at a loss to imagine by what means the Magistrates of the County of Berks can be competent to obtain such information ... the comparative statement ... will necessarily, I conceive, be little more than Guess work."[2] And, second, as the returns proceeded to demonstrate, "an account of the produce of the late crop" was not a phrase devoid of ambiguity.[3] Some returns gave the yield in bushels per acre, some in total acreage under the various crops, while yet others gave only a verbal statement such as: "Wheat, not so good this year as last, Barley, better than last year, Oats, a middling crop, not so good as former years, Beans, a pretty fair crop, about on an average."[4] Some gave the information by parishes,

---

[1] H.O. 42, 36–7.   [2] H.O. 42, 36, f. 244.

[3] Some of these returns are to be found in H.O. 42, 37. Additional Gloucestershire returns are to be found in the Shire Hall, Gloucester, and some Leicestershire returns (for information about which I am indebted to Dr W. G. Hoskins and Dr Joan Thirsk) in the County Record Office, Leicester. No doubt other returns will be found in other local collections.

[4] The return for Hinton, Gloucestershire.—H.O. 42, 37, f. 138.

some consolidated them by hundreds, while others stated the details of individual holdings. An extract from a parish in the last category, Quedgely (Gloucestershire),[1] reads as follows.

Occupier	WHEAT			BARLEY			BEANS		
	Acres	Yield per acre (bushels)	Total Produce (bushels)	Acres	Yield per acre (bushels)	Total Produce (bushels)	Acres	Yield per acre (bushels)	Total Produce (bushels)
Chas. Hayward Esq.[1]	—	—	—	—	—	—	—	—	—
Mr Jno. Beach									
1794	23	14	322	8	18	144	20	10	200
1795	20	15	300	3	9	27	28	20	560
John Bailey									
1794	28	10	280	8	14	112	28	8	224
1795	27	12	324	8	16	128	25	20	200
Ann Miles[2]									
1794	7	15	85	2	10	20	8	8	64
1795	4	15	60	5	15	75	4	20	80
John Purser[1]	—	—	—	—	—	—	—	—	—

[1] No tillage.   [2] Not in the Hundred.

Thus the returns varied in the information they contained, varied in format—only in Warwickshire does a printed form appear to have been issued—and lacked a common standard of comparison. Nor could their accuracy be guaranteed. As the magistrates of one district reported, "We had hoped to convey an accurate account . . . (but we are) disappointed by the Jealousy and miserable Policy of the Farmers and others who in order to conceal, from the Government and from the Landlords, the real state of their Produce have to our full Conviction in many instances estimated their several Crops not less than one-third below the actual amount."[2]

Although they were for the most part collected expeditiously, it was not till the Third Report of the Select Committee that the returns received mention. In their First Report they stated that "the crop of the other sorts of grain has been on the whole abundant but the produce of wheat has proved so far deficient as to require the adoption of the speediest and most effectual measures for the alleviation of so great an evil."[3] And the returns generally, as the following table based on the returns for a single county—Gloucestershire—shows, confirmed that the main failure in both 1794 and 1795 was the wheat crop. In both years the best yield of wheat fell considerably short of the best average yield.

[1] Shire Hall, Gloucester. Some of the Leicestershire returns (County Record Office, Leicester) also give information about individual holdings.
[2] H.O. 42, 37, f. 28. Hundred of Lonsdale South of the Sands (Lancashire).
[3] Cited in *Annals of Agriculture*.

The Yields of 1794 and 1795 compared with the Average Yield[1]
(bushels per acre)

	Wheat	Barley	Oats	Beans	Peas
1794	7–18	5–24	2–24	1–15	1½–2½
1795	6–15	11–26	7–24	8–24	10–24
Average	8–24	14–25	12–24	12–25	8–20

The Second Report was mainly concerned with the shortage of rye. Then, in the Third, the Select Committee reported that they had received "a considerable number of returns, made by the *custodes rotulorum* of the different counties, respecting the state of the last crop, together with much additional intelligence communicated by many of their members." But, they continued, we "find it impossible as yet to draw, either from these returns or from any other quarter, a precise conclusion. The returns are so incomplete in their number and founded upon so many different principles ... that it is extremely difficult to combine and compare them, so as to state accurately the result of the whole."[2] And with this judgement we must concur. These returns do not provide a satisfactory assessment of the state of English agriculture in 1794–5, though studied in detail by the local or parish historian they may yield information of value.

As the returns failed to provide the government with the information it needed, it was forced to resort to emergency measures. The export of corn was forbidden, the manufacture of hand and hair powder—which, according to one correspondent, accounted for a seventh part of the whole consumption of wheat in the kingdom[3]—and the use of grain for the malt distillery, "which consumes large quantities of wheat and all Barley," were prohibited. Bounties were given for imported grain, attempts were made to popularize a standard wholemeal bread and to reduce consumption of wheaten bread,[4] and enclosure and the increased cultivation of arable land were encouraged. A scheme for public granaries was dropped after a fierce attack by Edmund Burke.[5] The activities of middlemen were discussed and criticized. Of these measures, it was the greatly increased import of grain—879,000 quarters—which brought relief in 1796. With harvests at home improving, the price of wheat fell to 53s. 9d. a quarter in 1797 and 47s. 10d. in 1798, the lowest price since 1792. The question of grain supplies was, for a time, less pressing.

[1] H.O. 42, 36, f. 138.   [2] Cited in *Annals of Agriculture*, XXVI, 1796, p. 209.
[3] H.O. 42, 34.   [4] See J. L. and B. Hammond, *The Village Labourer*, pp. 99–108.
[5] *Thoughts and Details on Scarcity Originally presented to the Rt. Hon. William Pitt, in the Month of November*, 1795.

III

In 1797 and 1798 a more urgent problem confronted the government, the threat of invasion, as with the withdrawal of Austria England stood alone against France. The government made plans for a withdrawal from the coast —a 'scorched-earth policy'—and to this end detailed returns were called for, particularly from those parishes within twelve miles of the sea. In addition to details about the yeomanry, about the waggons and horses available, the number of mills and baking ovens, the lords lieutenant were asked to make a return of live and dead stock.[1] Early in 1798 the Home Secretary suggested that a form drawn up by the county of Dorset should be generally adopted for this purpose.[2] This provided space for the number of livestock (horses, cows, sheep, deer, and pigs) and the number of acres under crops (wheat, barley, oats, beans, pease, rye, buckwheat, vetches, hemp, flax, potatoes, and hay) to be entered.

Although the lieutenancy records for all counties are not available, these returns are known to exist for Essex,[3] Sussex,[4] Dorset,[5] and for a few parishes in south Gloucestershire.[6] For some parishes, as for Kidford (Sussex), the stock lists of individual farmers survive. Similar returns were called for in 1801 and 1803,[7] so that in some cases a comparison is possible. This has been done by G. H. Kenyon for Sussex for the two years 1798 and 1801 as follows:[8]

	Cattle	Sheep	Pigs	Horses
1798	60,885	549,991		18,414
1801	62,047	346,589	63,094	22,620

Further examination of these returns, a by-product of the government's concern for defence, may well amplify our knowledge of both the general livestock position and the holdings of individual farmers in England at the end of the eighteenth century.

---

[1] A. Young circulated queries on horses in 1797. *Annals of Agriculture*, XXVIII, 1797, p. 405.
[2] H.O. 42, 39.
[3] County Record Office, Chelmsford. See J. L. Cranmer-Byng, *Essex Prepares for Invasion* (1953).
[4] Lieutenancy records, County Record Office, Lewes. See G. H. Kenyon, 'The civil defence and livestock returns for Sussex in 1801'; *Sussex Archaeol. Coll.*, LXXXIX, pp. 57–84.
[5] H.O. 42, 39.
[6] In the parish chest, Bitton, Gloucestershire. I am indebted to Miss E. Ralph for this information.
[7] The returns for 1801 exist for Sussex; those for 1803 for Essex, Sussex, and Somerset (Robertson-Glasgow Collection).
[8] *Sussex Archaeol. Coll.*, LXXXIX, p. 62.

IV

The summer of 1799 was wet and the harvest failure of that year forced the government to reimpose the restrictions on the use of grain and to renew the bounties on imports which rose slightly to 463,185 quarters in that year. Despite these measures the price of wheat rose, unrest became widespread during the cold wet winter, and the government was forced to extend the emergency provisions. Nevertheless a proposal in March 1800 that the Lords should set up a committee to examine the evidence as to the "Deficiency of the last Year's Crop of Wheat, the Stock in Hand at the time of the Harvest, and the supply now remaining in the Country"[1] was defeated as favourable reports about the forthcoming harvest began to come in. Meanwhile the price of wheat continued to rise, reaching 134s. 5d. in June 1800, and less optimistic forecasts were made about harvest prospects. An analysis of the replies to a circular letter sent out by the Board of Agriculture showed that "the produce of the wheat harvest in the whole country will be considerably under the average crop."[2] The price of wheat remained high and there were reports of unrest and incendiarism (either actual or intended) from many parts of the country.[3]

In these conditions of shortage, something like panic swept the country. As W. F. Galpin has written, "Impressed by the idea of his own self-sufficiency, the Englishman became visibly excited whenever self-sufficiency was threatened. On every hand he saw visions of impending famine."[4] To allay these fears, while pamphleteers were active in diagnosis,[5] the government made frantic attempts to obtain accurate information about the state of the harvest. The duke of Portland asked the bishops to secure answers to the following four questions:[6]

"1. What has been the produce of the late Crop in your district and county, so far as you have means of information, comparative with former crops, or if you can state it, what is the estimated number of Bushels per Acre, distinguishing Wheat, Barley, Oats, and Potatoes and also stating the comparative Crops of Hay, Beans, and Turnips?

"2. What is the Price in your Market Town of Wheat, Barley, Oats, Potatoes, Hay, and Beans, and Mutton and Beef in the month of October 1800 comparatively with the same period in 1799 and 1798?

---

[1] *Lords' Journal*, XLII, p. 402.
[2] B.T. 1, 18. See W. F. Galpin, *The Grain Supply of England during the Napoleonic Period*, New York, 1925, p. 15. The monthly prices for wheat are taken from Appendix 5, p. 213.
[3] H.O. 42, 49–51. [4] Galpin, *The Grain Supply of England*, p. 13.
[5] See D. G. Barnes, *A History of the English Corn Laws*, bibliography, pp. 308-9.
[6] H.O. 42, 52.

"3. Has the produce of the late Harvest been consumed? Is there any reason to believe that there is any considerable quantity of old wheat in store?

"4. Has much foreign Wheat or Flour been brought into your part of the Country? Is there much use made of Rice, Barley or Oats as Substitutes?"[1]

These questions were sent by the bishops—in some cases on printed forms—to such clergymen as appeared to them to be best qualified. The returns, completed with varying degrees of diligence, were collected by the bishops and sent by them to the Home Secretary.[2]

In the same months the Lords' Committee on the Dearth of Provisions called for reports "from respectable and well-informed persons" about the harvest.[3] These are to be found, consolidated by counties, as an appendix to the Second Report of the committee. The Warwickshire summary indicates the form in which the material is available:[4]

	Average Crop, as stated by the Evidence				Proportion of an Average Crop at the late Harvest, as stated by the Evidence.
	Q	B	Q	B	
Wheat	2	4 —	2	5	2-3ds — 3-5ths — 2-3ds
Barley	3	4 —	4	0	2-3ds — 3-5ths — 13-18ths
Oats	5	0 —	5	5	3-4ths — Average — 11-18ths
Rye	3	0			
Pease	2	2 —	2	5	2-3ds — Average
Beans	2	4 —			2-3ds — Average
Potatoes	150 bushels				2-3ds — Nearly Average

"The Consumption of the New Crop began as soon as possible after the Harvest was in, and much of it was threshed out for immediate Use, the Stock of Old Corn being, comparatively speaking, none (the Case in most of the Midland Counties); in general there used to be enough to carry on the County for three Months. Land sown with Wheat in 1799, 1800—not so much, on account of the Badness of the Season."

The Board of Trade[5] and the Board of Taxes[6] made similar investiga-

---

[1] The appendix to the *Second Report of the Commons' Committee on the Scarcity of Corn* was devoted to "Modes of preparing Rice."

[2] They exist for almost all the dioceses of England and Wales in H.O. 42, 52–55.

[3] *Second Report of the Lords' Committee on the Dearth of Provisions*, p. 4. (Parliamentary Papers, 1801, II)

[4] *Ibid.*, p. 170. Cited in Pelham, *Trans. Birmingham Archaeol. Soc.*, LXVII, 1952, p. 91. In the table Q stands for quarters and B for bushels.

[5] Galpin, *Grain Supply of England*, p. 16, n. 24. See B.T. 6,139.

[6] Treasury Letter Books, Board of Taxes, 17 Nov. 1800. I owe this reference to L. S. Pressnell.

tions in the autumn of 1800. Thus not one but several enquiries were on foot at the same time. Rarely in the history of English agriculture can there have been so fevered an attempt to find out the facts.

All this material appears to have been made available to the Commons' Committee on the High Price of Provisions. In their First Report, dated 24 November 1800, they stated:[1]

"Having many documents before them, which could be examined without much delay, and which, checked by the very extensive information of members from different parts of the country, appeared likely to enable them to form a general estimate of the crop, your Committee have thought it right to avail themselves of those materials for that purpose. These documents consist of very numerous returns to those enquiries which different departments of Government have directed to be made, by the receivers of the land tax, by the various officers employed under the boards of taxes, stamps, and excise, and by those amongst the clergy to whom circular letters for that purpose had been addressed by the bishops in each diocese. Though the returns are not complete from every county, yet the omissions upon the whole are neither numerous nor important."

When they had made their examination of the whole of this information, the Committee reported there was "reason to believe that the general deficiency of the crop of Wheat in England and Wales, below an average crop, does not amount to quite so much as one-fourth." They also commented on the harvest of the other crops, but the wheat harvest was the crucial crop. Wheat prices had fallen from their peak of June to 114s. 5d. in October, but when the facts about the harvest became known they rose again. Although imports reached a record figure of 1,264,520 quarters in 1800, the price of wheat had risen to 137s. a quarter by the end of December. The committee had seen "no ground for believing that any result attainable by the most detailed enquiry, could lead to any practicable conclusion, applicable to the present emergency." Its remedy for the situation was economy in the use of grain.

As prices continued to rise in 1801—to a peak of 154s. 8d. in April—further proposals were put forward—that the growing of potatoes should be encouraged, that those in extreme and peculiar distress should be helped financially, and that increased efforts should be made to secure foreign grain. The improvement of agriculture was also urged, and the passage of the General Enclosure Act was a result of a recommendation of a Lords' Committee in May.

[1] *Parliamentary History*, xxxv, col. 778. I am indebted to Dr R. A. Pelham for this reference.

Despite the apparently small use it had hitherto made of the agricultural returns, the government continued its quest for accurate statistical information about the condition of agriculture. In the words of Lord Pelham "it occurred to His Majesty's Confidential Servants that if they could be furnished with an annual return of the number of acres under Tillage it would be a circumstance highly beneficial to the Public Interests, as it would form the best criterion whereby to judge of the effects which the provisions of Parliament, both in regard to inclosures and other matters, produce on the Agriculture of the County."[1]

Accordingly in the summer of 1801 printed forms were distributed by the Home Office to the bishops and by them to incumbents in England and Wales. The clergy were asked to state the acreage sown since last year's harvest with wheat, barley, oats, potatoes, beans, peas, turnips (with rye, vetches, or dill sometimes entered in addition). A space was provided for General Remarks. The completed returns were sent to the Home Secretary.[2] Only one diocese, Peterborough, is completely unrepresented, though returns are meagre for a number of counties (Devon, Dorset, Nottingham, Norfolk, Oxford, Suffolk, and Westmoreland).[3] These returns were sent for comment to the Board of Agriculture, which reported that "as far as the Members present can ascertain by their personal knowledge of particular Parishes, they are so extremely erroneous that they cannot safely be at all relied on in forming any general conclusions respecting the quantities of Land sown with any species of Grain."[4] And with this somewhat harsh and hasty judgement the returns were laid aside to be ignored for more than a century.

v

Of recent years, the 1801 acreage returns have been re-examined,[5] and the published results suggest that if they were regarded as inadequate by some contemporaries they are nevertheless of some value to the historian.

[1] Home Office Domestic Entry Book (H.O. 43, 13, pp. 285–6).   [2] H.O. 67.
[3] H. C. K. Henderson, 'Agriculture in England and Wales in 1801,' *Geog. J.*, CXVIII, 1952, p. 339.
[4] Minute Book of the Board of Agriculture (R.A.S.E.), pp. 310–11 (15 April 1802).
[5] The following articles have so far been published: W. G. Hoskins, 'The Leicestershire crop returns of 1801' in *Studies in Leicestershire Agrarian History*, ed. W. G. Hoskins; W. E. Minchinton, 'Agriculture in Gloucestershire during the Napoleonic Wars', *Trans. Bristol and Glouc. Archaeol. Soc.*, LXVIII, 1949, pp. 165–83; D. Williams, 'The acreage returns of 1801 for Wales', *Bull. Board of Celtic Studies*, XIV, 1950–1, pp. 54–68, 139–54; K. G. Davies and G. E. Fussell, 'Worcestershire in the acreage returns for 1801', *Trans. Worcs. Archaeol. Soc.*, XXVII, N.S., 1951, 15–23; H. C. K. Henderson, 'The 1801 crop returns for Wiltshire', *Wilts. Archaeol. and Nat. Hist. Mag.*, LIV, 1951, pp. 85–91; 'The 1801 crop returns: geo-

These studies are generally agreed that the returns of 1801 err on the side of understatement as far as the figures of actual acreage are concerned but that the information they contain about the distribution of crops, about yields and courses of husbandry, should not be ignored. They tend to show that many of the commentators underestimated the acreage under turnips and were sometimes unduly biased in favour of enclosure as a means of improvement. P. A. Churley writes that for part of Yorkshire "open field parishes . . . had not lagged too far behind the best contemporary practice and the cropping was quite different from the traditional open-field pattern."[1] In addition to the information about crop acreages, the returns often contain some analysis of the causes of the present discontents—high prices, the profiteering of middlemen, paper currency, and restrictive covenants. Some incumbents, particularly in Wales, give information about the advance of industrialism, others criticized "the iniquitous system of the monopolizing of lands by our rich farmers," and yet others, echoing Arthur Young, urged enclosure and the cultivation of the waste. Finally, some of the returns include comment about other matters, such as tithes and poor relief. Thus the 1801 returns provide both statistical information and a commentary on rural life, as viewed through the eyes of the local parson.

Since the enquiries of 1795, 1800, and 1801 did not require the same categories of information to be obtained, direct comparison is not generally possible between them. But in some instances acreage returns are available for several years. Dr Joan Thirsk has drawn on the Leicestershire returns for 1794-5 (which also include estimates for 1793) and 1801 for her discussion of Leicestershire agriculture in a forthcoming volume of the Victoria County History, and the table which follows is taken from that account.[2] The arable acreage in the Guthlaxton hundred of Leicestershire increased considerably between 1793 and 1801 and an examination of the returns for some other Leicestershire hundreds yielded a similar result.

graphical distributions', *Trans. Leics. Archaeol. Soc.* XXVII, 1951, pp. 100–2; 'The 1801 crop returns for Sussex', *Sussex Archaeol. Coll.* XC, 1952, pp. 51–9: 'Agriculture in England and Wales in 1801', *Geog. J.*, CXVIII, 1952, pp. 338–45 (includes a discussion of the returns for Herefordshire); R. A. Pelham, 'The agricultural geography of Warwickshire during the Napoleonic Wars', *Trans. Birmingham Archaeol. Soc.*, LXVIII, 1952, pp. 89–106; and P. A. Churley, 'The Yorkshire crop returns of 1801', *Yorks. Bull. Econ. and Social Research*, V, 1953, pp. 179–97. (The returns for the Yorkshire parishes in the dioceses of Chester and Durham are not included.) H. C. K. Henderson is to publish maps for the remaining counties for which returns are available.

[1] *Yorks. Bull. Econ. and Social Research*, V, p. 189.

[2] I am indebted to the Editor of V.C.H. Leicestershire and to Dr Joan Thirsk for permission to print this table.

Table showing crop acreages in Leicestershire between 1793 and 1801
(Guthlaxton Hundred: Totals for 9 parishes)

Year	Wheat	Barley	Oats	Beans	Peas	Rye	Turnips	Potatoes	Maslin	Total
1793	459	534	403	$125\frac{1}{2}$	—	—	—	—	2	$1523\frac{1}{2}$
1794	518	$566\frac{1}{2}$	503	$129\frac{1}{2}$	$3\frac{1}{2}$	—	—	—	$2\frac{1}{2}$	1723
1795	558	586	517	165	$4\frac{1}{2}$	11	—	—	36	$1877\frac{1}{2}$
1801	$705\frac{1}{4}$	818	$749\frac{1}{2}$	24	$40\frac{1}{2}$	5	445	$26\frac{3}{4}$	—	2814[1]

[1] $2342\frac{1}{4}$ excl. turnips and potatoes

A comparison of the Gloucestershire returns (for 1794, 1795, 1801, and the acreage of the common years) for the fifteen parishes for which this was possible was much less conclusive. In only six was cultivation expanded appreciably in this decade. For other counties such an examination may yield different results. If such figures are accurate, they may provide a statistical statement of the extension of cultivation under the stimulus of high prices during the Napoleonic Wars. In this and other ways the arable returns of 1794, 1795, 1800, and 1801, and the livestock returns of 1798, 1801, and 1803, can provide a useful supplement to the other accounts of English agriculture available for these years. Particularly where returns for individual farmers for both arable acreage and livestock exist, it should be possible to get behind the generalization of the surveys and so show the detail and diversity of English farming in the late eighteenth century.

VI

Thus the 1801 returns were not the first attempt in this country to obtain agricultural statistics on a national scale but the latest of a series of attempts, on which in two important respects, they are, for all their defects, an advance. First, as the detailed evidence produced earlier shows, the 1801 enquiry was more limited in scope than the previous surveys, and the information required for a single year was defined more precisely. From the elaborate questionnaires of Arthur Young the range was narrowed to a specific and limited set of questions. As the vicar of Hatton (Warwickshire) remarked in 1801: "The foregoing Questions seem to me more judicious, and more inoffensive, more easy to be answered with precision, and far more likely to be answered with fidelity, than those which were sent last year."[1] And to ensure that the material was presented in 1801 in a comparable manner, printed forms were distributed, as had been done in a few cases of local initia-

---

[1] H.O. 67. See *Trans. Birmingham Archaeol. Soc.*, LXVIII, p. 90.

tive for the earlier returns.[1] Secondly, the ecclesiastical machinery of collection, as suggested by Sir John Sinclair in 1793, was used and forms were sent to all incumbents and not merely to those best suited, as in 1800. Although his interest in tithes may have made him the object of suspicion, the parson, as an educated man, apparently proved better qualified for this task than either the receiver of taxes or the magistrate. Neither these nor the previous returns were used, as far as is known, as the basis for government policy.

There were suggestions in 1801 that a regular annual return of the number of acres under tillage should be made parish by parish by the overseers of the poor or the assessors of "the Land or other King's Taxes",[2] but no further action appears to have been taken. Bad harvests provided the spur for both private and governmental enquiry and the period of pressing scarcity was past. The years from 1795 to 1801 show the government, lacking paid civil servants in the localities, endeavouring to find the best machinery for the collection of information about the food supplies of a country at war. This has been a neglected strand in the study of the history of England during this period. In the past historians have used the reports on agricultural conditions available in Home Office Papers and elsewhere to document the literature of social protests. But it is also possible, without ignoring the picture they have presented, to use this material for other purposes. From it can be gained a clearer picture of the conduct of agriculture in England and Wales at the end of the eighteenth century, of the attempts to collect accurate statistical information to be used as a basis for policy to meet pressing social, economic, and military questions, and of the administrative problems and difficulties in the way.

[1] For Warwickshire in 1795, for Dorset in 1798, and for the diocese of Chester in 1800.
[2] H.O. 43, 13, pp. 285–6 and Minute Book of the Board of Agriculture (R.A.S.E.), pp. 310–11 (15 April 1802).

BIBLIOGRAPHICAL NOTE

In addition to the articles listed on p. 116, note 5, the returns discussed in this article have been used by J. P. Dodd, 'The state of agriculture in Shropshire, 1775–1825', *Trans. Shrops. Archaeol. Soc.*, LV (1954), 1–31, and 'South Lancashire in transition, a study of the crop returns for 1795–1801', *Trans. Hist. Soc. Lancs. & Ches.*, CXVII (1965), 89–107; D. B. Grigg, 'The 1801 crop returns for south Lincolnshire', *East Midland Geographer*, XVI (1961), 43–8; H. C. K. Henderson, 'The agricultural geography of Derbyshire in the early 19th century', *East Midland Geographer*, VII (1957), 16–20; W. E. Minchinton, 'Agriculture in Dorset during the Napoleonic wars', *Proc. Dorset Nat. Hist. & Archaeol. Soc.*, LXXVII (1955), 162–73, and 'The agricultural returns of 1800 for Wales', *Bull. Board of Celtic Studies*, XXI (1964), 74–93; R. A. Pelham, 'The 1801 crop returns for Staffordshire in their geographical setting', *Collections for a History of Staffordshire*, (1950–1), 231–42, and 'The agricultural revolution in Hampshire with special reference to the acreage returns of 1801', *Papers & Proc. Hants. Field Club & Archaeol. Soc.*, XVIII (1953), 139–43; and D. Thomas, 'The acreage returns of 1801 for Wales: an addendum', *Bull. Board of Celtic Studies*, XVII (1956–7), 50–2; 'The statistical and cartographic treatment of the acreage returns of 1801', *Geog. Studies*, V (1959), 15–25; 'The acreage returns of 1801 for the Welsh borderland', *Trans. & Papers*, Institute of British Geographers XXVI (1959), 169–83; 'The acreage returns of 1801; a test of accuracy', *Bull. Board of Celtic Studies*, XVIII (1959–60), 379–83; and *Agriculture in Wales during the Napoleonic Wars* (Cardiff, 1963).

AGRICULTURAL WAGES IN ENGLAND AND WALES DURING THE LAST HALF CENTURY

A. Wilson Fox

AGRICULTURAL WAGES *in* ENGLAND *and* WALES *during the* LAST FIFTY YEARS. *By* A. WILSON FOX, C.B.

[Read before the Royal Statistical Society, 21st April, 1903. MAJOR PATRICK GEORGE CRAIGIE, C.B., President, in the Chair.]

CONTENTS :

Introduction
Methods of obtaining Information
Terms of Engagement of Farm Labourers, Systems of Payment, &c.
Effect of Poor Law Administration upon Wages
Rates of Weekly Wages
Yearly Earnings
Value of Food

Irregularity of Work
Earnings of Women and Children
Condition of Cottages, and Rent
Position of the Agricultural Labourer in 1903 compared with 1850
Migration from the Country Districts

APPENDICES

Introduction.

WHEN Major Craigie did me the honour to ask me to read this Paper, I felt diffident of undertaking such a task, because of the great difficulty in obtaining satisfactory information about the total annual earnings, particularly in former years. The rates of weekly wages present much less difficulty, but the annual amount received from this source does not represent the labourer's income.

Methods of obtaining Information.

The methods of obtaining information for this paper have been as follows :—

Records of weekly wages, summer and winter, for periods of thirty years and upwards, have been collected from 119 farms in nearly every county in England, and from 6 in Wales, amounting in all to 125 returns. Information has also been obtained from these farms about rates for piecework, remuneration in harvest and payments in kind, in certain cases about total annual earnings, and also about the employment of women and children at field work in former times. I have endeavoured to obtain these particulars as far as possible from tenant farmers, as the wages paid on the home farms of estates are not infrequently rather higher than those paid in the surrounding district, and are usually less susceptible to change on account of low prices and unfavourable seasons.

A number of correspondents from nearly every county, with special knowledge of the economic condition of the agricultural classes, have sent particulars of the kind of food eaten by the labourers at the present time and fifty years ago, the quantities consumed, and prices; also benefit societies, and other matters. These correspondents consist of landowners, Local Government Board inspectors, members of Local Authorities, farmers, clergymen, relieving officers, village tradesmen, and labourers. I have also visited various counties in England and Wales during the last six months for the purpose of making personal inquiries, and have made a special point of interviewing the older farmers and also a number of old labourers. In Appendix V will be found the questions asked of correspondents.

Terms of Engagement of Farm Labourers, Systems of Payment, &c.

In most counties weekly engagements prevail for ordinary agricultural labourers, while men specially in charge of animals are frequently engaged on longer terms. Piecework is, of course, more suited to the work of ordinary labourers than to that of men in charge of animals, and it is more common in arable than pastoral districts. The annual earnings of ordinary labourers, therefore, comprise not only the ordinary weekly wages, but also extra payments for piecework, harvest, and overtime, and in some counties certain payments in kind. In the northern counties and in Wales most of the men are hired by the year or half-year, and piecework, and extra payments at harvest, are not generally customary in such cases, though beer and also some extra food are often given at harvest time. Extra money payments in these districts are usually only given to casual men. The single men living in the farmers' houses are provided with all their food. The married men in these districts are more usually on weekly engagements, and, in addition to their weekly wages, frequently have free cottages, potatoes, or potato ground, fuel, and other allowances. Therefore no useful comparison can be made between the rates of weekly wages in the low and high wage counties. The only comparison which can properly be made is between the actual yearly earnings, including all extra money payments, and the value of payments in kind.

However, as the weekly wages have formed the principal part of the labourer's earnings during the period under review, a comparative statement of the rates paid for a series of years would give, at any rate, a substantial indication of the fluctuations in the labourer's circumstances. The figures which I shall presently give will, I suggest, show that the fluctuations in weekly wages determine, to some extent, the fluctuations in annual earnings, that is to say, that within comparatively narrow limits the ratio of earnings to wages is fairly constant.

The wages and earnings of ordinary agricultural labourers only have been taken for the purposes of this Paper. The higher paid classes, namely, shepherds, and men specially engaged in the charge of cattle and horses, who have greater responsibilities, and generally longer hours and Sunday work, have been excluded, because the ordinary labourers comprise much the largest class, their rates of wages are generally more uniform in a given district, and they receive fewer payments in kind than the other classes referred to.

Further, the wages and earnings of ordinary labourers were given in greater detail than those of other classes by the Royal Commission on the Employment of Children, Young Persons, and Women in Agriculture in 1867-69, by the Royal Commission on Agricultural Interests (Richmond Commission) in 1879-82, by the Royal Commission on Labour in 1891-94, and in the Board of Trade Report in 1900, and I desire on the present occasion to make some comparison with those figures.

Effect of Poor Law Administration upon Wages.

Before the reform of the Poor Law in 1834, the rates of wages in many counties, though not as a rule in the north, were affected by the prevailing system of Poor Law Administration.[1] Generally speaking, where the rate of expenditure per head on relief was high, wages were lower than in the districts where the rate per head was low.

The "Report from the Select Committee on Labourers' Wages" in 1824, appointed to inquire into the practice of paying the wages of labourers out of the poor rates,[2] said, " able-bodied labourers are " sent round to the farmers, and receive a part, and in some instances " the whole of their substance from the parish, while working upon " the land of individuals. . . . Persons who have no need of farm " labour are obliged to contribute to the payment of work done for " others."[3]

The "Report from the Select Committee on Agriculture" in 1833 said that the labour rate interfered directly "with the

---

[1] "Extracts from the Information received by the Commissioners for Inquiring "into the Administration and Practical Operation of the Poor Laws" (1833), p. 169. See also Purdy, "Earnings of Agricultural Labourers in England and "Wales, 1860," *Journal of the Royal Statistical Society*, 1861, pp. 345 and 346.

[2] Out-door relief of the able-bodied was given in (1) kind by payment of rent (partially or wholly); (2) in money by (a) relief without labour, (b) the allowance system, (c) the roundsmen system, (d) parish employment, (e) the labour rate system.

[3] pp. 3 and 4 of Report.

"natural demand for labour, levying, in many cases, the wages of labour from those who are not its employers."[4]

The Report on the Further Amendment of the Poor Law in 1839, said that "various contrivances for confounding relief with wages had enabled the predominant interest in each locality to force their weaker neighbours to contribute to a common fund from which they did not derive an equal benefit."[5]

Sometimes the farmers had to level their wages up to higher wages given by the Poor Law Authorities to the unemployed for unproductive labour, while on the other hand, it is on record that some farmers agreed to pay low rates of wages, so that the men could get something from the parish in addition, in the form of money, food, tickets on shops, or allowances for children.

In Worcestershire, in the parish of Kidderminster, a committee appointed by the vestry to inquire into the management of the poor and the expenditure on poor relief, reported in 1832 that "a practice had, in some degree, obtained, of labourers being engaged at one-half, or even one-third of the average rate of wages, upon an understanding with their employers that the difference will be made up to them from the parochial rates."[6] The labourers of course did not exert themselves over their work, as they were certain of obtaining from one source or the other sufficient to maintain their families.[7]

The Assistant Commissioner, reporting on east Sussex to the Poor Law Commissioners in 1833, said that "Farmers turned off their men or refused to employ them at fair wages, thereby causing a surplus fraudulently; they then took the men from the parish at reduced wages paid out of the poor rates."[8]

The Assistant Commissioner in Buckinghamshire reported that "wages, considered as the result of a bargain between the capitalist and the labourer, for the advantage of both parties, can hardly be said to exist. The farmer, like the parish, commonly pays every

---

[4] p. 7 of Report.
[5] "Report of the Poor Law Commissioners on the Continuance of the Poor Law Commission and on some Further Amendments of the Laws relating to the Relief of the Poor" (1840), p. 10. See also p. 66.
[6] "Reports of the Assistant Commissioners to the Commissioners for Inquiring into the Administration and Practical Operation of the Poor Laws." Part II (1834), p. 36.
[7] See "Report from the Select Committee on Labourers' Wages," 1824, pp. 3 and 4; and "Report of the Poor Law Commissioners on the Continuance of the Poor Law Commission, and on some Further Amendments of the Laws relating to the Relief of the Poor" (1840), pp. 64 and 65.
[8] "Reports of the Assistant Commissioners to the Commissioners for Inquiring into the Administration and Practical Operation of the Poor Laws." Part I (1834), p. 203.

"man according to the wants of himself and his family, and then gets what work he can out of him."[9]

But the farmer had to pay both wages and rates, and the fund from which these came was not inexhaustible.

I will quote an interesting illustration of the apparent inelasticity of this fund, at any rate in one district, from the report of the Poor Law Commissioners published in 1833.[10]

At Eastbourne, in Sussex, in 1830, under the pressure of riots and incendiarism, it was agreed that the surplus labourers should be paid according to a certain scale varying with the number of children, a system which was a common one in the southern counties after the Act of 1782, in connection with the fixing of the rate of wages. A single man 18 years of age received 6s. a week, a man and his wife with three children 12s. a week and a gallon of flour, or else a total money payment of 13s. 4d. If there were ten children the sum paid was 18s. 8d. a week. Under such a system, to quote the Report of 1824 to inquire into the practice of paying the wages of labourers out of the poor rates, "men who receive but a small pittance know that they have only to marry, and that pittance will be augmented in proportion to the number of their children."[11]

The amount spent in labour and rates by the principal occupier of this parish in 1830 and 1831 was, in round figures, as follows:—[12]

	1830.	1831.
	£	£
Labour	900	700
Rates	300	500
Total	1,200	1,200

Very soon after the reform of the Poor Law in 1834, a radical change was effected in the system of relief. The Report of the Commissioners on the Further Amendment of the Poor Law, 1839, states "that systematic relief of able-bodied men in aid of wages only exists in a few Unions which do not yet possess an efficient workhouse. All the other pernicious varieties of the old mode of relief,

---

[9] "Extracts from the information received by the Commissioners for Inquiring into the Administration and Practical Operation of the Poor Laws" (1833), p. 77.

[10] "Reports of the Assistant Commissioners to the Commissioners for Inquiring into the Administration and Practical Operation of the Poor Laws." Part II (1834), pp. 187 and 188.

[11] "Report from the Select Committee on Labourers' Wages," 1824, p. 4.

[12] See Note 10, above.

"which are described by the Commission of Inquiry as being then "in full vigour—the allowance system, the roundsmen system, the "labour-rate system—have ceased."¹³

But during the "forties," at any rate, the provision of work by the farmers in many districts for surplus labour for which they had no need, in order to keep the men off the rates, tended to keep the wages low.

The "Report on the Burdens on Land," 1846, states that "in "order to reduce the Poor's Rate, the farmers in many parishes "employ more hands than the economical working of the land "requires."¹⁴

Farmers on large holdings in Beds, Essex, Norfolk, Surrey, Wilts, Devon, Kent, Hunts, Cambs, Rutland, Herts, Bucks, Oxford, Hants, Suffolk, gave striking evidence before the Committee as to their practice of employing considerably more men than they required, finding it more economical to have them doing some work on the land than doing nothing, and being supported with their families out of the poor rate. Consequently preference was frequently given to the men with large families, who might not be the best workers, both by the farmers, and also by the local authorities, for employment at road work. Some of these witnesses stated that they did not use machinery, in order to be able to employ these men. Threshing with the flail was often resorted to for the sake of giving employment. As a Huntingdonshire farmer said to the Committee, they had "either to employ or maintain."¹⁵

Again, Caird¹⁶ refers to a similar state of things in 1850-51, the farmers in certain districts dividing up the surplus labour by arrangement.

This superabundance of labour was very unsatisfactory, both for the labourer, who got a low rate of wages, if employed, and for the farmer, who often had to employ inferior men, and also more than he required at certain seasons.¹⁷

---

¹³ "Report of the Poor Law Commissioners on the continuance of the Poor "Law Commission, and on some Further Amendments of the Law relating to the "Relief of the Poor" (1840), p. 10.

¹⁴ "Report from the Select Committee of the House of Lords on the Burdens "affecting Real Property," 1846, p. v.

¹⁵ *Ibid.*, pp. 4, 7, 23, 24, 42, 49, 64, 70, 71, 73, 78, 87, 93, 105, 106, 112, 116, 118, 124, 136, 137, 146, 153, 154, 166, 169, 171, 177, 189, 380, 521, 539, and 551.

¹⁶ "English Agriculture in 1850-51," pp. 18, 84, 148, and 515—51

¹⁷ Speaking of a district in Wiltshire, where the wages were very low, Caird says: "Both farmers and labourers suffer in this locality from the present over-"supply of labour. The farmer is compelled to employ more men than his "present mode of operations require, and, to save himself, he pays them a lower "rate of wages than is sufficient to give that amount of physical power which is "necessary for the performance of a fair day's work." *Ibid.*, p. 85.

Rates of Weekly Wages.

I will now proceed to deal with the records of weekly wages for the last half-century.

I have obtained records showing for thirty years or more the rates of weekly cash wages paid in each year to ordinary labourers employed on 125 farms in England and Wales. In Appendix I a few of these records will be found printed in detail. Of the 125 records, 67 cover the whole of the period from 1850 to 1902, and I have used these 67 returns as the basis of the charts shown with Appendix II on pp. 333—5.

Although I have only included in the charts the records of weekly wages since 1850, I have obtained information as to the rates of wages on some farms at an earlier period. One return from Hertfordshire commences in 1789, one from Essex in 1800, one from Herefordshire in 1819, one from Wiltshire in 1824, one from Warwickshire in 1825, one from Northumberland in 1831, one from Shropshire in 1835, and one from Suffolk in 1836.

The first chart shows the percentage fluctuations in the rates of wages paid on the 67 farms in each of the years 1850-1902, as compared with the year 1871, which I have selected as a standard year, being one in which the average rate of wages was about midway between the minimum and maximum years.

The second chart shows a corresponding curve for the eastern counties, and as wages there for many years were more or less regulated according to the price of corn, a curve has been added showing the percentage fluctuations in the average price of British wheat in each of the years for which the changes in wages are shown.

The third chart shows the course of wages, on the same method as in the first and second diagrams, in the northern, midland, and southern and south-western groups of counties respectively.[18]

Where the summer rates differed from those paid in winter, an average has been taken of the summer and winter rates, it being reckoned that the ratio of summer to winter weeks is as 3 to 2. The period varies in different districts according to circumstances. In times of falling wages the winter rates may begin soon after harvest; in good times the fall does not take place (if at all)

---

[18] The counties included in the different groups are as follows:—*Northern Counties.*—Northumberland, Cumberland, Westmorland, Lancaster, York. *Midland Counties.*—Derby, Chester, Nottingham, Leicester, Rutland, Salop, Worcester, Warwick, Northants, Bucks, Herts, Beds. *Eastern Counties.*—Huntingdon, Lincoln, Norfolk, Suffolk, Essex. *Southern and South Western Counties.*—Surrey, Sussex, Hants, Wilts, Dorset, Somerset, Gloucester, Hereford, Monmouth, Devon, Cornwall. No chart is given for Wales only, as the returns are not sufficiently numerous to yield a representative curve.

until nearly Christmas, and the change in the spring depends on similar considerations.

While the figures for these 67 farms may not accurately represent the average rate of wages for the whole body of ordinary farm labourers in England and Wales in any one year, they, at any rate, form a connected picture of the fluctuations in rates of wages, year by year, during the last half-century.

It will be seen from the chart for England and Wales that the lowest point touched was in the early fifties, a time of great agricultural depression. A few years before 1850 both prices and wages were higher. In 1846 the Corn Laws were repealed, and prices rose in 1847, the year of the Irish famine. Some indication of the comparative lowness of wages in 1850 is afforded by the following figures, based on the records for 10 farms in which the figures are available as far back as the year 1843.

Average Rate of Weekly Wages in—																
1843.		1844.		1845.		1846.		1847.		1848.		1849.		1850.	
s.	d.	s.	d.	s.	d.	s.	d.	s.	d.	s.	d.	s.	d.	s.	d.
9	1¼	9	1¾	9	4	9	5	10	0½	9	3	8	10½	8	7½

Wages rose sharply in 1853 and 1854, the years of the Crimean War, and from this period until 1871 the upward movement continued, with slight interruptions coincident with falls in the price of corn. In 1872 and 1873, just after the Franco-German War, rates of wages again rose considerably, and the agitation amongst the labourers, led by Joseph Arch, helped to maintain the high level until the period of agricultural depression which followed the disastrous season of 1879. The upward movement was resumed in 1889 and, with the exception of slight decreases in 1893 and 1894 (a period of general agricultural and commercial depression), it continued up to 1902.

If we turn to the charts for the different groups of counties we find that the general characteristics of the curve for England and Wales are repeated, but it will be noticed that in the southern and south-western group the fluctuations in wages were comparatively slight, while in the eastern counties, where the farmers' profits mainly depend on the prices of grain, the variations in the rates of wages have been greater than in the other groups, where cattle and sheep are more generally bred and fattened, and mixed farming is carried on.

In many districts, chiefly in the eastern counties, up to and including the "sixties" at any rate, wages used to be frequently adjusted according to the price of wheat; sometimes in accordance with a regular scale, sometimes in a more rough and ready fashion. A Buckinghamshire farmer giving evidence before the Committee on the Burdens on Land in 1846, spoke of a bushel of wheat as representing the price of a week's wages in some former time. In parts of the eastern counties the price of a bushel of wheat added to half-a-crown used to be the weekly wage. Then when wheat was selling at 30s. a coombe (4 bushels) wages were 10s.[19] Subsequently the relation between the wages and the price of wheat became less precise, but still up to a comparatively recent period wages were roughly adjusted according as the price of corn rose or fell.

The highest and lowest rates of weekly wages shown in individual returns in the four groups are as follows :—

Group.	Year.	Highest Rates of Weekly Wages.	County.
ENGLAND.		s. d.	
Northern counties	1875	24 –	Northumberland
Midland ,,	1890–1902	20 –	Derby
Eastern ,,	1873–78	18 –	Lincoln
Southern and south-western counties	1900	18 –	Devon

Group.	Year.	Lowest Rates of Weekly Wages.	County.
ENGLAND.		s. d.	
Northern counties	Early 50's	10 –	Cumberland, Lancaster, York
Midland ,,	1853	7 –	Herts
Eastern ,,	1852	7 –	Suffolk
Southern and south-western counties	Early 50's	6 –	Somerset, Gloucester

[19] "Report from the Select Committee of the House of Lords on the Burdens "affecting Real Property," 1846, pp. 7, 8, 37, 50, 77, 84, 108, 109, 115, 138, 139, 170, 171, 185, 527, 529, 530, 545–-547, and Appendix, p. 6; Mr. H. Raynbird (see "Journal of the Royal Agricultural Society of England," 1847) said it was the practice of some farmers in East Suffolk to pay labourers according to the following scale :—

When wheat was 5s. per bushel and under 6s., wages paid were 8s. a week.
,, 6s. ,, 7s., ,, 9s. ,,
,, 7s. ,, 8s., ,, 10s. ,,

See also Lowe, "The Present State of England in regard to Agriculture, Trade, "and Finance," 1823, Appendix to Chapter x, pp. 99 and 100; Clare Sewell Read, M.P., in an address to the Tunstead and Happing Agricultural Association, "Norfolk News," 9th November, 1867; Clifford, "The Labour Bill in Farming," Journal of the Royal Agricultural Society of England, 1875, p. 73; H. J. Little's contribution to the "Memoir on English Agriculture, prepared for the International Congress at Paris, 1878," Journal of the Royal Agricultural Society of England, 1878, p. 771; Rew, "Report to the Royal Commission on Agriculture," C–7915 of 1895, pp. 43 and 44.

It is interesting to observe that when wages on the 67 farms were at their lowest (9s. 2½d. per week in 1851), the average price of wheat was 38s. 6d. per quarter, while in 1902, when wages reached their highest point (14s. 7d. per week), the price of wheat was only 28s. 1d. per quarter.

In the following table a comparison is made between the average rates of wages paid on the 67 farms, with the figures given by certain other authorities for England in certain years during the period under review. Notwithstanding the different methods adopted in arriving at these figures, they show a rough correspondence.

Year.	Authority.	Average Weekly Rate of Wages.	Average Weekly Rate of Wages on 67 Farms.	Year.
		s. d.	s. d.	
1850-51	Caird, "Agriculture in England in 1850-51"	9 7	9 3½	1850
'60	Purdy, *Journal of Royal Statistical Society*, 1861	11 7	10 11	'60
'67-69	Little, "Commission on Labour"	12 2	12 0¼	'68
'70-71	Druce, "Journal of Royal Agricultural Society of England," 1885	12 2	11 10¼	'70
'80-81		14 2	13 2¼	'80
'91-94	"Royal Commission on Labour"	13 5	13 5	'92
'98	"Board of Trade Report"	14 5	13 8½	'98

Yearly Earnings.

I will now pass to the question of how weekly wages are supplemented by other payments. Speaking generally, the amount by which the total weekly earnings exceeds the weekly rate of cash wages is greatest in those counties in which the rate of cash wages is low, and least in those in which the cash wages are high.

The following figures, giving the average weekly wages, and also the excess of average weekly earnings over average weekly rates of wages, in certain counties in 1898, illustrate this:—

High Wage Counties.	Average Weekly Rates of Wages in 1898.	Average Weekly Earnings during 1898.	Excess of Average Weekly Earnings over Average Weekly Rates of Wages.	Low Wage Counties.	Average Weekly Rates of Wages in 1898.	Average Weekly Earnings during 1898.	Excess of Average Weekly Earnings over Average Weekly Rates of Wages.
	s. d.	s. d.	s. d.		s. d.	s. d.	s. d.
Derbyshire	18 2	19 11	1 9	Suffolk	11 5	14 5	3 –
Lancashire	18 1	19 4	1 4	Dorset	11 8	14 9	3 1
Cumberland and Westmorland	17 –	18 9	1 9	Wilts	11 9	15 –	3 3

One result is that in the high-wage counties the labourer's income, whether paid in cash or kind, is more evenly distributed over the year, while in the low-wage counties, which are the arable ones, the labourer's weekly wages are increased at irregular intervals according as the season enables him to work at piecework or harvest.

This has, I think, been a great advantage to the men in the high-wage counties. It has enabled them to live on a uniform scale of diet throughout the year, and they have been better nourished in consequence. It has also kept them from getting into debt in the winter, and from the temptation of drinking when a lump sum is paid, as is the case of the harvest money in the eastern counties. But old customs are very difficult to alter, and it is quite likely that a suggestion in the eastern counties to raise the rate of weekly wages by 3s. to 4s. in lieu of the present system of harvest and piece-work payments, would meet with more opposition from the men than from the employers. The men would very likely think they were going to be the losers. Moreover, they have got accustomed to paying their rent for the year and buying some clothes, or paying some debts out of the harvest money.

Speaking generally, ordinary agricultural labourers in England get comparatively few allowances in kind excepting potato ground and beer at harvest. But in the northern and some of the western counties cottages and fuel are also frequently given free, and in some counties in the latter group cider is often given as a daily allowance.[20]

Although almost every class of farm work is the subject of piecework to some extent, most of the operations which are "put out" to piecework are undertaken between spring and autumn, and they are chiefly those connected with hoeing and the gathering of the corn and root crops. Much piecework is also given on the hop farms and fruit and flower gardens. More piecework is undertaken on large farms than small ones, as on the former the work can be better organised and supervised, and the prices more easily fixed. Moreover, where the farmer has a large range of roots to hoe, or potatoes to gather, he finds it to his interest not only to have it accomplished in the shortest possible time, but also to ascertain the cost of the operation.

---

[20] Men in charge of animals, in addition to higher wages than ordinary labourers, usually get more payments in kind. The married men generally have cottages and garden free, and frequently have potato ground. Among other allowances sometimes given are straw for pigs, coal, milk, vegetables, and certain allowances of food, beer, and cider. They also often receive some extra cash payments, such as lamb money, journey money, and Michaelmas money.

The harvest payments are highest in the great corn growing counties in the East of England, namely, Essex, Norfolk, Suffolk, Lincolnshire and Cambridgeshire, a month's harvest there being worth in 1902 between 7*l*. and 8*l*. per man, and up to 10*l*. per man in some of the fen districts of Cambridgeshire and Lincolnshire. Thus a man whose ordinary weekly wages are 12*s*., earning 7*l*. 10*s*. for a month's harvest, receives at least 5*l*. extra for the month's work.

In the Eastern counties the harvest is commonly undertaken by piecework. The amount earned depends a good deal on whether the crop is a light or a heavy one, and whether it is so laid by storms or wind that some of it has to be cut by hand instead of with the self-binder. In Norfolk and Suffolk it is the usual practice for the men to contract for the whole harvest, the ordinary staff undertaking to do the harvest for a certain sum per head, taking the risk of bad weather. In the midlands and the southern and south-western counties the harvest payments for a month are generally worth between 3*l*. 10*s*. and 5*l*.

In most districts a good deal of beer is given free at harvest, and in some districts extra food.

The component parts of the annual cash earnings on a few farms in different parts of England are shown in the following table :—

Year.	Number of Ordinary Labourers Employed throughout the Year on the Farms included in the Table.	Average Cash Earnings per Man during Year.				
		Ordinary Wages (Exclusive of Piecework and Corn Harvest).	Piecework Earnings (Exclusive of Corn Harvest).	Corn Harvest.	Other Cash Payments.	Total.
		£ s. d.	£ s. d.	£ s. d.	£ s. d.	£ s. d.
1897....	61	27 14 1	4 7 9	5 18 2	- 11 -	38 11 -
'98....	59	28 19 9	4 - 1	6 13 11	- 14 6	40 8 3
'99....	55	29 9 4	4 18 9	6 9 2	- 13 3	41 10 6

The following table shows in the case of these same men the amount of the component parts of the yearly earnings expressed in percentages :—

Year.	Percentage Proportion of Total Cash Earnings Derived from				Total.
	Ordinary Wages.	Piecework.	Corn Harvest.	Other Cash Payments.	
1897	72	11	15	2	100
'98	72	10	16	2	100
'99	71	12	15	2	100

I now come to the figures I have obtained from certain farms in England and Wales, showing the total annual earnings of ordinary labourers at decennial intervals between 1851 and 1901. The gentlemen who were good enough to supply me with these figures were asked to take the earnings of three or four representative men from their books, and not necessarily the men who earned the most.

The Society will understand the difficulty of making an inquiry into the earnings of forty or fifty years ago. Very few books kept for so long a period are now available, and where they are, in many of them no records of piecework payments to individual men are to be found, the course most usually adopted being for the employer to pay the total sum earned by a number of men on a piecework job to a particular man, who settles up with the rest of the "company." It is not known from these books what share the respective men took, and it is not possible to make even an estimate, because the "company" may have included some casual men whose names do not appear on the farm books at all.

In Appendix III a table will be found showing for ordinary agricultural labourers their rates of weekly wages and their total annual cash earnings, including weekly wages, payments for piecework and overtime, and for extra money earned at harvest, and a statement of the payments in kind, on farms in 21 counties in England and Wales at decennial intervals from 1851 to 1901.

The following are the earnings on 6 of these farms in the counties of Durham, York, Warwick, Lincoln, Essex and Sussex. In the case of the Essex farm I have added the earnings of the men in charge of animals for comparison.

County.	Total Cash Earnings of certain Individual Ordinary Agricultural Labourers, including Amounts Earned at Weekly Wages, Hay and Corn Harvest, Piecework, and Overtime during the Year.																	
	1851.			1861.			1871.			1881.			1891.			1901.		
	£	s.	d.	£	s.	d.	£	s.	d.	£	s.	d.	£	s.	d.	£	s.	d.
Durham	33	16	–	39	–	–*	40	–	–	47	2	–	54	12	–	57	15	6
	31	4	–	34	–	–*	39	3	9	46	16	–	52	–	–	47	16	–
	28	12	–	36	8	–*	40	3	5	49	8	–	49	8	–	52	–	–
	28	12	–	36	8	–*	39	–	–	46	16	–	44	4	–	49	8	–
Yorkshire: North Riding	29	19	11	36	1	7	39	9	1	42	19	–	39	7	–	42	–	–
	30	2	1	39	1	2	30	10	2	42	19	–	39	7	–	38	12	–
	26	13	5	35	2	6	41	6	11	42	19	–	39	7	–	44	8	–
Warwick	27	8	–	30	–	–	30	–	–	35	–	–	33	18	–	34	12	–
	27	8	–	30	7	–	30	–	–	35	4	–	34	–	–	34	12	–
	30	–	–	32	12	–	32	12	–	37	16	–	36	10	–	37	5	–
Lincoln	45	12	5†	42	18	6	40	11	3	38	17	5	43	4	2½	45	3	11
	45	2	9†	37	13	11	41	6	11	41	3	–½	44	1	–	43	17	8
	45	6	10†	45	8	11	50	19	9½	39	9	1½	42	13	–	43	–	6
Essex—																		
Common labourer	26	–	–	30	–	–	32	–	–	36	–	–	41	–	–	41	–	–
Capable task workman	27	–	–	32	–	–	35	–	–	39	–	–	43	–	–	44	–	–
Horseman	30	–	–	35	–	–	40	–	–	40	–	–	45	–	–	45	–	–
Stockman	29	–	–	33	–	–	35	–	–	39	–	–	44	–	–	44	–	–
Sussex	33	10	5	37	8	5	37	10	10	33	10	11	33	19	11	36	11	8½
	31	3	1	34	4	5	33	14	10	33	14	7	35	14	9	38	19	0½
	31	9	2	35	2	5	36	13	3	37	15	1½	38	14	1	36	12	–
	27	4	8	30	5	10	34	1	9	41	4	–	34	8	–	37	19	1

* Figures relate to the year 1859.
†   ,,   ,,   1855.

Allowances in Kind in addition to Cash Earnings.

DURHAM.—Cottage and garden rent free, coals, 40 stones potatoes, and beer during haytime and harvest.

YORKSHIRE.—Cottage and garden rent free; coals led; sticks for fuel found; potato ground found, manured and ploughed; 2 pints of beer each day during haytime and harvest, and if leading late, another pint and cheese and bread; straw for pigs.

WARWICK.—Formerly a gallon of beer or cider each day for 4 weeks in haytime and for 4 weeks in harvest. Now 1*l*. is paid in lieu of beer or cider for haytime, 1c*d*. or 8*d*. per day during harvest, and 6*d*. per day when threshing.

LINCOLN.—None.

ESSEX.—Home-brewed beer. At present time abstainers get 1*s*. per week, and for harvest 2c*s*., in lieu of beer. Horsemen and stockmen have a cottage and large garden at a low rental.

SUSSEX.—Up to 1855 all old wood was carted free. Subsequently over-hours were paid for and cartage was charged.

The following table gives the percentage increase in total annual earnings, and also in the rates of wages in each decennial period from 1851-1901 on the 14 farms for which information is given for the whole of the periods. An estimated allowance for payments in kind based upon the actual particulars supplied by the employers has been added.

	Increase Per Cent. in	
	Rates of Weekly Wages.	Total Earnings.
1861 as compared with 1851	22·2	17·3
'71 ,, '61	9·8	8·5
'81 ,, '71	11·8	11·8
'91 ,, '81	0·3	1·3
1901 ,, '91	6·9	5·1
1901 ,, '51	60·8	51·3

It will be seen that the percentage increases during these periods in the total annual earnings and in the rates of weekly wages respectively show a fairly close correspondence. Although I am not in a position to separate the total amount earned in each year by weekly wages and that earned by harvest and piecework, I am informed that on these farms the men were generally in constant employment during the entire period. But I have shown in this Paper that, in many districts, men were often irregularly employed in former years.

On a large farm in Cambridgeshire, where regular employment was usually given, and for which particulars of earnings will be found in the Appendix, the employer states that "the men were not paid "for any time when they were absent excepting certain holidays— "Christmas Day, Good Friday, and two fair days." The number of days lost by the men whose earnings have been furnished, exclusive of the holidays mentioned above, were as follows:—

	1871.	1881.	1891.	1901.
1st labourer	17 days	12 days	20 days	6 days
2nd ,,	17 ,,	6 ,,	2 ,,	4 ,,
3rd ,,	21 ,,	20 ,,	5 ,,	18 ,,
4th ,,	No record of any absence	15 ,,	19 ,,	8 ,,

Dividing the total annual earnings, including the value of allowances in kind into fifty-two weekly amounts, and comparing them with the rates of weekly wages, we get the following results:—

	Weekly Rates of Wages.	Weekly Earnings.	Excess of Earnings Over Wages.	
			Amount.	Per Cent.
	s. d.	s. d.	s. d.	
1851	9 9¼	12 2¾	2 5½	25·3
'61	11 11¼	14 4¼	2 5	20·3
'71	13 1¼	15 6¾	2 5½	18·8
'81	14 7¾	17 4¾	2 9	18·8
'91	14 8¼	17 7¼	2 11	20·0
1901	15 8¼	18 6	2 9¾	17·9

Turning now to figures given by other authorities as to total annual earnings, I do not find that there are any reliable ones before 1867 based on particulars relating to the country as a whole. Mr. Purdy in his Paper before this Society in 1861 found this to be the case, and Mr. Bowley, who has examined the available statistics on the subject with much care, appears to agree with this view.[21]

The general excess of earnings over wages in England, based on the information given by the Royal Commission on the Employment of Children, Young Persons, and Women in Agriculture (1867-69), the Royal Commission on Labour (1892-94), the Board of Trade Report on the Wages and Earnings of Agricultural Labourers, 1900, is as follows :—

Authority.	Year.	Excess of Earnings Per Cent. of Wages.
Royal Commission on the Employment of Children, Young Persons, and Women in Agriculture........................	1867–69	20
Royal Commission on Labour....................	'91–94	19
Board of Trade Report, 1900	1898	18

This question is of importance, for if it could be proved that there is a fairly constant relation between wages and earnings in each period, a rough and ready calculation of earnings can be made, when the weekly wages are known, without a laborious inquiry.[22]

[21] Purdy, "Earnings of Agricultural Labourers in England and Wales, 1860," *Journal of the Royal Statistical Society*, 1861, pp. 342, 343, 353, and 354; Bowley, "The Statistics of Wages in the United Kingdom during the last "Hundred Years," Part IV *Journal of the Royal Statistical Society*, 1895, pp. 555—557.

[22] Summing up the whole of the evidence before him in 1899, Mr. Bowley said: "There seems no reason to suppose that the ratio of earnings to wages has "changed to any great extent on the average since Arthur Young's time, and it "appears that the former are about 17 per cent. higher than the latter." *Ibid.*, p. 556.

I find that on the farms in question the payments in kind (if any) made to the class of men whose wages and earnings are being considered, have varied very little, if at all, during the period under review. It may, however, be observed that the old labourers state in some counties that since 1874 fewer gifts have been given by the farmers, such as an occasional meal, milk, broth, beer, cider, and fuel.[23] Generally the tendency is to substitute money payments for payments in kind, to all classes of farm labourers, and this is more particularly observable in the districts near towns. I may add that even the shepherds in Northumberland and over the Border, who have up to the present time been paid largely or wholly in kind, are now showing a decided preference for cash wages.

As regards the rates for piecework, they have, as would be expected, gradually increased along with the increase of weekly wages, and they are now about 50 per cent. higher than they were in 1850. On the other hand, the amount of piecework per man now given by the farmers is generally said to have decreased. This is partly due to the introduction of machinery, which has displaced hand labour at such operations as mowing at hay and corn harvest, and threshing. In some districts also the area of arable land has been reduced, and there are fewer crops of the character to which piecework is applicable. The smaller profits derived from agriculture since the "seventies" have also prevented the farmer from hoeing and weeding or keeping his ditches and hedges as tidy as formerly, and, lastly, the labourer himself, now that his wages are higher, is not so anxious to obtain piecework as formerly, and when he gets it he will seldom work overtime, as he frequently used to do.

[23] John Woollas, a Herefordshire labourer, aged 75, said to me in October, 1902: "Fifty-six years ago there were more allowances. A man could get a bag of wheat at market price from the farmer, and if he wanted a pig he could buy it from the farmer and pay for it in instalments. Broth and milk were given to the children 'graciously' in the old days, and if a man was kept late he was given supper. The men had as much cider as they liked then." An old farmer in the same county, who had farmed for fifty years, and was once a waggoner, said: "In the old days men bought wheat from the farmers, ground the grain, and used the offal for the pigs. They all had ovens then, and now they are not used. After Arch came they had more money and less perquisites. When bread was so dear the labourers often got dinners from the farmers, say twice a week. Farmers gave food rather than raise wages."

James Bullock, 82 years of age, said: "In the old days farmers used to give a can of broth or some victuals, and you could fetch a drop of milk when you wanted it, and a bit of fuel sometimes. You were bound to get a bit of summat extra over if you had seven or eight to feed. Farmers also gave more potato ground then."

It is alleged by some authorities that some farmers paid the wages partly in inferior wheat at a price they could not realise in the market. Caird refers to this being the case in Dorsetshire (English Agriculture in 1850-51, p. 72). See also the late Sir Thomas Dyke Acland, "On the Farming of Somersetshire" (Journal of the Royal Agricultural Society of England, 1850, pp. 750 and 751).

In Appendix I will be found some examples of rates for piecework in 1850 and 1902.

As regards earnings at corn harvest in 1901 compared with 1851, the information sent by employers also shows that about a 50 per cent. increase has taken place. But since the introduction of self-binding machines the number of men required for harvest operations has decreased. This has consequently also affected the Irish migratory labourers.

The amount paid for corn harvest on two farms for a series of years is shown in the following table :—

County.	Amount Paid for Corn Harvest on certain Farms in						Allowances in Kind in Addition to Cash Payment.
	1851.	1861.	1871.	1881.	1891.	1901.	
	£ s. d.	£ s. d.	£ s. d.	£ s. d.	£ s. d.	£ s. d.	
Suffolk	5 7 6*	7 13 –	8 1 –	—	8 12 6	8 13 6	
Essex....	5 – –	6 – –	6 10 –	7 10 –	7 10 –	7 15 –	Home-brewed beer

* 1853.

Piecework at hay harvest has disappeared since the introduction of machinery for cutting, but overtime money, beer, and sometimes extra money are given.

I have shown from the figures I myself obtained, and also from those collected by other authorities, that the earnings of the labourers have been almost continuously increasing since 1850. Taking the financial position of the labourer as a whole, and comparing it during the period 1850-70 with 1870-1900, there are three important elements which should be considered in connection with his position in the former period, namely, the higher prices paid for the necessaries of life, the greater irregularity of the men's employment in many districts, and the earnings of the women and children.

Value of Food.

I do not propose in this paper to go into any details on the question of prices, though it is essential to allude to it when considering the position of the labourers fifty years ago and now. It is a generally accepted fact that the prices of most of the necessaries of life — food, clothes, furniture and lights — have cheapened to a considerable extent.

Taking a few of the principal articles of food of the labourer in 1850 and in 1901, the reduction in prices is approximately as follows :—Flour, 25 to 30 per cent. ; sugar, 60 to 70 per cent. ; tea, 65 to 70 per cent. ; cheese, 25 per cent. ; potatoes, 8 per cent. On the other hand, pork has increased in price by about 20 per cent. and bacon nearly 15 per cent.

In the last fifty years the food of the labourer has generally increased in quantity in the low-wage districts, and in all districts in quality and variety. In some counties more meals are taken now, the whole family sitting down to tea as well as supper. In the north the hired men get substantial refreshments at ten o'clock and four o'clock, in addition to three other meals a day.

In the "forties," "fifties," and "sixties," it is evident that the amount of food eaten by the labourers' families was barely sufficient in some localities. In the winter, the season when food was most required, the labourers and their families in the low-wage districts often had to live on poor diet.[24] Regular employment was often scarce, there was little or no piecework, while extra money was required for fuel and clothing.

I do not think that there is much evidence from the low-wage districts that the food available was insufficient for men in normal health, but there is certainly medical evidence to show that if there was a disposition to disease, then the quality was found to be defective. Further, as the husband had necessarily to have the largest share of the food, and also the most strengthening diet, such as pork and bacon, the women and children frequently suffered from insufficient nourishment.[25]

In the "thirties," "forties," and "fifties," the principal diet of the agricultural labourers was wheaten bread or other food made from flour. Barley bread was, however, frequently eaten in the western counties; and, in the north, barley bread, oat cake, and porridge. In some counties nearly half a man's weekly wages appears to have been spent on bread for his family. Other articles of diet were bacon, pork (the latter frequently salted), cheese, dripping, lard, milk, potatoes, onions and other vegetables. The high price of tea prohibited much being drunk. Fresh meat (beef or mutton) was seldom eaten, except in some of the northern and north midland counties (chiefly on Sundays), but the men who were boarded in the farm houses had it more frequently.

---

[24] See "Reports of Special Assistant Poor Law Commissioners on the Employ-"ment of Women and Children in Agriculture," 1843, pp. 17 and 18; also Dr. Edward Smith's "Report on the Food of the Poorer Labouring Classes in "England," Appendix No. 6 to the Sixth Report of the Medical Officer of the Privy Council, 1863, p. 264.

[25] See "Reports of Special Assistant Poor Law Commissioners on the Employ-"ment of Women and Children," 1843, p. 18; also Dr. E. Smith, in his "Report "on the Food of the Poorer Labouring Classes in England," Appendix No. 6 to the Sixth Report of the Medical Officer of the Privy Council, 1863, p. 262, and the Report of Dr. Simon, Medical Officer of the Privy Council, p. 12.

In the low-wage counties the monotony of the bread diet was relieved by eating it soaked in broth or spread with dripping or lard. Toast water was often taken in lieu of tea. Skim milk or butter-milk was also drunk. Bacon or pork was, as a rule, eaten on Sundays only; and, at times when this could not be obtained for the Sunday dinner, potatoes were eaten with melted butter or grease.

In some of the western counties potatoes, swedes, and cheese made from skim milk formed a considerable portion of the diet. A good deal of cider was given free to the labourers in these counties by the farmers.

Since the "sixties" a great change has taken place in the labourer's diet. At the present time wheaten bread is universally eaten, but a good many people deplore the substitution of fine for coarse flour, which, they assert, was more nourishing. Fresh meat— beef or mutton—is now generally within the reach of all, though I do not think that in the low-wage counties it is eaten more than once a week, as a rule. In the north, however, fresh meat is eaten daily in many cases. Other articles of food now partaken of, some of which were practically unknown in the "fifties" and "sixties," but which are now brought round in carts to the labourer's door, are tinned meats, fish, jam, pickles, tea, butter, sugar, fruit, eggs, coffee, cocoa, currants, and cake.

Correspondents in various parts of the country state that one effect of the lower prices and larger earnings has been that many of the labourers have given up keeping pigs, and also cows, in the few districts where this was customary, and also cultivating allotments.

In Appendix IV I have given instances of the food most usually eaten at meals by a labourer and his family forty or fifty years ago and at the present time, in the counties of Norfolk, Suffolk, Huntingdon, Cambridge, and Essex, and also in Wales, and of the food eaten by hired men in the farm houses in Cumberland.

The following table shows the average quantity of the principal kinds of food consumed in a week by an agricultural labourer, his wife, and four children in 1902 in certain groups of counties:—

[Based on 114 returns furnished by landowners, farmers, Local Government Board Inspectors, members of Local Authorities, the clergy, relieving officers, tradesmen, and agricultural labourers.]

	Northern Counties.	Midland Counties.	Eastern Counties.	Southern and South-western Counties.	England.
Beef or mutton	74 ozs.	60 ozs.	28 ozs.	53 ozs.	53¾ ozs.
Pork	3 „	21 „	33 „	14 „	17¾ „
Bacon	55 „	48 „	32 „	38 „	43¼ „
Cheese	12 „	21 „	18 „	26 „	19¼ „
Bread	5 lbs.	27 lbs.	17 lbs.	29 lbs.	19½ lbs.
Flour	23 „	7 „	20½ „	9 „	14¾ „
Oatmeal and rice	1¼ „	1½ „	1 „	1¼ „	1¼ „
Potatoes	26 „	22 „	24 „	31 „	25¾ „
Tea	8 ozs.	7 ozs.	6½ ozs.	9 ozs.	7½ ozs.
Coffee or cocoa	1 „	5 „	1 „	3½ „	2½ „
Butter	22 „	15 „	14½ „	15 „	16¾ „
Lard, margarine or dripping	29 „	10 „	15 „	12 „	17 „
Sugar	4¾ lbs.	4¾ lbs.	4 lbs.	3¾ lbs.	4¼ lbs.
Syrup, treacle or jam	1¾ „	1½ „	1 „	2¼ „	1½ „
Milk new or skimmed	6½ pints —	4 pints or 9 „	3½ pints or 7¾ „	4 pints or 9¼ „	4½ pints or 8¾ „
Average total value	14*s.* 10½*d.*	13*s.* 6½*d.*	12*s.* 4½*d.*	13*s.* 4¾*d.*	13*s.* 6½*d.*

Particulars of the quantities of fish and eggs were asked for, but in many cases expenditure under these headings is very occasional and, in some cases, was not in addition but in place of one of the items included above.

From the varying quantities of bread and flour it will be seen that while baker's bread is largely consumed in the midland and southern and south-western counties, very little bread other than home-baked bread is consumed in the northern counties. In the eastern counties the consumption of baker's and home-made bread is nearly equal.

The proportion which the value of the articles of food shown in the preceding table bears to the average earnings of ordinary labourers is shown below:—

England.	Average Total Earnings of Ordinary Agricultural Labourers in 1898.	Average Value of Principal Articles of Food consumed by Families of Agricultural Labourers.	Percentage Proportion of Value of Food consumed to Earnings.
	s. *d.*	*s.* *d.*	Per cent.
Northern counties	19 1	14 10½	78
Midland „	16 11	13 6½	80
Eastern „	15 9	12 4½	79
Southern and South-western counties	16 9	13 4¾	80
England	16 10	13 6½	80

In the case of horsemen, cattlemen and shepherds, whose earnings are generally about 1s. to 2s. higher than those of ordinary labourers, the margin between the value of the food consumed and earnings would, of course, be greater.

The percentage proportion of the principal articles of food seems high, but it should be borne in mind that no account is taken above of the profit a labourer may derive from a garden, an allotment or potato ground, pig or poultry. He may also have a son over 14 years of age, living at home and in regular work, or his younger children may perhaps earn small sums occasionally. His wife, too, may earn a little. Further, children who are out in service or employed away from home, sometimes send money to their parents, especially when there is sickness. It should be added that at the present time the wages are higher than in 1898.

Although the details of the domestic economy of households in various parts of the country differ so widely, it will be seen from the following table that of the total value of foodstuffs consumed weekly, the proportion represented by the chief necessaries (meat and bread) is almost equal in the different groups of counties :—

	Northern Counties.		Midland Counties.		Eastern Counties.		Southern and South-western Counties.	
	s.	d.	s.	d.	s.	d.	s.	d.
Meat (including beef, mutton, pork, and bacon)	5	2½	4	9¾	3	2	3	5½
Bread and breadstuffs	3	1	3	3¾	4	0	4	0¼
Total	8	3½	8	1½	7	2	7	5¾
Total value of principal articles consumed	14	10½	13	6½	12	4½	13	4¾
Percentage of total value of principal articles consumed	56		60		58		56	

The following statement gives, side by side, the results of Dr. E. Smith's inquiry and my own, and shows the average quantity of the principal kinds of food consumed by an agricultural labourer's family in 1863 and 1903 respectively :—

[Based on returns relating to 370 families in England, without distinction as to number included in family.]		[Based on 114 returns relating to families in England, consisting of man, wife, and 4 children.]	
	1863.		1903.
		Beef or mutton	53¾ ozs.
		Pork	17¾ ,,
Bacon, meat and bone	72¾ ozs.	Bacon	43¼ ,,
Cheese	24 ,,	Cheese	19¼ ,,
Bread, flour, oatmeal, rice, and other kinds of grain (all reckoned as bread)	55¾ lbs.	Bread	19½ lbs.
		Flour	14¾ ,,
		Oatmeal and rice	1¼ ,,
Potatoes	27 ,,	Potatoes	25¾ ,,
Tea	2¼ ozs.	Tea	7½ ozs.
		Coffee or cocoa	2½ ,,
Butter, dripping or lard, suet	25 ,,	Butter	16¾ ,,
		Lard, margarine or dripping	17 ,,
Sugar, treacle	2 lbs.	Sugar	4¼ lbs.
		Syrup, treacle or jam	1½ ,,
New milk, skimmed milk, butter milk	7·3 pints	Milk, new or	4½ pints or
		,, skim	8¾ ,,

Irregularity of Work.

As regards the question of irregularity of work I may say that, after studying the authorities on the subject, I think that many of the published figures of annual earnings probably relate to the men in fairly regular work attached to the staff of the larger farms, and therefore do not disclose the losses incurred by men employed by smaller farmers with but little capital, or by men dependent on casual employment, working for different farmers. There were a considerable number of these casual men in many villages until well into the "eighties."

It is, I think, obvious that the figures must have this tendency, because to approach any accuracy they must of course be taken from books, and detailed labour books are, as a rule, only kept on the large farms occupied by men with a fair amount of capital. Such farmers can afford to employ their men the most regularly. They have more buildings and sheds than smaller farmers, and therefore greater opportunities of providing work under cover in wet weather.

Since 1896 the difficulty of estimating the average earnings in a district has become much less, as labour has, generally speaking, been scarce, and consequently nearly all the available labour has been regularly employed. Thus the earnings taken from the books of the larger farms are now probably fairly typical of the general body of labourers in the same districts. The "Board of Trade "Report" in 1898 comprised the wages of the whole of the ordinary labourers attached to the staff of the farms from which particulars were obtained, and these include time lost for sickness, holidays, and other causes.

When I was an Assistant Commissioner on the Labour Commission in 1892-93, I certainly felt the difficulty of gaining a correct idea of the average earnings in a district. For instance, in Norfolk and Suffolk the ordinary labourer's wages in 1891-92 were 12s. a week, and the earnings, which I took from the books of farmers, came to about 15s. on an average throughout the year.

But the labourers at the meetings I held in the open parishes generally said that those working on a farm where it was not customary to give regular employment, or men who worked for different farmers, lost 1s. a week, on an average, in the year from bad weather, sickness, or because they could not always get a job, and some said 2s. Some of them also said that they got little or no piecework on the smaller farms. Putting the loss of employment of such men at 1s. a week, and their piecework earnings at 1l. a year, their average weekly earnings, including harvest, would even then have been about 13s. 4d. a week, or 1s. 4d. a week higher than the current rate of weekly wages prevalent in the district. If any men had lost 2s. a week, the earnings in that case would have only been about 12s. 4d. My point on these facts is, that if I could have taken an earnings census in those districts, the earnings I published in 1902 of 15s. a week would have probably been found to be above the average.

Mr. Rew's report on Norfolk in 1895 to the Royal Commission on Agriculture[26] supports my contention. Weekly wages at that time had generally fallen to 10s., though in some parishes they were 11s., and in others 9s. Mr. Rew states that the "evidence goes to prove that with a current weekly wage of 10s. the "average weekly earnings of a *regular* labourer, taking the year "through, would be from 13s. to 14s." But speaking of the supply of labour he says, "in winter many men are thrown out of em-"ployment."

That very considerable irregularity of employment existed in a number of the southern counties in the "thirties," "forties," and "fifties" is apparent from the "Report from the Select Committee

---

[26] C–7915 of 1895, pp. 40, 41, and 43.

"on Agriculture" in 1833, the "Reports of the Poor Law Com-
"missioners" in 1833 and 1834, the "Reports from the Select
"Committee appointed to inquire into the state of Agriculture" in
1836, the "Report on the Burdens on Land" (1846), the "Reports
"of the Special Assistant Poor Law Commissioners on the Employ-
"ment of Women and Children in Agriculture" in 1843, and from
Sir James Caird's letters to the "Times" in 1850 and 1851.[27] It
is also referred to in the "Reports of the Assistant Com-
"missioners on the Employment of Children, Young Persons, and
"Women in Agriculture" in 1867-69, by Mr. Clifford in 1875,
and in the Reports of some of the Assistant Commissioners to the
Royal Commission on Labour in 1892-93, and to the Royal Commission on Agriculture in 1893-95, and in the Final Report of that
Commission, published in 1897.[28]

Earnings of Women and Children.

It can be no matter of surprise that when weekly wages of
ordinary labourers were so low between the "thirties" and the
"seventies," and work for a good many men frequently irregular, the
assistance of the wives and children either upon the land or in local
industries were essential to make both ends meet.

Mr. Austin, reporting on the counties of Wilts, Dorset, Devon,
and Somerset, in 1843, on the employment of women and children
in agriculture, speaking of the out-door employment of married
women, said, "Their earnings are a benefit to their families which
"cannot be dispensed with without creating a great deal of
"suffering."[29]

Referring to the condition of the labourers in South Wilts,
where weekly wages were 7s. a week, and in one large parish 6s.,
Caird says, in 1850: "Where a man's family can earn something at
"out-door work, this pittance is eked out a little, but in cases
"where there is a numerous young family, great pinching must be
"endured."[30]

Dr. Edward Smith, in his Report to the Medical Officer of the
Privy Council in 1863, says, "The labour of women in the fields
"(whatever may be its disadvantages and however desirable it may
"be that it should not be necessary,) is under present circumstances

---

[27] Subsequently reprinted in book form. See "English Agriculture in "1850-51."

[28] C–8540 of 1897, pp. 37—40.

[29] "Reports of Special Assistant Poor Law Commissioners on the Employment "of Women and Children in Agriculture," 1843, p. 28.

[30] "English Agriculture in 1850-51," p. 84. Caird states that in 1850 the common rate of wages for day labourers in the Cotswold Hills did not exceed 6s. and 7s. a week, women getting 6d. a day (*ibid.*, p. 32).

"of great advantage to the family, since it adds that amount of income to the family which relieves from the pressure of want."[31]

Old labourers have frequently told me of the struggles they had when young married men with several young children unable to do any work. Mr. J. J. Henley, C.B., who was an Assistant Commissioner on the 1867 Commission on the Employment of Children, Young Persons, and Women in Agriculture, informed me that that was the hardest period in a labourer's life, and that his advice to young labourers used to be, "marry and get your troubles over as early as you can."

In most parts of England and Wales women and children were often employed between the "thirties" and "seventies" at field work to a greater or less extent, but where there were opportunities for them to earn money at other industries, either in factories or at home, such as at spinning, hand-loom weaving, ribbon weaving, button making, lace making, knitting, glove making, straw plaiting, and making up garments, women and girls generally did less on the land. It would appear, as might be expected, that, generally, more field work was done by married women and by children in the low wage than the high wage districts. In the early part of the "seventies," owing to the higher wages, the demand for domestic servants in towns, and the Education Acts, the practice of employing women and children on the land largely declined. Machinery at harvest also began to displace their labour, and in the early "eighties" it had almost entirely ceased in many districts.

In 1892-93 the reports of the Assistant Commissioners to the Labour Commission show that women were not often employed on the land except in a few districts. The Senior Assistant Agricultural Commissioner, Mr. W. C. Little, wrote: "One very marked feature distinguishing the present inquiry from any of the previous investigations of a similar character is the lessened employment of women in farm work." He also said: "The universal withdrawal of women from field work is evidence of an improvement in the circumstances of the labourers."[32]

Mr. Spencer reported that "Women are occasionally employed at farm work in Dorset, Wilts, Essex, Worcestershire, and Surrey, and but rarely in Somerset,"[33] a very different state of affairs to what I have shown existed in the "forties" and "fifties."

[31] Appendix No. 6 to the "Sixth Report of the Medical Officer of the Privy Council, 1863," p. 262.
[32] "General Report on the Agricultural Labourer (Royal Commission on Labour)," C-6894—xxv of 1894, pp. 54 and 163.
[33] "Reports from Assistant Agricultural Commissioners (Royal Commission on Labour)," C-6894—v of 1893, p. 10.

I myself found very few women employed in the districts I reported on to that Commission, except in Northumberland, where the Scottish system prevails, and in Norfolk, where a good many were engaged at singling, pulling and cleaning roots, weeding corn, and raking after the waggons in hay and corn harvest. Some girls and widows were still working at Swaffham in a gang. The labourers in all my districts, with the exception of those in Northumberland, were averse to the employment of women.

At the present time women, except in Northumberland and Durham, are very seldom employed at field work in any counties, except for fruit and flower picking, pea picking and hop picking, and occasionally a little weeding, singling roots, and picking potatoes, and helping at hay harvest. I am not, of course, referring to the wives and families of the small farmers in England and Wales, who often help them on the land in certain seasons.

It will be readily understood that before the introduction of machinery at hay and corn harvest, the assistance of women and children was a great advantage to farmers, by enabling them to gather their crops as quickly as possible and to save them from the effects of bad weather. It was also of value to them to have a large supply of cheap labour for certain operations for which men's wages have now to be paid.

The employment of women and children is stated by several authorities to have been a factor in keeping the wages of the men low. The late Sir Thomas Dyke Acland stated that when a man had a family old enough to work, he was content to take a lower wage himself if they were employed.[34]

Generally the work of women and children was irregular, and they usually got but little employment in the winter months, the period when the men were also earning the least and were often in irregular work themselves.

In the early "forties" boys not infrequently began to do light work in the fields in the low wage counties as early as 6 years or soon after, bird scaring or watching cattle. Girls usually began to work later, about 11 or 12 years of age. As the elder boys and girls could not easily obtain situations elsewhere, the whole family were available for agricultural work. The boys at the age of about 12 or 13 used often to be hired in the farm houses, but when boys of between 13 and 18 lived at home, the family earnings were, of course, increased. The cost of the clothes and food, however, of boys of this age was not inconsiderable. In the north the boys

---

[34] "On the Farming of Somersetshire," Journal of the Royal Agricultural Society of England, 1850, p. 754.

generally appear to have begun out-door work at a somewhat later age than in the south.

Regular out-door employment must have been a very hard life for a married woman. She had to be up very early in the morning to see after the children and get the breakfast ready before she started, she had often to walk a considerable distance to and from her work, her clothes and boots were often unsuitable for field work, and frequently she had no change. On her return she had her household duties to perform, often in wet clothes, the supper to prepare, and the children to put to bed. In such circumstances as these the children were neglected and the home comforts of the men were sacrificed. The daughters who worked on the land also grew up without a knowledge of domestic duties, and when they married it is stated that they frequently were almost entirely ignorant of cooking or the economical management of a household which was so essential on a small income. I saw something of this in 1892 in Norfolk, when I was reporting for the Labour Commission.[35]

The information procurable as to the payment of women and children almost entirely refers to the rates of daily pay, and not to the total amount earned in the year. The reason is that the names of the women and children were seldom entered in the farmer's labour books, as they did not work regularly, and indeed they often worked for different farmers. Further, the farmer often paid the man what he owed to the other members of his family.

I have examined the evidence obtained by the Poor Law Commissioners in 1832-34, the interesting paper read in the year 1838 to this Society by Dr. Kay, an Assistant Poor Law Commissioner, the evidence obtained by the Assistant Poor Law Commissioners on the inquiry into the Employment of Women and Children in Agriculture in 1843, and of the Assistant Commissioners on the

---

[35] Mr. Austin, reporting to the Poor Law Commissioners on the counties of Wilts, Dorset, Devon, and Somerset in 1843, said: "There is not the same order "in the cottage, nor the same attention paid to his comforts as when his wife "remains at home all day. On returning from her labour she has to look after "her children, and her husband may have to wait for his supper. He may come "home tired and wet; he finds his wife has arrived just before him; she must "give her attention to the children; there is no fire, no supper, no comfort, and "he goes to the beershop. . . . . . Her own clothes, and those of her husband "and family, are rarely in such cases properly attended to" (Reports of Special Assistant Poor Law Commissioners on the Employment of Women and Children in Agriculture, p. 27). Mr. Austin also said that "When the mother of young "children is absent from home the whole or the greater part of the day, the "mischief to them is very great. They are neglected in every way, morally and "physically" (*Ibid.*, p. 26). See also Dr. E. Smith's "Report on the Food of "the Poorer Labouring Classes in England." (Appendix No. 6 to the Sixth Report of the Medical Officer of the Privy Council for 1863, p. 262.)

inquiry into the same subject in 1867-69, and I have also examined all the papers in the "Journals of the Royal Agricultural Society of "England," and have read other authorities. In addition, my own correspondents who have sent me particulars as to wages for a long series of years from their books, have given me information as to the annual sum generally earned by a labourer's wife and three or four children in the "fifties" and "sixties."

Having regard to all the available information which I possess, I should say that a farm labourer's wife and family of children, not more than four in number and not exceeding 12 or 13 years old, would have generally earned in the period named between 5l. and 12l. a year, varying of course according to the number of the children, their ages, the health of the wife, and the opportunities of work, that is, an addition of from 2s. to 5s. a week to the man's earnings.

With regard to the earnings at local industries of married women and of the older daughters who lived at home, there is a good deal of information in the reports of the Assistant Commissioners on the 1867-69 Commission. 3s. to 3s. 6d. a week appears to be about the usual amount earned, and the hours appear to have been long. Sometimes 4s. and 5s. a week was earned for a twelve hours' day or more. But assume a girl earned 4s. every week, she would only have earned about 10l. in a year, which could scarcely have fed and clothed her. A girl could now earn say 12l. to 15l. in domestic service, and be well fed in addition.[36]

Condition of Cottages, and Rent.

The condition of the cottages, and the overcrowding in many of the open villages, where they are often owned by speculators and small tradesmen, was frequently most deplorable in the earlier part of the period under consideration. Though much has been done since the sixties in the direction of improvement, much still remains to be done.

The evidence of reliable witnesses such as medical men and the clergy in certain districts given to the Commission of Inquiry into the Employment of Women and Children in Agriculture in 1843, and also the Reports of the Assistant Commissioners themselves, are sometimes simply appalling.

[36] I found a good deal of outwork done by the wives and daughters of agricultural labourers in the neighbourhood of Bury St. Edmunds in 1892, which they got from clothing factories in the neighbourhood or from London.

The women with large families in Suffolk told me what a great advantage the extra money earned at factory work was to them. But it will be understood that the noise of a machine in the only living room was very trying to the man, who not infrequently went to the public house to escape it.

Reporting on Wilts, Dorset, Devon, and Somerset, Mr. Austin said: "The want of sufficient accommodation seems universal. "Cottages generally have only two bedrooms (with very rare "exceptions); a great many have only one. The consequence is, "that it is very often extremely difficult, if not impossible, to "divide a family so that grown-up persons of different sexes, "brothers and sisters, fathers and daughters, do not sleep in the "same room."[37]

Cases are mentioned of lodgers being taken into the cottages in addition to a family of some size. It is not therefore surprising that we find the clergy talking about immorality, and the doctors about disease.

Dr. (afterwards Sir J.) Simon, the Medical Officer of the Privy Council, in his report for 1864, referring to Dr. Hunter's Inquiry on the State of the Dwellings of Rural Labourers, says:—"To "the insufficient quantity and miserable quality of the house-"accommodation generally had by our agricultural labourers, almost "every page of Dr. Hunter's report bears testimony. And gradually "for many years past the state of the labourer in these respects has "been deteriorating,—house-room being now greatly more difficult "for him to find, and, when found, greatly less suitable to his "needs, than perhaps for centuries has been the case. Especially "within the last twenty or thirty years the evil has been in very "rapid increase, and the household circumstances of the labourer "are now in the highest degree deplorable."[38]

The "First Report of the Royal Commission on the Employment "of Children, Young Persons, and Women in Agriculture" in 1868, stated as follows:—[39]

"The evidence received by our Assistant Commissioners in "every county hitherto visited by them proves that many land-"owners, both large and small, have, especially within the last "thirty years, expended in the aggregate immense sums of money "in improving and enlarging old and providing new cottages on "their estates.

"Nevertheless, it is lamentably evident that, although much has

---

[37] "Reports of Special Assistant Poor Law Commissioners on the Employment "of Women and Children in Agriculture" (1843), p. 19. See also evidence of the Hon. and Rev. (afterwards Rev. Lord) S. Godolphin Osborne, p. 73. Also evidence of Mr. Phelps, an agent of the Marquis of Lansdowne, p. 62, and Mr. Spooner, a surgeon, pp. 82 and 83. See Report on Kent, Surrey and Sussex, by Mr. Vaughan, one of the Assistant Commissioners, pp. 148 and 149. See also "Report from the Poor Law Commissioners, on an Inquiry into the Sanitary "Condition of the Labouring Population of Great Britain" (1842).

[38] "Seventh Report of the Medical Officer of the Privy Council, for 1864," p. 9.

[39] p. liv.

" been done towards remedying the omissions and the errors of past
" generations in that respect, a large proportion of the agricultural
" labourers throughout the country are still under the disadvantage
" of being housed in dwellings in which they cannot fail to be
" subjected to great and serious discomfort, and in which the
" decencies of life are often impossible."

The Hon. Edward Stanhope, one of the Assistant Commissioners of the Commission of 1867-69, afterwards Secretary of State for War, speaking of Dorset, said that while the great majority of landowners had effected great changes on their estates, there were many cottages unfit for habitation.[40] The Rev. Mr. Fraser, afterwards the Bishop of Manchester, who reported on the counties of Norfolk, Essex, Sussex, and Gloucester, said that " the majority of the " cottages that exist in rural parishes are deficient in almost " every requisite that should constitute a home for a Christian " family in a civilised community."[41]

In Mr. Frederick Clifford's book entitled " The Agricultural " Lock-out of 1874," which was originally published in the form of letters to the " Times " in that year, he thus describes the cottages in a Suffolk village :—" Habitations like these are enough to crush " nearly all sense of decency, or notion of tidiness and comfort " among the women, while they must inevitably drive the husband " to the public-house."[42] In my report to the Labour Commission in 1892, I quoted this and endorsed it as applicable to the state of things then existing nearly twenty years later in some of the open villages where I made a minute inspection.

In my final report to the Labour Commission on the condition of the cottages in the northern and eastern counties, I pointed out that although it was encouraging to be able to say that cottage accommodation was improving owing to the action of the landowners, who build without making profit their primary object, " there are many houses left more fitted for animals to inhabit than " men or women, and in which no human being could be either " comfortable or contented."[43]

The late Mr. W. C. Little, who was the senior Assistant Agricultural Commissioner, and who was charged with the task of writing a report summing up all the Assistant Commissioners'

---

[40] Appendix, Part I, to "Second Report of the Royal Commission on the " Employment of Children, Young Persons, and Women in Agriculture" (1869), p. 6.

[41] Appendix, Part I, to "First Report of the Royal Commission on the " Employment of Children, Young Persons, and Women in Agriculture" (1868), p. 35.

[42] p. 36.

[43] C-6894—III of 1893, p. 17.

reports to the Labour Commission, wrote as follows in 1894: "Very generally an improvement has taken place, and is still in progress, but this is chiefly on the estates of large proprietors, and it is to be feared that a large proportion of the cottages inhabited by labourers are below a proper standard of what is required for decency and comfort, while a considerable number are vile and deplorably wretched dwellings."[44]

On the Agricultural Commission in 1894-95 I had further opportunity of examining the cottage question. As I found the cottages more uniformly bad in Cambridgeshire than in any other county I visited, I will refer to the evidence given at Wisbech by a very representative body of farmers invited by the late Mr. W. C. Little to meet me. They said "the cottages are very bad in North Cambridgeshire, with the exception of those on large estates, and a lot are not fit to live in. If the sanitary authorities did their duty a lot would be condemned." A well-known farmer and land agent near Cambridge said that "the wretched homes of the labourers have had much to do with their migration from the villages." I myself said that "I venture to reiterate that until the inspection of cottages is undertaken by the county councils or a Government Office, through capable and disinterested officials, influenced by no local prejudices or interests, so long will the housing of the labourers remain a great blot on our rural life."[45]

The facts relating to this question require great care in collecting and handling. A great deal of evidence from a large number of districts is necessary to enable a general opinion to be formed of the condition of the cottages in rural districts. It is an easy matter to write a sensational report by visiting a number of open villages containing cottages of the older type made of lath and plaster, or clay lump, often owned by comparatively poor people, frequently without the means to keep them in decent repair, and to whom it is important to obtain the largest possible return. It is also an easy matter to write a rosy account of the cottage accommodation in the close villages, or on farms belonging to large and wealthy

[44] C-6894—V of 1894, p. 92.

[45] C-7871 of 1895, p. 15. Comparing the condition of the cottages in Northumberland, Cumberland, Westmorland, Lancashire, Norfolk, Suffolk, Lincolnshire, and Cambridgeshire in 1892-95, according to my experience as Assistant Commissioner on two Royal Commissions, the cottages in Lincolnshire were the best, and in Cambridgeshire the worst. In Norfolk and Suffolk the best and the worst class of cottages were to be found. Taking the average, the cottages in Northumberland, Cumberland, Westmorland, and Lancashire were better than in Norfolk and Suffolk. (See also Rew's Report on Norfolk to the Royal Commission on Agriculture. C-7915 of 1895, p. 46 and 47; and Mr. H. Rider Haggard's "Rural England" (1902), vol. II, pp. 59—64.

landowners, who have spared no expense to erect dwellings equipped with every modern convenience.

The contrast between the classes of cottages often in the same parish is extraordinary. In the old type of cottage there is often overcrowding in the sleeping rooms, low ceilings, small windows, ricketty stairs; while down stairs the living room is often a small kitchen possessing no back door, where the cooking and washing have to be done. The discomfort in case of illness in such places can be imagined. Add to this, dampness on the ground floor, general want of repair, little or no garden, no proper outhouse or sanitary arrangements, and water to be fetched from some distance, and occasionally nothing but pond water to be obtained, and you get some of the influences which make the agricultural labourer not disinclined to move elsewhere when he gets the chance. In the new type of cottage there are often three bedrooms, a kitchen, and scullery or pantry; also a parlour, good outhouses, including a washhouse with a copper, or a bakehouse, and a garden and pig stye. This class of cottage is not merely a dwelling but a home. Health, decency, cleanliness and comfort can be obtained; the wife need not be a slut, nor the husband a drunkard, nor the children little "hooligans."

The decline in the number of farm labourers during the last decade has resulted in the decrease of overcrowding in the cottages, as the following figures for certain agricultural counties show:—

Table showing for certain Agricultural Counties the Population, and the Percentage of the Total Population of those Counties, Living in Tenements, more than Two per Room, according to the Census of 1891 and 1901 respectively.

County.	1901.		1891.		Decrease in Percentage in 1901 as Compared with 1891.
	Population Living More than Two per Room.	Percentage of Total Population.	Population Living More than Two per Room.	Percentage of Total Population.	
Westmorland	1,804	2·80	3,229	4·88	2·08
Lincoln	12,581	2·52	20,384	4·30	1·78
Norfolk	17,357	3·64	28,020	5·98	2·34
Suffolk	12,912	3·46	21,478	5·93	2·47
Berkshire	6,118	2·42	11,396	4·83	2·41
Sussex	11,095	1·84	16,108	2·94	1·10
Hampshire	13,040	1·63	18,339	2·65	1·02
Gloucestershire	34,815	4·91	53,710	8·21	3·30
Somerset	12,428	2·82	20,067	4·67	1·85
Devon	51,723	7·81	65,219	10·31	2·50
Cornwall	12,742	3·95	21,282	6·60	2·65

The rent paid for cottages in the rural districts has generally very little relation to the accommodation or comfort provided, or to the earnings of the occupier. Indeed, the best cottages are not infrequently the lowest rented. 1s. to 2s. a week are the usual rents in the rural districts, 1s. 6d. being, I believe, the most usual. In the purely rural districts rents do not appear to have risen much in the last forty or fifty years, notwithstanding the improved class of new cottages, and the increase in the cost of building. But I think that there are fewer cottages now rented as low as a 1s. a week than formerly.

As between county and county, the rents in the purely rural districts appear to be generally about the same, notwithstanding the difference in wages. But rents of cottages near towns, not belonging to owners of estates, where other classes compete with the farm labourers for them, have certainly risen. Thus, a man on the Essex side of Hertfordshire may be earning 14s. to 15s. a week and paying 1s. 6d. for his cottage, while a man on the Middlesex side may be earning 17s. to 18s. a week, and paying 2s. 6d. to 4s. for his cottage.[46]

It is also satisfactory to be able to say that local authorities are often more active than formerly in administering the Sanitary Acts; and, further, that many landowners, with decreasing rentals and with the cost of building increasing, have spent, and are continuing to spend, considerable sums of money on erecting good cottages, from which no direct remunerative return is obtainable. Landowners and estate agents generally say that a pair of cottages now cost at least 350*l.*, and many put the sum higher. It is apparent that with rents at 1s. 6d. per week, and with rates to pay and repairs to execute, there is no direct profit on such an outlay.

But in order to attract a good class of tenant, a farm must be equipped with good accommodation for man and beast, and the landlord has to look at his profit from the rental of each farm as a whole, rather than at the profits arising from the component parts.

As showing how one evil leads to another, it is worth while

---

[46] In his General Report to the Royal Commission on Labour, Mr. W. C. Little compared the cottage rents in districts where the yearly earnings of ordinary labourers averaged 17s. a week and upwards with the rents of cottages in districts where the earnings averaged under 15s. a week, and came to the following conclusions:—" It is clear from this comparative statement that cottages which " are rented of those who are not estate owners are frequently let for as much " money in districts of low earnings as in those of higher earnings, and that the " rents of estate or farm cottages vary very little as between districts of high " and low earnings." C–6894, xxv, of 1894, p. 120.

to turn our attention back to the first half of the past century when the lavish administration of the Poor Law and the provisions concerning Settlement and Chargeability, which gave direct encouragement to idleness, thriftlessness and early marriages,[47] were also responsible for bad cottage accommodation and overcrowding, immorality and other attendant evils. Until the Union Chargeability Act (1865), which threw upon the union instead of the parish the maintenance of the poor, each parish had a direct interest in reducing the number of its resident labourers. Numerous landowners, in order to avoid high rates, and to prevent an increase of birth settlements, adopted the policy of not only refraining from building cottages on their properties, but of keeping empty or pulling down existing ones. Dr. Simon, in his Report to the Privy Council in 1865, said that the practice prevailed " on a very large " scale."[48]

But, to say the least of it, the practice was a selfish one, for it enabled the landlord to have his estate cultivated by men to whose support he contributed nothing in sickness or old age, or, as Mr. H. J. Little put it, "the landlord had, in fact, often been " obtaining a portion of his rental at the expense of his neighbours."[49] The labourers, where the landlords had thus acted, had to seek shelter in the dilapidated and often crowded open villages with high rents, resulting in a state of things which became a great reproach to rural life, and which has left its mark to the present day in some districts.

A further consequence was that the labourers, their wives and children often had to walk long distances to their work from the open villages. Caird states, in 1851, that it was "the commonest " thing possible" to find agricultural labourers lodged at such a distance from their regular place of employment that they had to walk an hour out in the morning and an hour home in the evening— from 40 to 50 miles a week. The distance to the villages from the farms was so great that in one county the farmers used to provide their men with donkeys.[50]

Dr. Simon, in his report to the Privy Council for 1864, said :—

[47] The " Report from the Select Committee on Agriculture " in 1833, says: " The great abuse would seem to be more prevalent in the southern counties, " where wages are paid out of the rate, where the system of roundsmen has been " longest established, where the father of the family receives an increased " allowance on the birth of each child, where the supply of labour is redundant, " and where a premium is thus indirectly offered to improvident marriages and to " an increase of population " (pp. 6 and 7).

[48] "Seventh Report of the Medical Officer of the Privy Council," 1864, p. 10.

[49] "Memoir on English Agriculture." See " Journal of the Royal Agricultural " Society of England " for 1878, p. 779.

[50] "English Agriculture in 1850-51," p. 516.

"While great owners are thus escaping from poor-rates through the
"depopulation of the lands over which they have control, the
"nearest town or *open* village receives the evicted labourers :—the
"nearest, I say; but this 'nearest' may be three or four miles
"distant from the farm where the labourer has his daily toil. To
"that daily toil there will then have to be added, as though it were
"nothing, the daily need of walking six or eight miles for power of
"earning his daily bread. And whatever farm-work is done by his
"wife and children is done at the same disadvantage. Nor is this
"nearly all the evil which the distance occasions him.

"In the open village, cottage-speculators buy scraps of land
"which they throng as densely as they can with the cheapest of all
"possible hovels. And into these wretched habitations (which, even
"if they adjoin the open country, have some of the worst features
"of the worst town residences) crowd the agricultural labourers of
"England."[51]

Another evil following this chain of evils was the gang system. The labourers being congregated together in the open villages, frequently in irregular work, and long distances from the farms, it became the practice for gangs of men, women, lads, girls, and children to be formed, by a gang-master, who contracted with the farmers to do certain operations. He was, therefore, the middleman, and he appears to have been frequently a sweater of the worst kind, trading on the poverty of all, and on the necessities of those who had no characters to enable them to obtain any other class of employment. He also made money by selling necessaries to the members of his gang.

The bargain the gang-master made with the farmer was based on a piecerate contract, but he paid the workers day wages, and extracted from them the longer hours and the increased exertions incidental to piecework; thus putting in his pocket the extra profit they would have made if their bargains had been direct with the farmer. The workers, including children, had sometimes to walk six or seven miles to their work, and if the distances were too great, the gang-master sometimes drove them in carts or the farmer sent for them.[52]

Immorality appears to have been often rife in these gangs, and the example of some of the gang-masters appears to have been degrading and ruffianly. As the result of the Sixth Report of the Children's

[51] "Seventh Report of the Medical Officer of the Privy Council," 1864, p. 11.
[52] "Reports of Special Assistant Poor Law Commissioners on the Employment "of Women and Children in Agriculture," 1843, pp. 222—25. Also see "Sixth "Report of Royal Commission on the Employment of Children and Young Persons "in Trades not already Regulated by Law" (1867).

Employment Commission in 1867, legislation happily interfered by the passing of the Agricultural Gangs Act of 1867. Children under 8 years of age were prohibited from working in gangs; mixed gangs of males and females have also been prohibited, and gang-masters for men gangs and women overseers for women gangs have to be licensed by the magistrate.[53] The Education Acts of the "seventies" subsequently were the means of preventing children working to the same extent in the fields. The higher wages in the "seventies" were responsible for the withdrawal of many of the women, particularly the married ones, from field work, and since then the gradual and steady demand for country girls as domestic servants and shop assistants has almost wholly deprived the English farmers of this class of labour.

Position of the Agricultural Labourer in 1903 compared with 1850.

I will now proceed to shortly state in what respects the farm labourers are better off at the present time than they were in 1850.

1. Their earnings are greater, due both to higher payments and more regular employment.
2. They are, in fact, better off than when they had the additional assistance of their wives and children, and they have not to sacrifice the comfort of their homes, the economy of their household arrangements, and the education and worldly prospects of their children.
3. Prices of most of the commodities of life are cheaper. Rent in rural districts has scarcely risen if at all. The result is that the labourers and their families have a greater quantity and a better quality of food than formerly. They furnish their cottages better, dress better, and have money to spend on trips, thus getting their views and ideas enlarged.
4. Work is less arduous owing to shorter hours, the introduction of machinery and to better tools.
5. There are more opportunities of obtaining allotments.
6. Education is free.
7. Sanitary arrangements and water supplies in the villages are better attended to.
8. Cottage accommodation, while not dearer, is better, due both to the superior class of buildings now erected to replace the old ones, and also to the decrease in the population in a good many rural villages, which has tended to reduce over-crowding and to leave the worst cottages empty.

[53] The powers of magistrates have since been transferred to the District Councils (56—7 Vic., c. 73).

9. Compensation can be obtained for accidents in the course of their employment.

Migration from the Country Districts.

According to the 1901 census, the number of male agricultural labourers (including foremen and bailiffs) in England and Wales was 631,728, as compared with 774,762 in 1891, a decrease of 18 per cent. The decrease in the acreage of arable land in the same period was 785,296 acres, or 6 per cent., and the increased use of farming machinery would account for a certain decline. But the fact that at the time of the 1901 census 49 militia battalions were embodied, and numbers of army reserve men were also serving with their regiments, should also be taken into consideration. At this period, too, the mining and other industries were active and wages high, and men were attracted to them from the rural districts. As compared with 1851 there was a falling off in the number of male agricultural labourers of about 40 per cent., and, making every allowance for exceptional circumstances attending the census of 1901, it is evident that the number of labourers engaged in farm work has, from one cause or another, considerably diminished during the last half-century.

Many people may perhaps say that an ordinary farm labourer even in the low-wage counties, earning, at the present time, from 15s. to 16s. a week, with 1s. 6d. a week to pay for his cottage, is perhaps not in such a bad position, particularly if he is comfortably housed and has a garden, and a young son at home also earning money. He may also derive some assistance from an allotment, from keeping a pig or poultry, from clothing or coal clubs, and he may also belong to a sick club or benefit society. Still, it requires very careful management, even with these advantages, for a family of four or five in such circumstances as these, to feed and clothe themselves,[54] having regard to the standard of modern living.[55]

---

[54] A labourer in the western counties said to me last autumn: "You are bound to dress the children better now they go to school and meet other children, and they must be dressed up to the mark or they would be thought nothing of now."

[55] According to the Board of Trade "Report on the Wages and Earnings of "Agricultural Labourers in the United Kingdom" (Cd–346 of 1900), the average total weekly earnings of ordinary farm labourers (including the estimated value of allowances in kind) in England in 1898 were 16s. 10d.; the earnings in ten counties were from 14s. 5d. up to 15s. 6d.; in nineteen counties from 15s. 6d. up to 18s.; in nine counties the earnings were from 18s. up to 20s. In Northumberland and Durham they were between 20s. and 21s. Generally speaking the earnings of men in charge of animals were 1s. to 2s. higher than those of ordinary farm labourers.

Still the farm labourer's position, improved as it is, does not appear to be sufficiently good, nor the conditions sufficiently attractive, to restrain him from accepting work in the populous centres, or in such occupations as the police force, the postal service, the railways, the mines, the brickyards, or the building trades.

The fact is that he is now able to sell his labour in other markets than the agricultural one, and he would have probably done so years ago if he had had the opportunity. He goes where he can earn the highest wages, and he does not differ in this respect from any other class of the community. He and his wife also go where life is less monotonous, and to some extent, perhaps, to raise themselves in the social scale.

We are seeing the effect of education for the first time upon a new generation of farm labourers. Fifty or sixty years ago the farm labourer commenced to work on the land at 6 or 7 years of age. He grew up uneducated, narrow-minded, and unenterprising. If he had had the wits, he had no means of locomotion, nor facilities for obtaining employment elsewhere. The young women were in a similar position. The then existing law of settlement also tended to keep him in his parish.[56] The farmer then had a complete monopoly of the rural labour market.[57] He could employ as many or as few as he liked, when he liked, and as long as he liked. There were the agricultural gangs, and any amount of cheap labour of women and children. Every dog has his day. The farmer has now to compete with other employers for his labour, and the labourer can select his employment and his employer.

No longer the ignorant, ill-clad yokel, but educated, and able to use the press, the posts, railways, and bicycles, and with the aid of friends and relations already employed in various pursuits elsewhere, he can now sell his labour outside his own parish. Unless agriculture can offer him as good terms as other callings, he is not likely to remain on the land on smaller wages for the sake of fresh air, or for breeding healthy children to cultivate it. Anyhow, it is better for him and for the country generally that he should leave the rural districts voluntarily to obtain employment elsewhere, than to be driven out for lack of it.

---

[56] Purdy, "Earnings of Agricultural Labourers in England and Wales, 1860," *Journal of the Royal Statistical Society*, 1861, p. 345. Caird, "English Agri-"culture in 1850-51," pp. 516 and 517. "Report from the Select Committee on "Agriculture," 1833, p. vii. "Report from the Select Committee of the House "of Lords on the Burdens affecting Real Property," 1846, p. xii.

[57] H. J. Little's contribution to the "Memoir on English Agriculture," Journal of the Royal Agricultural Society of England, 1878, p. 505.

The farmer may bemoan his absence, but some other employer is profiting by his presence.

Most of us, I expect, would like to see as many people as possible living in the agricultural districts either as small farmers or farm labourers. We should like to see them leading simple, healthy lives, surrounded by the fewest temptations. It is all very well, however, to say that more people should be employed on the land, but under what conditions ? Does any one want to go back to the period between the "twenties" and the "fifties," when the rural population was so plentiful in many counties outside the northern ones that there was not enough employment to go round; when landowners and farmers had to support large bodies of able-bodied men and their families, and were nearly overwhelmed by the rates in some districts in consequence ?[58] In 1851 Caird said "the "agricultural labourer in the southern counties, while he derives "from his labour the means of a very scanty existence, is almost "everywhere felt as a burden instead of a benefit to his employer."[59] I do not believe that any of the agricultural classes want those days again.

In the "twenties" farmers, in some counties, did not use machinery, in order to employ men who would otherwise have been out of work.[60] In the "thirties" there were constant disturbances in some of the low-wage counties, "a general feeling of insecurity "and alarm throughout the southern and eastern counties of "England,"[61] and according to the report of the Poor Law Commission in 1833,[62] the resentment at the condition in which they lived found frequent expression in rick burning and other acts of violence.

This is what Mr. Thurnall, a farmer and corn merchant of Duxford, Cambridgeshire, told the Select Committee on Agricultural Distress in 1836 :—

"With respect to the labourers, we are paying 50 per cent. more "for labour than we ought to do, as a sort of premium of insurance,

[58] "Report from the Commissioners for Inquiring into the Administration and "Practical Operation of the Poor Laws," 1834, pp. 36—38; "Report of the "Poor Law Commissioners on the Continuance of the Poor Law Commission, and "on some Further Amendments of the Laws relating to the Relief of the Poor," 1840, pp. 9 and 10.

[59] "English Agriculture in 1850-51," p. 513.

[60] "Report from the Select Committee on Labourers' Wages" (1824).

[61] "Report of the Poor Law Commissioners on the Continuance of the Poor "Law Commission, and on some Further Amendments to the Laws relating to the "Relief of the Poor" (1840), p. 10.

[62] "Report from the Commissioners for Inquiring into the Administration and "Practical Operation of the Poor Laws" (1834). Part V of Appendix B 1, "Answers to Rural Queries.—No. 53."

" to prevent our farms being burnt down . . . . . .   In the village
" near me we had 13 fires in one year and a half."

"To what," he was asked, "do you attribute those?" His reply was: "To the desperate state of the labouring class . . . . . . The " difficulty is to get employment . . . . . ."63

In 1846 a large Essex farmer told the House of Lords Committee on the Burdens on Land, that he employed a very considerable number more men than he required, to keep them off the parish; and that since the disturbances took place in the neighbourhood, he had put away his machinery in winter, very much to his detriment. He added: "*If I were to use machinery to any great " extent some resentment would be exhibited upon my premises.*"64

In 1851 Caird refers to frequent rick burning in some districts. In Cambridgeshire and Huntingdonshire he says that rick burning was of almost nightly occurrence, that the farmers there went in fear of their lives, and that "a man might as well expose his life " to the risk of a shot from a Tipperary assassin, as live, like a " Cambridgeshire farmer, in constant apprehension of incen- " diarism."65

Then proceed to the period from 1854 to the end of the "sixties," which is looked back on as a halcyon time for farmers, when many of them lived well, saved money, and bought land. I do not for one moment suggest that many farmers did not show much consideration towards their men, and often made sacrifices to employ them as regularly as possible, and to keep old men off the rates who had given them their life service. Neither do I say that a number of labourers, somehow or other, to their lasting credit, did not find it

---

[63] Mr. Thurnall also said: "Last year they were in a very deplorable state " indeed, and a great number are now where they cannot get employment, and " particularly the young men; the farmer frequently will employ the men with " large families, to prevent their being relieved by a rate, and it makes the young " men very desperate indeed, so much so, that they have told me lately, the " married men as well, that they would go upon the highway and rob. I am an " overseer at this moment, and several of the best and honest labourers have said " to me, that they are shocked to make a declaration of that kind, but that before " they will go to the union workhouse they will rob on the highway."
Asked if the want of employment had any demoralising effect on them, he replied: "It has demoralised nearly the whole of them, they are in a very " desperate state, they are in such a state of excitement, that they are ripe for " everything in the world" ("First Report of Select Committee appointed to " Inquire into the State of Agriculture," 1836, pp. 119 and 120).
Mr. Henry Morton, who farmed in Bucks, Herts, and Middlesex, also told the Committee that wages were high at one time owing to fear on the farmer's part of rick burning (*ibid.*, p. 186).

[64] "Report from Select Committee of the House of Lords on the Burdens " affecting Real Property" (1846), pp. 23 and 24.

[65] "English Agriculture in 1850-51," pp. 467 and 468.

possible to bring up large families honestly and respectably. But I do say that for numbers of the labourers these were still days of comparatively low wages, irregular work, and bad and overcrowded cottages; and no one would wish to see again many of the circumstances existing which were referred to in the reports of the medical officers to the Privy Council for 1863 and 1864, and in the Reports of the Royal Commission in 1867-69 on the Employment of Children, Young Persons, and Women in Agriculture. In 1874 the labourer revolted against the conditions of his employment, and a great unexpected fight was made by him for higher wages. The bitterness then exhibited by the labourers leads one to believe that they must have been long harbouring a sense of injustice.

In 1875 Mr. Frederick Clifford said that the labourer " must " migrate in order to work." He also said, " we must remember, too, " that the agricultural districts will bear a great deal of depletion, " not only without injury to farmers and labourers, but with positive " advantage to both. It is not really to the advantage of farmers " in any district that there should be a redundant population; for if " the nominal rate of wages be thereby kept somewhat lower than it " is elsewhere, the rates are higher. Moreover, low wages generally " mean depression and discontent among the labourers, and bad, " nerveless, dear work." . . . . . . " Will the taste for emigration " grow, and, after a time, sensibly affect the farm labour market ? " Or will it do more than restore a healthy balance between supply " and demand ?" . . . . . . Even then, when the weekly wages were higher than they are now by 1s. a week in Norfolk and Suffolk, Clifford said, " it is questionable whether, out of his " present earnings, the married labourer, however thrifty, can " support a family and pay the weekly sum which is necessary to " secure for himself an adequate provision in sickness and old age."[66] No doubt, in the " seventies," the position of the labourers had become a considerably better one than in the " fifties " and " sixties," and in 1878 Caird said that " The general condition of the " agricultural labourer was probably never better than it is at " present."[67] But I have already shown that as late as 1895, in some districts, certainly in some of the eastern counties,

---

[66] "The Labour Bill in Farming," Journal of the Royal Agricultural Society of England, 1875, pp. 125—127.

[67] See Caird's contribution to "Memoir on English Agriculture," Journal of Royal Agricultural Society of England, 1878, p. 302. Published also separately, under the tiile of "The Landed Interest and the Supply of Food."

all the men were by no means regularly employed.[68] Since 1896 I believe that, generally speaking, they have been regularly employed, and farmers have complained of a shortage of men, particularly in 1900 and 1901, when there was an exceptional demand for labour in the towns, owing to commercial prosperity, and when the country districts had men called up for active service in South Africa. Under what conditions, I therefore ask, is the labourer to remain on the soil? The conditions of larger numbers, crowded cottages, low wages and irregular work, or smaller numbers and the reverse. Is it to be when the farmer or the labourer has the whip hand of the labour market?

It is doubtful whether we shall see an agricultural millennium quite yet, when the farmers shall tell us they have sufficient men at the wages they can afford to pay, and the labourers, that their wages are sufficient and their work regular. But pending the arrival of that desirable time, it will certainly be to the advantage of the economic condition of the labourers, if competition enables them to bargain on fairly even terms with their employers.

Who can say whether the migration from the country districts to the towns will continue to the same extent as recently? Is it not possible that new methods of locomotion will open up the more remote country districts, and make farming more profitable and life less monotonous for the labourer? May it not enable more people to visit the country, and also to live there, and make it possible for manufactories to be erected outside the large urban centres, thus giving direct and indirect employment in the neighbouring villages and on the farms at good wages. And if more decentralisation of government should exist in the future, giving more importance to, and creating greater activity in, provincial districts, may not this all operate in the direction of increased employment in the rural districts?

We have been told by witnesses at various inquiries during the past thirty or forty years, that the farm labourer is decreasing in

---

[68] I reported to the Royal Commission on Agriculture on the county of Suffolk in that year, and I stated that in 1893 and 1894 in a number of districts men were in irregular work even in the summer time, that I had often seen men standing idle in several villages, and that evidence was given that this state of things was not uncommon.

In the winter of that year I stated that a very considerable number of men were in irregular employment, and in fact I went down in the early part of 1895 to try and get some idea of their numbers. This is fully borne out by the fact that a number of farmers in west and north-west Suffolk reduced the wages to 9s. a week in the autumn of 1894 (C–7755 of 1895, pp. 75 and 76).

See also Rew's Report on Norfolk (C–7915 of 1895, p. 40), and the Final Report of the Royal Commission on Agriculture (C–8540 of 1897, pp. 37 and 38).

stamina owing to migration to the towns. This allegation, I think, is somewhat apt to come from people of mature age, who think that their own times produced the high water mark of excellence. I remember the late W. G. Little, a great authority upon agricultural labour, and a well-known tenant farmer himself, saying to me, "if all my friends the farmers have said about the deterioration of the " farm labourer is true, they must be a race of monkeys by now." Reporting to the Royal Commission on the Employment of Children, Young Persons, and Women in Agriculture in 1867-69, a generation ago, the late Hon. Edward Stanhope, an Assistant Commissioner, said: "The younger portion of the labourers are being attracted into " the towns, leaving only the old or the ignorant behind."[69] The Vicar of Bures in Suffolk in a communication to the Rev. J. Fraser, another Assistant Commissioner, states that the farmers were complaining that all the sharper lads were migrating to London and other large towns, and that "'the clods of the valley' alone remain."[70] The Chairman of the Board of Guardians in the Hungerford Union, Berks, also said that "the farm work is now practically left to boys " and old men."[71] I heard much evidence of this character on two Royal Commissions ten years ago. In Herefordshire, a few months ago, an old labourer of 80 years said to me, "the men get weaker " every generation, and so do horses and stock."

Is there not, perhaps, too great a tendency on the part of the older farmers to remember the days when the hours were longer, the work more arduous owing to there being no machinery and inferior implements? Days when wages were low, and the labourer often worked excessive hours at piecework at hay and corn harvest to enable him to pay his way. Days when corn was threshed with the flail, ploughs were made of wood, stacks were made without elevators, and hay and corn were cut by hand.[72] Old labourers have told me, and farmers have corroborated it, that to earn extra money they sometimes reaped corn till 9 or even 10 o'clock at night by moonlight, and slept in the fields for a few hours till they could commence again at dawn. But because economic and scientific causes have combined to make the labourer's work less arduous than formerly, is there proof that he is incapable of the same exertion and the same endurance as the men of a former generation?

[69] Appendix, Part I, to First Report (1868), p. 91.
[70] Appendix, Part II, to First Report (1868), p. 183.
[71] Appendix, Part II, to Second Report (1869), pp. 405 and 401.
[72] See Caird's "English Agriculture in 1850-51"

Clifford said in 1875, "I cannot help thinking that there is, among the mass of our English peasantry, a great reserve of power waiting to be called out, and ready for use if adequate inducements are offered"[73] May this not be true to some extent to-day?

The medical authorites I have consulted as to the deterioration of our rural population doubt if there is evidence to warrant such an allegation. At any rate they say that it requires proof.

Has the better feeding during the last twenty-five years of higher wages and lower prices, the improvement in cottages, in drainage, water supply, the cessation of married women working in the fields, done nothing to maintain if not to improve the stamina of the race? Has medical science and skill been of no avail? Is it not possible, indeed, that the men on the land now, notwithstanding the migration, are quite as good as the average man of fifty years ago? If this is so, it may be better to breed from a small, well-nourished race than a large ill-fed one.

If evidence is required to prove that stamina, strength and courage are still to be found in the lads from the rural districts, the graves around Colenso, Spion Kop, and Waggon Hill are surely witnesses.

Compare the condition of the farm labourers in the Northern counties during the last century with those of the South. In the North there have been mines, and the big manufacturing centres which competed with the farms, and kept labour comparatively scarce, wages high, and work regular.[74] The men in the North

---

[73] "The Labour Bill in Farming," Journal of the Royal Agricultural Society of England, 1875, p. 97.

[74] The "Report from the Select Committee on Labourers' Wages" in 1824, alluding to the system then prevailing of paying labourers' wages out of the rates, said: "The effects of this system very clearly show the mistake of imagining that indiscriminate relief is the best method of providing for the happiness of the labouring classes. Employers, burdened with the support of a surplus population, endeavour to reduce the wages of labour to the lowest possible price. Hence, where the system to which we allude has gained ground, the labourers are found to live chiefly on bread, or even potatoes, scarcely ever tasting meat or beer, or being able even to buy milk; while in other parts of the country, where high wages are still prevalent, the food and whole manner of living of the labourer are on a greatly better scale" (p. 5).

See also evidence of Mr. Charles Howard (East Yorks) upon the "Select Committee to Inquire into the State of Agriculture" in 1836, Second Report, pp. 53 and 54.

Also evidence of Mr. George Culley, C.B., accompanying my Report on the Agricultural Labourer to the Royal Commission on Labour, C–6894—III of 1893, p. 138; also see Dr. E. Smith's "Report on the Food of the Poorer Labouring Classes in England," Appendix No. 6 to the "Sixth Report of the Medical Officer of the Privy Council," 1863, p. 265.

were not pauperised by the old Poor Law system, nor underfed. They have had the intelligence and the means to spend money on the education of their children, who, in their turn, endeavour to preserve their parents' old age from the stigma of pauperism.[75] Their wages have been sufficient to enable many of them to save money and start on small farms. Scores of farmers in the North, or their fathers before them, have been farm servants. They have been right away through from the beginning of last century a finer race, physically and intellectually, than the Southerner, as every report and book bears testimony, and to-day they are still a splendid race.[76] Good feeding for generations has

[75] Caird's "English Agriculture in 1850-51," pp. 513—515; "Report from the Select Committee on Agriculture," 1833, pp. vi and vii; "Extracts from information received by the Commissioners for Inquiring into the Administration and Practical Operation of the Poor Laws," 1833, p. 169; "Report from the Select Committee on Labourers' Wages," 1824, p. 5.

[76] Speaking of Northumberland, Sir Francis Doyle said, in 1843: "It is a rare thing to find a grown-up labourer who cannot read and write, and who is not capable of keeping his own accounts." ("Reports of Special Assistant Poor Law Commissioners on the Employment of Women and Children in Agriculture," p. 300.)

Mr. Grey, of Dilston, a noted Northumberland agriculturist, wrote in 1831: "In contrasting the condition of the peasantry in the Southern with that of the Northern parts of the Kingdom, it would be highly improper to pass over unnoticed the superior education of the latter, and the effect which is produced by it upon their worldly circumstances, as well as upon their moral and religious character . . . . . . In the school attached to almost every village, children are found not only able to read and write at a very early age, but most expert in all the common rules of arithmetic, and not unfrequently capable of extracting the square and cube root with great expedition and accuracy. And even the young men, who labour in the fields all the day, often spend a couple of hours in the evening in school, to advance themselves in such acquirements." See Statement appended to the article by Mr. L. Hindmarsh "On the State of Agriculture and Condition of the Agricultural Labourers of the Northern Division of Northumberland," *Journal of the Royal Statistical Society*, 1838, p. 414.

See Clifford, "Labour Bill in Farming," Journal of the Royal Agricultural Society, 1875, pp. 91—98. Mr. Clare Sewell Read is reported to have said in 1874, when addressing an agricultural association in Norfolk: "And I also come reluctantly to the conclusion that the highly paid Scotch hind is a cheaper and better man than the Norfolk labourer, and that, after all, there is no such thing as cheap labour." (*Ibid.*, pp. 95 and 96.)

See also my Report on the Agricultural Labourer to the Royal Commission on Labour, C–6894—111 of 1893, p. 24, comparing position of farm labourer in the North with that of those in the Eastern counties. Also see pp. 12 and 13. Also evidence of William Gray, a Scotchman, who had collected gangs of men for railway work during a period of thirty years: "Certainly in the counties where they are better fed they work better," p. 12 (note). See also evidence of the late Mr. George Culley, C.B., p. 138. See also evidence of Mr. Hindmarsh, p. 103 (note).

The Scottish farmers who were farming in Suffolk when I was reporting on that county to the Royal Commission on Agriculture, informed me that the cost of labour was greater in Suffolk than in Scotland. C–7755 of 1895, p. 78.

done much for them in body and brain.[77] Will anyone deny that a healthy competition for labour in the North has been a benefit not only to the labourer but to the community? Which is the better race to breed from now, the Northerner, or the Southerner?

The proposition that the labourer is less skilled is, I suggest, more capable of proof, though the inefficiency is probably exaggerated. The modern labourers are not trained to farm work from early childhood. In former times they frequently did piecework at 8 or 9 years of age under their fathers' eyes, while many lads were brought up in the farm houses and taught every branch of farm labour under the farmer's supervision.

It is certainly the case that many of the most enterprising of the labourers are finding employment on the railways, in the police force, and in other occupations. Farmers have suffered especially from the loss of horsemen, cattlemen, and milkers. This class of men, apart from the desire for higher wages, dislike the long hours and the Sunday work on the farms, and often seek situations in towns as carters or draymen. Their loss is a real inconvenience to farmers, and the competition for them is getting keener in the districts where the milk business is increasing. On farms where milk is sent away by train the work begins very early, and Sunday is by no means a day of rest. Men who really understand animals cannot easily be procured. The instinct is born in them, and they have to be bred. Many farmers, however, realise that it is very false economy to let men of this stamp go if they can be retained for a few shillings a week more, and some concessions made as to Sunday work. The extra expense is small compared with the welfare of a large herd of milking cows, a flock of sheep, or a valuable lot of horses. To quote Sir James Caird, "No labour is more unprofitable than that which is underpaid."[78] And it may be added, that an industry which depends so much on the weather for its success, requires willing workers as well as efficient ones.

---

[77] Dr. Edward Smith, in his "Report on the Food of the Poorer Labouring "Classes in England" in 1863, says: "Although the health and strength of the "people may be moderately well maintained on the existing dietary, it is more "than probable that mental vigour and activity, as well as moral courage and "enterprise, are less where the diet is low. The labourers and their families "in purely agricultural districts appear dull and unintellectual, not given to "think, ... and hence in a national point of view this class may be healthy, "but not equal in general value to others." Appendix No. 6 to the "Sixth "Report of the Medical Officer of the Privy Council," 1863, pp. 264 and 265.

[78] "English Agriculture in 1850-51," p. 73.

And where is the old-fashioned all-round man, the older farmers ask, who could mow, thatch, make ditches and fences ? Gone, is the reply, because machinery does some of his work; gone, because the thatching is largely gone, and because barbed wire takes the place of fences. But if the labourer has become less efficient for want of training, it is surely possible to provide the village boy with some theoretical and practical knowledge of rural economy to a far greater extent than it is at present done, without interfering with his general education. The report of the Inter-Departmental Committee on the Employment of School Children in 1901 says that the general effect of the agricultural evidence was "that the "present education of country children has been too literary and "not sufficiently practical, and has done little to interest children "in agricultural work. The present education tends to fit them "only for town life and give them a distaste for agriculture."[79]

Botany and elementary chemistry could be taught in all rural schools, and lectures on the rearing, feeding, and tending of animals and fowls given, while practical instruction could be given outdoors in all branches of farming, including information about machinery and engines to some of the older boys. Again, the girls will be all the more useful if instructed in fowl rearing and feeding, and butter making.

The passing of the Education Acts of the "seventies" has deprived this generation of farm labourers of their early agricultural education, and, having trained them to be clerks, we marvel that they become clerks.

Some agricultural education in the schools will at any rate give the farmers a more useful lot of labourers, even if it does not result in retaining many more on the soil. And agricultural knowledge may prove of use some time or another to many a man in his career. It would be another string to his bow, and if he failed in a town and joined the numbers of the unemployed, he would not be incapable of undertaking work on the land in this country, or in the Colonies, which are asking for men.

But agricultural education is not the only thing necessary in the rural districts to attract the labourers to remain on the land; higher wages have to be paid, and, I take it, if the farmers can get more efficient men, they will not grudge the money.

The farmers cannot, and, indeed, do not, I am sure, expect to return to their former monopoly of labour. If they now have to pay higher wages, they have, on the other hand, saved in the number

---

[79] Cd–849 of 1901, p. 15.

of men they employ by the use of machinery, which has also given them the additional advantage of securing their crops quicker. They have also saved labour by altering their system or course of farming. On the other side of the account the farmers may, however, put shorter hours of work, perhaps less efficient labour, and the loss of the lower paid labour of women and children. Whether the actual cost of cultivation has increased I will not attempt to discuss now, but if the land is to be cultivated, as I am sure it will be, with the demands of an increasing population for food for themselves, and fodder for animals, men are as necessary as manure, and their market value must be paid as in the case of any other commodity. Arrangements among the staff of the farm to minimise the Sunday work as far as possible, and concessions of "off" days, Bank Holidays and occasional half-holidays, are well worthy the consideration of employers, and the more amusement and recreation that can be given in the villages the better. It may be possible to increase the "three acres and a cow" labourer who is to be found in Cheshire, and, in some districts in the neighbourhood of the market towns, to encourage the creation of small holdings of a few acres, where a man with the rest of his family can have a cow or two, pigs and poultry, and grow vegetables, keep a pony and do a little carting, and also work for farmers at odd times. This class of men does exist in some localities, and they sometimes get on to larger holdings afterwards.

Then, again, the labourer must be provided with a decent and comfortable home, with a garden, as near other dwellings as possible, so that he and his family are not isolated from their neighbours, or from the shops and the schools.

All these things, it may be argued, cost money. So does every great undertaking, whether it be the reclamation of Egypt or South Africa, or the future prosperity of our own country districts, but is there any reason why the expenditure should not be reproductive in the end? The cultivation of this country is a great undertaking, not only from a monetary but from an economic and national point of view. Some share of securing the progress and development of agriculture may fall on the Government, but it can do little without the active assistance of the landowners and the farmers.

Modern farming, with the lower prices for grain and the keen competition which exists, requires men of business, whether landowners or tenants, and there is no reason why the country should lack them in the future. That there have been heavy losses among landowners, particularly, of course, those who bought land at the top price, and among farmers who farmed at the higher rentals, we are very well aware. But the men who have pulled through the period of declining prices, the men who have bought land at the large reduction, and are not encumbered by mortgages, and the new men who are farming at the lower rentals and on somewhat different systems than formerly, how do they stand to-day ? If farming is getting on to a sounder basis, and I have heard it asserted by men of large experience in the agricultural districts that this is the case, may not we still look forward to seeing a rural population earning a fair livelihood, and leading a healthy and contented life on the land ?

APPENDIX I.

Rates of Wages Paid by Messrs. J. and E. Lee and J. B. Lee, Stocksfield Hall, NORTHUMBERLAND.

Year.	Single Hind's Wages per Week.		Double Hind's Wages per Week		Women Workers (Ordinary) per Day.		Women Workers (Harvest) per Day.		Year.	Single Hind's Wages per Week.		Double Hind's Wages per Week.		Women Workers (Ordinary) per Day.		Women Workers (Harvest) per Day.	
	s.	d.	s.	d.	s.	d.	s.	d.		s.	d.	s.	d.	s.	d.	s.	d.
1831	11	–	—		–	8	1	6	1868	16	–	30	–	1	–	2	–
'32	11	–	—		–	8	–	10	'69	16	–	30	–	1	–	2	–
'33	11	–	—		–	8	–	10									
'34	11	–	—		–	8	1	6	1870	16	–	—		1	–	2	–
'35	10	6	—		–	8	1	6	'71	16	6	—		1	–	2	–
'36	10	6	—		–	8	1	6	'72	18	–	—		1	3	2	6
'37	10	6	—		–	8	1	6	'73	21	–	—		1	3	2	6
'38	10	6	—		–	10	1	6	'74	23	–	—		1	4	3	–
'39	11	–	18	–	–	10	1	6	'75	24	–	—		1	4	3	–
									'76	22	–	—		1	6	3	–
1840	12	–	20	–	–	10	1	6	'77	23	–	—		1	6	3	–
'41	12	–	18	–	–	10	1	6	'78	21	–	—		1	6	3	–
'42	—		19	–	–	10	1	6	'79	18	–	—		1	6	3	–
'43	—		20	–	–	10	1	6									
'44	—		22	–	–	10	1	6	1880	18	–	—		1	3	2	6
'45	—		18	–	–	10	1	6	'81	20	–	28	–	1	3	2	6
'46	12	–	20	–	–	10	1	6	'82	20	–	28	–	1	3	2	6
'47	13	6	22	–	–	10	1	6	'83	20	–	34	–	1	3	2	6
'48	12	6	22	–	–	10	1	6	'84	19	–	35	–	1	3	2	6
'49	12	–	23	–	–	10	1	6	'85	18	–	35	–	1	3	2	6
									'86	18	–	26	–	1	3	2	6
1850	11	–	22	–	–	10	1	6	'87	18	–	26	–	1	3	2	6
'51	11	–	22	–	–	10	1	6	'88	18	–	26	–	1	3	2	6
'52	11	–	—		–	10	1	6	'89	18	–	30	–	1	3	2	6
'53	12	–	19	–	–	10	1	6									
'54	14	–	26	–	–	10	1	6	1890	20	–	32	–	1	3	2	6
'55	14	–	27	–	–	10	1	6	'91	20	–	34	–	1	3	2	6
'56	14	–	27	–	–	10	1	6	'92	20	–	34	–	1	3	2	6
'57	16	–	27	6	1	–	1	6	'93	20	–	—		1	3	2	6
'58	16	–	27	6	1	–	1	6	'94	20	–	—		1	3	2	6
'59	15	6	27	–	–	10	1	6	'95	20	–	31	–	1	3	2	6
									'96	20	–	31	–	1	3	2	6
1860	16	–	27	6	–	10	1	6	'97	20	–	—		1	3	2	6
'61	16	6	28	–	–	10	1	6	'98	20	–	29	–	1	3	2	6
'62	15	6	28	–	–	10	1	6	'99	22	–	31	–	1	3	2	6
'63	15	6	27	6	–	10	1	6									
'64	15	6	27	6	–	10	1	6	1900	22	–	44	–	1	6	3	–
'65	15	6	28	–	–	10	1	6	'01	22	–	43	–	1	6	3	–
'66	16	–	30	–	1	–	2	–	'02	22	–	38	–	1	6	3	–
'67	16	–	30	–	1	–	2	–									

In addition to the above wages, hinds have their cottage and garden rent free, coals led, 60 to 80 stones of potatoes, 2 bushels of wheat in the year, and 20s. for extra hours in harvest.

The double hind's wages vary according to the age of the youth, who is almost always a son.

Of late years, since the binder came in, we have paid very little harvest wages to women; but last harvest (1902) was an exception, as the crop was so badly laid and twisted.

Particulars relating to Weekly Cash Wages, &c., of Ordinary Agricultural Labourers Employed on the Home Farm of an Estate in WARWICKSHIRE.

1. *Rates of Weekly Cash Wages,* 1825-1902.

Year.	Rates of Weekly Cash Wages in		Year.	Rates of Weekly Cash Wages in		Year.	Rates of Weekly Cash Wages in	
	June.	December.		June.	December.		June.	December.
	s.	s.		s.	s.		s.	s.
1825...	9	9	1851....	10	9	1877....	13	13
'26....	9	9	'52....	10	9	'78....	13	13
'27....	9	9	'53....	10	10	'79....	12	12
'28....	9	9	'54....	10	10	1880....	12	11
'29....	9	9	'55....	11	11	'81...	12	11
1830....	9	9	'56....	11	11	'82....	12	11
'31....	9	9	'57....	10	10	'83....	12	11
'32....	9	9	'58....	10	10	'84....	12	11
'33....	9	9	'59....	10	10	'85....	12	11
'34....	9	9	1860....	10	10	'86....	12	11
'35...	9	9	'61....	10	10	'87...	12	11
'36....	9	9	'62....	10	10	'88....	12	11
'37....	9	9	'63....	10	10	'89....	12	11
'38....	9	9	'64....	10	10	1890....	12	11
'39....	9	9	'65....	10	10	'91....	12	11
1840...	9	9	'66....	10	10	'92....	12	11
'41....	9	9	'67....	10	10	'93....	12	11
'42....	9	9	'68....	10	10	'94....	12	11
'43....	9	9	'69....	10	10	'95....	12	11
'44...	9	9	1870....	10	10	'96...	12	11
'45....	9	9	'71....	10	10	'97....	12	11
'46....	9	9	'72....	12	12	'98....	12	11
'47....	9	9	'73....	12	12	'99....	12	11
'48..	9	9	'74....	14	14	1900....	12	11
'49...	—	—	'75....	14	14	'01....	12	11
1850....	10	9	'76....	13	13	'02....	12	11

2. *Allowances in Kind.*—None.

3. *Variation in Allowances since Earlier Years.*—They once had a gallon of beer or cider per day for four weeks in haytime and four weeks' harvest, but now they have 1*l.* for haytime beer and 10*d.* or 8*d.* per day for beer in harvest, and 6*d.* per day for beer money when threshing.

4. *Amount of Piecework in* 1902, *as Compared with Fifty Years Ago.*—(*a*)—Hay and corn harvest.—Amount is less now than fifty years ago, as there is less grass and corn cut by hand. (*b*) Other work such as hoeing, &c.—Rather less piecework too under this heading.

5. *Earnings by Piecework in* 1902, *as Compared with Fifty Years Ago.*—If paid at old rates they would earn less, as they would do less, but they expect to be paid at a higher rate and to work shorter hours.

6. *Instances of Piecework Rates in* 1850 *and* 1901 *respectively*.

	Mowing Grass.	Reaping Wheat.	Cutting Beans.
	Per Acre.	Per Acre.	
1850..................	2s. 6d.	9s. to 10s.	9s. to 10s.
1901..................	5s.	14s. ,, 17s.	12s. ,, 14s.

7. *Amounts Paid for a Month's Hay and Corn Harvest respectively in* 1902 *and Fifty Years Ago.*—(*a*) Hay harvest.—No information as regards fifty years ago. The men have now 5*s.* per week beer money and 4*d.* per hour overtime after 5.30 p.m., in addition to regular wages, for four weeks. (*b*) Corn harvest.—It would be about 8*d.* per day more now than fifty years ago.

Particulars relating to Weekly Cash Wages, &c., of Ordinary Agricultural Labourers Employed on a Farm in HERTFORDSHIRE.

1. *Rates of Weekly Cash Wages, 1789-1902.*

Year.	Rates of Weekly Cash Wages.	Year.	Rates of Weekly Cash Wages.	Year.	Rates of Weekly Cash Wages.	Year.	Rates of Weekly Cash Wages.
	s. d.		s. d.		s. d.		s. d.
1789....	8 –	1818....	10 –	1847....	8/- to 9/-	1875....	13 6
1790....	8 –	'19....	8/- to 9/-	'48....	8/- „ 9/-	'76....	13 6
'91....	8 –			'49....	8/- „ 8/6	'77....	13 6
'92....	8 –	1820....	8/- „ 9/-			'78....	13 6
'93....	8 –	'21....	9 –	1850....	8 –	'79....	13 6
'94....	8 –	'22....	9 –	'51...	8 –		
'95...	8 –	'23....	8/- to 10/-*	'52....	8 –	1880....	13/- to 13/6
'96....	8 –	'24....	8/- „ 10/-	'53....	8 –	'81....	13/- „ 13/6
'97...	8 –	'25....	8/- „ 10/-	'54....	10 –	'82....	13/- „ 13/6
'98...	8 –	'26....	8/- „ 10/-	'55....	10 –	'83....	13/- „ 13/6
'99....	8/- to 9/-	'27....	8'- „ 10/-	'56....	10 –	'84....	12/- „ 13/6
		'28....	8/- „ 10/-	'57....	10 –	'85....	12 –
1800....	8 –	'29....	8/- „ 10/-	'58....	11 –	'86....	12 –
'01....	8 –			'59....	11 –	'87....	12 –
'02....	8 –	1830 ...	8/- „ 10/-			'88....	12 –
'03....	8 –	'31....	8/- „ 10/-	1860....	10 –	'89....	12 –
'04....	8 –	'32....	8/- „ 10/-	'61....	10 –		
'05....	8 –	'33....	8/- „ 10/-	'62....	10 –	1890....	12 –
'06....	8 –	'34....	8/- „ 10/-	'63....	10 –	'91....	12/- to 13/-
'07....	9 –	'35....	8/- „ 10/-	'64....	10 –	'92....	12/- „ 13/-
'08....	9 –	'36....	8/- „ 10/-	'65....	10 –	'93....	12/- „ 13/-
'09....	9 –	'37....	8/- „ 10/-	'66....	10 –	'94....	12 –
		'38....	8/- „ 10/-	'67....	11 –	'95....	12 –
1810....	9 –	'39....	8/- „ 10/-	'68....	11/- to 12/-	'96...	12 –
'11....	9 –			'69....	11/- „ 12/-	'97....	12 –
'12....	9/- to 10/-	1840....	8/- „ 10/-			'98....	13 –
'13....	10 –	'41....	8/- „ 10/-	1870....	11/- „ 12/-	'99....	13 –
'14....	10 –	'42....	8/- „ 10/-	'71....	11/- „ 12/-		
'15....	10 –	'43....	8/- „ 10/-	'72....	11/- „ 12/-	1900....	13 –
'16....	10 –	'44....	8/- „ 10/-	'73....	13 –	'01....	13 –
'17....	10 –	'45....	8/- „ 10/-	'74....	13 6	'02....	13 –
		'46....	8/- „ 10/-				

* Wages are stated to have rarely exceeded 9s. in the years 1823-46.

2. *Allowances in Kind Given in Addition to Cash Wages.*—Beer at harvest time.

3. *Variation in Allowances since Earlier Years.*—None.

7. *Payments for Haytime.*—Previous to 1840 men received ordinary wages in haytime, with 2s. and beer extra per week. At the present time [1902] 3d. per hour is paid for overtime, together with 6 pints of beer per day. *Payments for Harvest.*—Up to the year 1840 ordinary wages were paid during harvest but provisions and beer were given, Sundays included. In 1902 men received 3s. 6d. per day in harvest and 6 pints of beer per day.

Particulars relating to Weekly Cash Wages, &c., of Ordinary Agricultural Labourers Employed on Mr. Thomas Girling's White House Farm at Frostenden, SUFFOLK.

1. *Rates of Weekly Cash Wages, 1836-1902.*

Year.	Rates of Weekly Cash Wages in		Year.	Rates of Weekly Cash Wages in		Year.	Rates of Weekly Cash Wages in	
	June.	December.		June.	December.		June.	December.
	s.	*s.*		*s.*	*s.*		*s.*	*s.*
1836....	10	9	1859....	9	9	1881....	11	12
'37...	10	10	1860....	11	11	'82...	12	12
'38....	10	10	'61....	11	11	'83....	12	12
'39....	12	10	'62....	10	11	'84....	12	11
1840....	10	10	'63....	9	9	'85....	11	11
'41....	10	10	'64....	9	9	'86....	10	11
'42....	10	10	'65....	9	9	'87....	10	10
'43....	10	10	'66....	10	12	'88....	10	10
'44...	10	10	'67....	11	11	'89....	10	10
'45....	10	11	'68....	11	12	1890....	10	11
'46....	10	10	'69....	10	10	'91....	11	12
'47....	12	12	1870....	10	11	'92....	12	12
'48....	10	8	'71....	12	11	'93....	11	11
'49....	8	8	'72....	12	12	'94....	11	10
1850....	8	8	'73....	13	13	'95....	10	10
'51....	8	8	'74....	13	14	'96....	10	11
'52....	8	8	'75....	13	13	'97....	11	11
'53....	9	12	'76....	13	13	'98....	11	12
'54....	12	12	'77....	13	14	'99....	12	12
'55....	12	13	'78....	13	13			
'56....	12	12	'79....	12	12	1900....	12	12
'57....	11	11	1880....	12	12	'01....	13	12
'58....	10	10				'02....	13	13

2. *Allowances in Kind Given in Addition to Cash Wages.*—Beer would average about 10s. per man per annum. Fuel carted free.

3. *Variation in Allowances since Earlier Years.*—None.

4. *Amount of Piecework in 1902, as Compared with Fifty Years Ago.*— (*a.*) Hay and corn harvest.—Owing to machinery, piecework is now much reduced, and men are paid extra wages per day for hay harvest, up to, say, 3s. (*b.*) Other work, such as hoeing, &c.—Men will not, as a rule, take hoeing by piecework. They prefer day work.

5. *Earnings by Piecework in 1902, as Compared with Fifty Years Ago.*— Men would earn much more now by piecework, if they would only do it.

6. *Instances of Piecework Rates Fifty Years Ago, Compared with* 1902:—

	Hedging and Ditching.	Draining.	Hoeing.
	Per Rod.	Per Score Rods.	Per Acre.
Fifty years ago	9d. to 10d.	3s. 6d. to 4s.	2s. 6d. to 3s.
1902..................	1s. to 1s. 4d.	4s. 6d. to 5s. 6d.	3s. 6d. ,, 5s.

7. *Payments for a Month's Corn Harvest Fifty Years Ago and in* 1902.— Fifty years back harvest was 5*l.* to 6*l.* per month; now it runs from 7*l.* 10s. to 9*l.*

Agricultural wages in England and Wales during last half century 177

Particulars relating to Weekly Cash Wages, &c., of Agricultural Labourers Employed on a Farm in ESSEX.

1. *Rates of Weekly Cash Wages and Harvest Wages, 1850-1902.*

Year.	Rates of Weekly Cash Wages.			Harvest Wages (for Five Weeks).	Year.	Rates of Weekly Cash Wages.			Harvest Wages (for Five Weeks).
	Day Labourers.	Horse-men.	Stock-men.			Day Labourers.	Horse-men.	Stock-men.	
	s. d.	s. d.	s. d.	£ s.		s. d.	s. d.	s. d.	£ s.
1850	8 —	9 —	9 —	5 —	1877	12 —	13 6	13 6	7 10
'51	8 —	9 —	9 —	5 —	'78	13 —	14 6	14 6	7 10
'52	8 —	9 6	9 —	5 —	'79	13 —	14 6	14 6	7 10
'53	8 —	9 6	9 6	5 —	1880	12 —	13 6	13 6	7 10
'54	9 —	10 6	10 6	6 —	'81	12 —	13 6	13 6	7 10
'55	10 —	11 6	11 6	6 —	'82	12 —	13 6	13 6	7 10
'56	11 —	12 6	12 6	6 —	'83	12 —	13 6	13 6	7 10
'57	10 —	11 6	11 6	6 —	'84	12 —	13 6	13 6	7 10
'58	10 —	11 6	11 6	6 —	'85	11 —	12 6	12 6	7 —
'59	8 —	9 6	9 6	6 —	'86	11 —	12 6	12 6	7 —
1860	9 —	10 6	10 6	6 —	'87	11 —	12 6	12 6	7 —
'61	10 —	11 6	11 6	6 —	'88	11 —	12 6	12 6	7 —
'62	11 —	12 6	12 —	6 —	'89	11 —	12 6	12 6	7 10
'63	9 —	10 6	10 6	6 —	1890	11 —	12 6	12 6	7 10
'64	9 —	10 6	10 6	6 —	'91	12 —	13 6	13 6	7 10
'65	9 —	10 6	10 6	6 —	'92	12 —	13 6	13 6	7 10
'66	10 —	11 6	11 6	6 —	'93	12 —	13 6	13 6	7 —*
'67	11 —	12 6	12 6	6 —	'94	12 —	13 6	13 6	7 10
'68	12 —	13 6	13 6	6 10	'95	11 —	12 6	12 6	7 —*
'69	11 —	12 6	12 6	6 10	'96	11 —	12 6	12 6	7 —*
1870	10 —	11 6	12 6	6 10	'97	11 —	12 6	12 6	7 —*
'71	11 —	12 6	12 6	6 10	'98	12 —	13 6	13 6	7 10
'72	12 —	13 6	13 6	7 10	'99	12 —	13 6	13 6	7 10
'73	13 —	14 6	14 6	7 10	1900	13 —	14 6	14 6	7 10
'74	13 —	14 6	14 6	7 10	'01	13 —	14 6	14 6	7 15*
'75	12 —	13 6	13 6	7 10	'02	13 —	14 6	14 6	7 15†
'76	12 —	13 6	13 6	7 10					

* For four weeks.
† For five-and-a-half weeks.

2. *Allowances in Kind Given in Addition to Cash Wages.*—Home brewed beer. Abstainers have 1s. per week extra and 20s. extra for harvest in lieu of beer.

3. *Variation in Allowances since Earlier Years.*—None.

4. *Amount of Piecework in 1902, as Compared with Fifty Years Ago.*—(a) Hay and corn harvest.—Not much piecework at haytime but a quarter more wages. Corn cut by hand (piecework) fifty years ago, now by machinery. Men earn much more now with much less effort. (b) Other work such as hoeing, &c.—Men earn 3s. a day at hoeing, thatching, tying straw and hay for London.

5. *Earnings by Piecework in 1902, as Compared with Fifty Years Ago.*—The men earn at least a third more at piecework at the present time [1902] than fifty years ago, and have more than double the amount given them to do.

6. *Instance of Piecework Rates Fifty Years Ago, Compared with 1902.*—For hoeing beans, wheat and barley the price was 3s. to 4s. per acre fifty years ago. For the same work it was 4s. to 5s. per acre in 1902.

Particulars Furnished by Mr. W. F. Parsons relating to Weekly Cash Wages of Ordinary Agricultural Labourers Employed on Certain Farms at Wootton Bassett, WILTSHIRE.

1. *Rates of Weekly Cash Wages, 1824-1902.*

Year.	Rates of Weekly Cash Wages in June.		Rates of Weekly Cash Wages in December.		Year.	Rates of Weekly Cash Wages in June.		Rates of Weekly Cash Wages in December.		Year.	Rates of Weekly Cash Wages in June.		Rates of Weekly Cash Wages in December.	
	s.	d.	s.	d.		s.	d.	s.	d.		s.	d.	s.	d.
1824	7	–	6	–	1851	8	6	7	6	1877	12	6	11	6
'25	7	–	6	–	'52	8	6	7	6	'78	12	6	11	6
'26	7	6	6	6	'53	8	6	7	6	'79	12	6	11	6
'27	7	6	6	6	'54	9	6	8	6	1880	11	6	10	6
'28	7	6	6	6	'55	10	6	9	6	'81	11	6	10	6
'29	7	–	6	–	'56	10	6	9	6	'82	11	6	10	6
1830	7	–	6	6	'57	10	6	9	6	'83	11	6	10	6
'31	7	6	6	6	'58	10	6	9	6	'84	11	6	10	6
'32	7	6	6	6	'59	10	6	9	6	'85	12	6	12	6
'33	7	6	6	6	1860	10	6	9	6	'86	12	6	12	6
'34	7	6	6	6	'61	10	6	9	6	'87	11	6	10	6
'35	8	6	7	6	'62	9	6	8	6	'88	11	6	10	6
'36	8	6	7	6	'63	9	6	8	6	'89	12	6	11	6
'37	8	6	7	6	'64	9	6	8	6	1890	12	6	11	6
'38	8	6	7	6	'65	10	6	9	6	'91	12	6	11	6
'39	9	6	8	6	'66	11	6	10	6	'92	12	6	11	6
1840	9	6	8	6	'67	11	6	10	6	'93	12	6	11	6
'41	9	6	8	6	'68	11	6	10	6	'94	12	6	11	6
'42	8	6	7	6	'69	11	6	10	6	'95	12	6	11	6
'43	8	6	7	6	1870	11	6	10	6	'96	12	6	11	6
'44	8	6	7	6	'71	11	6	10	6	'97	13	6	12	6
'45	8	6	7	6	'72	11	6	10	6	'98	13	6	12	6
'46	8	6	7	6	'73	11	6	10	6	'99	14	–	13	–
'47	9	6	8	6	'74	12	6	11	6	1900	14	–	13	–
'48	9	6	8	6	'75	12	6	11	6	'01	15	–	14	–
'49	8	6	7	6	'76	12	6	11	6	'02	15	–	14	–
1850	8	6	7	6										

2. *Allowances in Kind, in Addition to Cash Wages.*—Free cottage, sometimes food for overtime in hay harvest, also from 3 quarts to a gallon of beer per diem.

3. *Variations in Allowances since Earlier Years.*—None stated.

4. *Amount of Piecework in 1902, as Compared with Fifty Years Ago.*—(a.) Hay and corn harvest.—No piecework in hay harvest, all mowing being now done by machinery, as well as much cutting of the corn. (b.) Other work, such as hoeing, &c.—Hoeing is still much done by hand, but there is little piecework besides.

5. *Earnings by Piecework in 1902, as Compared with Fifty Years Ago.*—He would earn far more [at the present time].

6. *Instances of Piecework Rates Fifty Years Ago, as Compared with 1902 :—*

	Reaping Wheat. Per Acre.	Cutting Hedges. Per Perch.	Making Faggots. Per 100.
Fifty years ago	7s. to 9s. (12s. if badly laid)	4d. to 6d.	2s. 6d.
Now (1902)	12s. to 14s. (20s. if badly laid)	7d. „ 8d.	4s. 6d.

7. *Amounts paid for a Month's Hay and Corn Harvest, respectively, in 1902 and Fifty Years Ago.*—A month's wages for an ordinary man fifty years ago would be about 40s. or 44s., with beer. Labourers employed in assisting to harvest the corn crops were paid about 3s. per diem on fine days.

Agricultural wages in England and Wales during last half century

Particulars relating to Weekly Cash Wages, &c., of Ordinary Agricultural Labourers Employed on Mr. J. H. Arkwright's Home Farm near Leominster, HEREFORDSHIRE.

1. *Rates of Weekly Cash Wages, 1819-1902.*

Year.	Rates of Weekly Cash Wages in June. s. d.	Rates of Weekly Cash Wages in December. s. d.	Year.	Rates of Weekly Cash Wages in June. s. d.	Rates of Weekly Cash Wages in December. s. d.	Year.	Rates of Weekly Cash Wages in June. s. d.	Rates of Weekly Cash Wages in December. s. d.
1819....	10 –	10 –	1847....	10 –	9 –	1875....	12 –	12 –
			'48....	9 –	8 –	'76....	14 –	14 –
1820....	10 –	9 –	'49....	9 –	8 –	'77....	14 –	14 –
'21....	9 –	9 –				'78....	14 –	13 –
'22....	8 –	7 –	1850....	8 –	8 –	'79....	13 –	13 –
'23....	8 –	8 –	'51....	8 –	8 –			
'24....	8 6	8 6	'52....	8 –	8 –	1880....	13 –	13 –
'25....	9 –	10 –	'53....	9 –	11 –	'81....	13 –	13 –
'26....	10 –	10 –	'54....	11 –	11 –	'82....	13 –	13 –
'27....	9 –	9 –	'55....	11 –	11 –	'83....	13 –	13 –
'28....	9 –	9 –	'56....	11 –	11 –	'84....	13 –	13 –
'29....	9 –	9 –	'57....	11 –	11 –	'85....	13 –	13 –
			'58....	11 –	11 –	'86....	12 –	12 –
1830....	9 –	8 –	'59....	11 –	11 –	'87....	12 –	12 –
'31....	9 –	9 –				'88....	12 –	12 –
'32....	8 –	8 –	1860....	11 –	11 –	'89....	12 –	12 –
'33....	8 –	8 –	'61....	11 –	11 –			
'34....	8 –	8 –	'62....	11 –	11 –	1890....	12 –	12 –
'35....	8 –	8 –	'63....	11 –	10 –	'91....	12 –	12 –
'36....	8 –	8 –	'64....	10 –	10 –	'92....	12 –	12 –
'37....	8 –	8 –	'65....	10 –	10 –	'93....	12 –	12 –
'38....	9 –	9 –	'66....	10 –	10 –	'94....	12 –	12 –
'39....	9 –	9 –	'67....	11 –	11 –	'95....	12 –	12 –
			'68....	11 –	11 –	'96....	12 –	12 –
1840....	9 –	9 –	'69....	11 –	11 –	'97....	12 –	12 –
'41....	9 –	9 –				'98....	12 –	12 –
'42....	9 –	8 –	1870....	11 –	11 –	'99....	12 –	12 –
'43....	9 –	9 –	'71....	11 –	11 –			
'44....	8 –	9 –	'72....	11 –	11 –	1900....	12 –	12 –
'45....	9 –	9 –	'73....	11 –	11 –	'01....	12 –	12 –
'46....	9 –	9 –	'74....	12 –	12 –	'02....	12 –	12 –

2. *Allowances in Kind Given in Addition to Cash Wages.*—Cider; fuel carted.

3. *Variations in Allowances since Earlier Years.*—No material variation.

4. *Amount of Piecework in 1902, as Compared with Fifty Years Ago.*—(*a*.) Hay and corn harvest.—Less now than fifty years ago. (*b*.) Other work such as hoeing, &c.—Rather less.

5. *Earnings by Piecework in 1902, as Compared with Fifty Years Ago.*—Men could earn more if they would work the same number of hours.

Particulars relating to Weekly Cash Wages, &c., of Ordinary Agricultural Labourers Employed on a Farm in DEVONSHIRE.

1. *Rates of Weekly Cash Wages, 1850-1902.*

Year.	Rates of Weekly Cash Wages in		Year.	Rates of Weekly Cash Wages in		Year.	Rates of Weekly Cash Wages in	
	June.	December.		June.	December.		June.	December.
	s.	*s.*		*s.*	*s.*		*s.*	*s.*
1850....	9	9	1868....	13	13	1886....	15	15
'51....	9	9	'69....	13	13	'87...	15	15
'52....	9	9	1870....	14	14	'88....	15	15
'53....	9	9	'71....	14	14	'89...	15	15
'54...	10	10	'72....	15	15	1890....	16	16
'55....	10	10	'73....	15	15	'91....	16	16
'56....	10	10	'74....	15	15	'92....	16	16
'57....	10	10	'75....	15	15	'93....	16	16
'58....	10	10	'76....	15	15	'94....	16	16
'59....	11	11	'77....	15	15	'95....	16	16
1860...	11	11	'78....	15	15	'96....	16 to 18	16
'61...	11	11	'79....	15	15	'97....	16 ,, 18	16
'62....	12	12	1880....	15	15	'98....	16 ,, 18	16
'63...	12	12	'81....	15	15	'99....	16 ,, 18	16
'64...	12	12	'82....	15	15	1900....	18	16
'65....	12	12	'83....	15	15	'01....	18	16
'66....	12	12	'84....	15	15	'02....	18	16
'67....	13	13	'85....	15	15			

2. *Allowances in Kind Given in Addition to Cash Wages.*—A quart of milk per day, cottage and garden, manure for garden, cider in haytime and harvest and other busy times in summer, some food when busy carrying hay.

3. *Variation in Allowances since Earlier Years.*—More cottages are provided now than formerly. In earlier years men had all their food for a month at corn harvest, but this has been abolished now that the hardest work is done by machinery, and money payment substituted (*see* below).

4. *Amount of Piecework in 1902, as Compared with Fifty Years Ago.*—(*a.*) Hay and corn harvest.—In consequence of machinery there is no piecework in hay and corn harvest as formerly. (*b.*) Other work, such as hoeing, &c.—Hoeing is mostly done by piecework, more so than formerly. Sheep shearing is done by piecework now, instead of the men having food.

5. *Earnings by Piecework in 1902, as Compared with Fifty Years Ago.*—Excepting hay and corn harvest, a labourer would earn considerably higher wages now by piecework, although men do not work so hard nor as long hours as formerly.

6. *Instances of Piecework Rates in 1850, Compared with 1902*:—

	Hedging.	Hoeing Twice.
	Per Perch.	Per Acre.
1850..................	6*d.*	10*s.*
1902..................	1*s.* to 1*s.* 3*d.*	15*s.*

7. *Payments for Hay and Corn Harvests in 1902 and Fifty Years Ago.*—(*a.*) Hay harvest.—Owing to use of machinery at present time, men do not get food, except cake or bread and cheese with their tea, but they often get 1*s.* per day extra when carrying. (*b.*) Corn harvest.—The old custom of giving men all their food for a month or six weeks' corn harvest has given way to a money payment of 30*s.* extra for harvest, with cider, and tea and cake at four p.m.

APPENDIX II.

*Average *Weekly Cash Wages of Ordinary Labourers employed on certain farms in England and Wales, and the Average Prices of British Wheat in each of the years* 1850 *to* 1902; *also the percentage fluctuations of such Wages and Prices Year by Year, as compared with the year* 1871. (*See annexed diagrams.*)

[The Cash Wages are exclusive of extra payments for piecework, hay and corn harvests, overtime, &c., and also of the value of allowances in kind.]

	Average Cash Wages per Week.										Percentage fluctuations in Wages as compared with the Standard Year 1871.					Average Prices of British Wheat.		
1.	2.		3.		4.		5.		6.		7.	8.	9.	10.	11.	12.		13.
Year.	England and Wales (67 farms). *		Northern Counties (8 farms).		Midland Counties (22 farms).		Eastern Counties (13 farms).		Southern and South-western Counties (21 farms).		England and Wales (67 farms).*	Northern Counties (8 farms).	Midland Counties (22 farms).	Eastern Counties (13 farms).	Southern and South-western Counties (21 farms).	Price per Imperial Quarter.		Per centage fluctuation in Prices.
	s.	*d.*	*s.*	*d.*	*s.*	*d.*	*s.*	*d.*	*s.*	*d.*						*s.*	*d.*	
1850	9	3½	11	5	9	8½	8	7½	8	5½	77·0	75·2	79·5	74·9	77·3	40	3	71·0
'51	9	2½	11	4¼	9	8¼	8	3¼	8	5¾	76·3	74·8	79·4	72·0	77·5	38	6	67·9
'52	9	3	11	4¼	9	7¾	8	6¼	8	6	76·7	74·8	79·0	74·0	77·7	40	9	71·9
'53	9	11¾	11	10½	10	4¼	9	11	9	–½	82·7	78·2	84·8	86·1	82·7	53	3	94·0
'54	10	9	12	7¼	11	2½	11	1¾	9	5¼	89·1	83·0	91·8	96·7	86·3	72	5	127·8
'55	11	–½	12	9	11	5¾	11	5	9	10	91·5	84·0	94·0	99·1	89·9	74	8	131·8
'56	11	1¼	13	4¼	11	6	11	4¼	9	9¾	92·1	87·9	94·2	98·7	89·7	69	2	122·1
'57	10	11½	13	7	11	3¼	10	10	9	10	90·8	89·4	92·3	94·0	89·9	56	4	99·4
'58	10	9	13	5½	10	10¼	10	4¼	9	10	89·1	88·6	88·9	89·9	89·9	44	2	77·9
'59	10	8¼	13	6½	10	9¾	10	1¼	9	9½	88·6	89·2	88·6	87·7	89·5	43	9	77·2
1860	10	11	13	7¾	11	0¼	10	7¼	9	11½	90·5	89·8	90·3	92·0	91·0	53	3	94·0
'61	11	–¾	13	8½	11	2¼	10	9¼	10	1	91·7	90·3	91·6	93·5	92·2	55	4	97·6
'62	11	–¼	13	7½	11	3¾	10	5½	10	1	91·4	89·7	92·7	90·8	92·2	55	5	97·8
'63	10	11¾	13	7¼	11	3½	10	–½	10	2¾	91·0	89·6	92·5	87·2	93·5	44	9	79·0
'64	11	–¼	13	7¼	11	3¼	10	2	10	3¾	91·4	89·6	92·3	88·2	94·3	40	2	70·9
'65	11	2¼	13	9¾	11	4¼	10	3¼	10	6	92·7	90·9	93·2	89·3	96·0	41	10	73·8
'66	11	6	14	2½	11	6¾	11	–½	10	8	95·3	93·6	94·7	95·8	97·5	49	11	88·1
'67	11	11¼	14	3¼	12	2¼	11	6¼	10	10¼	99·0	94·0	99·8	100·0	99·2	64	5	113·7
'68	12	–¼	14	7¾	12	2¼	11	8¼	10	10¾	99·7	96·4	99·8	101·4	99·6	63	9	112·5
'69	11	10	14	9	12	–	11	1¾	10	9¾	98·1	97·1	98·3	96·7	98·9	48	2	85·0

* Including 3 farms in Wales. The figures for these 3 farms are not included in any of the columns numbered 3 to 6 and 8 to 11.

Average Weekly Cash Wages of Ordinary Labourers—Contd.

	Average Cash Wages per Week.					Percentage fluctuations in Wages as compared with Standard Year 1871.					Average Prices of British Wheat.	
1.	2.	3.	4.	5.	6.	7.	8.	9.	10.	11.	12.	13.
Year.	England and Wales. (67 farms).*	Northern Counties (8 farms).	Midland Counties (22 farms).	Eastern Counties (13 farms).	Southern and South-western Counties (21 farms).	England and Wales (67 farms).*	Northern Counties (8 farms).	Midland Counties (22 farms).	Eastern Counties (13 farms).	Southern and South-western Counties (21 farms).	Prices per Imperial Quarter.	Percentage fluctuation in Prices.
	s. d.	*s. d.*	*s. d.*	*s. d.*	*s. d.*						*s. d.*	
1870	11 10¼	14 10½	12 –½	11 –¾	10 10½	98·3	97·9	98·6	96·0	99·4	46 11	82·8
'71	12 –¾	15 2¼	12 2½	11 6¼	10 11¼	**100·0**	**100·0**	**100·0**	**100·0**	**100·0**	56 8	**100·0**
'72	12 8¼	15 10¼	13 –¼	12 4	11 4	105·2	104·4	106·7	107·1	103·6	57 0	100·6
'73	13 3¾	17 2¾	13 9¼	13 –¼	11 6½	110·4	113·4	112·8	113·0	105·5	58 8	103·5
'74	13 6¼	17 8½	14 –½	13 2½	11 8	112·1	116·6	115·0	114·6	106·7	55 9	98·4
'75	13 6½	17 10	14 1	12 11½	11 8¼	112·3	117·4	115·4	112·5	106·9	45 2	79·7
'76	13 8	17 8½	14 1¼	13 –¾	11 11½	113·3	116·6	115·5	113·4	109·3	46 2	81·5
'77	13 8	17 9¼	14 1¾	12 10½	12 –½	113·3	117·0	115·9	111·8	110·1	56 9	100·1
'78	13 7½	17 5¾	14 –½	13 –	12 –¾	113·0	115·1	115·0	112·8	110·3	46 5	81·9
'79	13 3¼	16 7¼	13 8½	12 5¼	12 –	110·0	109·3	112·3	108·0	109·7	43 10	77·4
1880	13 2¼	16 8¾	13 8	12 –¾	12 –½	109·3	110·2	111·9	104·7	110·1	44 4	78·2
'81	13 2	16 8½	13 7½	11 11¾	12 –¾	109·2	110·0	111·6	104·0	110·3	45 4	80·0
'82	13 2½	16 9½	13 7	12 –¾	12 1¼	109·5	110·6	111·3	104·7	110·7	45 1	79·6
'83	13 3	16 10½	13 7¾	12 –¼	12 1½	109·8	111·1	111·8	104·3	110·9	41 7	73·4
'84	13 2¼	16 11¾	13 6¼	11 11	12 1¼	109·3	111·8	110·8	103·4	110·7	35 8	62·9
'85	13 0	16 11¼	13 3¾	11 4½	12 1	107·8	111·5	109·0	98·7	110·5	32 10	57·9
'86	12 10½	16 8¼	13 2¾	11 2	11 11¼	106·7	109·9	108·4	96·9	109·1	31 –	54·7
'87	12 8¾	16 6¾	12 11	10 11½	11 11¾	105·5	109·1	105·8	95·1	109·5	32 6	57·4
'88	12 8¼	16 8	12 10½	10 8	12 1	105·2	109·7	105·5	92·6	110·5	31 10	56·2
'89	12 9½	16 8	12 11	10 11¼	12 2	106·0	109·7	105·8	94·9	111·2	29 9	52·5
1890	13 –½	16 11¼	13 3¼	11 –¼	12 4¾	108·1	111·5	108·7	95·7	113·3	31 11	56·3
'91	13 4	17 3	13 5¾	11 9¾	12 5¼	110·5	113·6	110·4	102·5	113·9	37 –	65·3
'92	13 5	17 4½	13 7½	11 8	12 7	111·2	114·4	111·6	101·3	115·0	30 3	53·4
'93	13 3½	17 4½	13 6	11 4	12 6¾	110·2	114·4	110·6	98·4	114·9	26 4	46·5
'94	13 2¾	17 4½	13 4¾	11 –¾	12 6¾	109·7	114·4	109·7	96·0	114·9	22 10	40·3
'95	13 2¾	17 4½	13 4¾	11 –	12 7	109·7	144·4	109·7	95·5	115·0	23 1	40·7
'96	13 3¾	17 4½	13 5¾	11 1¼	12 8¾	110·4	114·4	110·4	96·4	116·4	26 2	46·2
'97	13 5	17 4½	13 6¼	11 5½	12 9½	111·2	114·4	110·8	99·5	117·0	30 2	53·2
'98	13 8½	17 5¼	13 8½	12 3	13 –	113·6	114·8	112·3	106·3	118·9	34 –	60·0
'99	13 11	17 5¾	14 –¼	12 6	13 1¾	115·4	115·1	114·8	108·5	120·2	25 8	45·3
1900	14 5¾	18 1½	14 5	13 –¼	13 8½	120·0	119·3	118·1	113·0	125·3	26 11	47·5
'01	14 7	18 2¾	14 5	13 1½	13 10	120·9	120·0	118·1	113·9	126·5	26 9	47·2
'02	14 7	18 2¾	14 5	13 1½	13 10¼	120·9	120·0	118·1	113·9	126·7	28 1	49·6

* Including 3 farms in Wales. The figures for these 3 farms are not included in any of the columns numbered 3 to 6 and 8 to 11.

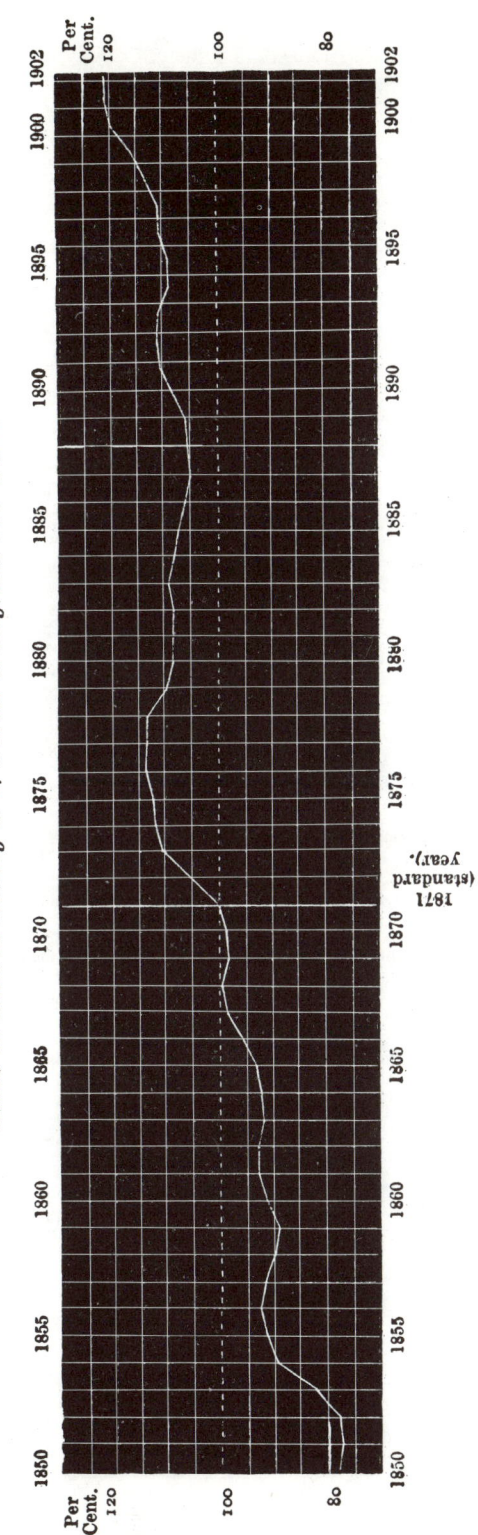

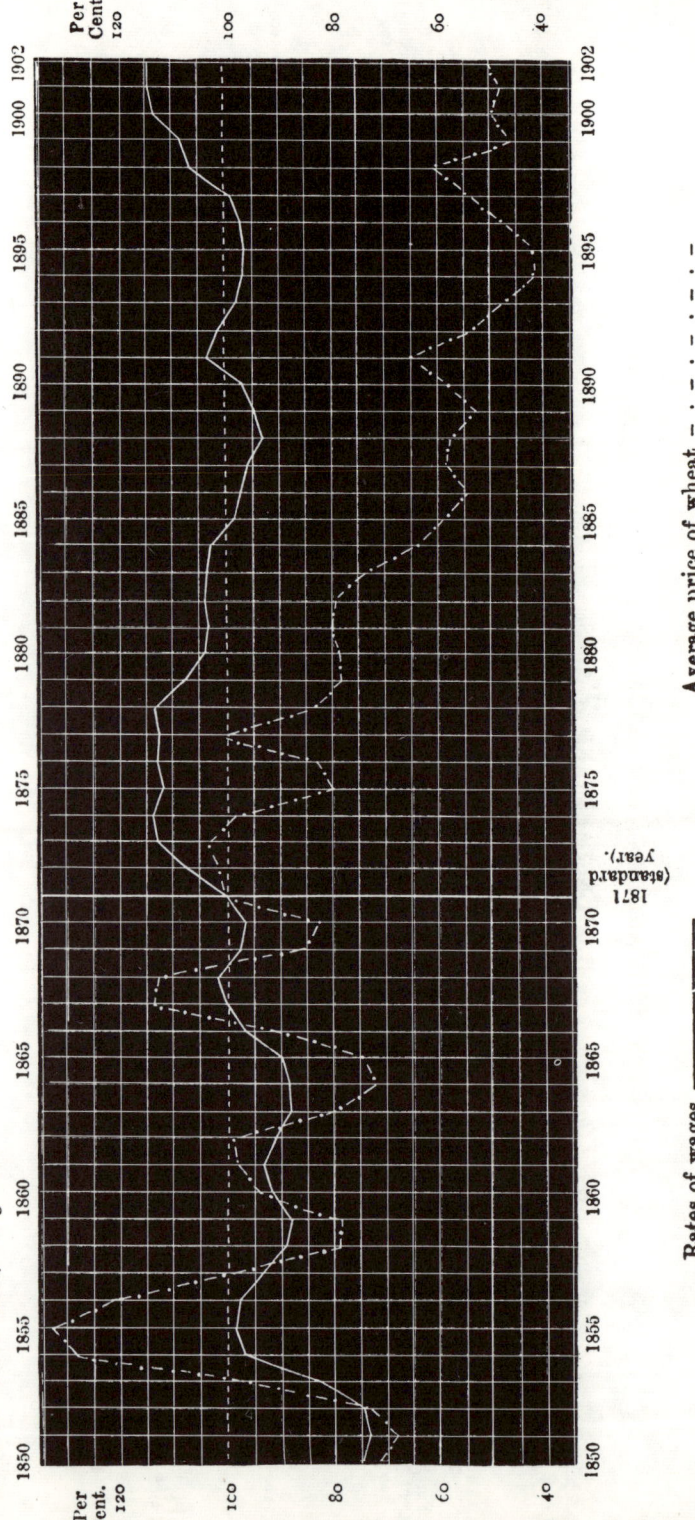

EASTERN COUNTIES OF ENGLAND.

Percentage Fluctuations in Weekly Cash Rates of Wages of Ordinary Agricultural Labourers, and in Average Prices of British Wheat, as compared with Rates and Prices prevailing in 1871. The Wages Curve is Based on Returns relating to 13 Farms in the Eastern Counties of England.

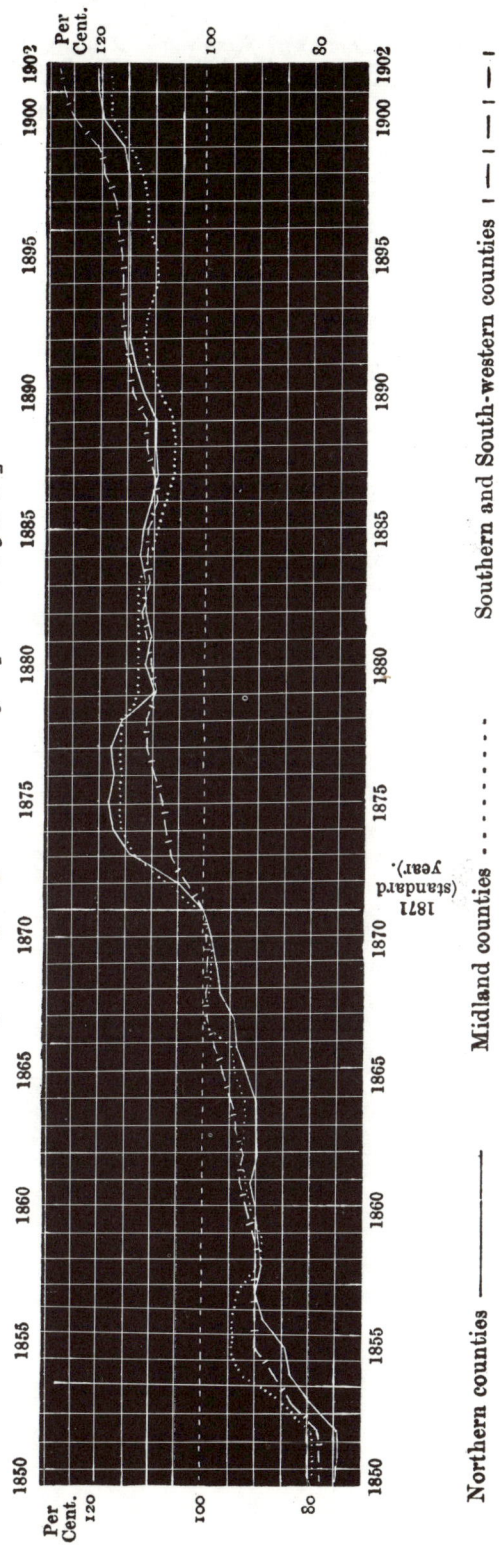

NORTHERN, MIDLAND, AND SOUTHERN COUNTIES OF ENGLAND.

Percentage Fluctuations in Weekly Cash Rates of Wages of Ordinary Agricultural Labourers as Compared with Rates prevailing in 1871, Based on Returns relating to 8 Farms in the Northern Counties, 22 Farms in the Midland Counties, and 21 Farms in the Southern and South-western Counties.

[NOTE.—The curves shown for these three groups of counties are each based on the average rates of wages in the particular group in 1871, not on the average rate of wages in the three groups taken together.]

Northern counties ——— Midland counties ·········· Southern and South-western counties ‒ ‒ ‒ ‒

APPENDIX III.

Table showing the Earnings of Individual Ordinary Labourers in the undermentioned made to such Labourers, and the Rate of Weekly Cash Wages prevailing

Ref. No.	County and Rural District.	1851	1861	1871	1881	1891	1901
		\multicolumn{6}{c}{Rates of Weekly Cash Wages.}					
1	NORTHUMBERLAND. Hexham	s. d. 11 – *11 –*	s. d. 16 6 *16 6*	s. d. 16 6 *16 6*	s. d. 20 – *20 –*	s. d. 20 – *20 –*	s. d. 22 – *22 –*
2	DURHAM. Stockton-on-Tees	12 6 *12 6*	13 6* *13 3**	15 4 *15 3*	18 – *18 –*	19 – *19 –*	20 – *20 –*
3	CUMBERLAND. Carlisle †			Paid Half-yearly.			a b c
4	WESTMORLAND. Kendal			Ditto			
5	Kendal	12 – *12 –*	13 – *13 –*	17 – *17 –*	18 – *18 –*	20 – *20 –*	20 – *20 –*
6	LANCASHIRE. Fylde ‡	12 – *12 –* 11 – *11 –* 10 – *10 –* 6 –§ *6 –§*	12 – *12 –* 12 – *12 –* 12 – *12 –* 12 – *12 –*	14 – *14 –* 14 – *14 –* 14 – *14 –* 13 6 *13 6*	18 – *18 –* 17 – *17 –* 16 6 *16 6* 16 – *16 –*	18 – *18 –* 17 – *17 –* 16 6 *16 6* 16 6 *16 6*	18 – *18 –* 17 – *17 –* 17 – *17 –* 16 6 *16 6*
7	YORKSHIRE. Thirsk	10 – *10 –*	12 6 *11 6*	13 – *13 –*	16 – *15 –*	15 – *15 –*	15 – *15 –*
8	DERBYSHIRE. Belper	— —	16 – *16 –*	17 – *17 –*	18 – *18 –*	20 – *20 –*	20 – *20 –*
9	RUTLAND. Ketton	9 – *9 –*	12 – *12 –*	13 – *13 –*	15 – *15 –*	13 6 *13 6*	15 – *15 –*

NOTE.—The Rates of Weekly Cash Wages in roman type refer to the summer months; *those in italics to the winter.*

* 1859.

APPENDIX III.

years, taken from Account Books by Employers, together with the Allowances in Kind on the Farms on which they were Employed in those years.

1851	1861	1871	1881	1891	1901	Allowances in kind given in addition to Cash Payments.	Ref. No.
colspan across cash columns: **Total Cash Earnings.** (Including amounts earned as weekly wages, hay and corn harvest, piece-work and overtime.)							
£ s. d.	£ s. d.	£ s. d.	£ s. d.	£ s. d.	£ s. d.		
29 12 –	43 18 –	43 18 –	53 – –	53 – –	58 4 –	Cottage and garden rent free; coals led; 80 stones potatoes and 2 bushels barley.	1
33 16 –	39 – –*	40 – –	47 2 –	54 12 –	57 15 6	Cottage and garden rent free; coals; 40 stones potatoes; and beer during haytime and harvest.	2
31 4 –	34 – –*	39 3 9	46 16 –	52 – –	47 16 –		
28 12 –	36 8 –*	40 3 5	49 8 –	49 8 –	52 – –		
28 12 –	36 8 –*	39 – –	46 16 –	44 4 –	49 8 –		
12 – –	20 – –	34 – –	34 – –	30 – –	36 – –	Board and lodging.	3
14 – –	25 – –	40 – –	42 – –	34 – –	40 – –		
8 – –	14 – –	18 – –	22 – –	26 – –	28 – –		
10 – –	16 – –	20 – –	26 – –	28 – –	30 – –		
8 – –	10 – –	12 – –	14 – –	16 – –	18 – –		
10 – –	12 – –	14 – –	16 – –	24 – –	26 – –		
—	22 – –	26 – –	28 – –	22 – –	27 – –	Ditto.	4
31 10 –	34 2 –	44 10 –	47 16 –	53 – –	53 – –	Beer was allowed during haytime and an allowance of skim milk each day up to and including 1891. From 1892 to 1901 there were no allowances. In 1902 6d. per day was paid during haytime in lieu of beer.	5
31 4 –	31 4 –	36 8 –	46 16 –	46 16 –	46 16 –	Beer during haytime and a load of firewood each year.	6
28 12 –	31 4 –	36 8 –	44 4 –	44 4 –	44 4 –		
26 – –	31 4 –	36 8 –	42 18 –	42 18 –	44 4 –		
15 12 –§	31 4 –	35 2 –	41 12 –	42 18 –	42 18 –	Cottage and garden rent free; coals led; sticks for fuel found; potato ground found, manured and ploughed; 2 pints of beer each day during haytime and harvest, and if leading late another pint and cheese and bread; and straw for pigs.	7
29 19 11	36 1 7	39 9 1	42 19 –	39 7 –	42 – –		
30 2 1	39 1 2	30 10 2	42 19 –	39 7 –	38 12 –		
26 13 5	35 2 6	41 6 11	42 19 –	39 7 –	44 8 –		
—	43 5 3	46 18 9	55 4 2	50 2 –	57 14 –	Cottage and garden rent free; potato ground; fuel carted, and beer in haytime and harvest. In 1850 beer was the only allowance. In some cases cottages were let at a moderate rent.	8
29 – –	36 – –	39 – –	44 – –	41 10 –	45 – –	None.	9

† Farm servants paid half-yearly:—(*a*) best men; (*b*) second-class men; (*c*) women.
‡ Men marked (*a*) are solely or partly in charge of animals, *e.g.*, cowmen, shepherds, teamsmen.
§ Lad.

Table showing the Earnings of Individual Ordinary

Ref. No.	County and Rural District.	1851.	1861.	1871.	1881.	1891.	1901.
		\multicolumn{6}{c}{Rates of Weekly Cash Wages.}					
		s. d.	s. d.	s. d.	s. d.	s. d.	s. d.
10	WORCESTER. Pershore	— —	10 - / 10 -	10 - / 10 -	11 - / 11 -	11 - / 11 -	12 - / 12 -
11	WARWICK. Stratford-on-Avon	10 - / 9 -	11 - / 10 -	13 - / 12 -	14 - / 13 -	14 - / 13 -	13 - / 13 -
12	Shipston-on-Stour	10 - / 9 -	10 - / 10 -	10 - / 10 -	12 - / 11 -	12 - / 11 -	12 - / 11 -
13	OXFORD. Banbury	—	10 - / 10 -	10 - / 10 -	11 - / 11 -	11 - / 11 -	12 - / 12 -
14	HERTFORD. Berkhampstead	—	—	12 - / 12 -	13 - / 13 -	13 - / 12 -	13 - / 13 -
15	Bishop's Stortford	—	—	—	14 - / 14 -	12 - / 12 -	14 - / 14 -
16	CAMBRIDGE. Newmarket †	—	—	12 0 / 11 0	12 - / 12 -	12 - / 11 -	13 - / 13 -

† The time lost by the four men (exclusive of Christmas Day, Good Friday, and two Fair days) was as follows:—

1871.	1881.	1891.	1901.
17 days	12 days	20 days	6 days
17 ,,	6 ,,	2 ,,	4 ,,
21 ,,	20 ,,	5 ,,	18 ,,
No record of any absence	15 ,,	19 ,,	8 ,,

Labourers in each of the undermentioned years—Contd.

1851.	1861.	1871.	1881.	1891.	1901.	Allowances in kind given in addition to Cash Payments.	Ref. No.
\multicolumn{6}{c	}{Total Cash Earnings (including amounts earned as weekly wages, hay and corn harvest, piece-work, and overtime).}		
£ s. d.	£ s. d.	£ s. d.	£ s. d.	£ s. d.	£ s. d.		
—	27 2 3	30 15 —	29 17 —	31 13 9	29 13 —	Two pints of cider each day up to about 1886, but since then from 1st April to end of year only.	10
—	25 4 3	28 3 6	29 1 5	30 9 7	27 4 9		
—	22 15 2	26 8 7	27 10 7	29 15 —	26 6 5		
30 — —	33 2 —	33 12 —	38 16 —	39 6 —	39 6 —	Beer during the summer months. Up to 1875 the allowance was greater.	11
27 8 —	30 — —	30 — —	35 — —	33 18 —	34 12 —	Formerly a gallon of beer or cider each day for four weeks in hay time and four weeks in harvest. Now £1 is paid in lieu of beer or cider for hay time, 10d. or 8d. per day during harvest, and 6d. per day when threshing.	12
27 8 —	30 7 —	30 — —	35 4 —	34 — —	34 12 —		
30 — —	32 12 —	32 12 —	37 16 —	36 10 —	37 5 —		
—	27 10 —	28 — —	30 — —	32 — —	33 10 —	Beer, but quantity not so great now as formerly.	13
—	28 10 —	30 — —	28 — —	30 — —	35 — —		
—	32 5 —	31 — —	30 — —	31 — —	32 — —		
—	—	37 14 —	41 12 —	34 14 —	39 16 —	Beer during hay time, harvest, for threshing days, and for some few special jobs throughout the year. Quantity varies from 2 pints per day up to 6 pints on busy days in harvest.	14
—	—	34 12 —	38 10 —	—	—		
—	—	—	44 7 7	46 7 2	47 2 8	Beer for thrashing, haytime, and when sowing artificial manure or carting coal.	15
—	—	—	42 4 11	45 2 2	43 17 11		
—	—	—	39 5 2	46 4 10	45 6 5		
—	—	—	43 4 3	47 17 1	44 18 3		
—	—	34 1 —	36 8 8	33 14 5	39 6 8	Three pints of beer per day during hay time and when threshing. For harvest, 3 bushels of malt and 3 lbs. of hops or its equivalent in money. The allowance of beer for threshing was formerly 2 pints per day.	16
—	—	33 16 2	38 6 6	39 11 11	38 6 6		
—	—	30 16 8	32 15 11	37 — —	37 9 —		
—	—	36 1 —	36 5 —	33 18 10	40 12 3		

NOTE.—The rates of weekly cash wages in roman type refer to the summer months; those in italics to the winter.

Table showing the Earnings of Individual Ordinary

Ref. No.	County and Rural District.	1851 s. d.	1861 s. d.	1871 s. d.	1881 s. d.	1891 s. d.	1901 s. d.
		\multicolumn{6}{c}{Rates of Weekly Cash Wages.}					
	LINCOLN.						
17	Louth	15 -* / *15 -**	13 6 / *13 6*	15 - / *15 -*	15 - / *13 6*	15 - / *15 -*	16 6 / *15 -*
	NORFOLK.						
18	Depwade	13 -† / *13 -†*	10 - / *10 -*	11 - / *11 -*	13 - / *13 -*	11 - / *12 -*	13 - / *13 -*
	SUFFOLK.						
19	Blything	8 - / *8 -*	11 - / *11 -*	12 - / *11 -*	11 - / *12 -*	11 - / *12 -*	13 - / *12 -*
20	Thingoe	8 - / *8 -*	10 -‡ / —	10 - / *10 6*	13 -§ / *12 -§*	— / —	— / —
	ESSEX.						
21	Tendring	9 - / *9 -*	12 - / *11 -*	12 - / *11 -*	13 - / *13 -*	12 - / *13 -*	14 - / *15 -*
22	Lexden and Winstree	9 - / *9 -*	11 - / *10 6*	12 - / *12 -*	14 - / *14 -*	12 - / *12 -*	14 - / *14 -*
23	Chelmsford ‖	8 - / *8 -* / 9 - / *9 -*	10 - / *10 -* / 11 6 / *11 6*	11 - / *11 -* / 12 6 / *12 6*	12 - / *12 -* / 13 6 / *13 6*	12 - / *12 -* / 13 6 / *13 6*	13 - / *13 -* / 14 6 / *14 6*
	SUSSEX.						
24	Rye	10 - / *10 -*	12 - / *12 -*	12 - / *12 -*	13 6 / *13 6*	13 6 / *13 6*	15 - / *13 6*
	SOMERSET.						
25	Wellington	—	8 -¶ / *8 -¶*	9 - / *9 -*	13 - / *13 -*	12 - / *12 -*	13 - / *13 -*
	MONMOUTH.						
26	Chepstow	—	12 - / *12 -*	12 - / *12 -*	13 - / *13 -*	14 - / *14 -*	16 - / *16 -*
	GLAMORGAN.						
27	Cardiff	9 - / *9 -*	12 - / *12 -*	14 - / *14 -*	13 - / *13 -*	15 - / *15 -*	18 - / *18 -*

Note.—The Rates of Weekly Cash Wages in roman type refer to the summer months; those in *italics* to the *winter*.

* 1855.   † 1854.   ‡ 1860.

Labourers in each of the undermentioned years—Contd.

1851	1861	1871	1881	1891	1901	Allowances in kind given in addition to Cash Payments.	Ref. No.
\multicolumn{6}{	c	}{Total Cash Earnings. (Including amounts earned at weekly wages, hay and corn harvest, piece-work and overtime.)}		

£ s. d.	£ s. d.	£ s. d.	£ s. d.	£ s. d.	£ s. d.	Allowances	Ref
45 12 5*	42 18 6	40 11 3	38 17 5	43 4 2½	45 3 11	} None.	17
45 2 9*	37 13 11	41 6 11	41 3 0½	44 1 –	43 17 8		
45 6 10*	45 8 11	50 19 9½	39 9 1½	42 13 –	43 – 6		
35 3 –†	31 9 6	33 13 6	38 19 –	36 5 –	39 7 –	} None.	18
33 4 –†	30 8 6	31 15 6	38 19 –	36 5 –	39 7 –		
28 – –	35 6 –	38 16 –	44 – –	46 – –	47 – –	Fuel carted, and beer to the value of 10s. per annum.	19
27 17 –	30 7 6‡	29 15 6	40 14 –§	—	—	Three pints of beer per day during haytime. For harvest, 3 bushels of malt up to and including 1871.	20
29 1 –	30 7 6‡	30 19 6	40 14 –§	—	—		
31 8 6	33 10 –	35 18 –	39 3 6	41 2 6	43 17 9	Fuel, straw for pig; and sometimes food and beer.	21
26 10 –	31 18 –	34 16 0	40 2 –	34 16 –	39 12 –	Home-brewed beer, valued at 1s. per week.	22
26 – –	30 – –	32 – –	36 – –	41 – –	41 – –a	Home-brewed beer. At present time abstainers get 1s. per week and, for harvest, 20s. in lieu of beer. Horsemen and stockmen have cottage and large garden at a low rental.	23
27 – –	32 – –	35 – –	39 – –	43 – –	44 – –b		
30 – –	35 – –	40 – –	40 – –	45 – –	45 – –c		
29 – –	33 – –	35 – –	39 – –	44 – –	44 – –d		
33 10 5	37 8 5	37 10 10	33 10 11	33 19 11	36 11 8½	Up to 1855 all old wood was carted free, but afterwards over hours were paid for and cartage was charged.	24
31 3 1	34 4 5	33 14 10	33 14 7	35 14 9	38 19 –½		
31 9 2	35 2 5	36 13 3	37 15 1½	38 14 1	36 12 –		
27 4 8	30 5 10	34 1 9	41 4 –	34 8 –	37 19 1		
—	24 15 0¶	28 – –	37 – –	38 – –	42 – –	Cider on threshing days, and during haytime and corn harvest. Up to 1873, 3 pints of cider each day. Straw for pigs. Good cottages and about 20 perches of land are let for 1s. per week. Within the last 25 years cottages have been improved and gardens enlarged.	25
—	38 2 –	39 1 –	41 15 –	43 6 –	45 16 –	Potato ground and beer or cider when threshing, harvesting, or doing extra work.	26
—	37 9 –	38 3 –	40 14 –	41 18 –	42 9 –		
—	37 1 –	38 12 –	39 7 –	41 2 –	42 3 –		
29 8 –	38 9 –	43 8 –	42 16 –	46 5 –	52 6 –	Cottage and garden rent free; firewood found; coals supplied at cost price, carted free; 9 gallons of beer for haytime and 18 gallons for harvest; food on threshing days; and straw for pigs.	27
28 15 –	36 7 6	43 8 –	42 16 –	45 14 –	—		

§ 1878.

|| The figures relate to the following classes of men :—(a) common labourer; (b) capable task workman; (c) horseman; (d) stockman.

¶ 1863–4.

APPENDIX IV.

Examples of the Food of Agricultural Labourers Forty or Fifty Years Ago, and at the Present Time, in Cumberland and Wales, and Summary for the Eastern Counties.

CUMBERLAND.

Men boarded and lodged in the Farm-house.

(i.) Forty or fifty years ago :—

Breakfast.—Porridge and milk, barley bread and cheese.

Dinner.—Boiled pudding, very little butcher's meat, and a good deal of bacon and pork, potatoes and bread.

Tea or Supper.—Boiled milk and brown bread. Sometimes cheese (Dutch). On Sundays, tea with bread or cake.

Present time :—

Breakfast.—Porridge with milk and treacle or sugar, tea or coffee, bread and butter.

Lunch ("ten o'clocks").—Tea, coffee, or milk, and bread or cake, on week-days only.

Dinner.—Pudding generally served first. Meat and potatoes. Sometimes broth and boiled beef. Vegetables other than potatoes rarely used.

Lunch ("four o'clocks").—Tea, bread and cake on week-days only.

Tea or Supper.—Tea, cake or bread and butter. Sometimes boiled milk.

(ii.) In 1850 :—

Breakfast.—Oatmeal porridge with skimmed milk, followed by brown bread, cheese and skimmed milk.

Lunch ("ten o'clocks").—Beer, perhaps, in harvest.

Dinner.—Beef or mutton (generally boiled) once or twice a week. Other days cold meat or bacon. When the meat was boiled, soup was served first course. Potatoes. Rice pudding or dumplings.

Lunch ("four o'clocks").—Beer or milk, brown bread and cheese in harvest only.

Supper.—Porridge made with oatmeal or flour, and skimmed milk.

In 1902 :—

Breakfast.—Oatmeal porridge with separated milk, or, in many cases, with new milk; followed by tea or coffee, white bread, butter and cheese. In many cases eggs in summer, and cold meat or bacon in winter.

Lunch ("ten o'clocks").—Tea, coffee, or milk, bread, butter and cheese.

Dinner.—Beef or mutton (generally roast) about three times a week, other days cold meat and pickles, stews, &c. (Bacon is not much used.) Potatoes and other vegetables always served. Milk puddings or dumplings.

Tea—Tea, white bread and butter, fruit cake or jam.

Supper.—Milk or tea, bread, butter, and cheese.

EASTERN COUNTIES (except LINCOLN).

The Diet of Agricultural Labourers Forty and Fifty Years Ago and at the Present Time.

	Huntingdon and Cambridge.	Norfolk and Suffolk.	Essex.

Forty or Fifty years ago.

	Huntingdon and Cambridge.	Norfolk and Suffolk.	Essex.
Breakfast	Bread and milk (skim), or bread and lard or dripping	Bread and butter, lard, or dripping, or cheese. Tea. In some cases bread and skim milk or bread and water sop	Bread—very often dry — occasionally butter or cheese
Dinner....	Pudding or dumpling. Vegetables, when procurable. [When there was any meat it was usually sufficient only for the husband, the wife and children sharing the crust in which the meat was cooked, or the gravy from it when cooked alone.] Sunday.—Sometimes a little pork	Bread and vegetables (turnips—swede or white; potatoes or onion), or cheese of an inferior quality Sunday.—In some cases a small quantity of pork, which was often eked out for a week	Bread and cheese Sunday.—Sometimes pork or bacon. In such cases tea consisted of bread and butter and tea
Tea .... Supper	Bread and lard or dripping with an onion, or sometimes a herring or a little cheese	Bread with an onion, or butter, lard, or dripping. Tea	Vegetable pudding (sometimes swede turnips and topping or carrot and parsnip). On rare occasions a little pork [In some places this meal was partaken of at midday. In such cases tea or supper consisted of bread and cheese]

EASTERN COUNTIES (except LINCOLN)—*Contd.*

	Huntingdon and Cambridge.	Norfolk and Suffolk.	Essex.
Present Time.			
Breakfast	Bread, tea, and, in some cases, bacon or pork.	Bread and butter, dripping or cheese. Tea. The husband in many cases has bread with cheese or meat (salt pork or bacon) or herrings when in season	Bread, butter and cheese, tea
Dinner	Salt or fresh pork, dumpling, potatoes, and vegetables, or pastry or suet roll or dumpling with jam or treacle. Sunday.—Small piece of fresh meat	Pork, potatoes, dumplings (the meat sometimes put in the dumpling). In some cases no meat, in others some beef Sundays.—In many cases beef or mutton; meat of some kind in all cases, with plain or fruit pudding in addition	Bread and cheese. Butter or jam, in some cases tea. Sunday.—Roast meat or meat pudding, potatoes, sometimes a rice pudding.
Tea	Tea, bread and lard, butter or jam. In some cases cheese or a little meat [If husband is working too far from home to have dinner at mid-day, the family make shift until supper, which takes the place of dinner or tea]	Tea, bread and butter, dripping or cheese Sunday.—Cake more general in addition	Boiled pork, potatoes, bread and butter, or suet pudding, with vegetables Sunday.—Bread, butter, or jam. Tea.
Supper			

WALES.

(1) *Food in Farmhouse.*

North Wales (forty or fifty years ago):—
    Breakfast.—Bread and milk or porridge and milk.
    Dinner.—Potatoes and bacon.
    Tea or Supper.—Bread and milk.

North Wales (present time):—
    Breakfast.—Bread and milk and tea, bread and butter.
    Dinner.—Broth, bacon, potatoes, carrots, cabbage and turnips. In most cases fresh meat on Sunday.
    Tea.—Tea, bread and butter.
    Supper.—Bread and milk and bread and butter.

WALES—*Contd.*

(2) *Food in Labourers' Cottages.*

South-West Wales (forty or fifty years ago) :—
  Breakfast.—Oatmeal gruel made with water, sometimes with skimmed milk, barley bread and cheese.
  Dinner.—Flummery (oatmeal steeped for some days in water and afterwards boiled; eaten with sugar or treacle), barley bread and cheese, sometimes roasted potatoes and bacon.
  Tea or Supper.—Bwdram (barley meal and water, sweetened with a little sugar), and barley bread and cheese to eat with it.

South-West Wales (present time) :—
  Breakfast.—Tea, bread and butter and cheese.
  Dinner.—Broth made from salted beef and bacon, thickened with oatmeal, with potatoes. On Sunday fresh meat and rice and milk.
  Tea.—Tea, bread and butter.
  Supper.—Broth rewarmed, with bread and cheese, and sometimes a little tea.

APPENDIX V.

The forms used for the collection of the information on which the Paper was based are as follows :—

QUESTIONS RELATING TO RATES OF WEEKLY WAGES.

Particulars relating to Wages, &c., of Agricultural Labourers employed on _____. Farm in the occupation of _____. County of _____.

1. Please state the **Rates** of **Weekly Cash Wages**, taken from Books, paid to **Ordinary Agricultural Labourers** in receipt of Men's full Wages on the above-mentioned Farm in the Months of **June** and **December** of each of the **Years 1850-1901**, or as many years as possible.

[*Ordinary Agricultural Labourers do not include Foremen, Shepherds, Cattlemen, Carters, Waggoners, Teamsters. Weekly Cash Wages are not to include payments for piecework, or extra payments during hay and corn harvest, or for overtime, or the value of any perquisites, or allowances in kind.*— See *questions 2 to 7.*]

Year.	Rate of Weekly Cash Wages in		Year.	Rate of Weekly Cash Wages in	
	June.	December.		June.	December.
	s. d.	s. d.		s. d.	s. d.

NOTE.—Should your records relating to Rates of Wages extend back beyond 1850, and if you would be good enough to give this additional information, I will send you another form for the purpose.

Will you be good enough to answer as many of the following questions as you are able:—

2. Please describe perquisites or allowances in kind given in 1901 to the ordinary agricultural labourers on your farm, in addition to their weekly cash wages, such as house, garden, potato ground, allotment, food, beer, cider, fuel or fuel carted, straw for pigs, &c.

3. Please state whether the perquisites or allowances in kind have varied in character or amount since 1850, or since the earliest period for which you give rates of wages. If so, kindly give particulars as far as possible.

4. Please state whether the amount of piecework given at the present time is, generally speaking, more or less than was customary fifty years ago in the case of—

   (*a.*) Hay and corn harvest.
   (*b.*) Other work, such as hoeing, &c.

5. Can you say, by reference to books or otherwise, whether an average able-bodied labourer would earn more or less by piecework in a year at the present time than fifty years ago.

6. If possible, please give a few instances of the rates paid for piecework fifty years ago, or at the earliest period for which you give rates of wages, compared with the rates paid for the same classes of work at the present time.

7. If possible, please give the amount paid for a month during hay and corn harvest at the present time, and also fifty years ago, or at the earliest period for which you give rates of wages—

   (*a.*) Hay harvest.
   (*b.*) Corn harvest.

*Name*_____

*Postal Address*_____

QUESTIONS RELATING TO YEARLY EARNINGS.

I. Actual yearly cash earnings of certain ordinary agricultural labourers in the undermentioned years :—

Note.—Ordinary agricultural labourers do not include men specially engaged in charge of animals, such as shepherds, cattlemen, carters, waggoners, &c.

(Please take three or four representative men in each year—not necessarily the same men in each year, or those who earned the most on the farm. If you cannot give figures for all of the undermentioned years, please give them for such periods as you are able.)

	Total Earnings in *Cash*, Including Amounts Earned at Weekly Wages, Hay and Corn Harvest, Piecework, and Overtime during the Year.					
	1851.	1861.	1871.	1881.	1891.	1901.
	£ s. d.	£ s. d.	£ s. d.	£ s. d.	£ s. d.	£ s. d.
1st labourer						
2nd ,, ...						
3rd ,, ...						
4th ,, ...						

II. Please state the rates of weekly cash wages paid to the ordinary agricultural labourers in each of the years for which you state annual earnings :—

	1851.	1861.	1871.	1881.	1891.	1901.
(*a*) in summer						
(*b*) in winter						

III. Please state about what annual sum a labourer's wife and, say, 3 or 4 children would have earned by farm work in the "fifties" or "sixties."

IV. About what period did women cease to be employed regularly at field work in your neighbourhood?

Name _____

Postal Address _____

QUESTIONS RELATING TO FOOD, &c.

(1.) Please state what is the usual food of farm labourers and their families at the present time in your neighbourhood, showing in detail what they generally have for breakfast, dinner, tea, and supper. If the food on Sundays differs from that eaten on week-days, please give particulars.

	Week-Days.	Sundays.		Week-Days.	Sundays.
Breakfast Dinner			Tea .... Supper....		

(2.) Can you also give information asked for in Question (1) for forty or fifty years ago? (Some of the older people in your neighbourhood will probably remember this.)

	Week-Days.	Sundays.		Week-Days.	Sundays.
Breakfast Dinner........			Tea .... Supper....		

(3.) About what quantities of the following articles are consumed in a week by a farm labourer, his wife, and four children? I should also be glad to know the prices usually paid by farm labourers for these commodities:—

	Quantity.	Price.		Quantity.	Price.
		s. d. per			s. d. per
Fresh meat (beef or mutton) .... }		,,	Butter		,,
			Margarine		,,
Pork		,,	Lard		,,
Bacon		,,	Cheese		,,
Fish (fresh or cured) .... }		,,	Sugar...........		,,
			Syrup or Treacle .... }		,,
Milk		,,	Jam		,,
Bread		,,	Tea		,,
Flour..................		,,	Cocoa...........		,,
Oatmeal		,,	Eggs		,,
Rice		,,			
Potatoes		,,			

(4.) Do the farm labourers in your neighbourhood generally keep pigs, and have they gardens or allotments?

(5.) Do the farm labourers in your neighbourhood generally belong to benefit societies, coal or clothing clubs, &c.? To what extent was this the custom fifty years ago?

Name_____

Postal Address_____

LIVESTOCK PRICES IN BRITAIN 1851—93

E. H. Whetham

Livestock Prices in Britain, 1851-93

By EDITH H. WHETHAM

IN assessing the fortunes of the different branches of British farming in the nineteenth century, historians have had to rely on the trends in prices collected mainly in urban areas for products often much altered from those sold by farmers. Beef and mutton at wholesale markets have undergone much processing and incurred many costs compared with the fatstock for which farmers were paid at country auction sales. And in selling fatstock, farmers also sold hides and tallow and skin wool as well as meat; further, their profits depended as much on the price of the store animals bought for fattening as on the price of meat in the ultimate market. Unfortunately, we have no regular series of fatstock prices for the nineteenth century, but some unofficial information on store stock prices can be used, in conjunction with meat and wool prices, to assess changes in profit trends for the mountain, hill, and upland farms devoted primarily to stock rearing, and for the lowland farms which fattened sheep and cattle for the meat market.

Three price series are here used: that published by the Teviotdale Farmers' Club, that published in the *Transactions of the Highland and Agricultural Society* from 1886 onwards, and that published by R. M. Barrington in the *Journal of the Royal Agricultural Society of England* in 1893. The first is presumably based on local prices recorded at the main autumn sales in each year, and was published for the years from 1859 to 1893 in Wilson Fox's report on Cumberland to the 1894 Royal Commission on Agriculture (*Report on Counties*, II, p. 47). These prices refer to draft ewes from Cheviot flocks and their progeny either by Cheviot or by Border-Leicester rams; to the wool from these flocks; and to shorthorn store cattle. The second series, which goes back to 1818, is derived from the records of the Inverness market;[1] it includes wethers, lambs, and draft ewes of both Cheviot and Blackface breeds, and the wool derived therefrom. The third series is taken from the autumn fair at Ballinasloe, in Ireland, described as being held mainly for store stock; as Ireland was a major exporter of sheep and cattle to Britain in the last half of the nineteenth century, it is not unreasonable to assume that prices here would reflect fairly closely price trends in store markets in other parts of Britain. When the prices derived from these different sources were converted to index numbers, with the decade 1865-74 as a base, both the trends and the fluctuations round the trends were seen to be remarkably similar.

[1] *Trans. High. & Agric. Soc.*, XVIII, Fourth Series, 1886, p. 297.

Yet the reliability of these prices is clearly no greater than the reliability of the original observations from which they were derived. It was customary to quote prices as a range, with no indication of the volume of business done at each end of the range, whose size varied greatly from year to year. The average taken of the quoted range inevitably ignores the greater variability of prices in some years than in others, a variability which reflects partly the skill of stockmen and farmers from whose holdings these beasts were sold; partly the conditions of soil and climate; and partly the influence of weather on the general condition of the flocks and herds. A single figure quoted for each year for each market is inevitably a highly condensed summary of a general trend in prices as recorded by one observer. Nor are these records attributed to any particular author, but it is probable that they were derived from the books or memories of the auctioneers functioning in each market. The departmental Committee on Agricultural Prices in Scotland (1902) commented on the imperfections of prices collected from this source, for auctioneers were unwilling to publicize low prices in the markets with which they were concerned, and might quote only a range of the higher prices.[1] Nevertheless, the close conjunction of these sets of prices, derived from such different sources, suggests that they can be used, with caution, to indicate trends over the forty years from 1851. Table I gives the price index for wool and for each class of stock, taking a straight average of available records for each class, with the average of 1865–74 as a base for each series.

WOOL

It will be seen that after the general rise in all prices in the 1850's, wool prices followed a pattern of their own. After a peak in 1864, six years of falling prices were followed by a short upward movement in 1871 and 1872; then the fall was again resumed until wool prices attained stability at some 60 per cent of the base period, and somewhat below the level of the earliest years. Prices of the fine Cheviot wool from Inverness fell less after 1871–2 than the prices of the Blackface wools or the Cheviot wools from Teviotdale, but nevertheless the fall was drastic and severe for all types of wool from 1872 to the end of the period here included. The growing imports of this product brought a permanent fall in its value from the 1860's onward, which especially affected the mountain farms with their wether flocks.

STORE SHEEP

Table I shows that a new pattern in sheep prices developed in the middle of the 1860's, a pattern of far wider fluctuations from a markedly higher level

[1] Cd. 805, p. xiv.

TABLE I

PRICE INDICES FOR WOOL, STORE STOCK, MUTTON, AND BEEF, 1851–93
(Average of 1865–74=100)

	Wool	Store Lambs	Store Wethers	Ewes	Store Cattle	Mutton (*a*)		Beef (*a*)	
						Prime	Middling	Prime	Middling
1851	63½	66½	64	61	55	72	69	65	62
2	63	60	68	64	63	72	69	65	64
3	89½	82	82	78	75½	89	86	80	80
4	59½	79	79	72	84½	89	86	88	88
5	69½	85½	81	72	86	87	84	88	90
6	86	76	77	73	92½	87	84	85	84
7	100½	82	85	72	96½	89	84	85	86
8	70½	78	82	75	87½	84	80	83	84
9	92	78	78	76	82	87	86	85	84
1860	120	85	83	77	84	92	91	88	86
1	91	80	83	79	85	90	91	87	86
2	100	81	80	79	85	87	87	81	80
3	117½	90	81	79	92	89	87	83	84
4	149	116	89	89	92½	90	93	88	90
5	119	134	96	114	98	105	106	94	94
6	117½	122½	111	118	96	100	100	94	97
7	88	70	91	83	95½	90	91	92	92
8	85½	62	80	67	92½	84	86	88	88
9	85½	78½	89	82	95	95	93	97	94
1870	82	87	102	93	99	95	95	99	99
1	115	119	108	114	112	103	107	106	109
2	115½	134	121	126	107	110	111	104	107
3	94	120	118	111	105½	116	115	115	115
4	103	78	95	92	99	102	97	110	105
5	102½	113	105	108	102½	116	107	113	113
6	86	114	115	105	94	118	106	110	107
7	86	120	117	109	95	113	98	108	101
8	77	121½	109	115	105	111	100	108	101
9	65½	93	98	82	93	105	95	97	92
1880	74½	102	103	99	108	108	98	103	101
1	67	106½	109	100	101	113	104	99	99
2	60	139	120	128	119	118	109	106	105
3	56½	140	123	130	118½	120	111	108	105
4	56	107	109	110	104	105	97	103	101
5	54½	87	91	81	86	92	86	92	90
6	59½	94	93	91	83	102	91	87	82
7	65	92	86	82	73	85	77	76	74
8	59	126	89	94	93	95	86	85	80
9	60	137	102	114	97	103	91	83	80
1890	59½	121	93	101	89	97	82	83	78
1	59	87	86	78	81½	87	77	83	82
2	55½	65	76	62	69½	87	77	83	78
3	55½	89	86½	69	75½	87	77	85	80

(*a*) Sauerbeck's meat prices from the London market, published in the *Journal of the Royal Statistical Society*, and converted to the base of 1865–74.

than was known in the previous decade. It seems likely that the change was brought about not only by the growing demand for meat from the towns, but also by the influence of the railways which in the 1860's effectively linked the great store stock markets in the remote areas to the arable farms in the east, south, and midlands, with their pastures for summer grazing and their fields of turnips and swedes for winter feeding. If the agricultural census of Scotland taken by the Highland and Agricultural Society in the years 1854–7 is compared with the official census begun in 1866, it will be seen that in Scotland the number of cattle on farms in June rose sharply in the north and west, the most remote districts, but fell in the east; and that though the number of sheep rose in all regions, the rise was greatest in the northern counties. More draft ewes, more wethers and lambs became available for fattening in the lowlands as the falling costs of sending them south or east raised prices to rearing farms, but much of this increased supply could only be fattened from the turnip crop which was at intervals seriously affected by drought and the 'fly'. Drought in 1867 and the really disastrous drought of 1868 brought down prices for store sheep for three successive years by one-third of the 1865–74 level; the dry year 1874 left a similar but smaller mark, as did that phenomenally wet year 1879, when many turnip fields were too wet to carry sheep in the autumn. Spells of dry weather in 1885 and 1887 brought already low prices lower still, as did a similar spell in 1892. Lamb prices fluctuated most, since lambs needed more and longer feeding than wethers, before being sold fat at 12–15 months; but ewes were often bought to be crossed again with a Border-Leicester or Down ram before being fattened for the butcher, and a poor turnip crop affected their prices almost as much as those for lambs.

The general trend in these sheep prices, and the timing, though not the size, of the fluctuations, follows pretty well the general trends in Sauerbeck's mutton prices, though the peak in 1865–6 must reflect the indirect result of the epidemics of rinderpest and pleuro-pneumonia of those years which disrupted the markets for cattle and for beef. But from 1851 to 1863 mutton prices were higher in relation to sheep prices than at any other period, indicating a high level of profitability for sheep fatteners; a similar difference on a smaller scale developed for six or seven years after 1873. The peak both in mutton and in sheep prices over these decades was reached in 1882–3, and it was not until 1891–2 that prices fell substantially below the level of the base years. After the epidemic of sheep rot in 1879–80, many farmers in the lowlands were restocking, and this demand kept up store sheep prices, whose supply had been drastically reduced by the two severe winters of 1879–80 and 1880–1. The losses then experienced on hill farms meant that a higher proportion of a smaller crop of lambs was required as replacements and smaller numbers were thus available for sale at a time when demand was exceptionally high. A similar conjunction followed the long winter of 1887-8 when lamb and ewe prices rose very sharply and to a far greater extent than the small rise in mutton prices. Such high prices did not therefore necessarily bring high profits for hill farms, but only mitigated the results of a reduced output, while they added to the costs of lowland farms.

Except for the immediate effects of severe winters, the number of sheep recorded annually in June increased generally in Scotland and in Wales over this period, starting with the first census in 1854 and 1866 respectively. But in England the highest numbers were recorded in 1867 and in 1874 at 19·8 millions; there was then a slight fall until the wet year of 1879 brought an epidemic of liver rot that swept away many lowland flocks and reduced the numbers year by year to just under 15 million in 1884. In the grassland counties there was then some recovery in numbers, but not in the five eastern counties of Cambridge, Essex, Huntingdon, Norfolk, and Suffolk, where the fall continued remorselessly throughout the depression years. Some of this fall was clearly due to the quicker fattening of sheep at earlier ages, for it was the number of sheep over one year in age which fell most from 1874 onwards; the numbers under one year old in June (which indicate breeding flocks) showed much less change, apart from those ill-favoured years of 1879-84. The larger number of hill lambs bought at autumn fairs must have been more frequently sold in their second spring before the June census was taken, partly because the fall in wool prices diminished the profits to be obtained from keeping them over a second summer to be sold fat and shorn at 15–18 months; wethers were similarly got away earlier and at lighter weights. In the north, too, there was a profitable trade in taking ewe lambs from the mountain farms for wintering on pasture or turnips; as the numbers of ewes rose in the hills, so did the pressure to find suitable wintering on which the young stock could build the constitutions required to face future winters on their own ground. This trade brought a steadier return with less capital outlay to lowland farms than the outright purchase of hoggetts or ewes for winter fattening.

STORE CATTLE

The prices of store cattle reflect pretty closely the trends in Sauerbeck's beef prices derived from the London market. But the cattle prices appear to have risen rather faster than beef prices up to 1871 and to have fallen slightly more in the subsequent decade; they were appreciably higher than beef prices from 1880 to 1884 and again from 1888 to 1891, when the feeders' margin must have been severely squeezed. All classes of meat producers, however, must have benefited from the long rise in prices over the first twenty years included in these statistics; again, it is noteworthy that cattle prices reached their highest point in 1882–3, thereafter falling sharply in 1887 and again after 1889. The peak in 1882–3 presumably reflects the high prices of store sheep in those years, for sheep and cattle were alternative enterprises for some farmers with pastures to be grazed or with turnips to be turned into manure. Others might be restricted to sheep through lack of buildings, while farmers with a surplus of straw, or with wet fields on heavy soils, necessarily relied on cattle for their muck-making.

In the lowland belt of arable farms running north of the Border, cattle fattened on oat straw and turnips, with a supplement of home-grown corn or, increasingly, of purchased cattle cake; sheep likewise consumed turnips with some trough feeding, while the ewes and their lambs would be run over the temporary leys in the summer. South of the Border, oat straw had less feeding value, and cattle used the straw as litter, while they fattened on turnips and hay, with, again, a growing consumption of cattle cake or maize. Stirks might be wintered cheaply on straw and turnips, before being fattened on summer pastures to the point where two or three months in the stalls or yards brought them out for the Christmas markets. But some fodder could usually be found for the cattle, even if turnips were scarce; the chaff-cutters and the turnip-slicers could be supplemented by green crops or by the wares of the provender merchants. Hence the demand for store cattle was less variable than that for store sheep, just as the supply was also less affected by seasonal variations in weather; prices did not show those huge fluctuations from year to year which were so marked a feature of the store sheep market.

PROFIT TRENDS IN HILL FARMING

In order to show the effect of these price trends on the profits of stock-rearing farms, three indices (base 1865–74) were compiled from the price data, referring to (*a*) Scottish mountain farms selling wool, two- or three-year-old wethers, and draft ewes from a Blackface flock; it has been assumed that these products provided over the period one-half, one-third, and one-sixth of the gross receipts; (*b*) hill farms in Sutherland or on the Borders which sold Cheviot wool, wethers, and draft ewes, together with some Cheviot or half-bred (Cheviot × Border-Leicester) lambs; the proportions are taken to be one-third for the wool and one-sixth each for the other four products; (*c*) upland farms selling half- or three-quarter-bred lambs, Cheviot wool, draft ewes, and store cattle, in the proportions 5 : 2 : 1 : 2.[1] These indices

[1] These weights are largely arbitrary, but originate in contemporary accounts, e.g. James Macdonald, 'Agriculture of Sutherland', *Trans. High. & Agric. Soc.*, XII, Fourth Series, 1880, pp. 76–8.

are shown in Table II. The distinction between these types of farming lies in the proportion of wethers to lambs. Mountain farms in a severe climate maintained flocks of wethers for the higher ground where ewes did not thrive; they sold each year their draft ewes and a proportion of two- or three-year-old wethers, keeping the greater part of their lambs to replace the drafts from the older sheep. They therefore had a high proportion of mature animals from which they sold several clips of wool; and a principal item of expense was that of wintering their lambs on the turnip fields or pastures of lowland farms. Border farms in a more kindly climate could keep all-ewe flocks and therefore sold primarily their surplus lambs, together with the draft ewes and the annual clip of wool from the ewes. According to the altitude and the feeding value of the pastures, such farms kept pure Cheviot flocks, selling either Cheviot lambs or the half-breds got by Border-Leicester rams; or half-bred ewes crossed again with the Border-Leicester to produce three-quarter-bred or 'park' lambs. These hill and upland farms might also run a certain number of breeding cows whose trampling helped to keep down the bracken and whose progeny by shorthorn bulls found a ready sale as yearlings or two-year-olds at the autumn markets.

The rising prices for the first twenty years of the period justify the remark made in 1878 that "there is perhaps no class of farming in Scotland that will at the present time give the same return of profits as that derived from Highland sheep farming;"[1] only the dry years from 1867–8 and the simultaneous check to wool prices disturbed the profits and rents of farms selling wool and store sheep. Nor was it only prices that rose over these years; the annual census showed that many farms were gradually increasing their flocks, and contemporary comment also shows that wire fencing, better drainage, and the application of lime had enabled many upland farms to change their breeding policy, so as to produce more highly priced animals. Writing in 1862, Sanderson commented that "all upland improvements tend to make the Cheviot breed supplant the Blackface; and again, the half-Leicester supplants the Cheviot and the full-bred Leicester goes on extending its range."[2] Another writer almost contemporary with Sanderson noted that in south-west Scotland there were "many farms from which a few years ago the Blackface lambs averaged 10s. per head that are now selling the produce of the same ewe by a Leicester ram at 24s."[3] These cross-breds or 'mules' were almost as

[1] James Mollison, 'Farming in the Central and North Western Districts' in *Report on the Present State of Agriculture of Scotland*, High. & Agric. Soc., 1878, p. 103.
[2] James Sanderson, 'Agriculture of Berwick and Roxburghshire', *Trans. High. & Agric. Soc.*, 1862, p. 354.
[3] G. Murray, 'Improved Value of Scotch Sheep', *J.R.A.S.E.*, Second Series, III, 1867, p. 575.

TABLE II

PRICE INDICES FOR LIVESTOCK REARING FARMS
(Average of 1865–74=100)

	A Mountain	B Hill	C Upland
1851	59½	66	66
2	65	66½	67
3	87	85	83
4	68½	72	77
5	75	78	83
6	78½	80	83
7	91	84	86
8	75½	73	78
9	78	82	82
1860	118	98	93
1	—	87	81
2	85	87	88
3	104	95	92
4	117½	116	113
5	106	97	117
6	137	119	105
7	—	83	77
8	70	77	68
9	75	84	90
1870	100½	90	90
1	124	106	115
2	105	132	129½
3	100	110	116
4	103	96	93
5	93	117	115
6	101	104	106½
7	99	115	108
8	81½	108	113
9	94	90	83
1880	79	96	97
1	87	98	94
2	94	103½	114
3	103	110	113
4	88	97½	94
5	77	83	80
6	79	86	88
7	73	84	81
8	77½	87½	95
9	90	96	106
1890	83	90	98
1	76	77	83
2	67	66	71
3	77	76	79

popular as the half-breds with lowland farmers buying sheep for their turnip fields. The fall in wool prices from 1864 onwards checked the upward movement in the composite indices and was the chief reason for the fact that between 1871 and 1884 they fluctuated across a downward trend, while stock prices tended to rise. It was the mountain farms whose profits were presumably most affected; they drew a high proportion of their receipts from Blackface wool whose price fell most in this period, bringing their composite index down by 1885 to less than 80 per cent of the base. The hill and upland farms suffered less, since a higher proportion of their income was derived from selling store animals, and their composite indices only fell below 80 per cent of the base level in the early 1890's.

The fact that store sheep and cattle prices fell between 1884 and 1888 and after 1890 in rough proportion to the general trend in meat prices implies that lowland farmers were then able to buy their raw materials at falling costs, while the price of feeding-stuffs had fallen earlier and further. There was thus a double economy to set against the shrinking receipts from the sale of livestock and against the adverse trend in prices in the store markets in the years 1880 to 1884 and 1888 to 1890. This advantage was no doubt only a small mercy in comparison with the general fall in prices, and especially in beef prices after 1884. It is curious, though, that English lowland farmers tended to increase their cattle stocks throughout the depression, but somewhat reduced their sheep numbers, while Scottish lowland farmers increased their sheep flocks more than their cattle herds; the explanation may lie in the greater growth of the dairy trade south of the Border. On the other hand, the mountain, hill, and upland farmers who reared animals for the store markets took the full brunt of falling prices after 1884 with no countervailing economies, for they bought few animals (except rams) and no significant quantity of the cheaper imported cereals. Yet they also increased their stocking of both sheep and cattle, presumably because they thus added little to their costs but considerably to their gross receipts.

THE CHANGING CATTLE ENTERPRISES OF ENGLAND AND WALES

E. H. Whetham

The Changing Cattle Enterprises of England and Wales, 1870–1910

EDITH H. WHETHAM

The factors of soil and climate have no doubt been the principal determinants in Britain of the location of the three types of cattle enterprise—rearing, fattening and dairying; but the development of communications and changes in profitability have also influenced their history. An analysis of the age groups recorded in the annual census of livestock (taken in June each year from 1866 onwards) is here used to show changes in England and Wales during the forty years from 1870 to 1910 under the influence first of the coming of the railways and then of later price changes, in particular the fall in cereal prices in the last third of the nineteenth century.

The Table gives the ratio of the numbers of cattle aged over and under two years of age per 100 cows and heifers in milk and calf for each county of England and Wales, grouped into the classes into which they naturally fell. The ratios distinguished sharply between those counties which, in 1870, were importers of cattle aged two years and over for fattening into beef; those which were exporters, with a lower ratio of the older cattle; and those devoted to dairying, which kept a low proportion of non-dairying animals. Middlesex and Dorset carried the fewest young stock, less than 30 to every 100 cows and heifers; these were the intensive dairying districts which reared few calves, fattened few cattle and imported young cows from other counties.

The statistics for 1890 and 1910 reveal several changes in the pattern established by 1870. There was, firstly, the general rise in cattle numbers throughout the country, from 4·7 million in 1871–5 to 5·8 million in 1906–10. Secondly, the ratio of the cattle aged two years and over to the cows and heifers fell from 62 in 1870 to 56 in 1890 and to 47 in 1910; with rising imports of frozen meat, it had become less profitable to fatten the older cattle to high weights and more of them were sold at younger ages. Thirdly, more calves were reared to provide this quicker turnover of beef stock, especially in the rearing districts; in Wales the proportion of the younger cattle rose from 86 in 1870 to 134 in 1910.

A fourth major change was the falling area of arable land and the rising area of permanent grass, especially on the heavy clays of Huntingdon and the mixed soils of Norfolk; these were the only two counties which showed a higher ratio of the older beef cattle in 1910 than in 1870, indicating a shift from the traditional winter fattening on the turnips and straw to more summer grazing. Finally, there was the extension of dairying as an alternative use of grassland, whether old or recently established. By 1890 the West Riding of Yorkshire had increased its population of cows by one-third of the 1870 level, and by 1910 the age structure showed that dairying had become the principal cattle enterprise. The growth of the milk market in London had a similar effect in Berkshire, Essex and Sussex which by 1910 had moved into Group 6, while Suffolk had moved half-way into Group 3. Of the fourteen counties in Group 6 in 1910, six showed by their low ratio of young cattle that they practised intensive dairying and imported some at least of their milking stock—Cheshire, Dorset, Hampshire, Lancashire and Wiltshire; these counties all carried less than twenty of the older cattle and less than thirty in each of the younger age groups for every 100 cows and heifers. The agriculture of London and Middlesex had by then been submerged under bricks and paving-stones.

By the first decade of the twentieth century, the London milk market drew supplies of liquid milk from farms over the southern half of England. Within 3 or 4 miles of the suburbs, farmers retailed milk from their own carts. Farther out, farmers within a couple of miles of a railway station—the limit of the twice-daily drive for the milk cob—sold to retailers or to the wholesalers, getting perhaps 6d–9d a gallon for their milk, from which price they paid rail charges averaging 1d per gallon for about 80 miles. Beyond this distance, the summer flush of milk was commonly bought by local factories which might in winter forward some milk to the large towns to supplement the diminished supply from the nearer farms. It was only dairy farms without easy access to a railway that continued the traditional manufacture of butter and cheese for which the net return was usually less than the price received by farms selling milk liquid, in spite of the greater work.

Within another decade, however, this equilibrium between cattle rearing, cattle fattening and dairying was again disturbed by the development of motor transport and of bulk refrigeration of liquid milk.

CATTLE ENTERPRISES IN ENGLAND AND WALES, 1870–1910

		1870			1890			1910		
	No. of Counties	Per 100 cows and heifers in milk and calf		No. of Counties	Per 100 cows and heifers in milk and calf		No. of Counties	Per 100 cows and heifers in milk and calf		
		Cattle 2 years and over	Cattle under 2 years		Cattle 2 years and over	Cattle under 2 years		Cattle 2 years and over	Cattle 1–2 years	Cattle under 1 year
1. Fattening on arable and leys	10	98	104	7	78	114	5	80	75	63
2. Fattening on grass	5	171	136	7	140	142	7	136	88	72
3. Mixed enterprises with some dairying on grass	5	61	77	6	59	97	5	51	60	52
4. Lowland rearing with some fattening	7	69	95	7	63	118	7	50	68	63
5. Hill rearing England Wales	5	57	92	4	43	115	4	42	65	69
6. Primarily dairying	10	27	51	11	29	64	14	25	32	31
England and Wales	—	62	83	—	56	98	—	47	53	50

1. Bedford, Cambs, Essex, Hunts, Norfolk, Nottingham, Suffolk, Sussex, Warwick, Yorks, E.R.; in 1890, Hunts and Norfolk shift to Group 2 and Suffolk to Group 3; in 1910 Essex, Sussex shift to Group 6.
2. Leics, Lincs, Northampton, Northumberland, Rutland; add Hunts, Norfolk in 1890 and 1910.
3. Berks, Bucks, Herts, Kent, Oxford; add Suffolk in 1890 and 1910; in 1910; Berks. shifts to Group 6.
4. Cornwall, Devon, Glos, Hereford, Monmouth, Salop, Worcs.
5. Cumberland, Durham, Westmorland, Yorks N.R. and W.R.; in 1890 Yorks W.R. shifts to Group 6.
6. Cheshire, Derby, Dorset, Hants, Lancs, London and Middlesex, Somerset, Staffs, Surrey, Wilts; add Yorks. W.R. in 1890; add Berks, Essex, Sussex in 1910.

THE CHANGING BASIS OF
AGRICULTURAL PROSPERITY
1853-73

E. L. Jones

The Changing Basis of English Agricultural Prosperity, 1853-73[1]

By E. L. JONES

MOST historians are familiar with the essential topography of English agricultural prosperity—or adversity—during the nineteenth century. This comprises a peak during the Napoleonic wars, a deep trough for twenty years thereafter, another peak rising steeply from 1837, after which the line dips once or twice during the 'forties, sags at midcentury, rises in a booming curve through the 'fifties and 'sixties, until it crashes down some time in the 'seventies. To the more sophisticated the line begins to rise again, a little, from 1894.

This stark outline, treating agriculture more or less as a single entity, owes most to the work of Lord Ernle, which for years was slavishly followed.[2] A renewal of interest in nineteenth-century agriculture is now evident, and, as Marc Bloch would have put it, we are again keeping faith with Ernle by striving to modify his findings. The single line, firm but very generalized, with which Ernle drew the depression of the last quarter of the nineteenth century, has already been split into two divergent paths, representing the fortunes of cereal growers and livestock producers, by Mr T. W. Fletcher.[3] Similarly, two or three regional studies have suggested that the depths of the depression after 1815, which Ernle described so vividly, were plumbed only in restricted localities and for only two or three short spells. The topography of this depression is likely to be re-shaped at the hands of the next serious student to treat it as a whole.

The most conspicuous hump in the line is formed by the period from the early 1850's to the early 1870's. These years are usually passed over lightly as a time of prosperity, and in marked contrast to the succeeding period as one of prosperity for the grain grower. My intention is not to try to invert this period into one of depression, for although the accounts of prosperity could be made much more precise than they are at present, its general character is

---

[1] I am indebted to J. R. Bellerby and J. W. Y. Higgs for commenting on a draft of this paper, which was read at the December 1961 conference of the British Agricultural History Society.
[2] Most notably *English Farming Past and Present*, 1912.
[3] T. W. Fletcher, 'Lancashire Livestock Farming during the Great Depression', *Agric. Hist. Rev.*, IX, 1961, pp. 17-42, and 'The Great Depression of English Agriculture 1873-1896', *Econ. Hist. Rev.*, 2 ser., XIII, 1961, pp. 417-32.

plain. Mr J. R. Bellerby's figures of farmers' incentive income, obtained by deducting estimates for net rent, wages, and interest on occupier-capital from an estimate of the total factor income of agriculture, and therefore showing the reward for management and risk, are:

    in 1851   £21·4 million
    in 1870–3 on average £43·9 million

Incentive income per man-week per farmer:
    in 1851   £0·514
    in 1870–3   £1·038

Incentive income relative to that for industrial occupations:
    in 1851   49·5 per cent
    in 1870–3   77·3 per cent[1]

These statistics cannot be used to show the differing experience of various groups of producers, although the different trends might be elucidated by a study of contemporary farm accounts.

My intention here is to examine the agricultural basis of this overall rise in the prosperity of the farmer. Ernle, I think, tended to overemphasize the rôle and prosperity of the cereal grower during the years in question, although he did recognize the growing importance of livestock. Not every subsequent writer has remembered this caveat, and some have depicted the period primarily as one of prosperity for the specialist grain producer. I think it fair to say that the 'fifties to the 'seventies form a sort of base period in the minds of agricultural historians and agricultural economists, as the persistence of the term 'Golden Age' would suggest, when the wind was set fair for arable England. A heartening number of writers do mention that there were far-reaching changes in the pattern of agricultural production at this time—"down corn, up horn," as Ernle said[2]—but this movement is overshadowed by the swing towards livestock production during the Great Depression, and its implications have not been much explored.

---

[1] J. R. Bellerby, 'National and Agricultural Income 1851', *Economic Journal*, LXIX, 1959, p. 103.

[2] R. E. Prothero (Lord Ernle), *The Pioneers and Progress of English Farming*, 1888, p. 106. See also J. H. Clapham, *An Economic History of Modern Britain*, II, p. 278; J. R. T. Hughes, *Fluctuations in Trade, Industry, and Finance*, 1960, p. 224; William Ashworth, *An Economic History of England: 1870–1939*, 1960, pp. 47–8. On the other hand O. R. McGregor has recently asserted that rotations were "unalterable" and "majestically though profitably insensitive to shifting market demands."—Introduction, Part II, p. cxviii, to Lord Ernle, *English Farming Past and Present*, sixth edition, 1961.

I

The expression commonly used for the agriculture of the mid-nineteenth century is 'high farming'. The economic and technical connotations of this term have often been confused. I prefer to restrict high farming to the economic sense in which it was used, loosely, by Caird and those who agreed with him, that is, the increase of inputs to farming in supposed attempts to offset falling prices by an increased output. In the technical sense, which is perhaps the commoner and with which we are concerned here, high farming is an extension of mixed farming, that is of any system which interlocks the growing of cereals and the keeping of either or both sheep and cattle. This was epitomized by the Norfolk four-course system, with its close-knit cycle of fodder and grain crops, its arable flock, and its yard-fed bullocks. What high farming adds—and here I prefer to use Philip Pusey's alternative term 'high feeding'[1]—is intensity of operation, the feeding of purchased oilcake to the livestock on a lavish scale, to produce both meat and dung; the latter, with purchased artificial fertilizers, in turn lavished on the arable land to promote high yields of grain, and of fodder crops for the stock. The greater the scale of feeding farm-grown and bought-in fodder and the heavier the applications of farm-produced and purchased fertilizer, the more the saleable produce and the more manure for the next round of cropping, that is, the higher the farming. This was the 'expanding circle' which Mechi advocated.[2]

Dr A. H. John has drawn attention to William Ellis's description of East Anglian farming in the early 1740's as having shown "many elements of what was subsequently called 'high farming'."[3] Turnips were sown before barley and fed to fatting cattle, which returned so much dung that the yields of barley were on the increase. Mixed farming of this type will undoubtedly be found to have been a development of the seventeenth century, when the requisite root-break and hay from rotation grasses became available. An increased yield of grain was usually held to be the *raison d'être* of such systems. This was the case in the 1840's, when Pusey stated that the practice of fattening cattle on arable farms was continued "not from a view to profit in the sale of meat, but for the production of dung, and the consequent increase of the corn crop."[4] To Pusey the liberal feeding of oilcake to stock for the sake of extra manure for the land under cereals was the "great distinction of English agriculture, and constitutes what is called high farming" and what he

[1] Philip Pusey, 'On the Progress of Agricultural Knowledge during the last Four Years', *JRASE*, III, 1842, p. 205.
[2] J. A. S. Watson and M. E. Hobbs, *Great Farmers*, 1951, p. 90.
[3] A. H. John, 'The Course of Agricultural Change, 1660–1760', in L. S. Pressnell (ed.), *Studies in the Industrial Revolution*, 1960, p. 146, n. 1.
[4] Pusey, *loc. cit.*, p. 205.

called alternatively high feeding. The principle was worked out in different ways, typically in the eastern counties by the winter-feeding of oxen bought-in at the autumn fairs, but in the southern counties, where a feeding-house of cattle was a rarity, by giving supplementary oilcake to sheep hurdled on turnips.

On soils derived from chalk, limestone, or sands, high feeding possessed great advantages for the cereal grower. Such soils tend to be very deficient in potash, and although easy to cultivate are 'puffy' and need to be consolidated. Before, and indeed long after, adequate supplies of imported potash became available (from the Stassfurt mines in 1861) and while the only consolidating implement was a light roller, these needs were met by a hurdled flock. Potash was transferred from the subsoil to the topsoil in the dung of sheep fed with turnips, the roots of which had tapped the subsoil supplies of potash. Moisture was retained in the soil in dry seasons in the crumb structure built up by the treading of the sheep in the fold. Sheep and bullock dung acted as the nitrogenous fertilizer and provided humus, which the one course of 'seeds' did not fully supply, for the course of wheat in the Norfolk-type rotations which predominated on these soils.[1] Clearly, the richer the feeding of livestock, the better the dung and the heavier the crops of grain which might be expected.

II

For a score of years after the Crimean war the price of wheat, apart from short-term fluctuations, showed no tendency to rise. There was now a large import every year. On the other hand the general level of prices and the prices of livestock products in particular rose with little pause.[2] This rise in the value of livestock products compared with the value of wheat became marked from 1857 and could not but affect the working of high feeding systems in which livestock and cereal enterprises were nicely combined. The proportions of cost to be ascribed to, and of profit accruing to, the meat- and grain-producing enterprises are the subjects of contemporary assertions which are not easy to evaluate, the more so because the nature of high feeding varied according to locality and changed as the balance between the prices for grain and livestock products shifted. Nevertheless an arrangement in chronological order of the statements as to the profitable end of high feeding

[1] Viscount Astor and B. Seebohm Rowntree, *Mixed Farming and Muddled Thinking*, n.d., pp. 55, 58.
[2] W. T. Layton and G. Crowther, *An Introduction to the Study of Prices*, 1938, p. 75, n. 1. I am indebted to Dr A. H. John for a copy of his graph of wheat, barley, and beef prices from 1816 to 1870.

sheds some light on the changing relation between grain and livestock production.

Until the 1850's it was held that the cost of stall-feeding oxen through the winter was not recovered from the sale of fat-stock in the spring, but only by charging the grain enterprise for the dung which had accumulated from the beasts. This, and the fact that wheat was stall-fed on a wide scale only when it was exceptionally cheap, as in 1835-6, suggests that before the Corn Laws were repealed wheat production was not so unprofitable as many of the producers claimed. It is probable that fatstock prices were inadequate to cover the purchase of store beasts and oilcake, and leave a profit, and that stall-feeding in many areas was only practised because in addition the price of wheat was high enough for it to pay, in effect, a good sum for the rich bullock dung. The differential of 1d. per lb. more for meat in spring than in autumn, of the days when the supply of beasts fattened on summer grass was much in excess of those winter-fed, had disappeared. The meat and hides of stall-fed oxen were directly profitable only when farm-grown fodder was used as a substitute for expensive purchased feed.

In the Welsh Marches it was worth while to winter stores on turnips and straw "chiefly for their manure," although this was not common practice. It was usual in eastern England. Lincolnshire farmers were prepared to winter other men's beasts on straw free of charge, although the stock-owner had to provide the oilcake, simply in order to acquire the dung. On thin, arable soils in Norfolk and on Lincoln Heath the dung was needed to turn the straw crop into good manure, and as C. S. Read added, "on the poor chalk hills, the hungry greensands, and the thin stonebrash, high farming is as necessary as in West Norfolk."[1] According to Clarke's essay on Lincolnshire farming in 1851, "*the Grounds of the present practice of consuming the Straw with Oilcake given to Beasts on light Arable Farms . . .* are . . . simply the natural infertility of the land and the expectation of bountiful crops from the ample investment of capital in manures."[2]

Equally, the dung seems to have been the justification for feeding extra oilcake or grain to sheep hurdled on turnips on the chalk uplands, where according to Pusey the effect was "distinctly seen along the line where the hurdles had stood in the following crop of barley, marking the efficacy of high feeding," while in east Berkshire one farmer would give another his turnip crop if the latter would put his sheep in to consume it in the field.[3] The heavy demand for manure for hop-growing alone justified the generous feeding of

---

[1] C. S. Read, 'Farming of Oxfordshire', *JRASE*, xv, 1854, p. 258.
[2] J. A. Clarke, 'Farming of Lincolnshire', *JRASE*, xii, 1851, pp. 398-9.
[3] Pusey, *loc. cit.*, p. 206; James Caird, *English Agriculture in 1850-51*, 1852, p. 100.

cattle in parts of Kent.¹ The conversion of their straw into manure kept up the practice among Nottinghamshire farmers even when meat prices were low: "they calculate," wrote Corringham in 1846, "how they shall use the greatest amount of cake, which they regard as an indispensable in good farming—at the least possible loss; for as prices both of beef and mutton have of late been, they must necessarily incur a loss if they expect their remuneration from the livestock, instead of from the land," and he repeated Pusey's aphorism that as in Lincolnshire cattle were "machines whereby to make manure."²

In Cumberland, by way of contrast, the farmer who fed cattle "reckons it an unprofitable season if any part of his profit requires to be charged to the dung-heap,"³ but the basis of the Cumberland feeding system was the swede and not costly oilcake. In more easterly arable areas, where a farmer might buy several hundred pounds' worth of oilcake each winter but sell his bullocks in spring for £1 or £2 per head less than they had cost the previous autumn, stall-feeding was only practised as an adjunct to cereal production.⁴ In 1851 the four principal farmers of Borough Fen, Northamptonshire, who were lavish feeders of oilcake, agreed that two-thirds of its cost were returned by the manure from cattle and only one-third from the sale of beef, one-third by the manure from sheep, and two-thirds from the mutton.⁵ It was this sort of ratio which led Pusey to regard the production of plenty of rich manure as "the whole object of all feeding."⁶ While Protection lasted, the price of cereals covered losses on meat production by stall-feeding; afterwards they did not, yet mixed farming as a whole continued to be profitable.⁷

In 1851–52, 1858, and the mid-sixties wheat was cheap enough to be fed to bullocks and pigs on a large scale, in the hope of a compensating return from fatstock. The prices for fatstock were high when the price of wheat was low. In this situation, the receipts from grain and livestock products helped to balance one another, and in 1864 when grain prices were low and prices for stock and wool high a correspondent in the *Farmer's Magazine* observed that in consequence the farmer's "business position would be about an

---

[1] G. Buckland, 'Farming of Kent', *JRASE*, VI, 1846, p. 273.

[2] R. W. Corringham, 'Agriculture of Nottinghamshire', *JRASE*, VI, 1846, pp. 20–1.

[3] W. Dickinson, 'On the Farming of Cumberland', *JRASE*, XIII, 1852, pp. 256–7.

[4] Philip Pusey, 'Some Introductory Remarks on the present State of Agriculture as a Science in England', *JRASE*, I, 1840, p. 18; A. Huxtable, *The 'Present Prices'*, 1850, p. 13.

[5] W. Bearn, 'On the Farming of Northamptonshire', *JRASE*, XIII, 1852, p. 71 (dated 23.2.1851).

[6] Pusey, 1842, *loc. cit.*, p. 207.

[7] This was stated categorically by T. J. Eliot, *The Land Question... as illustrated by twenty-three years' experience on the Wilton House Home Farm*, n.d. [1884], especially p. 37.

average one."¹ The complementary nature of the two groups of enterprises is revealed by the unusually frank account of a farmer as to the effects of the bad harvests of 1856 and '57 in Scotland. Sprouted grain was fed to the stock and potatoes were sold for seed instead of human consumption, so that on balance profits were almost if not quite what they might have been had the harvests been good.² The inverse movement of the prices and profitability of grain and sheep is further borne out by C. S. Read's comments on the relative fortunes of sheep farmers on the Norfolk heaths and grain growers on the dearer-rented Norfolk soils. It was held at the time a distinct advantage of mixed farming that when grain prices were poor, the crop or some part of it could be fed to the fatting stock.³

It is noteworthy that in the East Lothians oilcake and grain were fed liberally when grain prices were good in the early 1840's, were sharply curtailed when grain and stock prices were low at mid-century, and fed freely again in the mid-1860's when grain was cheap but stock fetched a good price.⁴ In 1858 oilcake was being fed in Norfolk on a scale which grain prices did not warrant.⁵ In other words, in the 1850's and '60's prices for livestock products were sometimes high enough to induce high feeding regardless of unremunerative prices for grain. Low grain prices of course meant low feed costs. As P. H. Frere noted in 1860, "whereas of old the bread consumer had to pay in part for the supply furnished to the consumer of meat, now, each kind of produce must in the main defray its own cost of production," and at times the production of meat became the mixed farmer's chief aim.⁶ The manure from stall-feeding was thought of as devoted not to the wheat crop, as it had been in the past, but to the roots as further feed for the livestock. There are plenty of signs that this new relationship was widely recognized by the mid-1860's.⁷

This account has been somewhat simplified for the sake of clarity: the

---

¹ 'The Present Position of the British Farmer', *Farmer's Magazine*, 3 ser., xxv, 1864, p. 207; see also 'The Causes of the Decline in the Price of Corn', *Farmer's Magazine*, 3 ser., xiii, 1858, p. 251.
² A. Simpson, 'High Farming with Profit', *Farmer's Magazine*, 3 ser., xviii, 1860, p. 239.
³ 'The Present State and Prospects of the Farming Interest', *Farmer's Magazine*, 3 ser., xxv, 1864, p. 193; C. S. Read, 'Recent Improvements in Norfolk Farming', *JRASE*, xix, 1858, p. 271.
⁴ R. S. Skirving, 'Ten Years of East Lothian Farming', *JRASE*, 2 ser., i, 1865, pp. 105-6.
⁵ Read, *loc. cit.*, p. 287.
⁶ P. H. Frere, 'On the Feeding of Stock', *JRASE*, xxi, 1860, pp. 233-4.
⁷ See e.g. J. Coleman, 'The Breeding and Feeding of Sheep', *JRASE*, xxiv, 1863, p. 623; 'Oilcake and Grain for Cattle', *Farmer's Magazine*, 3 ser., xxv, 1864, p. 216; H. Evershed, 'On Sheep', *JRASE*, 2 ser., i, 1865, pp. 332-5; 'Are the Present High Prices of Stock Likely to Continue?', *Farmer's Magazine*, 3 ser., xxx, 1866, p. 104. The opposite view taken by J. J. Mechi in 1867 and quoted by T. W. Fletcher, *Econ. Hist. Rev.*, 2 ser., xiii, 1961, p. 422, is exceptional, as Mechi's views tended to be.

proportions of profit due to grain and livestock cannot be learnt in detail since few farmers could make the distinction themselves. A Norfolk farmer told Sir Daniel Hall early this century that "it is impossible to show that any single operation on a farm pays by itself, it is the whole system taken together which succeeds or fails," and in the early days of cost accounting, as Hall agreed, this was not an entirely unreasonable position, because decisions as to how to apportion costs and receipts in the Norfolk system are necessarily very arbitrary.[1] Nevertheless, a general change in the profitable base of high feeding systems from about 1850 does seem to be indicated.

III

The long-term movements of product prices had been foretold by Caird as early as 1849, although he had exaggerated their immediacy.[2] Caird expected the price of grain (except malting barley, of which the British sorts were superior) to fall as imports increased, while with the growth of population he anticipated that prices for butcher's meat, dairy produce, vegetables, wool, and hides would rise. In consequence, he advocated turning attention to green crops which could be fed to livestock, partly for the saleable products and partly for manure to increase the yields of the grain crops. Caird was by no means the only one to recognize this trend, which became a source of general comment,[3] but he was the most constant in stressing the need to adjust the pattern of mixed farming to meet it. He returned to the topic in 1868 and pointed out how accurate his prognosis had been. "Since 1850 the price of bread on the average, has remained the same," he wrote, "while that of meat, dairy produce, and wool has risen fifty per cent... This and the steadily advancing barley, to which I then referred, is the true explanation of increasing rents and agricultural prosperity, notwithstanding increasing receipts of foreign corn."[4] Professor Clapham came to the conclusion from

---

[1] A. D. Hall, *A Pilgrimage of British Farming 1910–1912*, 1914, pp. 83–4.

[2] *High Farming, under liberal covenants* . . . 1849, pp. 6–7, 25–6.

[3] See e.g. 'On the Peculiarities of the Management of Farms', *Farmer's Magazine*, XXII, 1850, p. 396; 'The Wool Trade and Meat Trade—foreshadowing the change that must be made in our Agricultural System', *Farmer's Magazine*, 3 ser., III, 1853, pp. 8–9; C. S. Read, 'Farming of Oxfordshire', *JRASE*, XV, 1854, p. 256; 'Shall we cultivate corn or cattle?', *Farmer's Magazine*, 3 ser., XIX, 1861, p. 411; H. S. Thompson, 'Agricultural Progress and the Royal Agricultural Society', *JRASE*, XXV, 1864, p. 35: "The breeding and feeding of livestock have thus become such profitable operations that the growth of corn, *as a sequence to stockfarming*, has also become profitable, even at present prices." A Cumberland Landowner, *A Few Hints to Landowners & Cultivators, Horn or Corn. Which pays best*, 1873, *passim*; T. Farrall, 'A Report on the Agriculture of Cumberland, chiefly with regard to the Production of Meat', *JRASE*, 2 ser., X, 1874, p. 429.

[4] J. Caird, *Our Daily Food*, 1868, p. 33.

price data in the *Economist* that the rise in wholesale prices for meat and dairy produce was nearer 40 per cent, although it was calculated in the '70's that the price of beef in the Metropolitan market advanced 58 per cent and that of mutton 85 per cent between 1853 and '73.[1] Obviously the lowest of these figures is large enough to have brought about very considerable changes in the structure of agriculture. Caird's analysis in 1878 is probably the best formulation of his oft-repeated views and deserves to be quoted at length. "Thirty years ago," he says, "probably not more than one-third of the people of this country consumed animal food more than once a week. Now, nearly all of them eat it, in meat or cheese or butter, once a day. This has more than doubled the average consumption of animal food in this country... The leap which the consumption of meat took in consequence of the general rise of wages in all branches of trade and employment, could not have been met without foreign supplies, and these could not have been secured except by such a rise in price as fully paid the risk and cost of transport. The additional price on the home-produce was all profit to the landed interests of this country."[2] Before considering further the nature of these changes, it is worth examining how the disturbance in the relative values of farm products has usually been treated.

The accident of the long-delayed date when national agricultural statistics were first collected has imparted a somewhat false sense of discontinuity in agriculture about 1870. Many authorities take 1870 as the first year in which the statistics are reasonably complete and reliable, and many of them start with this date when tracing the development of present-day agriculture. As a result, the early 1870's are often made to appear as the high-water-mark of the 'Golden Age' as regards cereal acreages and production. The increased concern with livestock production from 1873, or '75, or '79 (the utter lack of agreement about the onset of the Great Depression in agriculture itself suggests that the change was not sudden, but part of a cumulative process), has thus been exaggerated at the expense of the more gradual, but fundamental, shift in the pattern of farming from the 1850's. That the alteration in the balance of prices could be and was met by adjustments within mixed farming systems, and only at comparatively late dates by a switch to the grassland production of livestock, has tended to conceal the extent of the transition. The years 1870–73 might more properly be regarded as marked by the final wave, apart from the brief surge in 1878, of high prices for grain and hence big acreages of cereals.

[1] J. H. Clapham, *op. cit.*, II, p. 278; J. A. Clarke, 'Practical Agriculture', *JRASE*, 2 ser., XIV, 1878, p. 476.
[2] James Caird, 'General View of British Agriculture', *JRASE*, 2 ser., XIV, 1878, p. 289.

Some recent writers, notably M. Olsen and C. C. Harris in the *Quarterly Journal of Economics* for 1959,[1] deny the growing emphasis on livestock as the profitable end of farming during the 1850's and '60's, and stress the importance of wheat. Their conclusions are based largely on the post-1866 acreage statistics, which cannot of themselves reveal which were the most profitable enterprises in close-knit farming systems, nor even which products were destined for sale and which for farm consumption, nor point to the considerable year-to-year changes in output per acre. The acreage statistics seem to have diverted attention from changes in production which took place without correspondingly large changes in land use. Since there was no clear increase of rotation grass and only a steady, slow expansion of permanent pasture during the '70's, the growing importance of livestock has been minimized.[2] Yet the value of the gross output of United Kingdom agriculture, as recalculated from E. M. Ojala's figures by T. W. Fletcher, was

	1867–69	1870–76
Arable products	£104·17 million	£94·99 million
Livestock products	£126·76 million	£154·87 million[3]

Earlier estimates of cereal acreages collected by Lawes and Gilbert[4] and Drescher,[5] and the figures of 'British corn sold' from 1849 to '72 given by Hasbach[6] show that the peak of arable expansion in the early 1870's was a temporary upswing after a contraction which had begun to set in during the later '50's. The increase in the total cultivated area of England and Wales which is usually said to have occurred between 1851 and '71 is not necessarily inimical to the view that the cereal acreage, especially the wheat acreage, was at its peak in the mid-1850's. In 1868 Lawes and Gilbert referred to "the

---

[1] 'Free Trade in "Corn"', in LXXIII, pp. 145–6, 165–8. For another account based on the acreage figures and minimizing the importance of livestock before the mid-1870's see J. T. Coppock, 'The Changing Arable in England and Wales 1870–1956', *Tijdschrift voor Economische en Sociale Geografie*, L, 1959, pp. 122–3.

[2] It was generally agreed in the 1860's that most of the increased production of meat came from turnips, clover, or sainfoin on land where intervening grain crops were taken, and not from grass. See e.g. 'W. W. G.', 'The Outcry about Meat', *Farmer's Magazine*, 3 ser., XXVIII, 1865, p. 134.

[3] T. W. Fletcher, *Econ. Hist. Rev.*, 2 ser., XIII, 1961, p. 432.

[4] J. B. Lawes and J. H. Gilbert, 'On the Home Produce... of Wheat, 1852–3 to 1879–80', *JRASE*, 2 ser., XVI, 1880, Table V.

[5] L. Drescher, 'The Development of Agricultural Production in Great Britain and Ireland from the Early Nineteenth Century', *Manchester School Econ. & Soc. Studies*, XXIII, 1955, Graph 1, p. 155.

[6] W. Hasbach, *A History of the English Agricultural Labourer*, 1920, p. 255, quoting *Statistical Abstracts Report*, XX, 1858–72.

general opinion... that the area under wheat has diminished during the last 15 or 20 years," and agreed that this was the case, especially in Scotland and Ireland.[1] All the signs point to a contraction of the wheat acreage in the less suitable northern and western areas, including parts of England, during those years, while there is additional confirmation that arable clays in England were being laid down to permanent pasture in the mid-1860's, as might be expected from the movement of wheat prices.[2] Olsen and Harris, taking the opposite view, say that "from the attention lavished on the repeal of the Corn Laws one might assume that all that was important in British agriculture ended in 1846. But it would be more appropriate to say that the downfall of British agriculture began, not in 1846, but in 1873."[3] Disregarding the emotive word "downfall," it can be shown that after the Repeal the altered relative value of wheat and livestock products, due to imports which prevented a rise in the price of wheat, the growth of population, and rising real incomes of which an increasing proportion was spent on livestock products, led to considerable modifications in the structure of farming.

IV

Greater production of livestock was attained primarily by increasing output from arable farms. In the 1850's and '60's stall-feeding and yard-feeding of cattle was intensified in mixed farming regions, and spread into districts such as the dairying parts of Cheshire and Gloucestershire, where it was hitherto unknown, on to chalk and limestone uplands where until the 1840's sheep had been almost the only stock, and into parts of Cornwall and Cumberland where the entire dependence had previously been on grain.[4] The spread of mixed farming and high feeding from its original homes in eastern England and on the chalk and limestone uplands was stimulated by the development of artificial fertilizers which were important to the root-break, and by the completion of a railway network by which oilcake and artificials could be carried quickly and cheaply all over the country. It was soon realized that yard- and stall- or box-feeding enabled more and better manure to be collected, and fatstock to be produced in more rapid succession than did feeding

---

[1] J. B. Lawes and J. H. Gilbert, 'On the Home Produce... of Wheat', *JRASE*, 2 ser., IV, 1868, pp. 365, 390.
[2] Anon., 'On the Price of Butcher-meat, and the Increase of Home Supplies of Cattle and Sheep', *Jnl. of Agric.*, xxv, N.S., 1865–6, p. 362; W. J. Moscrop, 'A Report on the Farming of Leicestershire', *JRASE*, 2 ser., II, 1866, p. 326; H. Evershed, 'Agriculture of Staffordshire', *JRASE*, 2 ser., V, 1869, p. 268, and 'Agriculture of Hertfordshire', *JRASE*, xxv, 1864, p. 283.
[3] Olsen & Harris, *loc. cit.*, p. 168.
[4] L. de Lavergne, *The Rural Economy of England, Scotland, and Ireland*, 1855, p. 185; Read, *loc. cit.*, p. 222; L. H. Ruegg, 'Farming of Dorsetshire', *JRASE*, xv, 1854, p. 412.

in the fields. A further impetus to high feeding came from the high prices of the Crimean war, which prompted the conversion of large acreages of the remaining remote downland, which could not be reached economically with the dung cart, to arable land fertilized by folded flocks.[1] The extension of systems involving hurdled sheep and stall-fed cattle did not, however, mean the end of fattening on the better permanent pastures. Lavergne was exaggerating the trend of the times when in 1855 he bade "adieu, then, to the pastoral scenes of which England was so proud."[2]

Nevertheless, the increased importance of livestock on arable farms is obvious. This is brought out neatly when the principal items of expenditure and receipts for a 'mixed soil farm' of 590 acres in East Suffolk and a 'heavy land' arable farm of 230 acres in West Suffolk are compared for the periods 1839–44 and 1863–67. Both farms show the trend, and taking them together between the two periods receipts from wheat fell slightly, whereas receipts from barley, peas, oats and beans, cattle, sheep, and pigs all rose markedly. The bill for feed for livestock nearly trebled and became the largest single item of expenditure in the latter period.[3]

Since the price of wheat did not fall catastrophically until the late 1870's, the joint production of cereals and meat was favoured in the meantime: if the grain enterprise were *given* the manure from the livestock, it could pay its way. On the other hand there were serious obstacles in the way of increasing the grassland production of livestock. Pasture of a sufficient quality to fatten stock was too scarce to provide the whole supply of meat for which there was a demand and could not in any case have provided an all-year-round supply. The three- or four-year leys which contemporaries were able to sow were said to be only half as productive as the 'artificial' feeding on arable farms.[4] As Frere argued in 1860, the additional supply had to come from feeding in the stall or the yard, and the cost of this would *"regulate the cost of the whole supply."*[5] As grain-growing could no longer bear the cost of stall-feeding for the sake of the manure, 'artificial' feeding had to be made directly profitable, and with existing methods this meant that the price of beef would gradually have to rise. But as long as receipts from mixed farming as a whole were adequate, only the economically more astute farmers, in districts where grass grew well, would lay land down to grass and specialize in what were becoming the most profitable farm enterprises, finishing cattle and sheep on

---

[1] See e.g. J. B. Spearing, 'On the Agriculture of Berkshire', *JRASE*, XXI, 1860, p. 16.
[2] Lavergne, *op. cit.*, pp. 54, 187.
[3] Royal Commission on Agriculture, *Particulars of . . . Farm Accounts*, 1896, pp. 167–8.
[4] 'The Outcry about Meat', *Farmer's Magazine, loc. cit.*, p. 135.
[5] Frere, *loc. cit.*, p. 234.

pasture with oilcake.¹ High feeding was not inflexible, since high inputs of oilcake were justified by reasonable prices for either grain or fatstock even if the price of the other happened to be low. The system was sufficiently viable, economically and technically, for the emphasis on the various products to be altered within wide limits before the grassland production of beef became a more attractive proposition for the arable farmer.

It might be expected that the increasing profitability of livestock would have led to a marked numerical increase of cattle and sheep. This, however, was offset by severe losses among breeding ewes in hill flocks during the hard weather of early 1860, by losses and liquidation sales in the summer droughts of 1864 and 1868, and by the rinderpest among cattle in 1865–66, which drew attention firmly to the short supply of fatstock. The demand for meat continued to grow, with the supply unable to keep pace.² In 1865 it was thought that meat would have become scarce sooner "had it not been for the war with Russia in the Crimea, which caused corn to rise to a high price, and capital therefore to flow back into the hands of farmers, which enabled them to hold their live stock and increase it, instead of forcing it into market half-grown and half-fat at certain seasons that they might meet their fixed expenses."³ Prices and costs favoured the expansion of sheep more than cattle production, but diseased turnip crops and consequently dear feed were alleged to have brought about a decline in the average weight of sheep. It seems likely that cattle were retained on free-draining land where sheep might have brought greater financial rewards because they were more efficient at converting straw into manure. On upland farms the quantity of straw was embarrassing and the insistence of landowners that it should not be sold off the farm was thought a great nuisance.⁴ Contemporaries were divided as to whether or not sheep numbers rose during the '50's and '60's; the most cogent among them argued that a rise was taking place.⁵ The official agricul-

¹ W. H. Heywood, 'The Comparative Profit from Making Cheese or Butter, Selling Milk, or Grazing', *JRASE*, 2 ser., I, 1865, pp. 342–3, considered grazing even more profitable than milk-producing. Country milking received a tremendous impulse, much of it lasting, when the rinderpest of 1865–6 half-emptied the London cow-houses, but the milk was diverted from the less profitable business of cheese or butter making and no great increase of cows was necessarily involved.—J. C. Morton, 'Town Milk', *JRASE*, 2 ser., IV, 1868, pp. 95–7.

² On the increased demand and high prices in the fatstock markets see Robert Herbert, 'Statistics of Livestock for Consumption in the Metropolis', *JRASE*, XIX, 1858, pp. 496–500, and annually thereafter.

³ 'The Outcry about Meat', *Farmer's Magazine*, loc. cit., p. 134.

⁴ Clement Cadle, *On the Management of a Breeding Herd of Cattle, on an Arable Farm..*, 1863, pp. 3–4.

⁵ W. Wright, 'On the Improvements in the Farming of Yorkshire', *JRASE*, XXII, 1861, pp. 129–30; J. D. Dent, 'Agricultural Notes on the Census of 1861', *JRASE*, XXV, 1864, p. 321.

tural statistics for England and Wales between 1867 and 1875 show a rise of approximately 21 per cent in cattle numbers, some of which may have represented recovery from the plague of 1865–66, although a negligible increase in sheep. Earlier maturity, with a quicker turnover of stock and perhaps heavier killing-out weights of cattle, probably increased the quantity of meat marketed still further. The capital value of the livestock of the U.K. increased almost 80 per cent between 1853 and 1878 according to Caird.[1]

Prices moved strongly against wheat in the mid-1860's and at that time the poorer clayland arable was laid to grass in many districts. Much opinion was as yet against this expedient, although that enthusiastic M.F.H. the duke of Beaufort remarked prophetically in 1861 that "the next generation will have much more grass to ride over than the present."[2] The change was slow. Many farmers regarded the wheat crop with an almost mystical reverence, and in public, at least, many of them took the price of wheat to be the index of agricultural fortunes. Frere in 1860 remarked, in rather muddled language, that "though all are conscious that we can no longer rely on the corn-crops for paying the rent, perhaps none of us have been able sufficiently to throw off the trammels of custom and association, which led him to look for profit first to the stack rather than to the stall."[3] A reason which was put forward in 1873 for the persistent emphasis on arable cultivation was that returns came in to the arable farmer throughout the year; "in short, he can as it were, live from hand to mouth on a comparatively less capital. It is not so however with a general stock farmer, who has necessarily to lie [sic] out his capital for extended periods."[4] Most farmers were in any case conditioned to act by the knowledge that a greater physical production of grain and meat could be obtained by feeding stock on arable farms than on grass, and they therefore sought the most profitable combination of stock and grain production.[5] In 1866 it was noted that "the fact that grass will pay, and pay much better for manure applied, than corn at its present selling price, is as yet recognized by a limited number of the agriculturists of the country;" the same observation had been made in 1858, another year in which grain prices had been especially low.[6] Capital and manure continued to be spent on the ploughland at the expense of all but the best pastures. All except the supreme fattening pastures and the dairy pastures of Cheshire, which were properly drained

[1] Caird, 1878, *loc. cit.*, p. 290.
[2] James Stratton, *A History of the Wiltshire Strattons*, n.d., p. 79 n.
[3] Frere, *loc. cit.*, p. 219.   [4] A Cumberland Landowner, *op. cit.*, p. 11.
[5] See e.g. 'Stock versus Corn; or rather the most profitable conduct of farming', *Farmer's Magazine*, 3 ser., XXIII, 1863, p. 142.
[6] Moscrop, *loc. cit.*, p. 337; H. Tanner, 'The Agriculture of Shropshire', *JRASE*, XIX, 1858, p. 38.

and fertilized with bone dust, seemed to contemporaries less profitable than they might have been, through continual mowing and depasturing by dairy cows and young growing stock which took more out of the land than they returned in manure. Such pastures were thought to be in a gradually deteriorating state.[1]

Conversion of arable land to permanent pasture was probably delayed by the rise of grain prices to a peak in the early 1870's, but by this time informed opinion was in favour of fattening stock on grass and finishing the beasts with oilcake. This ensured that the pastures were adequately manured, and besides being a cheaper mode of production than yard- or stall-feeding enabled the fatstock to be sold in June or July, when the price of beef was higher than at the end of summer. "The great difficulty," as it was seen in February 1872, "is in making a beginning. The routine of years, possibly handed down for generations, cannot be broken through without a pang; but such pangs seldom outlive the first favourable balance-sheet, and it may be confidently stated that for some time past the farmers who have made most money are those who have paid as much attention to the improvement of their grass as to the growth of fine crops of corn or roots."[2] Even later the trend was on occasion reversed for a brief spell, but the successive peaks of wheat and barley prices and acreages were lower and lower in the '70's and were looked on as transient. For example, at Aldbourne, Wiltshire, where in 1878 "corn growing superseded the making of meat," this was regarded as "a state of things which cannot last long,"[3] and indeed it did not last, for this was where Henry Wilson allowed a large acreage to go down to grass for the stock in which he was dealing, and where as a result the hamlet of Snap was eventually deserted.

There are signs that the growing profitability of mixed farming and the weakening position of the specialist cereal grower was not without influence on the size and type of farm holdings. The census returns of 1851 and '61 show a decrease of 6,132 farms below 300 acres, and an increase of 229 in those between 300 and 1,000 acres, for the ten very diverse counties for which figures are available for both dates. This change was explained as the engulfing of the smaller holdings, which had been occupied by men of little capital, "who were very much dependent upon corn crops for their living, and, at the

---

[1] Anon., 'On the Price of Butcher-meat', *loc. cit.*, pp. 363–4; J. C. Morton, 'On the Management of Grass Lands', *Jnl. of the Bath & West Soc.*, XIII, 1865, pp. 62–4, 68–9.

[2] H. S. Thompson, 'On the Management of Grass Land. . .', *JRASE*, 2 ser., VIII, 1872, p. 179.

[3] *Agric. Gazette*, N.S. VIII, 18.11.1878, p. 463, quoted by F. M. L. Thompson, 'Agriculture since 1870', *V.C.H. Wilts.*, IV, 1959, p. 97.

present prices of grain ... not having stock to back them up, cannot make farming remunerative."[1] In Cumberland in 1874 the growing number of livestock was attributed to the improved quality of the pastures more than to the increased acreage of grass, although many clayland farms which a few years earlier were heavily cropped to afford a precarious livelihood had been drained and converted into good grazing farms.[2]

V

High feeding had been so much extolled as the salvation of the farmer at mid-century (even Fred Vincy in *Middlemarch* was supposed to have written on the 'Cultivation of Green Crops and the Economy of Cattle Feeding')[3] that the shift of advanced opinion in favour of grassland fattening by the early 1870's comes as some surprise. According to Clapham, although lease covenants were in practice winked at, cropping changed in no essential way between 1850 and 1886.[4] But the agitation for more flexible rotations was so strong in this period that had lease covenants been so uniformly a dead letter, there would surely have been major cropping changes. In 1863 the [London] Farmers' Club was discussing how to meet the growing demand for meat and wool, "without materially disarranging our order of management, so objectionable to land-agents."[5] The summer droughts of the following year and of 1868, when the root-crops were severely damaged, brought home the need for freedom to amend cropping plans to meet contingencies of this sort,[6] quite apart from the desirability of tailoring rotations to suit the trends of prices. The agitation against cropping restrictions, although perhaps as Professor Ashworth claims in part a rationalization of antagonism to the continued political influence of landowners,[7] was underpinned by genuine economic considerations. It seems that the growing incentive to produce livestock could account for much of the uneasiness in landlord-tenant relations, in particular the demands for freedom to alter cycles of fodder crops and to insert catch crops of cereals, according to the swaying state of the markets, and for more livestock housing, without which no big increase of stock was possible.

With rising livestock prices as the attraction, fodder crops were at first extended at the expense of grain. On the clays the mangel acreage increased throughout the 1850's, but by 1865 farmers in many clayland districts were

[1] Dent, *loc. cit.*, pp. 323–4. [2] Farrall, *loc. cit.*, p. 407.
[3] George Eliot, *Middlemarch*, 1947 edn., p. 889. [4] Clapham, *op. cit.*, II, pp. 275–6.
[5] 'Stock versus Corn', *loc. cit.*, pp. 142–3.
[6] J. C. Morton, 'Some of the Agricultural Lessons of 1868', *JRASE*, 2 ser., v, 1869, pp. 54–5.
[7] Ashworth, *op. cit.*, p. 50.

finding it cheaper to feed stock on purchased grain than to grow roots.¹ In Worcestershire in 1867 mangels were still being extended on the clays, "from the high price of meat," and it was observed of Cumberland in 1874, that "the majority of skilled agriculturists do not go in solely for producing wheat; they would much rather sow the land with oats and barley than forgo the turnip crop, which is now looked on as the mainstay of arable farming."² But in the drier eastern counties, where roots, although more difficult to grow, occupied a larger proportion of each farm than in the west, the root-break had come to be viewed with a jaundiced eye by the mid-1870's. By that time, as Lawes showed, stock could beyond doubt be fattened more cheaply on grain and cut-straw than on roots. The insistence of landowners that 25 per cent of the farm acreage must be kept under roots, according to the dictates of the four-course system, was a source of some bitterness.³

VI

The retention of mixed farming systems in which livestock were replacing grain as the most profitable elements had in the 1850's and '60's been a reasonable adaptation to prices, which favoured now the one side, now the other, while gradually swinging farther and farther to the livestock side. Mixed farming was less well suited to the conditions of the '70's. The fall in the price of wheat was uneven and the temporary peak of the Franco-Prussian war period dissuaded grain-conscious farmers from a wholehearted change to fatstock production on grass, but after 1873 hesitation in following the trend of the previous twenty years evaporated. However, the persistence so late with cereal growing under the shelter of mixed farming and high feeding must have intensified the distress when bad harvests and the landslide in grain prices occurred at the end of the '70's. Until then, since mixed farming's strength lay in stabilizing income through the sale of several commodities, short-term, out-of-phase fluctuations in the prices of its various products could be accommodated. The collapse of grain prices and thus one whole side of the system was needed to effect the break-up of mixed farming. Even so, as has been shown from the income tax assessments, the rise in rent between 1851-52 and 1878-79 had been greater in the pastoral north and west and in the grazing counties than in the arable east of England. Indeed,

---

¹ P. D. Tuckett, 'On the Modifications of the Four-course...', *JRASE*, XXI, 1860, p. 262; H. Evershed, 'On Sheep', *JRASE*, 2 ser., I, 1865, p. 335.
² C. Cadle, 'The Agriculture of Worcestershire', *JRASE*, 2 ser., III, 1867, p. 452; Farrall, loc. cit., p. 407.
³ F. Clifford, 'The Labour Bill in Farming', *JRASE*, 2 ser., XI, 1875, pp. 123-4, and citing J. D. Lawes in *JRASE*, 2 ser., IX, 1873, pp. 373-4.

in arable districts, especially on the chalk and sands of the drier counties where grass does not thrive and leys are difficult to establish, and above all on the poor clays where expenditure by landowners may have been highest, there may have been a fall in real rent over these years.[1] This is a final indication that profits from livestock rather than grain had become increasingly the basis of agricultural prosperity. The structural changes in English agriculture during the Great Depression, which made livestock production far more prominent than cereal growing, had been foreshadowed by the transformation of mixed farming.

[1] Clapham, *op. cit.*, II, pp. 278–9; Caird, 1878, *loc. cit.*, p. 315.

POSTSCRIPT

A weakness of the argument in this paper may lie in its assumption that the trend of livestock product prices, or more narrowly meat prices and the prices of animals for slaughter, equated with that of feeders' margins. It would be difficult to test for any discrepant movement, since an index of feeders' profit margins would have to be arrived at not merely by subtracting the cost of store stock from receipts from fatstock but also by subtracting the intervening costs of feed and management. Collecting data on the cost of feed where so much of it was farm-grown, as was the case in the mixed farming of the nineteenth century, would be extremely hard. Farm-grown fodder crops contributed to fattening stock and through them produced dung which was applied in part to subsequent cereal crops. What part of the value of these fodder crops should be regarded as a charge on the cereal enterprises and how much on the fatstock side defies exact calculation. However, the general tenor of the evidence supports the view that price movements are an acceptable long-run proxy for profits at this time.

The trends towards more emphasis on the livestock enterprises within mixed farming seem sufficiently clear. It would certainly be useful to see spelt out more explicitly the rigidities which impeded a whole-hearted switch to livestock production during the entire second half of the nineteenth century. That there were serious rigidities is definite: part of such switching as did take place, for example the growth of dairying in south-eastern England, was achieved not by the existing arable farmers, who from the seventies failed, but by fresh operators (notably immigrant Scots dairy farmers in Essex) working under tenurial conditions which landowners were forced to make more attractive and employing a dairy technology which they understood but which the men they replaced emphatically did not. Professor Charles Kindleberger has offered an interesting interpretation of the constraints on a swing to livestock as late as the last quarter of the century—'The Failure of British Agriculture to Transform', pp. 239–47, in his *Economic Growth in France and Britain, 1851–1950* (Cambridge, Mass., 1964).

Finally, one point which the original article does not take into account is how far a rise in the horse population over the years 1853–73 may have brought about more attention to the forage crops within mixed farming rotations, perhaps with a sale of feedstuffs to urban horse owners in mind. Unfortunately there appears to be no series of horse numbers for England starting before 1870.

E. L. J.

THE GREAT DEPRESSION OF ENGLISH AGRICULTURE 1873–96

T. W. Fletcher

THE GREAT DEPRESSION OF ENGLISH AGRICULTURE
1873–1896

By T. W. FLETCHER

I

THE nature and extent of the Great Depression of trade and industry during the last quarter of the nineteenth century have been argued for many years. In contrast, the existence of a great depression in agriculture was, and is, universally accepted, and farmers' sufferings have been wept over by generations of mourners. 'Since 1862 the tide of agricultural prosperity had ceased to flow; after 1874 it turned and rapidly ebbed'—Ernle's splendid narrative leaves us in no doubt as to the severity of depression.[1] Venn, discussing the supply of gold and the price level, believed agriculture to have suffered more than most industries, 'being plunged indeed into the abyss'.[2] The general opinion is perhaps best summarized by Halévy; 'if the position of industry was doubtful, about agriculture there could be no doubt. It was in an advanced state of decay'.[3]

The evidence for this sort of textbook generalization is of two kinds, the statistical, with the Gazette price of wheat and Sauerbeck's food index illustrating the fall in farm prices and the Agricultural Returns mirroring output, and the descriptive, which leans heavily on Ernle and the proceedings of the two Royal Commissions of 1879–82 and 1894–7. Additional evidence, but playing little or no part in the genesis of this orthodox view, is the Schedule A assessments of the Inland Revenue Board and the recent work on rent by Mr Rhee and on output by Dr Ojala.[4] It is the view of the present writer that much of this evidence is biased in that most commentators have adopted, albeit unconsciously, an attitude towards agriculture and consequently towards the Great Depression that is inappropriate and misleading in the economic climate of Victorian, and later, England.

The depression is usually dated 1873–96, which fairly coincides with the turning points of both the wheat price and Sauerbeck's index. This seems satisfactory until the question is asked, how important was wheat to the English farmer and what does Sauerbeck's index measure? According to Dr Ojala, who does not underestimate its importance, the wheat crop contributed 13 per cent of the gross output at current prices of the agriculture of the U.K. in the period 1867–76 and this fell to four per cent by 1894–1903.[5]

---

[1] R. E. Prothero (later Lord Ernle), *English Farming Past and Present* (4th. ed. 1927), p. 374.
[2] J. A. Venn, *The Foundations of Agricultural Economics* (2nd. ed. 1923), p. 474.
[3] E. Halévy, *A History of the English People in the Nineteenth Century* – V (2nd. ed. 1951), pp. 293–4.
[4] H. A. Rhee, *The Rent of Agricultural Land in England and Wales* (Central Landowners Association, 1946); E. M. Ojala, *Agriculture and Economic Progress* (1952).
[5] Computed from Ojala, *op. cit.* Table XVI, p. 208.

An estimate for England alone shews percentages of 22 and seven.¹ Sauerbeck's index, from the point of view of the commodities and prices selected, is probably a better measure of price changes of foods entering international trade than it is of the products of English farms; for example, the whole of English dairying is represented by one price series, that of Friesland butter, out of 19, all equally weighted, and 14 of these series relate to import not home product prices.² A further drawback is that the weighting remains unaltered throughout the period and by the eighteen nineties is ludicrously unrepresentative of the output from English farms.

Neither the coincidence of Sauerbeck's vegetable food index with the curve of the wheat price nor the relatively small part played by wheat in farm output would matter so much if changes in the price of wheat accurately reflected changes in agricultural prices generally or if Sauerbeck's import prices were representative of prices received by English livestock producers. But neither of these suppositions is tenable: the price of wheat notoriously fell by more than other cereal prices and very much more than livestock prices (except wool), and although home livestock prices are neither abundant nor easily found, such price series as can be constructed exhibit a smaller fall during the Great Depression than the respective import series.³ On the output side, to judge by the *Agricultural Returns*, there is little evidence of any contraction of production, except in the case of wheat and, to a much smaller extent, of barley; on the contrary the acreage of oats, fruit and vegetables, and the numbers of most categories of livestock increased significantly.⁴

Thus the most widely used statistical evidence of agricultural depression appears, on examination, to relate mainly to the price and acreage changes of wheat. A closer look at the Great Depression seems called for; it is proposed to begin with the general demand and supply situation and pass on to a consideration of the nature of English agriculture and of the contemporary scene.

II

The demand situation facing English farmers was encouraging. Between 1851 and 1871 the population of England increased at the rate of 1·3 per cent per annum; between 1871 and 1901 the annual rate of growth was 1·5 per cent, or, in absolute terms, whereas in the twenty years of the 'Golden Age' less than five millions were added to the population, in the thirty years covering the Great Depression an additional 10 million mouths appeared. Again, between 1851 and 1871 real wages rose by less than one per cent per annum; between 1871 and 1901 the rate was approximately two per cent.⁵ The contrast is the more marked in that there was little change for a decade and a half after 1851 and the 'take-off' into significant growth of real wages occurred as late as the half dozen years after 1868. Thus with population increasing faster than during the Golden Age and accompanied for the first time by a marked upward surge in real wages the aggregate demand situation for food was exceedingly favourable for the producer.

¹ See Appendix.
² Sauerbeck's food index, base 1867–77, is an unweighted average of 19 price indices, eight of them forming his vegetable food index, seven his animal food index, and four covering sugar, tea, and coffee; details can be found in the *Journal of the Statistical Society*, XLIX (1886), 592–648.
³ See p. 319 below.
⁴ The numbers of cattle, pigs, and farm horses in England increased by 22, 18, and 19 per cent respectively; the number of sheep fell by 18 per cent, between 1868–71 and 1894–8.
⁵ W. T. Layton, *An Introduction to the Study of Prices* (1912), p. 150.

It is a commonplace that with rising income civilized man prefers to purchase the more expensive and appetizing proteins rather than the cheaper starches. And when, as during the Great Depression, the price of bread and cereals falls by more than the price of animal products, a growing fraction of income becomes available for expenditure on protein. Contemporary references to the changing pattern of food consumption abound and were neatly paraphrased by Graham in 1899 in his wellknown phrase, 'the sort of man who had bread and cheese for his dinner 40 years ago now demands a chop'.[1]

The effect on English farmers of this changing pattern of demand was naturally to stimulate the production of meat, milk, and dairy products at the expense of wheat and potatoes. Not that this shift began in the seventies. Since 1846 the price of meat and dairy products rose slowly relative to the price of wheat, but the prophesied flood of cereal imports was unexpectedly restricted until the seventies; it was in this decade that a revolutionary change in relative livestock and cereal prices began to be observed.[2]

Demand forms only one blade of the economist's 'abhorred shears': on the supply side a prominent feature of the period was the growth in food imports. The quantity of wheat and flour imported into the U.K. increased by 90 per cent, that of meat by 300 per cent, and that of butter and cheese by 110 per cent between 1871–5 and 1896–1900; the repercussions on home output were not, however, identical.

To judge from estimates of total supply available for consumption in the U.K., demand for wheat increased more slowly than population. Foreign supplies were plentiful following the opening up of virgin territory abroad and the fall in rail and shipping rates, and the price at English ports fell drastically. Wheat was to all intents a homogeneous product, it sold on the classic international wheat market, and the price received by the English farmer was a direct function of the world price; it fell from 56s. 0d. a quarter in 1867–71 to 27s. 3d. in 1894–8 [3] and was accompanied by a decline in the English acreage from over three to one and three quarter million acres.

The situation was different in the case of meat. Demand grew faster than population, and home output rose by some 10 per cent in spite of a severe thinning of the country's sheep flocks by outbreaks of disease in the years 1879–81. Imports were generally inferior in quality to the home product and priced accordingly, and price differentials widened over the period of the Great Depression.[4] Imports of butter and cheese, already considerable, increased further to satisfy the growth in consumer demand which, in face of the attractions of the lucrative liquid milk trade, could not be supplied by English farmers. Most foreign supplies on the English market fetched lower

---

[1] P. A. Graham, *The Revival of English Agriculture* (1899), p. 9.

[2] Early advocates of a change from corn to meat, dairy and green crop production include J. Caird, *English Agriculture in 1850–51* (1852), pp. 483–7 *passim* and G. Beasley, *A Report on the State of Agriculture in Lancashire* (Preston, 1849), who argued 'upon the presumption that permanently low prices of grain will in future be established' (p. 67).

[3] *Gazette* prices. The period 1867–71 is chosen, whenever possible, as more representative of pre-depression prices than say 1870–6 which covers the marked cyclical peak of the early seventies; 1894–8 is taken as the end of the depression in the trough of the nineties.

[4] For example, the price of best English beef at Smithfield between 1867–71 and 1894–8 fell by 11 per cent compared with imported fresh beef which fell by 23 per cent. Imported mutton was even less competitive; first quality light-weight mutton and lamb rose by eight per cent as against a fall in average import prices of some 30 per cent (*Agricultural Returns*).

prices than the home product and, as with meat, the price difference widened.¹ The responsible factor, apart from quality, was undoubtedly the price of liquid milk which, immune from foreign competition, shewed little or no overall fall. To generalize in terms of grave import competition reducing agricultural prices is inadmissible against a background of generally falling prices. Some farm prices fell, others did not; some fell in the seventies, others in the eighties and nineties.

A fourth group of imports was that comprising maize, coarse grains and oilcakes. In that the quantity imported doubled between 1867–71 and 1894–8, during which time the average price fell by about 40 per cent, whilst livestock numbers increased by only about 10 per cent,² a significant increase in productivity is suggested, in the form, for example, of higher yields per cow. The question is prompted, what changes occurred in the output of English agriculture during this period?

III

The one published estimate that provides sufficient data to check the various series contributing to the final sum is Dr Ojala's, and it is unfortunate that it is computed for the U.K. as a whole, so divergent were the interests and experiences of farmers in the four countries concerned, but the difficulty of allocating imports within the U.K. and the paucity of figures relating to Anglo-Irish trade may well justify Dr Ojala's decision in this respect. It is otherwise with some of his price series which rely overmuch on Sauerbeck's import prices, in particular for meat and dairy output. Using Dr Ojala's basic data but substituting home for import prices, a revised index of the U.K.'s gross farm output at current prices moves from 100 in 1867–9 to 108 in 1870–6 to 90 in 1894–1903.³ An estimate for England falls from 100 in 1867–71 to 87 in 1894–8.⁴

A net output calculation to determine the margin of farmers' profits is hazardous, in that small opposed movements of gross output and total costs squeeze or magnify the margin severely; nevertheless the subtraction may be attempted for the U.K. Deducting from the revised gross output figures for 1867–76 and 1894–1903 Dr Ojala's costs—to which must be added 'rent' and 'wages etc.' derived from Mr Bellerby's estimates—the total net income at current prices of U.K. farmers declined from £85·4 million to £79 million, a fall of some 7·5 per cent.⁵ In view of the predominance of imports in farm costs it is impossible to assign a figure to English farmers alone, but their fall in income was perhaps greater than in the U.K. as a whole, because of the

---

¹ Sauerbeck's best imported Friesland butter fell in price by 22 per cent between 1867–71 and 1894–8; Lancashire farm butter by about 13 per cent. Cheese imports declined in price by over 20 per cent; best Lancashire and Cheshire by some 10 per cent. (For Lancashire prices see my forthcoming article 'Lancashire Livestock Farming During the Great Depression' in *British Agricultural History Review*.)

² In terms of Livestock Units, which provide a method of adding different categories of livestock standardized in terms of feed requirements; see *Rations for Livestock*, Ministry of Agriculture, Bulletin No. 48.

³ Dr Ojala's estimates are for the groups of years 1867–9, 1870–6, 1877–85, 1886–93, 1894–1903.

⁴ For details see Appendix.

⁵ See J. R. Bellerby, *Agriculture and Industry Relative Income* (1956), Table 1, p. 56. These farmers' net income figures are of the same order of magnitude as those shewn by Dr Ojala (less Mr Bellerby's rent and wages), but are significantly larger than those computed by Mr Bellerby.

greater importance of wheat. Wales, Ireland and Scotland were predominantly livestock farming areas. It would seem, however, that although English farmers as a group did not, as did farm labourers,[1] manage to augment their money incomes during the Great Depression, although their real incomes appreciated, they did not suffer to the same extent as landowners, to judge by the fall in gross rents.[2] But in all these cases crude average figures mask crucial differences. The contrast between the movement of wages, rents, and profits in arable and livestock counties is noticeable. In the northern counties wages rose by some 17 per cent between 1867-71 and 1894-8; in the eastern counties the gain of the seventies was lost by the mid-nineties.[3] The experiences of landowners were more extreme; for example, the earl of Derby's Fylde rents, which rose by 18 per cent between 1870-1 and 1896, may be compared with those of the Cambridgeshire estates cited by Mr Rhee which declined by 35 per cent between the same dates.[4]

Profits are not directly measurable but output changes are. At constant 1894-8 prices, arable output declined from 1867-71 by about five per cent, livestock output increased by some 20 per cent; using 1867-71 prices the changes shew as -9 and $+18$ per cent, respectively. The fall in gross output, at current prices, is entirely accounted for by the decline of wheat, and if the gross output sum be divided into its two components, crops and livestock, the distinction is clear; whilst arable output declined from £65 million to £41 million, livestock output increased from £64 million to £71 million. On the eve of depression arable output equalled that of livestock; by the mid-nineties it was only three fifths its value. Wheat is pre-eminent in 1870; it accounts for nearly a half of total arable output and over a fifth of gross output, and equals in value beef and mutton together. By the mid-nineties wheat accounts for little over a sixth of the diminished arable output and has been surpassed not only by dairy produce, beef, mutton, and pigmeat severally but is rapidly being overhauled by poultry.[5] Thus, whilst livestock farmers increased their quantum of output appreciably and even significantly raised its value, wheat growers suffered the brunt of the price fall and cut back their acreage severely.

There are a number of considerations relevant to such a gross and net output computation. Firstly, helped by the greater freedom of cropping achieved by the tenant farmer during the period, an increasing proportion of cereal growers sold oats, hay, and straw off the farm as feed for non-farm horses the numbers of which in England may well have increased by as much as 50 per cent, although no census returns were collected after 1872.[6] Fertility was raised and yields increased on the shrinking arable acreage by the greater supplies of

---

[1] Whose wages on average rose by 11 per cent; see A. Wilson Fox, 'Agricultural Wages in England and Wales During the Last Fifty Years', *Journal of the Royal Statistical Society*, LXIV (1903).

[2] See Rhee, *op. cit.* Table II, pp. 44-6. Mr Rhee's rent series are heavily weighted by rents from the corn growing counties and thus probably overestimate the national average fall in rents.

[3] Wilson Fox, *loc. cit.*

[4] Lancs. R.O., DDK (Fylde Rents); Rhee, *op. cit.*

[5] See Appendix.

[6] Dr Ojala's estimate shews an insignificant increase in non-farm horses in G.B. during the Great Depression. The only available census figures are for Ireland, where the non-farm horses almost doubled in number. In that the population of England increased by roughly 50 per cent, as did both the volume of trade and of railway freight, an equivalent increase in the number of non-farm horses seems not improbable. For the numbers of non-farm horses 1831-72 inclusive, see *Report from the S.C. of the House of Lords on Horses*, H.C. 325 of 1873; it was called to investigate the 'alleged scarcity of horses in this country'.

town manure available, the growing numbers of farm livestock, the larger manurial residues from the growing import of feeding stuffs, and the increasing import of fertilizer.

Secondly, there were changes in the quality of products and in the relative quantities sold by farmers of the several qualities of a single product, themselves changing in relative price, as exemplified in the shift from wether mutton to lamb that is apparent from an analysis of sheep numbers given in the *Agricultural Returns*. And when this shift from a lower to a higher quality output is reinforced by a widening of the price differential in favour of the better qualities, an upward bias in farmers' returns results which is not reflected in a simple quantity times average price computation.

Thirdly, although the emphasis in this brief appraisal of the Great Depression is on the overall change between 1867–71 and 1894–8, a further contrast between livestock and crops emerges when the timing of price changes is considered. Corn prices plunged after 1874 from their 'Golden Age' plateau and never recovered, declining further in the mid-eighties and again in the mid-nineties. Livestock prices on the other hand rose rapidly in the sixties and early seventies and, apart from the one year 1879, hardly fell significantly from these new heights until the mid-eighties. Even then they did not fall below their 1867–71 level and the further fall in the mid-nineties was slight compared with that of cereal prices. In 1896 a corn grower could look back on over twenty years of almost continually falling prices; a livestock farmer would be gradually reacclimatizing to a price level regrettably somewhat lower than in the prosperous seventies and early eighties but not very different from that of twenty five or thirty years earlier, and in compensation he could always point to his lower feed costs.

Finally, there is the nature of the information provided by aggregate models of the gross output kind. An abstraction like the 'national farm' can neither suffer depression nor enjoy prosperity: suffering and joy are attributes of human beings, in this context of the thousands of farmers who form part of the agricultural community. What is ideally needed are the numbers of English farmers to whom wheat was the lynch pin of their systems and the numbers who were in livestock, in sheep, milk, or beef. At the one extreme were those livestock farmers who had abandoned the plough before or during the Great Depression, together with many others whose arable acreage was negligible. At the other extreme there were no farmers specializing solely in wheat, although a significant number, concentrated in certain localities such as the Fens, southwest Lancashire, and the neighbourhood of large towns, kept few if any livestock and were wholly dependent on the sale of arable crops such as corn, hay, straw, and potatoes. Between these extremes was to be found every conceivable type of farming, classifiable into two main groups, those farmers who relied primarily on the sale of corn and to whom livestock were principally a source of fertility,[1] and those mainly dependent on livestock and whose ploughing was ancillary to their needs. During the Great Depression the numbers in this second group increased as mixed farmers abandoned the plough or fed their corn to stock rather than sell it on the market.

---

[1] As late as 1867, J. J. Mechi, the well-known Essex farmer, was 'of the opinion that, although livestock do not pay directly, they are essential to the well-being of the farm as providers of the best and cheapest manure'; more categorically, 'will any livestock (pigs, sheep, or cattle) pay market price for their food? – No' (*Chester Courant*, 16 October 1867).

IV

Accurately to divide the total number of farmers in the country into these categories is impossible, but, as a first approximation, use can be made of the division of England into agricultural regions introduced into the *Agricultural Returns* in 1868. Basically this is a single division into the 'grazing' counties of the north and west and the 'corn' counties of the south and east, following a line not unlike that drawn by Caird [1] and an argument used by Cobbett [2] even earlier. There were of course arable farms in the grazing counties, but they were undoubtedly out-numbered by livestock farmers in the south and east, from the Lincolnshire and Leicestershire graziers, the dairymen of the midland vales and the environs of towns, to the sheep masters of Romney Marsh, with the result that a simple comparison of 'grazing' with 'corn' counties exaggerates the relative number of arable farmers. Nevertheless the comparison is worth making. The greater area, 18 million acres as against 14·5,[3] lay to the north and west and contained many more agricultural holdings over five acres in size, 172 thousand compared with 118 thousand in the south and east. The average size of these holdings was smaller in the 'grazing' counties, 70 acres as against 100 in the 'corn' counties,[4] as was the ratio of farm workers to farmers at approximately 220 : 100 compared with 600 : 100 in the south and east.[5] Justification for the descriptions 'grazing' and 'corn' applied to these two areas is provided by the statistics of crops and livestock. For example, the ten leading wheat growing counties were all situated in the east of the country and, although covering less than a quarter of the area of crops and grass in England, provided almost a half of the wheat acreage: at the other extreme, the ten counties with the highest numbers of milk cows contained between them practically a half of the country's total population of milk cows; these counties all lay in the north and west. The 'grazing' counties between them supported 68 per cent of England's milk cows,[6] that branch of farming which, together with hill sheep and their crosses, another activity predominant in the north and west, proved most continuously profitable during the Great Depression.

Without wishing to press the geographical division too closely, it is this distinction between the livestock farmer and the arable farmer that is crucial to an understanding of the Great Depression. It was not simply that arable farmers, mainly in the south and east, suffered a steep fall in the prices of their principal output products whilst livestock farmers, predominant in the north and west, enjoyed more favourable prices, but that every fall in the price of cereals, so damaging to corn growers, was to them, the livestock producers, clear gain, because it meant a reduction in the price of their most important input—feed. Further, every fall in the price of bread to the consumer, other things equal, stimulated the demand for livestock products. Livestock farmers gained on either hand and their economic interests were

---

[1] J. Caird, *op. cit.* map, p. 1.
[2] W. Cobbett, *Rural Rides* (1930), ed. G.D.H. and Margaret Cole, III, 696–9.
[3] These figures represent total acreage; the acreage of crops and grass (excluding rough grazing) was 12·0 million in the north and west, 11·8 million in the south and east.
[4] *Agricultural Returns*, 1885; all these figures are insignificantly different from those of the next size of holding investigation in 1895.
[5] Census of 1891.
[6] These comparisons refer to the year 1896; there is little difference between the nineties and the seventies, e.g. the figure quoted was 69 in 1872. For a geographer's views on this division see W. Smith, *An Economic Geography of Great Britain* (1949), p. 53 et seq.

aligned with those of the manufacturing population to the extent that cheap bread meant cheap livestock feed and an expanding industry meant full employment, high wages, and a stronger demand for meat, milk, eggs, and dairy products.[1] Attempts to assess the impact of the Great, or any other, depression upon agriculture considered as a single form of economic activity are not very meaningful. Agriculture in these islands is not one industry but several; in particular it consists in the two sectors, arable and livestock, whose aims are basically incompatible. Arable farmers want a high price for their output of cereals, hay, and straw: livestock producers want low cereal and fodder prices because corn is to them an input not an output.

This division was not of course a phenomenon suddenly emerging in the eighteen seventies; throughout our history, for geographical reasons, the east and south have yielded most of our corn, whereas the north and west have been in the main producers of livestock.[2] But in the second half of the nineteenth century two developments, on the one hand improvements in transport, the opening up of foreign supplies, and the extension of international trade, and on the other, rising living standards and changing patterns of food consumption among the working classes, helped to produce a situation in England in which livestock products were in rapidly growing demand, especially so relative to the arable bread and potatoes, and cheap cereals were in abundant supply.

This was the hard truth that faced English corn growers as the prophecies of thirty years earlier were demonstrably fulfilled in the seventies and eighties. There was no lack of warning in the agricultural press; contributors to the *Journal of the Royal Agricultural Society* in the sixties pointed to the growing importance of livestock farming [3] and in 1872 a leader writer in the *Agricultural Economist* went so far as to ask why grow corn at all? Why not pursue a rotation of two year's pasture, one year's meadow, and one year's green crop in order to keep more stock? But such a radical suggestion was premature and received the traditional reply, 'wheat and barley are the breakfast and dinner and something more to the farmer'.[4] The same belief was expressed, and with more justice, in the eighteen thirties; [5] it continued to be voiced by such as 'Squire' Chaplin, owner of some twenty three thousand Lincolnshire acres and for fifty years agriculture's spokesman in the House of Commons.[6]

The persistence among influential agriculturalists of this belief in the crucial importance of corn growing and the desirability, if inexpediency, of protection was paralleled by the persistence in the public mind of that tripartite image of an immutable English agriculture based on 'Squire', 'Giles', and 'Hodge' so beloved of successive generations of cartoonists. But was this general, 'official' picture adequately representative of the views and practices of the scores of

---

[1] This was explicitly recognized by some livestock farmers; for examples of anti-corn law, Free Trade farmers see W. Cooke Taylor, *Tour of the Manufacturing Districts* (1842), p. 87 and *Preston Guardian*, 27 September 1884, 10 December 1892, 13 April 1895.

[2] The implications of this division in the field of agrarian history are far reaching and little explored. Cf. the highland and lowland zones in R. G. Collingwood and J. N. L. Myers, *Roman Britain and the English Settlements* (2nd. ed. 1937), pp. 1–15.

[3] For example, *J.R.A.S.* 2nd. series, II (1866), p. 45.

[4] *Agricultural Economist*, 1 August 1872 and 1 September 1872.

[5] See *Report from the S.C. of the House of Lords on the State of Agriculture* (H.C. 464 of 1837), QQ. 528–9, 3267–3271.

[6] See, for example, *The Economist*'s report (5 December 1879) of 'Mr. Chaplin on Protection', and *R.C. 1879–82, Final Report*, C. 3309 of 1882, supplementary memorandum by H. Chaplin, pp. 37–8.

thousands of farmers throughout the country, few of whom subscribed to the agricultural journals,[1] and even fewer read *The Times, Punch,* or *The Economist,* and whose farming, to judge by the *Agricultural Returns* and the *Journal of the Royal Agricultural Society*,[2] was not in fact so indissolubly attached to wheat growing as one is led to believe? Whom in reality did 'Squire' Chaplin represent?

V

The weather of 1879 was so bad that in July Chaplin moved for a Royal Commission.[3] He was opposed by S. C. Read, member for South Norfolk and the only 'legitimate tenant farmer'[4] in the House. Read expressed the opinion that less corn and more grass should be grown, and cited Suffolk, which he said was all dairies before the Napoleonic War and should now be sown down again. It may be noted that Read lost his seat in the election of the following year. Chaplin's view prevailed and a commission was appointed. Its title was the Royal Commission on the Depressed State of the Agricultural Interest. Who or what was the 'Agricultural Interest'?

The members of the Commission were classified by the *Agricultural Economist* as four 'aristocrats',[5] including the chairman the duke of Richmond, and two 'landed gentry',[6] all of whom were extensive landowners south of the Trent, six 'others'[7] who 'may be considered farmers' representatives', together with two future Chancellors, G. J. Goschen and C. T. Ritchie, Bonamy Price and Sir William Stephenson, 'both great in political economy',[8] Joseph Cowen, M.P. for Newcastle,[9] and three spokesmen for Ireland.[10] Excluding the Irishmen, twelve of the seventeen members were directly concerned in or considered to be sympathetic to the fortunes of agriculture.

Assistant Commissioners went out to their selected districts. Druce, Assistant Commissioner for the Home Counties, was also secretary to the Farmer's Club, and, in December, attended an important meeting of the Central Chamber of Agriculture in London where it was decided that local associated chambers should be circularized and local committees formed to furnish Assistant

---

[1] The *Agricultural Economist* (1 February 1882) was of the opinion that 'farmers do not read'; it declared itself the only paying agricultural journal on the occasion of Morton's appeal, as editor, for more readers, in the *Agricultural Gazette* (26 December 1881).

[2] The Farm Prize Reports in the *J.R.A.S.* between 1870 and 1891 illustrate the diversity of English farming.

[3] This was not universal; for instance, a Cornish farmer later asserted that 1879 was his best year (*R.C. 1894-7*, Q. 37432).

[4] *Agricultural Economist*, 1 August 1879.

[5] The duke of Richmond (1818–1903), the 'farmers' friend', Lord President of the Council and first chairman of its agricultural committee, 1884; the duke of Buccleuch; earl Spencer and lord Vernon, the former also a member of the Privy Council's agricultural committee. For this classification see *Agricultural Economist*, 1 September 1879.

[6] Chaplin and Col. R.N.F. Kingscote, chairman of the finance committee of the R.A.S. and governor of the Royal Agricultural College, for whose family background see *Gloucestershire Studies*, ed. H.P.R. Finberg (Leicester, 1957), pp. 159–173.

[7] C. Howard, Wm. Stratten, J. Wilson (later Agricultural Adviser to the Board of Agriculture and Director of the Land Division), H. Rodwell, J. Clay, R. Patterson.

[8] Price was Drummond Professor at Oxford; Stephenson began his career with a clerkship in the Treasury in 1827 and was for fifteen years chairman of the Inland Revenue Board.

[9] Described in *Who Was Who* (1897–1916) as an 'old radical, imperialist, and anti-socialist', and assumed by the *Agricultural Economist* to be the 'representative of the working man' on the Commission.

[10] M. Henry, J. L. Naper, J. Rice.

Commissioners with the 'facts' and to 'select men who could supply the information required, viz., evidence of fall in profit or fall in output or rise in cost of production'.[1] Besides Druce, two other Assistant Commissioners were present at this London meeting and, after some debate, the Chamber's business committee was instructed to 'observe' all this activity because some members of the committee served on the Commission and were thus unable to 'act'.

Among the witnesses called before the Richmond Commission, together with landowners, land agents for both individuals and corporate bodies, civil servants and others, were 35 farmers, almost all tenants. Of these 35 only one farmed less than 100 acres, 31 farmed more than 300 acres, 25 of them farming more than 500 and ten more than 1000, at a time when the average size of farm in England was perhaps less than 100 acres.[2] It is also illuminating to notice where these witnesses farmed. Twenty-six came from the 'corn' counties of the east and south and nine from the 'grazing' counties of the north and west; only four of the 35 hailed from north of the Trent, and of these four, two farmed in the arable East Riding. The ten leading wheat growing counties produced between them 14 witnesses; the ten leading dairy counties contributed only five.

Decided views and attitudes regarding, for instance, size of farm—270 acres was described as 'small'—and the nature of agriculture—almost synonymous with corn growing—were unconsciously revealed.[3] Moreover, as appears in their questioning of witnesses, members of the Commission assumed *a priori* that depression was general, and much of their interrogation consisted in the kind of amicable discussion, with hearsay evidence prominent, of the weather, markets, taxes, yields, diseases, and so on that is indulged in at all times among farmers, agents, merchants and others of the agricultural community when all participants share a common interest and expertise.[4]

Thus with the Commission itself firmly led by the landowning aristocracy and gentry, all with large properties in the south and midlands, with farmers' views screened and organized by the Central and Associated Chambers of Agriculture whose headquarters, like those of the Farmers' Club and the Royal Agricultural Society, were in London, with farmer witnesses overwhelmingly reflecting the interests of corn growers, and with almost all concerned sharing a similar set of assumptions as to the nature of English agriculture, a fairly clear idea emerges of what was meant by the 'agricultural interest' and of where its centre of gravity lay.

The evidence before the Commission shewed that the immediate cause of depression was the weather, and that the only price fall, other than the short lived general fall of 1879, was that of wheat which no longer rose in price as compensation for a diminished output. Nevertheless the view prevailed that depression was universal, 'no description of estate or tenure has been exempted',[5] and critics of this view received short shrift.[6]

---

[1] *Agricultural Economist*, 1 December 1879. In its *Final Report* the Commission put on record its view that the 'evidence [was] collected, we believe, with the greatest care and impartiality' (*R.C. 1879–82*, C.3309 of 1882, p. 33).

[2] No precise figure is available, but the average size of 'holding over five acres' in England, according to the *Agricultural Returns*, was 84 acres in both 1885 and 1895.

[3] *R.C. 1879–82*, QQ.49768–9, 33138–9.

[4] *Ibid.* QQ.33109–10, 138.

[5] *R.C. 1879–82, Preliminary Report*, C.2778 of 1881, p. 24.

[6] As, for example, did Giffen on calculating that agriculture's gross output had fallen by no more than six per cent between 1870 and 1880 (*ibid.* Q.64733 foll; *The Times*, 7 January 1882).

In its *Final Report* the Commission listed an impressive number of burdens on the farmer, including tithe and local rates, farm labour which was increasingly costly and, as always, less efficient—the 'very widespread complaint among farmers that the present system of education operates prejudicially to the interests of agriculture', meaning simply that children were kept at school when they might be 'usefully employed upon the farm',[1] rents that had been unduly raised, railway rates that discriminated in favour of imports and so on. The numerous recommendations ranged from a 'shift in the incidence of Local Taxation from real property to the Consolidated Fund'[2] to the desirability of one public department for agriculture. The government in its turn did little beyond introduce a second Agricultural Holdings Act in 1883, approve Lord Cairn's Settled Land Bill in the following year, and in 1889 create a Board of Agriculture.[3] By how much all this raised farmers' incomes is a nice question.

However the weather improved, prices held, the threat of imports seemed to slacken, and grumbling among themselves, the agricultural interest carried on, some in new ways, others in the old. Prices, and this time including livestock prices, fell in the mid-eighties but subsequently recovered somewhat and the later eighties witnessed some mild rejoicing.[4] The next outcry had to await another bout of deplorable weather initiated by the drought of 1893. But the weather experienced in different parts of the country varied even more markedly than in the seventies; in 1893 London experienced 114 days without rain, Manchester and Stoneyhurst only 30,[5] whilst in north Derbyshire the 'oldest inhabitant could scarcely remember a more productive year'.[6] Nevertheless the cry of distress was formidable and a second Royal Commission was granted; against the advice of *The Economist* which maintained that, in respect of what might be *done*, the Richmond Commission had already elicited all the facts, that no new developments had occurred, and that another Commission would merely waste time and money:[7] but time on occasion can be a valuable commodity to government.

VI

The members of the new Commission appointed by Gladstone's government were a mixed body compared with their predecessors. The 'aristocracy' had shrunk to lords Cobham and Rendel, the one a liberal Lyttleton, the other an ex-engineer, although the 'landed gentry' were still powerfully represented in the persons of Chaplin, Kingscote, and W. H. Long.[8] The Commons also provided the chairman, Shaw-Lefevre,[9] first commissioner of works with a seat in the Cabinet, R. L. Everett, an East Anglian farmer, and F. A. Chan-

---

[1] R.C. *1879–82, Final Report*, p. 27.
[2] *Ibid.* p. 25.
[3] Of which Chaplin was first president with a seat in the Cabinet.
[4] See the annual reviews of the preceding year in the *Agricultural Economist* of 1 January for 1889, 1890, and 1891.
[5] Weather statistics from *J.R.A.S.* LXIV (1893), 849–856.
[6] R.C. *1894–7*, Q.5133.
[7] *The Economist*, 15 July 1893.
[8] The Long estate of some 14,000 acres in Wiltshire was of ancient descent; for the family see *V.C.H. Wiltshire*, VII (1953), index, 233–4.
[9] G. J. Shaw-Lefevre (1831–1928); lord Eversley, 1906; ex-member of the Privy Council's agricultural committee, and a member of every Liberal government, except Gladstone's of 1885, since 1866. In lord Rosebery's administration of 1894–5 Shaw-Lefevre remained in the Cabinet as president of the Local Government Board.

ning,[1] ex-chairman of the Central and Associated Chambers of Agriculture, also, and untypically, Liberals. The Civil Service contributed R. Giffen, late of *The Economist* and now at the Board of Trade, C. N. Dalton, an expert on local government taxation, and C. Whitehead, technical adviser to the Board of Agriculture. The Committee was completed by W. C. Little, another East Anglian farmer and late Assistant Commissioner to the Richmond Commission, G. Lambert, C. I. Elton, a lawyer, O. Thomas from Wales, and J. Gilmour and J. Clay from Scotland.

As compared with the Richmond Commission, agriculture's representatives had both declined in number and changed in character. Whereas in the seventies leadership of the agricultural interest was firmly in the hands of the landed aristocracy, prominent in the House of Lords and the Privy Council, in the nineties the farming interest was struggling to wean itself from the now politically embarrassing aristocracy and to make its voice heard in the more hostile Commons. The establishment of a Board of Agriculture in 1889 opened a new avenue of advance for the agricultural interest via Whitehall and 'delegated legislation'.

Change is also noticeable among the farmer witnesses; not perhaps in terms of size of farm, as only five of the 39 whose acreage is known farmed less than 300 acres and 27 farmed more than 500 acres, but certainly in their regional dispersion. The majority, 22, still came from the east and south, but the north and west were now represented by no fewer than 18, and although the corn counties provided 13 witnesses, the dairy counties followed them close with 12.

Happily for the agricultural interest the Conservatives were returned in June 1895 and the balance of power within the Commission shifted decisively. Chaplin and Long joined the government as presidents of the Local Government Board and the Board of Agriculture respectively, Everett and Channing moved into opposition, and the chairman, Shaw-Lefevre, lost both office and seat.

Conflict of interest among the members of the Commission was apparent on the publication, after nearly two years work, of the second report in February 1896. Although the chief cause of depression was 'unanimously attributed' to the fall in prices,[2] the majority Report, with Cobham,[3] Chaplin, Long, and Kingscote as leading signatories, was expressly confined to a discussion of rates and land tax and the question of State loans to agriculture. It concluded with a nasty rider to the effect that 'it would be inexpedient for any member of the commission to submit for presentation to the Secretary of State a counter report or memorandum in connexion with the ad interim report agreed to by the members of the commission dealing with questions which have not been considered by the commission'.[4] A minority of three, led by the chairman, now clearly powerless to curb Chaplin and Long, and backed by Rendel and Giffen, expressed their disgust at this majority resolution and ignored it. Their own position was clear. 'The depression has been and still is far more serious in the eastern and southern counties of England, over an area of rather more than one third of England and Wales, than in the other parts of Great

---

[1] Author of *The Truth About Agricultural Depression* (1897).

[2] *R.C. 1894–7, Second Report*, C.7981 of 1896, p. 7. The first report of one page appeared in May 1894 as C.7400 of 1894; cf. *The Economist*, 7 March 1896, pp. 290–2 – 'Divided Counsels on Agricultural Relief'.

[3] It would seem that Cobham's support was less than wholehearted in view of what Sir H. Fowler in the Commons described as his 'singular reservation' disagreeing with any reduction in the rate of assessment of land (*Parliamentary Debates*, 4th ser. XXXIX, 20 April 1896).

[4] *R.C. 1894–7, Second Report*, p. 21.

Britain'.¹ The causes of this were (1) the east and south suffered unfavourable seasons beginning in 1892 and including two years, 1893 and 1895, of exceptional drought, the former being 'quite unprecedented', whilst the north and west had 'enjoyed far more favourable conditions'; (2) the east and south suffered greater in proportion because they were the chief wheat growing districts; (3) there was a comparative absence of small farms in the south and east and small farmers had done better owing to a preponderance of family labour, more attention to smaller products, and more dairying than corn growing; (4) 'burdens on land' in the south and east in the shape of tithe, land tax, and local rates were as a rule much heavier.²

The minority then proceeded to discuss prices, wages, and remedial measures, which latter, as might be expected, were limited to landlord-tenant agreements, rent levels, railway rates, 'co-operation with a view to getting rid of middlemen' and the mitigation of some of the grosser inequalities of the so-called 'burdens on land'. This was as much as could be done 'short of tampering with the currency, debasing the gold standard, or adopting protective duties'.³ The intrepid trio then demolished the 'burdens on land' case by shewing that in fact the 'burdens' had diminished, and the chairman, in a supplementary solo, stated, 'there appears to be a general impression among farmers and others connected with the agricultural interest that the actual average payments in respect of local rates on land have considerably increased during the last 25 years. This however is not in accord with the facts supplied from official sources, or with the experience of the great majority of individual cases so far as they have been laid before the Commission'.⁴ Two months later, in April 1896, Shaw-Lefevre resigned.

The gravamen of Shaw-Lefevre's charge against the majority of the Commission was that Chaplin and Long privately prepared an Agricultural Rating Bill at the Local Government Board and then bulldozed the Royal Commission into endorsing its recommendations in the fortnight between the 26 January, when they first acquainted the Commission with their plan, and the 11 February when Chaplin, ignoring Shaw-Lefevre's plea for longer consideration, gave notice in the Commons of his intention to introduce the Bill. In Shaw-Lefevre's words, bearing in mind the 'constitution of the Royal Commission, how could they refuse a scheme for relieving land of three quarters of its rates put before it by the government?' ⁵

The *Final* (majority) *Report* in 1897 ⁶ under the signature of Cobham as chairman, and which was almost rivalled in bulk by memoranda, reservations and two impressive minority reports, took the form of a tour of the country and vindicated Shaw-Lefevre's views. Beginning with Essex, the worst hit county, eight pages described the 'corn' counties; two sufficed for the 'grazing' counties. Recommendations were insubstantial and the only concrete financial

---

¹ *R.C. 1894–7, Second Report*, p. 22.
² *Ibid.*
³ *Ibid.* p. 23.
⁴ *Ibid.* p. 32.
⁵ *The Times*, 27 April 1896; for the controversy between Shaw-Lefevre and Chaplin see *The Times*, 29 and 30 April and 1 May, and *Parliamentary Debates*, 4th ser. XXXIX, 27 April, when Chaplin referred to Shaw-Lefevre's letter in *The Times* and was strongly attacked by the opposition.
⁶ *R.C. 1894–7, Final Report*, C.8540 of 1897.

measure was the Agricultural Rates Act of 1896,[1] the result of the Commission's two year deliberation of the 'burdens on land'.

The *Final Report* is a discordant compendium of many voices. Pertinent questioning by Liberals and free traders, who were not prepared to accept uncritically the agricultural interest's cry of a ruined agriculture, disclosed new problems and discredited some of the evidence. For example, Giffen's survey of world agricultural output unexpectedly revealed that the supply of wheat was not running ahead of population and therefore the fall in price must have been due to restricted demand.[2] Farm accounts submitted to the Commission as evidence of depression were criticized as unrepresentative, '50 of the 69 [which 'gave sufficient detail to enable them to be checked'] relate to the eight chief corn growing, and therefore most depressed, counties, and the whole 69 are collected from only 16 of the 52 counties of England and Wales'. In the same context, the sceptical view is expressed that 'opinions of tenant farmers ... cannot, any more than those of landlords and agents, be accepted as the views of disinterested witnesses'.[3]

For all the gathering and sifting of evidence no common understanding of the decisive changes that were occurring in the agriculture of the western world is to be observed among the members of the Commission. In particular, although the *Final Report* was cast in the form of a comparison of the north and west with the east and south, the Commission seemed curiously blind to the full implications of this contrast. The differential fall in farm prices, the growth of dairying and so on were pointed to and no more; out of nearly two hundred pages exactly two were devoted to production costs and these included three paragraphs only on feeding stuffs and manures.[4] That the fall in price of feed relative to changes in the price of livestock products during the great depression was of more importance to livestock farmers than this space apportionment would indicate is suggested by what may be termed the livestock: feed price ratio, which expresses the relationship between the average of dairy and livestock prices and the cost of feed in the two periods 1867–71 and 1894–8. It moved in the producer's favour from 100 to about 150.[5]

VII

Very clearly the basic conflict of interest, felt rather than formulated, between the two main groups of English farmers, and masked by the ambivalent rural-urban, protection-free trade division, prevented the formulation of any co-ordinated view, any single, forceful, agricultural policy, any effective co-operation.[6] And in the absence of unanimity, with on the one hand a declining

[1] 59 & 60 Vict. Cap. 16; by which the Exchequer was to contribute annually a sum equal to half the amount raised from agricultural land in 1895.

[2] *Final Report*, App. V. p. 73; 'people consume less cereals per head because with increase of resources, they consume more meat, which *pro tanto* displaces the cereals'.

[3] *Ibid.* pp. 118–19. The Commission was also interested to know why 'in 16 instances (seven of which refer to Essex), profits were earned between 1889 and 1894 from five to 24 per cent on the capital employed, the rents ranging from 9s. 7d. to 34s. 5d. per acre'.

[4] *R.C. 1894–7, Final Report*, pp. 87–9, paras. 313–15.

[5] Average livestock and dairy prices are assumed to have fallen by 10 per cent; the cost of imported maize and oilcakes fell by 40 per cent.

[6] The great London agricultural conference of December 1892, convened by the Central Chamber of Agriculture and addressed by Chaplin and Lowther, split on the question of protection which Prof. J. P. Sheldon described as the '*ignis fatuus* leading our southern and eastern farmers away from their true interests' (*The Future of British Agriculture* (1893), p. 142). A similar conflict obtained among the members of the Royal Commission on Agriculture of 1919–20 over the problem of whether to continue government support of corn prices (see *Interim Report*, Cmd. 473 of 1919).

corn growing interest nostalgically looking to the past and on the other hand thousands of livestock farmers—with the small hard-working family farmer in the majority, motivated by profit and with a keen eye to the main chance—quietly increasing their output with the aid of cheap, imported cereals, the vacuum left by these divergent interests was easily filled by the confused idealism of Free Land Leaguers, Georgists and anti-landlord radicals, bimetallists, and all the advocates of peasant ownership, small holdings, and the return to the land.

Finally, it may be asked why, if arable farming did not pay and livestock farming did, East Anglian corn growers persisted in unprofitable practices? The short answer is that time was needed to distinguish an apparent cycle from an unmistakeably secular trend, and it may be argued that a certain rigidity, not merely of system but of mind, was the penalty paid by the third generation for the undoubted success of their forebears' 'Norfolk system'. The earl of Leicester, son of the great Coke, grassed down his home farm and ran sheep at a profit, but, as he explained in a letter to Shaw-Lefevre, he almost despaired of his tenants having the sense to follow his example.[1] As a Lancashire farmer observed after touring Essex in 1896, 'new-comers are going in for milk, cheese, butter, fruit, and sheep but with the average Essex farmer it is corn, corn, corn'.[2] The difference in attitude is apparent in the evidence of farmers and landowners before the two Royal Commissions. Some, and not only in the north, farmed for the market and produced only that which paid them to do so; others continued in the ways of their fathers.[3]

The outcry died down as the century drew to its close and the agricultural interest learned to accept, if not embrace, the new England. Apart from the social problems associated with the spread of urban values and the political decline of the landed interest, what, in the narrower economic field, did the Great Depression achieve? It dethroned 'orient and immortal wheat' and turned English farmers in a new direction, that is to the production of quality livestock products. It inflicted suffering on a particular section of farmers, the large corn growers. Output figures shew that agriculture was not ruined; on the contrary an important internal revolution was effected during a period of falling prices. Seemingly unheedful of the cries of distress that sounded for over twenty years, the majority of farmers pursued the path of self interest as they saw it; others, protesting loudly or lamenting quietly, were impelled by the logic of their bank balances to change their systems; some few, to whom cowkeeping, the laying down to grass, or the selling of hay and straw were distasteful violations of the canon, went to the wall.[4] It needed war or the threat of war to revive their kind.[5]

University of Manchester.

[1] *R.C. 1894–7*, C7400 of 1896 IV, 596–7.
[2] *Preston Guardian*, 24 October 1896.
[3] See also the examples of successful farming during the depression described in the minority reports of Lambert and Channing (*R.C. 1894–7, Final Report*, pp. 204–379), and by Shaw-Lefevre (*ibid*. C.7400 of 1896, IV, 611–14); for instances of change in Essex, see R. Hunter Pringle's series of articles in the *Agricultural Gazette* of 1887, July onwards, especially 10 October 1887.
[4] This latter frame of mind is well treated in the earlier novels of A. G. Street, as, for example, in *The Gentleman of the Party* (1936).
[5] The traditional view of farmers as men who grow corn persisted into the twentieth century. For example, the first effective post-1921 legislation gave help to sugar beet (1925) and wheat (1932), such was the persuasive, political power of the 'voice of Norfolk' against which Viscount Astor and Dr K. A. H. Murray pleaded vigorously in the nineteen thirties (see *Land and Life* (1932) and *The Planning of Agriculture* (1933)).

APPENDIX

Two gross output estimates, one for the agriculture of the U.K. and one for that of England, have been computed. They are based on Dr Ojala's work, the main change being the substitution of more appropriate home prices for the Sauerbeck series of import prices used by Dr Ojala, in the case of Hay and Straw, Fruit, Vegetables, Beef, Mutton, Pigmeat, Milk, Poultry and Eggs. Beef and Mutton prices are based on the Smithfield series of home produced beef and mutton given in *Agricultural Statistics*. Milk and Poultry and Egg prices are derived from material in *Report on Wholesale and Retail Prices in the U.K.* (1903), the two Royal Commissions of 1879–82 and 1894–7, and Lancashire sources (see *supra*, p. 320 n. 1). The Hay and Straw, Fruit, Vegetables, and Pigmeat prices are estimated from data in *Agricultural Statistics*, Lancashire newspapers, and *Agricultural Statistics of Ireland* 1910 (Cd. 5882). Revised quantities for the output of Oats and Hay and Straw follow from the re-estimate of the numbers of non-farm horses (*supra*. p. 321 n. 6) and of Potatoes from a reconsideration of the Irish potato crop.

The final series are not claimed to be definitive; in particular the dairy, the poultry and the fruit and vegetable outputs could be improved by the discovery of further prices and by the estimation of more accurate quantities. It is considered, however, that these crude alterations to Dr Ojala's estimates contribute to a more realistic measure of the Great Depression. Details of individual series and of methods of estimation may be obtained from the author.

The Gross Output of the Agriculture of the U.K. and England (£ million)

	U.K.			England	
	1867–9	1870–6	1894–1903	1867–71	1894–8
Wheat	35·38	27·56	7·72	28·44	7·64
Barley	16·78	17·56	9·43	12·62	7·54
Oats	10·54	9·07	8·07	4·28	4·23
Potatoes	14·02	13·82	11·34	3·00	3·00
Hay & Straw, Fruit, Vegetables	20·11	19·40	21·75	14·00	17·00
Other crops	7·34	7·58	3·64	3·09	2·06
ARABLE	104·17	94·99	61·95	65·43	41·47
Beef	34·90	45·67	42·05	14·59	16·02
Mutton	25·92	30·51	25·20	14·60	12·59
Pigmeat	18·60	22·95	19·13	9·59	10·52
Horses	1·50	2·00	3·00	1·00	2·00
Milk	33·78	38·51	43·56	15·40	20·29
Wool	7·49	8·27	3·24	5·62	2·36
Poultry & Eggs	4·57	6·96	10·00	3·50	7·00
LIVESTOCK	126·76	154·87	146·18	64·30	70·78
TOTAL	230·93	249·86	208·13	129·73	112·25
Index	100	108	90	100	87

POSTSCRIPT

I don't know of any 'more recent work' that is not familiar and the only change in my views worth recording is that I believe, more strongly than ever, that advances in historical understanding, of the Great Depression or of any other problem, will be achieved by the proper and imaginative use of language, with all that this implies in terms of training, tradition and sources, rather than by whoring after 'numeracy' and tagging at the coat-tails of econometricians.

T. W. F.

THE DISTRIBUTION OF FARM INCOME IN THE U.K. 1867–1938

J. R. Bellerby

Distribution of Farm Income in the United Kingdom, 1867-1938

J. R. BELLERBY

It appears to be well established that in its consequences for farm workers the Golden Age of Agriculture by no means deserved this title, for price increases offset much of the rise in cash wages before 1873; and it is known that in the later depression, when conditions for farmers were catastrophic, those agricultural labourers who still retained their employment gained considerably from the fall in prices. The position was reversed in 1896-1920 when farmers at times again prospered greatly; and from 1920 onwards both parties suffered, though not in the same degree. An account of agricultural welfare during such periods would not be representative if it were based solely on trends in farm income as a whole. Distinction would seem desirable at least between the farmers' and farm workers' income, and if possible between the return to property and to human effort.

The need for breaking down farm income has arisen on several other grounds during the Institute's enquiry into the relationships between agriculture and industry. Following the decision to study this question, a review of the farm and non-farm income statistics of selected countries showed that for many decades before 1939 there had been a large difference in the return per head in the two spheres; and it was decided to study first the economic and social causes underlying the difference. Since a separate system of causes affects the return to each factor of production, it was necessary to distinguish the share of each as far as possible.

Moreover, in the comparison of the rewards in farm and non-farm enterprise it seemed desirable to compare the farmer's income with as many indexes as possible of non-farm income, including industrial average wages. For such a purpose the appropriate income is the return to the farmer for effort and enterprise, excluding all revenue from property.

This return is described here, for brevity, as the farmer's 'incentive income'. The term arose from consideration of the economic calculations made by any entrepreneur when facing a choice of occupation. In deciding whether to enter one trade in preference to another, he compares the prospective net revenue from each, after making allowance for a fair return on capital invested. This net revenue is the measure of the financial incentive attracting 'enterprise' as such.

The chief preparation needed for the study of relative income was therefore to construct a historical series of the farmer's incentive income, with a view to comparing this with various categories of non-farm income.

With the farmers are included their relatives actively engaged on the work of the farm. For purposes of estimating their income per man-equivalent, the women[1] in the group are assessed at two-thirds of a man-unit and the youths at two-thirds or three-quarters according to the dividing age between youths and adults. The aggregate incentive income of the group is obtained by the deduction, from the total factor income of agriculture, of net rent, interest on tenant's capital, and the wages or incentive income of all active farm personnel not included in the farmer-and-relative group.[2]

Table I gives the conclusions in summary. The estimates in all tables are averages for groups of years, each group representing a fairly well-defined economic phase, described in the following notes. The information obtained on crops is not comprehensive before 1884.

Period	Principal Features
1850–1857	Rising prices from 1851. High employment. Beginning of the Golden Age of Agriculture, with good harvests from 1852.
1858–1866	A period of fluctuation including two trade cycles. Severe depression and falling prices, 1858. Thereafter, quick recovery and later slight recession. Good yields, 1858, 1863–5.
1867–1873	Prices initially stable but rising rapidly in a general inflationary movement, 1870–3. Variable crops.
1874–1878	Good yields. Generally declining prices. End of the Golden Age. Year of transition, 1878.
1879–1883	Trade crisis and exceptionally bad harvest in 1879, leading to the great depression in agriculture. Persistently low farm prices, 1880–3.
1884–1896	Falling prices, 1884–7, 1893–6. Unemployment severe except in 1889–91 and 1896. Grain imports depress the market.
1897–1910	General recovery of prices, with slight recessions in 1901

[1] Female relatives are excluded entirely before 1901 for Great Britain and before 1926 for Ireland—see F. D. W. Taylor, 'Numbers in agriculture', *Farm Economist*, VIII, No. 4 (1955), 36–40.

[2] The *residual* character of the incentive income should be emphasized as having a bearing on the discussion at many points. Partly because it is defined as a residual amount, this category of income reflects the greater part of the fluctuation in total agricultural income. Interest, as assessed, shows only gradual change; aggregate net rent and wages are in fact comparatively stable quantities. When these have been deducted from total farm income, the residue is the return for the manual effort, management and enterprise of the farmer and his relatives, and ordinarily shows wide annual variation.

and 1908. Improving yields. High employment except in 1908–9. Beginning of the phase of tranquillity, 1902 onwards.

1911–1914   Culmination of the upward price movement, 1913. Fair harvests except in 1912. End of tranquillity.

1923–1929   General post-war depression following deflation. Battle of the Gold Standard. High interest rates. Persistently falling farm prices, 1923–7. Some advance in yields.

1930–1932   Crisis and intense depression. Gold Standard abandoned, 1931. Bad harvests, 1930–1.

1933–1935   Price recovery. Diminishing unemployment. Better harvests. Unprecedented and increasing Government aid to agricultural organization and finance. Falling interest rates.

1936–1938   Culmination of general wholesale price recovery, 1937. Further development of agricultural support policy. Low interest rates. Some reaction in industry and agriculture, 1937–8.

1939–1945   War.

1946–   Full employment. High and rising prices.

TOTAL FACTOR INCOME OF AGRICULTURE

Total farm income, Table I, col. 1, was obtained by the subtraction, from the gross agricultural output of the United Kingdom, of the value of inputs bought from outside the 'national farm', and by other adjustments. Annual series of gross output from 1867 to 1938 were compiled —mainly from the *Agricultural Statistics, Censuses of Agricultural Output*, the *Abstracts of Statistics* and professional journals—separately for wheat, oats, barley, potatoes, other vegetables, milk and milk products, cattle, sheep, pigs and eleven other principal products, and for a residual miscellaneous group comprising mainly game, rabbits, flowers and nursery stock. Inputs separately assessed include feeding-stuffs, fertilizers, seed, store livestock, machinery, fuel and repairs, and maintenance expenses. Both Ojala and Boreham relied to a considerable extent on J. H. Kirk's valuations of input given in the June 1946 issue of the *A.E.S. Journal*, and worked back from these with the aid of indexes of change.

The subtraction of input from gross output leaves a figure which needs adjustment in three ways to give the net income estimate in col. 1. First, rates and taxes on land, together with tithe,[1] have been deducted, and subsidies direct to farmers have been added. Secondly, the self-supplies of farmers have been raised to a retail valuation. When the 'gross output' of a farm product is measured either by a disappearance formula or by

[1] See J. R. Bellerby and F. D. W. Taylor, 'Aggregate tithe rentcharge on farm land in the United Kingdom, 1867–1938', *J.A.E.*, February 1955.

TABLE I

UNITED KINGDOM: DISTRIBUTION OF FARM INCOME, 1867-1938

	Total Factor Income of Agriculture	Net Rent		Interest on Occupiers' Capital		Wages, etc.		Farmers' and Relatives' Incentive Income*			Farm Labourers' Weekly Earnings‡	Ratio (10):(11)	Ratio Including Interest§
	(1) £ mil.	(2) Aggregate £ mil.	(3) %	(4) Aggregate† £ mil.	(5) %	(6) Aggregate £ mil.	(7) %	(8) Aggregate £ mil.	(9) %	Per-man week (10) £	(11) £	(12) %	(13) %
Annual Average Including all Ireland													
1867-1873	150·7	35·2	23	20·0	13	53·4	35	42·1	28	·998	·653	153	225
1874-1878	149·0	36·4	24	20·3	14	54·4	37	37·9	25	·837	·738	113	174
1879-1883	121·9	32·8	27	16·7	14	48·7	40	23·7	19	·490	·724	68	115
1884-1896	112·3	26·0	23	14·6	13	44·5	40	27·2	24	·562	·728	77	119
1897-1910	119·2	23·0	19	14·3	12	43·6	37	38·3	32	·786	·804	98	134
1911-1914	143·4	26·5	18	17·6	12	47·6	33	51·7	36	1·084	·874	124	166
Excluding Eire													
1923-1929	165·6	22·3	13	29·8	18	67·6	41	45·9	28	1·823	1·582	115	190
1930-1932	148·2	18·5	12	24·2	16	64·0	43	41·6	28	1·733	1·560	111	176
1933-1935	166·6	17·4	10	18·0	11	60·7	36	70·5	42	2·947	1·552	190	238
1936-1938	169·0	20·0	12	17·8	11	62·3	37	68·9	41	2·880	1·713	168	212

* See footnote 2, p. 262.
† The varying current rate of interest has been applied to estimates of tenants' capital.
‡ Calculated from the wage rates of ordinary farm labourers, adjusted for excess of earnings over basic rates, and for fluctuations in employment imputed from evidence of the variation of industrial unemployment.
§ Ratio of farmers' and relatives' income, including interest, per man-week, to farm labourers' weekly earnings—see text, p. 269.
Because of rounding, the constituents in cols. (2) – (9) do not always add to totals in col (1) or to 100%.

the estimation of total production less seed, feed and waste, the amount consumed by the farm personnel is automatically included in the figure of gross output; but unless correction is made later the valuation is at farm realization prices. The correction in Boreham's estimates was based for much of the earlier period on records contained in reports of the Royal Commission on Agriculture of 1896. Information which the Northern Ireland Department of Agriculture were good enough to supply in considerable detail, and the Eire official paper, P 7356, *National Income and Expenditure*, 1938–44, show that in Ireland self-supplies have formed a particularly high proportion of farm income. Data in the 1937–8 Family Budget enquiry assist in determining the margin between the farm gate and retail prices of the commodities chiefly composing the self-supplies. Thirdly, adjustments have been made for changes in stocks held on farms. No amendment is needed where the estimate of gross output is based on total production less feed on farms, seed and waste, for such an estimate shows the result of the year's productive activity regardless of whether the product is held in store or sold. A disappearance formula, as applied to livestock, leads however to an estimate of gross *realized* output, and in order to bring this into conformity with the concept of the total yield of the year's effort, adjustment for inventory changes is necessary. Stock increases have been valued as far as possible according to the price prevailing at the time of later realization.

RENT

As a step towards the measurement of agricultural net rent, an estimate of gross rent is first needed; for this, two types of data have been used. Gross rent may be determined as the product of average rent per acre and total acreage if enough is known about the rents for different sizes of farms and the separate acreage of cultivated and rough land. For England and Wales this method gives good results, but it cannot be used independently for Scotland or Ireland.

The alternative is to take as basis the Inland Revenue assessments of the 'annual value' of land and adjust them to conform to a suitable definition of gross rent. The annual value of all farm land in the United Kingdom has been periodically assessed for income tax for more than a century, and the total valuations appear under 'Schedule A' in the Inland Revenue's *Annual Reports*. In England and Wales the basis of the assessment is, broadly, the best rent that could be obtained on a year-to-year tenancy if the landlord undertook repairs and the tenant paid the rates; in other words, it corresponds to gross rent in concept, though in fact the assessments *exclude* farm dwellings occupied by the owners, and all farm cottages, and *include* certain non-farm land such as pleasure grounds. Moreover, these Schedule A assessments take no account of rent remissions in times of depression; and the fact that they are made at intervals of three or more years implies a considerable lag in the series as a reflection of actual rents. When allowance is made for such distinctions, however, the Schedule A series provide a valuable check on the results obtained from average rent per acre and total acreage.

The figures used for England and Wales for purposes of Table I have been based chiefly on acreage returns contained in the *Agricultural Statistics* and estimates of rent per acre in *The Rent of Agricultural Land in England and Wales, 1870–1946*, published by the Central Landowners' Association. A. W. Ashby there suggests a figure of 34s 6d for the average rent of all cultivated land in 1872–3, and we have made an adjustment for the relatively small area of occupied rough grazing. When the estimate of aggregate rent for that date is associated with acreage changes and with R. J. Thompson's index of rent per acre in the Minutes of Evidence of the Royal Commission on Tithe Rentcharge, p. 44, it yields a series from 1867 to 1914 which agrees well with the Schedule A assessments.

For 1923–38, use has been made of the findings of the National Farm Survey of 1941–3 and other material assembled by D. K. Britton, J. J. MacGregor and H. A. Rhee in the C.L.A. publication already quoted.

In respect of Scotland and Ireland the principle followed for 1867–1914 was to adjust the Schedule A assessments for those countries to produce series comparable to the Schedule A series for England and Wales, and then further adjust the resulting series to yield figures comparable to actual gross rent in England and Wales.

The Inland Revenue assessments for Scotland have been reduced by 6 per cent to eliminate the allowance for the landlord's responsibility for a share in the rates. Further reductions were then made to allow for rent abatements, the assumption being that the abatements have been proportionate to those observed in England and Wales.

For Ireland a detailed investigation by Lord Stamp, the results of which appear in *British Incomes and Property*, provides the means of adjusting the Irish valuations to accord with true annual value. After correction in this way, allowance was made for default in rent payment.

Similar methods have been used for the inter-war period, with additional support in the case of Scotland from the official records of *The Profitableness of Scottish Farming*, from which the trend of rents may be broadly gauged.

The United Kingdom totals of gross rent, thus derived from regional estimates conforming as far as possible to a common definition, have been converted to net rent by a series of percentages suggested by A. J. Boreham after enquiries including a study of the financial records of the Royal Commission which reported in 1896 and by reference to more recent sources.[1]

[1] A revised series of gross and net rent was published in the *Journal of the Proceedings of the Agricultural Economics Society*, March 1954, use being made of additional material, analysed by F. D. W. Taylor, from accounts in the Royal

CAPITAL AND INTEREST

For evaluating tenant's capital there are again two types of source available. The direct approach, used by A. J. Boreham,[1] was to prepare annual series of the value of (1) livestock, (2) farm machinery and implements, (3) harvested crops, (4) growing crops, cultivations and reserve cash, and (5) other items. The aim in such an inventory is to discover how much capital or cash reserve farmers must possess in order to maintain their current level of business. Considerable difference of opinion may arise as to the amount of reserve needed in respect of certain items, such as grain before harvest and market garden produce. However, the annual series resulting from the summation of the above five groups is by virtue of its construction a good index of change, so that confirmation of the level of the index at any date gives confirmation for a considerable period before and after the date. Reference has therefore been made to the second type of source—historical estimates by experts in this field—to obtain means of confirming the series for as long a period as possible.

Since 1867, statements of the value of tenant's capital have been made on the basis of (1) the capitalization of yield, (2) appraisal of the requirements of capital per acre or (3) inventories of farmers' capital and cash, by Giffen, Caird, Craigie, Stamp, *The Economist*, Turnbull, Harris, Kendall and several others. The series derived from Boreham's inventory traces a course through the constellation of other estimates, starting in 1938 at a point where two authorities agree within 1 per cent, and passing through other points in 1893–5 where there is a convergence of opinion by Turnbull, Harris and *The Economist*. In the years before 1880 the series runs somewhat above most of the estimates then current, though it is below that of Giffen for 1875.

The proper rate of interest to apply to the capital value depends on the purpose in view, and if the object is to indicate the amount the entrepreneur might earn from alternative forms of investment, 1 per cent above the current yield on consols seems not unreasonable. This figure can be carried back reliably to the beginning of the series, and has been used throughout in comparisons between agricultural and industrial incentive income.

Commission's Report of 1896, and of the estimates in Dampier-Whetham's address to the Agricultural Economics Society in the Journal of 1930. These and other sources mentioned in the article of 1954 led to adjustments reflected in the revised Table I herewith.

[1] Further details of the method of assessing tenant's capital are given in two papers, one by A. J. Boreham, the other by the present writer, in the *Farm Economist*, VII, No. 6, 1953. The change in the interest charge shown in the revised col. 4 of Table I is due to a change in the method of smoothing the annual estimates—see the *Journal of the Royal Statistical Society*, 1955, p. 340, where the series of tenant's capital, as extended from 1937/8 to 1952/3 by F. D. W. Taylor, is reproduced.

AGGREGATE WAGES, ETC.

The third deductible class of income, 'wages, etc.,' is composed chiefly of the wages and salaries of agricultural labourers, stockmen, ploughmen, market gardeners, bailiffs, salaried managers and others commonly recognized as being engaged in agriculture. It includes also the revenue of various *independent* producers not ordinarily classed as farmers, and of their employees. Chief among these are farm machinery proprietors and attendants, agricultural nurserymen and florists, drainage attendants, estate workers, vermin destroyers, drovers and various classes of seasonal workers. There is no escape from attempting to assess the income of these contributors, for they receive their income, in so far as they serve agriculture, from the gross revenue realized by the farmer-and-relative group from the sale of farm produce; and in order to arrive at the net income of the farmer-and-relative group it is necessary to subtract the payments to all others.

As regards the measurement of the principal section of this labour income, the wages of ordinary farm workers, an appraisal is necessary of normal cash wages, income in kind, harvest pay, and sundry forms of supplementary or piece-work payment. Largely compensating the evident difficulty of assembling material on each of these from the records of three administratively separate Kingdoms, is the fact that farm wages have been the object of a remarkable concentration of effort by official and professional statisticians, especially in the nineteenth century when agriculture was still the predominant national industry. For England and Wales, farm labourers' weekly cash wages have been presented *by groups of counties* for as many as nine periods from 1824 to 1898 by Orwin and Felton in the *R.A.S.E. Journal* for 1931, the county figures being derived mainly from official sources. J. J. MacGregor extended the series in *Forestry*, 1946. Farm wages in Ireland and Scotland, as well as in England and Wales, have been extensively studied by a succession of statisticians including Purdy, Little, Bowley, Wilson Fox and George Wood. Wood's article in the *Statistical Journal* for 1909 comes at the end of this accumulation of research, and his farm wage indexes have been used here for the period 1867–1906 coupled with returns in the *Labour Gazette* and detailed information in the *Earnings and Hours Report*, Cd. 5460, relating to 1907. For the later period we have been assisted by direct advice, for which we are under a heavy obligation to the Departments of Agriculture in London, Edinburgh and Belfast.

The problem of estimating aggregate wages has one point in common with that of measuring net farm income as a whole: there are certain items greatly preponderating over the rest, and if the more significant quantities can be assessed reasonably well, the fact that the smaller ones are numerous is not itself a cause of inaccuracy. The main items are (1) the cash wages of ordinary farm labourers for a normal week, (2) cash supplements which raise their earnings above the normal wage and (3) their income in kind. Broadly, the procedure has been to construct an annual series from 1867 to 1938 showing the aggregate of these three items per agricultural farm labourer and then to adjust the series to account for the higher pay of the numerically smaller classes of specialized farm employees and independent workers not in the farmer-and-relative group. As regards the independent operators such as florists, machinery owners and drovers, only their incentive income is considered, as rent and interest are included elsewhere; and their incentive income probably does not greatly exceed the receipts of their employees.

INCOME PER MAN-EQUIVALENT

The sequence of deductions here described gives the aggregate of the farmer's incentive income, which must be divided by the number of man-equivalent units in the farmer-and-relative group. The sources used by F. D. W. Taylor[1] in ascertaining the number in this group are the Occupations Tables in the Censuses of Population relating to every tenth year from 1871 to 1911, and later the Occupations Tables and the Industries Tables in the Censuses of 1921 and 1931, the Northern Ireland Census of 1926, and the annual returns of the Departments of Agriculture. The three types of source with differing classifications present the inquirer with the choice of figures, and there is again scope for judgment.

THE RATIO

Weekly incentive income per man-equivalent unit in the *farmer-and-relative group*, Table I, col. 10, may be compared with the figures in col. 11, which are the estimated *average weekly earnings*, not of the whole group of all others, but of *ordinary farm labourers*. Col. 12 gives the ratio of the two; and in col. 13 there is added a second ratio showing what *would be* the relationship of farmers' and labourers' income if all farmers owned their capital without offsetting loan, and if the interest on it were included in their income for purposes of the ratio. Since farmers' borrowings have sometimes been heavy, as in the period covered by the Royal Commission's report of 1896, the figures in the last column are liable to mislead unless it is recalled that part of the interest is not received by the farmer himself.

CHANGES IN REAL INCOME

Table II shows the estimated change in the real income of farmers and farm workers since 1867. The rural retail price index for adjusting the current value of the income has been based primarily on Bowley's retail price series in *Wages and Incomes since 1860* and on the *Ministry of Labour's cost-of-living index*. Since the Ministry's index relates to national prices, we have adjusted it to reflect rural price changes by assuming

[1] *Farm Economist*, VIII, No. 4, (1955).

certain percentage differences in average national and rural retail prices. These percentages are derived from a study of the disparity between urban and rural retail prices in 1904 and 1937–8, the findings of which were given in the *Journal of the Royal Statistical Society*, 1953, pp. 47–56.

TABLE II

UNITED KINGDOM: CHANGES IN REAL FARM INCOME, 1867–1938

	Rural Retail Price Index	Index of Farmers' and Relatives' Real Incentive Income per man-week	Incentive Income as in (2) plus Interest on Tenants' Capital	Index of Farm Labourers' Real Weekly Earnings
	(1)	(2)	(3)	(4)
Including all Ireland*				
1867–1873	100·0	100·0	100·0	100·0
1874–1878	95·7	87·7	91·3	118·1
1879–1883	89·2	55·0	63·6	124·3
1884–1896	76·6	73·5	76·5	145·6
1897–1910	78·9	99·8	93·0	156·0
1911–1914	87·3	124·4	113·0	153·3
Excluding Eire				
1923–1929	152·6	119·7	133·8	158·8
1930–1932	135·1	128·5	137·8	176·8
1933–1935	128·0	230·7	196·3	185·7
1936–1938	138·7	208·1	177·5	189·1

* In 1871 there were in the United Kingdom approximately 801,700 farmers and co-working relatives, in man-equivalents, of whom 424,100 were in Ireland, living in conditions not much changed from those which gave rise to the Great Famine.

COMPARISON WITH INDUSTRY

Subject to these differences in retail prices the weekly incentive income of farmers, shown in col. 10 of Table I, may be compared with the average weekly wage *rate* for industry in col. 2 of Table III.

The agricultural rates in Table III refer to the payment for a full week without overtime of 'ordinary farm labourers' and include allowances in kind. For the industrial weighted average, similar rates for a normal week have been ascertained for fourteen predominantly male occupations comprised in Bowley's wages index, the representative character of which has been subjected to considerable test over a period extending into the nineteenth century. For the period 1906–47, the rates are derived partly from details given by Bowley in the London and Cambridge Economic Service publications, and partly from the *Abstracts of Labour Statistics*. Uniformity in construction could not be maintained in the earlier part of the series, for which extensive use was made of G. H. Wood's indices in the *Statistical Journal* for 1909 associated with his unpublished collection, *Rates of Wages and Hours of Labour*, 1851–1906, in the R.S. Society's Library. The aim has been to ensure that each of the annual figures on which the period-averages are based relates to a date, season or period for which comparable quotations are available for agriculture and industry. After 1913 the annual figures refer to a date or period in the second half of the year.

TABLE III

AGRICULTURAL AND INDUSTRIAL WAGE RATES, 1850–1947

	Weekly Wage-rates		Ratio, Agriculture: Industry	
	Agricultural	Industrial	Unadjusted	Adjusted for Retail Price difference
	(1)	(2)	(3)	(4)
	s. d.	s. d.	%	%
1850–1857	10 0	22 10	44	49
1858–1866	11 0	23 7	47	52
1867–1873	12 2	25 11	47	52
1874–1878	13 9	27 11	49	55
1879–1883	13 7	27 0	50	56
1884–1896	13 8	27 9	49	55
1897–1910	15 0	31 4	48	53
1911–1914	16 2	32 11	49	54
1923–1929	30 6	60 10	50	54
1930–1932	31 4	59 2	53	56
1933–1935	30 11	58 9	53	55
1936–1938	33 5	62 11	53	56
1939–1945	56 9	83 7	68	70
1946–1947	87 11	112 4	78	80

INTERPRETATION

The break in continuity after the First World War, due to the partition of Ireland, should be emphasized especially in relation to Tables I and II. Farming in Ireland has been on the basis of a much smaller unit than in Great Britain, as is indicated by the difference between the two countries in the number of acres cultivated per man-equivalent in the farmer-and-relative group. This was 28·3 in Ireland in 1911, compared with 51·4 for the United Kingdom as a whole. After the withdrawal of 26 of the 32 counties of Ireland, the average for the United Kingdom, in 1931, was 70·4. Such a change may be less significant in itself than as the evidence of the withdrawal of the major part of a system in which the unit was different in several respects. The change may in any event be expected to have been associated with an appreciable increase in the average incentive income of farmers.

Moreover, in Ireland, in 1911, the farmer-and-relative group outnumbered all others in agriculture by more than 5: 2, whereas in Great Britain the farmer-and-relative group was less than a third of the whole. Thus the low income of Irish farmers depressed the average of farmers' income in the United Kingdom much more than the low income of Irish farm wage-earners depressed the general average of farm wages in the United Kingdom.

The effect of this on the ratio of the farmers' income to that of the farm worker must have been particularly marked in the earlier years of our period. In 1867, Irish agriculture was still not far removed from the conditions which had produced the Great Famine. The potato blight of 1845-6 came at a time when the peasantry had already, after a long period of decline, sunk to a state bordering on starvation in many areas, and it is inconceivable that after a million deaths and distress causing emigration in even greater numbers the income of farmers could have been raised much above bare subsistence level in less than a generation.

It may be possible in due course to obtain figures separately for Ireland and Great Britain, but meanwhile the overall figures for the nineteenth century may be assumed to conceal wide variations in experience and to give a picture revealing average conditions much less satisfactory than would be expected from series relating to Great Britain alone.

The quickest description of the trends from 1867 to 1938 is obtained by considering Tables I, II and III in reverse. Col. 4 of Table III suggests that if allowance be made for retail price differences, there was virtually no change in the ratio of farm to industrial wage *rates* over the whole period. The ratio was 52 per cent in 1867-73 and subsequently varied from 53 to 56 per cent till 1939. This means that, when the farmer's income is being compared with the farm worker's income, the comparison with industrial wages is concurrently made by recalling this fairly constant ratio of just over a half. Owing to the small size of the Irish wage-earning group, the influence on the ratio of the change in 1921-2 was not significant.

Table II indicates that the real earnings of wage-earners on the land moved steadily upwards, apart from a slight setback during the upswing of prices before the First World War; and at the end, in 1936-8, the level was nearly twice that recorded in 1867-73. Among farmers and their relatives the rise in incentive income may appear to have been greater; but again it must be said that the groups were much changed after 1922. If comparable group incomes could be assessed separately, the farmers' real incentive income in Great Britain might well be shown to have risen less from 1867-73 to 1936-8 than farm workers' real earnings.

Table II gives evidence of the see-saw effect of price fluctuations on the incomes of farmers and farm workers.

In conclusion, certain points may be noted chiefly from Table I, some of which have a bearing on more general questions of income distribution.

FARMER'S INCENTIVE INCOME

(1) Harvest and price fluctuations are reflected to a much greater degree in the variations in the farmer's incentive income than in the movements of rent, interest or wages. Rent, for example, is affected by price movements only if they persist. In so far as the laws of rent imply that it is a residual quantity determined by, rather than determining, the movement of prices, the farmer's incentive income conforms to these laws in the short- and medium-term much more fully than does rent itself.

(2) The pre-1914 figures suggest that when farming is conducted as a family business, as in most of Ireland and much of Great Britain, the farmer's incentive income does not in the long run appreciably exceed farm wages. Indeed, for much of the period there was no excess, but a deficit. Assuming that the excess which sometimes arises is the return for the farmer's extra effort, there is no net positive money return for either management or risk. The exercise of independent power and managerial and other faculties and the assumption of risk may be partly their own reward in farming as elsewhere, but the average monetary return has been negligible in family-farm husbandry.

(3) The social status of the farmer in the rural community has been maintained by the possession and control of capital.

(4) An increase in the size of the farm and in the scale of production is accompanied by a positive money return to management, as is apparent in the rise in the long-term average ratio of the farmer's incentive income to farm wage-earnings after 1922.

(5) The increase in the ratio of farmers' to workers' incomes in 1933-8 was due to a considerable range of influences, among which were the wheat, cattle, sugar and milk subsidies, the Government's protective policies and the creation of Marketing Boards. Taken as a whole the figures for this period are evidence that in the United Kingdom public intervention is capable of substantially raising the farmer's incentive income, even during general depression.

(6) Other factors tending to increase this residual incentive income were the fall in the rate of interest and some decline in rent. Yields were relatively good after 1931. Feeding-stuffs prices were low.

(7) When all Ireland was within the United Kingdom the farmer's incentive income never reached parity with average industrial wages except in certain years of unusually good harvest during the Golden Age. After 1933 it rose to about equality with the average industrial wage rate, as a result of the influences indicated in (5) and (6) above.

Farm Wages

(8) The stability of the relationship between agricultural and industrial wage rates from 1867 to 1938 has some relevance for substitution theories of wages. It seems to suggest that substitution may be much delayed by frictions and non-monetary considerations, and that these have been of fairly constant strength for more than eighty years.

(9) Direct Government intervention is capable of overriding such frictions, according to the evidence from 1939 onwards.

(10) Farm wages have been remarkably independent of short-term fluctuations in the profitableness of farming.

(11) The long-term rise in real wages, coupled with the rise in the farmer's real incentive income from 1867 to 1938, is associated with a steady decline in the proportionate return to property. The validity of theories of distribution may be tested according to their ability to give a reasoned explanation of these combined trends.

Rent and Interest

(12) The decline in the interest proportion, due mainly to the fall in the rate of interest, was associated with a fall in the rent proportion. It may be useful to consider (a) whether the change in the rate of interest has any implication for the level of rent per acre, (b) how far capital is a substitute for land, and (c) whether extra-farm capital, by increasing the accessibility of remoter lands and external resources, tends to reduce rent.

(13) The decline in the return to property, coupled with the rise in the return to the human agent, was accompanied by a substantial fall in the number of employees engaged, while the three other factors of production remained fairly stable in quantity, i.e. in terms of acreage, man-equivalents in the entrepreneur group, or physical implements or assets.

One of the chief aims in obtaining estimates of British agricultural income and its component parts has been to compare the results with those for other countries, and then to draw inferences regarding causation. It has been found, however, that the wider and more varied the field of comparison, the greater is the variation in the findings; and because of the variation nothing of any significance can be inferred directly from the statistics. Their value consists in the check they provide for theories of distribution deductively established. There clearly must be some combination of theories capable of explaining every known fact, and the greater the collection of facts the more complete will be the test of the tentative theories. Thus the ultimate interest of any discoveries relating to the United Kingdom—apart from their adding detail to the description of the historical situation—rests in the contribution they make to the international evidence whereby conclusions drawn from such situations may be made more reliable through test.

METHODS AND COMPARISONS

In a symposium at a Conference in Oxford in 1952, a paper by L. Napolitan, published in the *Farm Economist*, 1953, described the principles on which the official United Kingdom estimates of farm output and income were constructed. A second paper by O. J. Beilby discussed the 'expanded sample of farm accounts' as a source of alternative independent estimates, the method being commended by reference to official farm-account sampling in Scotland.

For compiling estimates relating to historical periods, when none but large-scale or exceptional farmers kept accounts, only one basic method of construction is available. It is capable, however, of yielding valuations corresponding to widely varying definitions of output and income. Table IV illustrates the method. Each series in it serves a different aim of historical research, but all are obtained by the same procedure.

Estimates corresponding to the widest definition, 'domestic supply' are given in col. 1. They exceed the aggregates of 'net output', col. 3, by about £100 m. or more. Whereas Table IV contains only one 'output' series between these extremes, several other intermediate series or estimates have been presented by statisticians in the past. A comparison of these with any category employed in Table IV entails the means of placing them at some point in the scale of definitions in the Table.

'Domestic supply' is a classification of greater practical use in wartime than in peace: it is a total containing the quantities of basic food supplies which a wartime Minister of Food would take as his starting point in planning the distribution of farm products for both human and animal consumption. The amounts of grain and potatoes comprised in it represent the total harvested crop, without deduction for seed or fodder. In respect of livestock the category used is 'realized gross output', which differs from total production only to the extent of inventory change; and for other goods, including milk and milk products, vegetables and fruit, the category is similar. In peacetime this large denomination is useful as a special form of index: when adjusted by a price series such as that in col. 7,[1] it reveals, more clearly and comprehensively than any other evidence, the overall fluctuation of the country's food-supply industry due to natural, seasonal causes. The annual variations shown in Table IV are appreciably more reliable from 1884 onwards than for earlier years.

'Gross output', col. 2,[2] shows the home food supply after the producers have withdrawn the quantities they need for seed and farm animal fodder. Nutritional studies are based on gross output data, after allow-

---

[1] The weighting of this price series makes it more suitable for adjusting 'gross output' data, but for short-term comparisons it may be applied to wider categories without risk of significant error.

[2] This series has been adjusted for inventory change.

ance for consumption by non-farm animals, and by non-food industries, and the addition of net import.

'Net output', col. 3, indicates the contribution of British agriculture to society, after allowance for the cost of all 'productive inputs' bought from abroad by farmers and from non-farm sources. This cost includes depreciation. It takes into account also the landowners' extra-estate payments for upkeep.

To obtain 'net income', col. 4, from net output, it is necessary, as observed in the earlier text, to add any subsidies[1] which are not already in the price of the net output, and deduct land tax, rates paid by the landowners, and tithe. For fair comparison with non-farm producers' incomes, adjustments are made for retail valuation of farmers' self-supplies. Col. 4 gives the annual data, thus adjusted, from which the period averages in Table I, col. 1, have been drawn. As the mutually offsetting corrections are almost equal, net income differs little from net output.

In a reply to discussion in 1952 it was noted that when grain-growers suffer, much of their loss is gain to livestock farmers who use grain for feed. Historically there has been a seesaw movement in the fortunes of the

Table IV

UNITED KINGDOM AGRICULTURE, 1867–1914

Annual Estimates of the Current Value of Specified Classes of Output and Income, and Index of Agricultural Prices

| | | | | | Adjusted Gross Revenue | | |
	Domestic Supply	Gross Output	Net Output	Net Income	Grain (incl. Straw)	Livestock and Livestock Products	Agricultural Prices (at Farm)
	(1)	(2)	(3)	(4)	(5)	(6)	(7)
	£m.	£m.	£m.	£m.	£m.	£m.	1867–77 = 100
1867	246·8	205·5	155·0	153·8	73·9	79·4	97·1
1868	250·5	207·9	150·4	150·0	79·2	73·3	93·7
1869	230·7	193·1	134·2	132·6	63·0	71·0	93·2
1870	249·9	209·0	149·8	148·8	71·9	69·0	94·8
1871	254·2	216·7	152·5	151·4	68·3	78·0	99·6
1872	254·1	221·4	153·8	153·0	66·7	83·3	103·3
1873	271·8	233·1	166·0	165·4	75·7	88·2	108·3
1874	273·4	227·6	157·1	156·3	77·5	79·4	100·1
1875	281·0	230·4	155·8	154·4	71·8	79·1	103·6
1876	283·5	230·3	153·9	152·4	76·4	71·4	102·9
1877	254·9	214·8	145·7	144·6	67·2	74·9	100·3
1878	249·3	210·6	138·2	137·2	62·9	68·8	94·0
1879	215·8	180·3	115·9	113·4	52·0	62·5	89·0
1880	233·4	191·6	122·4	120·7	59·4	58·2	91·9

[1] Not, however, relevant to the period covered by Table IV.

1881	233·8	192·7	125·0	123·1	59·5	60·0	91·2
1882	227·3	194·8	130·6	129·3	55·4	71·1	92·0
1883	226·3	194·8	124·6	123·2	52·3	66·6	88·5
1884	212·4	184·6	121·4	120·4	50·9	66·0	83·7
1885	208·6	178·8	115·1	114·5	47·8	62·2	78·6
1886	200·6	171·2	113·4	113·2	41·7	63·9	77·4
1887	197·5	166·7	110·3	110·2	40·5	61·0	73·8
1888	195·4	165·9	109·4	110·4	41·6	61·9	75·1
1889	197·3	172·3	109·9	111·3	45·1	57·0	76·2
1890	199·7	178·8	115·7	117·7	49·0	61·3	76·2
1891	213·3	185·4	121·7	124·3	48·4	68·4	75·7
1892	203·1	173·2	112·1	114·4	40·4	65·0	75·8
1893	199·2	164·1	106·7	108·6	36·8	61·3	76·5
1894	187·5	158·2	101·3	103·6	35·2	60·3	73·0
1895	181·5	156·6	101·6	104·0	30·6	64·6	70·9
1896	186·7	161·1	105·1	107·4	36·8	61·9	68·6
1897	191·4	165·8	108·9	111·7	41·3	61·5	74·2
1898	195·3	169·2	105·5	108·8	41·3	55·3	70·9
1899	204·0	178·6	112·4	115·4	38·9	62·9	72·3
1900	204·7	179·9	112·5	115·4	36·8	64·6	76·5
1901	209·7	179·7	112·6	115·6	38·7	62·7	76·7
1902	213·4	187·6	120·1	123·2	39·2	67·9	78·3
1903	204·0	178·8	110·5	112·8	33·1	64·1	76·5
1904	204·8	177·6	111·6	113·6	33·3	65·8	75·2
1905	213·5	185·6	115·7	118·3	37·1	64·8	77·8
1906	222·3	194·1	123·6	126·3	38·5	68·0	80·9
1907	228·3	201·4	125·1	127·8	40·2	68·5	82·7
1908	226·3	198·7	130·1	133·4	39·7	75·8	79·6
1909	225·7	196·9	120·0	123·4	39·8	64·3	80·2
1910	227·1	198·0	120·5	122·6	37·7	63·4	83·1
1911	249·9	212·7	137·8	140·9	44·1	72·3	85·1
1912	251·8	218·9	134·1	136·9	40·0	72·7	89·8
1913	243·5	210·0	127·8	131·3	41·0	65·5	88·8
1914	279·3	237·7	160·9	164·7	57·5	86·9	94·8

two classes of farmers, some examples of this being reflected in the series in cols. 5 and 6. The adjusted gross revenue in col. 5 is the value of the total crop of wheat, barley and oats, including straw, less seed. In col. 6 is given the value of gross output of cattle, sheep, pigs (plus inventory increase or minus decrease), milk and milk products, and clipwool, less purchases of manufactured feed and imports of store livestock.

In col. 7 is an index of prices at farm based on the Paasche formula. The aggregate value of the gross output of fifteen farm products assessed at the prices current in a given year, divided by their aggregate value at base-period prices, gives the price relative for that year.

STARTING POINT FOR ESTIMATES

For compiling the historical series shown in Table IV, the point of focal interest is the estimation of 'gross output', separately, for each principal farm product. There are two broad types of formula for valuing the gross output of *crops*—one based on production, the other on consumption—and in addition there is a 'realization' or disappearance formula for *livestock*. These formulae have been described in the third paper of the symposium published in the *Farm Economist* 1953; and variants of the formulae are illustrated in research papers under the general title 'Gross Output of Farm Products in the United Kingdom, 1847–1938'—copies of which are obtainable from the Agricultural Economics Research Institute, Oxford, or from the writer.

INFERENCES

The aim in analysing farm income into rent, interest, wages and the farmer's incentive income has been to derive, from historical evidence of the fluctuation of these components, deductions regarding the strength of the various influences which have depressed wages and incentive income in agriculture below the levels in the rest of the economy. In Chapter XVI of *Agriculture and Industry: Relative Income*[1] long-term statistical evidence is given from twenty-eight countries, and inferences are drawn for the due ranking of the principal factors which depress the return to agriculture.

Although the low level of farm income is an almost world-wide phenomenon, sharp distinction is needed between the complex of influences tending to reduce the level of consumption in subsistence areas, and the causal system where commercial farming predominates. In the sixties it is now becoming necessary to distinguish a third category of agricultural regime, to which a third type of economic analysis is appropriate. New developments in production techniques, permitting a final breaking of the 'scale barrier' which has restricted British agriculture for 150 years, have enabled considerable sections of this industry to develop conditions and organization akin to those of manufacture. To the extent that this tendency persists in the future, say, under the guiding and modulating influence of the equivalent of Factory Laws and codes, it will be necessary to evolve a new composite theory, an amalgam of the theory of the individual (industrial) *firm* and the traditional theory of the individual *farm*. It is here suggested that for the purpose both of distinguishing the two systems of analysis and of indicating how they may be merged, a great store of useful data is to be found in the farm and non-farm statistics of the last third of the nineteenth century—a time when the scale barrier in agriculture was apparently unbreakable, while typical firms in industry, transport and finance were expanding into mammoth joint stock undertakings and trusts.

[1] London: Macmillan, 1956.

POSTSCRIPT

When this paper was read at the A.E.S. Conference in July 1952 and published in 1953, the series in it were stated to be provisional, and later they were re-examined. Reprinting has made possible the inclusion of the revised figures. The corrections have not entailed material changes in the inferences, except as regards yields before 1884. To the commentary a section has been added, beginning with 'Methods and Comparisons', p. 275, and comprising Table IV which gives data not previously published by the writer as annual series.

Several past and present members of the Agricultural Economics Research Institute, Oxford, contributed to the cumulative work on the estimates. In a note introducing the original text it was said: 'The compiling of farm income series was first undertaken here by E. M. Ojala, whose results have lately been published by the University Press in *Agriculture and Economic Progress*—the Appendix to which contains estimates of agricultural net output and income in the United Kingdom for groups of years from 1867 to 1938. In his Preface Ojala makes acknowledgments, which we warmly reciprocate, and refers especially to A. W. Ashby's part in the work. Ojala was good enough to leave his farm-income material with the Institute, and A. J. Boreham, a member of a team studying the relationships between agriculture and industry, combined this with other data to produce annual estimates for the same period. K. E. Hunt and D. K. Britton who had independently prepared series of the gross output of certain farm products made these available, and assisted in the further construction of the output and income figures. For purposes of the breakdown of income, studies of rent by A. W. Ashby, D. K. Britton and H. A. Rhee were used. A. J. Boreham was chiefly responsible for the estimates of tenant's capital and the aggregate interest on it. The wage figures were produced by the present speaker, who acknowledges especially the many months of work by W. D. McMullen in compiling wage-rate series and by F. D. W. Taylor in making the computations involved in editing and completing the present series.'

Acknowledgment is made also to J. J. MacGregor, whose inquiries into rent and wages have provided valuable historical data.

OWNER-FARMING IN ENGLAND AND WALES
1900–1950

S. G. Sturmey

Owner-Farming in England and Wales, 1900 to 1950

This article discusses the re-emergence in the present century of owner-occupation [1] as a significant tenurial form in the agriculture of England and Wales. In 1900, 13·5 per cent. of the cultivated area was farmed by its owners; by 1950 the percentage had risen to 37·5 per cent. We start with a brief discussion of the events which led up to this change, the first of which occurred in 1867. The early discussion concerns the period between 1867 and 1908, the last year in the present century of decreasing owner-farming. The years from 1909 to 1927 are dealt with in considerable detail, these being the years in which the bulk of the increase occurred. The years after 1927 are treated as briefly as those before 1909, and the article concludes with a brief examination of the present position.

I. THE PRELIMINARY YEARS: 1867 TO 1908.

This period opens with the Reform Act of 1867 and covers the agricultural depression of the late 1870's, the slow process of adjustment of English farming to changing conditions, and the re-emergence of prosperity in the new century.

The Reform Act, by further extending the franchise, weakened the incentive for politically minded men to hold, or build up, agricultural estates in order to secure the votes of their tenants. Between 1832 and 1867 very little land passed into owner-occupation, despite the general prosperity of farming, as the ownership of a number of £50 leaseholds, together with the growing device of yearly tenancies, enabled land-owners to secure for themselves the votes of their tenants who knew that failure to use "correctly" the votes given them in 1832 would lead to the termination of their tenancies.[2] After 1867 the relative importance of these votes diminished.

[1] The terms "owner-farmer" and "owner-occupier" are used interchangeably to describe those farmers who own the land which they work. The term "farmer-in-hand" will be used to describe land-owners, classed as owner-occupiers, who are temporarily farming land as an alternative to letting it.

[2] cf. G. Broderick, "English Land and English Landlords," *Cobden Club*, 1881, p. 205).

This, coupled with agricultural prosperity, led to land being sold for owner-occupation in the early 1870's.[1] These sales, and the concurrent increase in owner-occupation, ceased in the depression of 1874, depression intensified by the entry of American farm produce to British markets and by adverse weather conditions between 1875 and 1879. Failure among farmers was widespread, rents often could not be paid and mortgage payments usually not maintained. Many owner-farmers lost their farms or became the tenants of the mortgagees: landlords, unable to let land, often farmed it in hand.

In the early 1880's, owner-occupation was fairly widespread, brought about not by the ownership of their farms by farmers, but by the farming of their land by owners who were unable to let the farms to suitable tenants. Rents fell continuously as agriculture adjusted itself to the new competitive conditions; in 1877 gross rents in England and Wales were £48·6 million while by 1899 they had fallen to £33·9 million.[2] The index of gross rent per acre (28/- per acre = 100) fell from 107 to 71 in the same period.[3] In the circumstances, the inducements to land-owners to sell land were greatly increased, but land was difficult to sell. In 1890 however, the reports preceding the Agricultural Returns speak of purchases of small farms for owner occupation in Wales. Such purchases began about 10 years later in England. Alongside of these purchases went the letting of farms in hand which became possible as rents were adjusted to the new circumstances and as agricultural conditions improved.

During the early years of the present century the letting of farms in hand continued, reducing continuously the extent of owner-occupation. This process was more or less completed by 1908, save for some large farms. At the same time, the number of working owner-farmers was increasing. As farms became in greater demand to rent due to increasing prosperity,

[1] cf. *Report of the Royal Commission on Agricultural Depression*, Cd., 7400, 1897, particularly the evidence of Mr. C. S. Read.
[2] J. R. Bellerby, "Gross and Net Farm Rent in the United Kingdom, 1867-1938," *Journal of Agricultural Economics*, March, 1954, pp. 357-8).
[3] H. A. Rhee, "The Rent of Agricultural Land in England and Wales, 1870-1943," in *The Rent of Agricultural Land in England and Wales, 1870-1946*. Central Landowners Association.

a tenant, if his holding was for sale, could not lightly forgo the chance to purchase in case the sale was accompanied by a notice to quit and another farm to rent proved difficult to obtain. Despite the increasing prosperity, reflected in an increase in the average annual agricultural income of the United Kingdom from £119 million in the period 1894 to 1903 to £131 million in the period 1904 to 1910,[1] gross farm rents in England and Wales rose from £34·1 million in 1900 to only £34·7 million in 1908.[2] The incentive to landlords to sell was, therefore, undiminished.

The first statistics relating to owner-occupation refer to 1888. Prior to this date only general statements relating to the extent of this form of tenure are available, for example, Caird's statement in 1878 that the " . . . land of the United Kingdom may be said to be almost . . . wholly cultivated by tenant farmers." [3]

Using the figures available for 1888, adjusted slightly to obtain comparability with those relating to 1908, the position was :—

Holdings over 1 acre	1888 %	1908 %
Owner occupation of number of holdings...	14·5	12·8
Owner occupation of area of crops and grass	15·4	12·3

Sources : 1888—from *Agricultural Returns*, 1888, omitting the estimated number of, and area covered by, holdings of 1 acre and under.
1908—from *Agricultural Statistics*, 1908.

The striking thing about these figures is that, whereas in 1888 owner-occupation was more important when measured in terms of area than in terms of number of holdings, in 1908 the reverse was true. Accepting that farms in hand tend to be of larger than average size, the figures confirm that considerable farming in hand existed in 1888. The change in the figures in twenty years, and, in particular, their altered relationship, was produced by a combination of larger than average sized farms passing out of owner-occupation and smaller than average sized farms passing into owner-occupation. That this occurred is

[1] E. M. Ojala, *Agriculture and Economic Progress*, p. 215.
[2] Bellerby, *op. cit.*
[3] James Caird, "General View of British Agriculture," *Journal of the Royal Agricultural Society*, 1878, p. 32.

supported by the annual reports of land agents published in the *Estates Gazette* during the period. It is also significant in this connection that in 1888 the average size of the owner-occupied holding of over 1 acre was about 64 acres compared with 61 acres in 1908; the average size of all holdings was about 63 acres in both years.[1]

During the period 1867 to 1908 the inducements to own agricultural estates were severely weakened, both politically and financially. A readiness to sell land resulted. As agricultural conditions improved, unaccompanied by any marked rise in rents, land was often sold, sometimes to tenant-farmers, who, with increasing prosperity, were more frequently than formerly in a position to contemplate owning their land. This affected mainly small farms, the demand to rent large farms not being sufficiently great to lead a tenant to buy for fear of being served a notice to quit. At the same time, however, a decrease in owner-occupation occurred as farms in hand were let. By 1908, this letting was practically completed and only some large farms were being involuntarily farmed in hand.

II. THE INCREASE OF OWNER-OCCUPATION : 1909 to 1927.

Between 1909 and 1927 the extent of owner-occupation began to increase, slowly at first, then at increasing speed after 1917, culminating in a wild buying spree immediately after the war. Depression again struck British agriculture in 1921, temporarily halting the increase in owner-farming which, recommencing in 1924, was halted again in 1926. By 1927 the extent of owner-occupation was greater than it had been, probably since the seventeenth century.

[1]Reflection will show that the combination of a decline in :—
   the percentage of holdings owner-occupied by 2%
   the percentage of acreage owner-occupied by 3%, and
   the average size of the owner-occupied holding by 5%
could only be produced if large holdings move out of owner-occupation. When the difference in average size between owner-occupied holdings and all holdings is small, very large shifts of average-sized holdings into or out of owner-occupation are required to produce even small changes in the average size of owner-occupied holdings. Given the change in the extent of owner-occupation, the decline in the average size of owner-occupied holdings is significant as showing the impossibility of the changes being produced other than in the manner stated.

The published statistics relating to owner-occupation in this period show movements which, it is believed, did not occur. The statistics relating to the post-war years, 1919 to 1924 inclusive, were admitted as inaccurate.[1] For 1927, however, a careful and successful attempt was made to secure greater accuracy. The admittedly inaccurate figures will not be reproduced here. It is the contention of this paper that the published statistics for the years 1910 to 1914 are also inaccurate and do not accord with the other evidence relating to the period; this section will be largely concerned with this evidence.

In Table I are given what may be regarded as the reasonably accurate statistics relating to 1909 and 1927, together with the more doubtful figures relating to the years 1910-14. No statistics were collected after 1914 until 1919.

TABLE I

OWNER-OCCUPATION IN ENGLAND AND WALES, 1909 TO 1914 AND 1927

Holdings of over 1 acre

Year	Number of owner-occupied holdings	Percentage of holdings owner-occupied %	Area of crops and grass owner-occupied (acres)	Percentage of area owner-occupied %
1909	55,920	13·0	3,337,456	12·2
10	55,433	12·8	3,329,015	12·2
11	54,176	12·4	3,246,971	11·9
12	50,972	11·7	2,954,491	10·9
13	48,760	11·2	2,890,559	10·6
14	49,204	11·3	2,961,979	10·9
27	146,887	36·6	9,225,734	36·0

Source: *Agricultural Statistics*, 1909 to 1914 and 1927.

(a) *The pre-war period*: 1909 *to* 1914. It has been seen that land was being bought for owner-occupation in the years before 1909. After 1909, particularly in 1909-11, these purchases increased. Land agents from all over England and

[1] *Agricultural Statistics*, Part 1, Vol. 59, 1924, p. 5).

Wales, reporting in the *Estates Gazette* were practically unanimous on this point. Land had been sold before 1909 without any marked increase in owner-occupation, but, whereas before 1909 estates were rarely broken up for sale, this was not the case in later years. "It has become very general to break up the large estates.... Farmers ... cannot be sure of remaining on except by purchasing for themselves—this has created a new and large demand."[1] "Owing to the breaking up of ... estates an enormous amount of land has been on the market, the greater portion of which has been purchased by the tenants."[2]

Additional evidence that land was sold extensively in these pre-war years is provided by the appointment of the Haversham Committee in 1911. As the terms of reference limited the inquiry of this Committee to the position of tenant farmers on the sale of their holdings, their report does not mention purchases of land for owner-occupation. In his minority report, however, Mr. H. Trustram Eve comments on the fact that farmers had frequently purchased land by raising both first and second mortgages, often from mortgagees who refused to accept repayments, either regularly or intermittently. It was, he said, "... under these unsatisfactory conditions that a very large quantity of farms have been purchased during the last two years."[3]

It is clear that in the years 1909-1914, farmers were purchasing farms for their own occupation. There is some evidence that credit difficulties may have acted as a brake on purchases in the years 1912-14. "It would appear ... that in some parts of the country the mortgage market is tight, and that rates of interest for money borrowed for the purchase of farms are rising somewhat uncomfortably."[4] Mortgages were sometimes called in when lenders became worried about their

[1] Report of John Francis, Carmarthen, *Estates Gazette*, Vol. 78, 23rd December, 1911, p. 995.

[2] Report of Wheller & Laing, Exeter, *op. cit.*, Vol. 80, 21st December, 1912, p. 999.

[3] *Report of the Departmental Committee appointed to inquire into the position of tenant farmers on the occasion of any change in the ownership of their holdings*, (Haversham Committee), Cd. 6030, 1912, Minority report by Mr. H. Trustram Eve, para. 15, p. 24.

[4] *Estates Gazette*, Vol. 83, 3rd January, 1914, p. 19.

security. Some farmers had to give up farming in the years after 1912, as evidenced by the increased number of bankruptcies in the years 1912 and 1913. The numbers of Receiving Orders issued against, and Deeds of Arrangement entered with, farmers for the years 1905-14 were:

1905	..	389	1910	..	245
06	..	318	11	..	305
07	..	279	12	..	336
08	..	298	13	..	326
09	..	310	14	..	189

(*Figures by courtesy of the National Farmers Union*).

There is, however, no evidence that these influences were strong enough to cause an overall decline in the extent of owner-occupation such as that shown in the statistics reproduced in Table I.

There is a possible explanation, alternative to calling the statistics into question, of the difference between the course of events outlined for the years 1909 to 1914 and the statistics relating to the period. If, alongside of purchases of holdings for owner-occupation, there was extensive letting of farms in hand, it would be possible to reconcile the statistics and the argument of this paper. There is no doubt that some large farms which were in hand in 1909 had been let by 1914. If this had been the dominant factor in the period, a decline in the average size of the owner-occupied holding, as shown by the statistics, should have occurred, whereas an increase from 59·7 acres to 60·2 acres in 1914 is shown. A reconciliation along these lines between the statistics and the general evidence relating to the period is, therefore, impossible. The increase in the average size of owner-occupied holdings as shown by the statistics results from an incomplete record of the increase in owner-occupation, particularly of smaller than average sized holdings.

The combination of rising land prices and low rents, which led land-owners to sell their properties in the years immediately before 1909, continued after 1909,[1] supplemented by the campaign against land-owners which was in progress at the time. This campaign moved from a mere vilification of landlords as a class, to threats of the nationalisation of land or the imposition of heavy taxes thereon. In this regard, the Finance (1909-10) Act, 1910, was crucial, in particular Form 4 on which land-owners were required to give particulars of their holdings. With this, the attack seemed to shift to cover all land-owners, not only the large landlords, and it is suggested that this shift of emphasis accelerated the break up of estates which commenced about this time. At the same time, the owner-occupier may have felt a strong incentive to hide the fact of his land-ownership. So long as only large estates were being attacked this did not apply, but once the attack was turned, or appeared to be turned, against all land-owners, the situation was different. However irrational it may now appear, at a time when it seemed to be regarded politically as almost a crime to own land, it is quite reasonable to suppose that landowners took every opportunity to conceal the extent of their land-ownership.

There is no evidence that land was actually adversely affected by existing legislation, for example, taxes were only threatened, not imposed; the situation was " . . . a striking illustration of the evil that may be worked by mere threats of what is going to happen." [2] Added to this attack was the Agricultural Holdings Act, 1908, designed to give to tenants a much greater security of tenure than they had previously enjoyed, coupled with a freedom of cropping. This Act

[1] Although rents were low in the period 1909-14, they were not falling. Lowness is relative; gross rents in England and Wales in 1909, estimated at £34·8 million, were low in relation to the £48·6 million of 1877. Between 1908 and 1914, gross rents rose from £34·8 million to £35·5 million; at the same time the ratio of net rents to gross rents for the United Kingdom rose from 48·7 per cent. to 52·0 per cent. . . . (Bellerby, *op. cit.*). If these ratios applied equally to England and Wales, net rents must have risen from £17·0 million to £18·5 million. This being the case, landlords apparently had no incentive, if all other factors are disregarded, to sell their land after 1909, if they had not wished to sell it before 1909. However, at the same time, agricultural incomes had risen to an annual average of £142 million for the years 1911-13 compared with £119 million for 1894-1903 and £131 million for the period 1904-1910 (Ojala, *op. cit.*).

[2] *Estates Gazette*, Vol. 77, 14th February, 1911, p. 61).

appeared, at the time, to take from landlords the control of their land, and, far from giving greater security to tenants, land-owners steered around the Act by selling their properties. It is plausible to argue that, with an apparently water-tight security code for tenants, land-owners were no longer interested in retaining their land, and sold for that reason alone.[1]

Tenants purchased their land, partly because they could afford to and, at the prices ruling, it often seemed to be a good investment, partly because the freedom of cropping and rights to compensation were not markedly better after 1908 than before, and partly because the farmer was not compensated for disturbance on the sale of his holding. The tenant had no security on the sale of the holding and knew that another holding to rent would be difficult to obtain if he had to leave that on which he was the sitting tenant. In 1913 tenants became entitled to compensation if disturbed after the sale of their holdings.

Having bought his holding for such reasons, the farmer, apparently was often not classed as an owner-occupier when the statistics of owner-occupation were compiled. This may, in some cases, have been because, having a mortgage on his holding with the mortgagee holding the title deeds, he was uncertain of his status. This could only apply to farmers who had purchased farms after 1909, the statistics for previous years appearing to be reliable. Much more important was the concealment of the fact of ownership; it was the success of these attempts which led to the statistics becoming deficient:

(b) *The War Years*: 1915 *to* 1918. During the war years, owner-occupation continued to increase, once the first period of uncertainty was over. The 1913 compensation provision might have been expected to lessen the willingness of tenants to buy their holdings; despite compensation the difficulty of finding another farm remained and farmers showed ". . . an increasing desire to purchase their holdings. . . ."[2]

In the later years of the war, farmers had a taxation incentive to purchase their farms. With the general increases in

[1] *cf.* H. M. Conacher, "The Relation of Land Tenure and Agriculture," *Journal of the Agricultural Economics Society*, 1936, p. 184.
[2] Report of Brodwell & Son, Nottingham, *op. cit.*, Vol. 90, 29th December, 1917, p. 60.

income taxation during the war, the basis of farmers' taxation assessments was changed. Whereas their taxable income from farming had been taken as equal to the rent or rental value of their holdings, it now became twice that amount in the absence of accounts showing a lower income. A tenant on an old estate where rents were low knew that if his farm was sold his rent would probably be increased, possibly to double its previous level. With the change in the basis of the taxation, this would have meant a further doubling of the taxation assessment to four times its previous level, to avoid which farmers were often anxious to buy their farms; rental values as calculated for taxation purposes tend to be extremely "sticky," being re-calculated only at intervals of three or more years.

On 5th April, 1917, the Corn Production Act came into operation. The guarantees given under this Act are usually cited as the cause of the increase in owner-occupation which the Agricultural Statistics show as beginning after 1919. It has been shown that, in fact, the increase began in 1909. Even without this Act, the increase in owner-occupation would have continued because of the high product prices and the high level of incomes ruling at the time.[1] Because of these prices, the guarantees given under the Act were not utilised, save for some small payments in 1920. The Act applied only to cereal growers, yet, as will be shown later, the greatest increases in owner-occupation occurred in counties other than cereal growing counties. In view of the fact that the increase in owner-occupation had started before the Act was passed, and that product prices were extremely high in the relevant years, it is impossible to credit the Act with more than a marginal influence on the number of owner-farmers.

(c) *The Post-war Years*: 1919 *to* 1927. The story of the years 1919 to 1921 is clear. Farms were in demand to rent and farmers, despairing of renting farms, were spilling over into the purchase market. "The scarcity of farms to let compels many farmers to purchase."[2] There was a demand for land from

[1] The average annual agricultural income of the United Kingdom for the years 1920-2 was £327 million, compared with £142 million in 1911-13. (Ojala, *op. cit.*).

[2] Report of A. J. Burrows, Ashford, *op. cit.*, Vol. 95, 17th January, 1920, p. 118.

investors and from the newly-rich of the war. Tenant farmers themselves saw in their farms an investment for their surplus funds and a possible source of profit on re-sale. In addition, those farmers who remained tenants under a new landlord often found themselves, for example because of increased rents, in a less fortunate position than formerly; this encouraged other tenant farmers to purchase if they possibly could. In consequence, land prices were high, reaching an average of £35 per acre in 1920.[1]

The high land prices had two main effects on land-owners. With rising costs of estate maintenance, net rents on estates often gave a very poor return on the capital invested and an even poorer return on the capital value of the land represented by the market sale price. Some landlords raised rents, particularly on a change of tenancy, but many preferred to sell their estates, leaving to the buyers the unpopular course of raising rents. Further, in 1919 a new basis of land valuation was adopted for the purpose of calculating death duties; the valuation became the sale price of land. In times of high land prices, such as 1920 and again in more recent years, this meant that the value of land for death duties exceeded the capitalised value of the income from that land. The new valuations, therefore, constituted a strong inducement for heirs to sell land, rather than other assets, in order to pay the duties.

Speculators often took a hand, selling land to farmers at inflated prices, but while many tenants bought their land as a consequence of threats of eviction, many others bought willingly. The period was one of enormous increase in owner-occupation. "With the continual breaking up of innumerable ancestral domains, all England seemed to be changing hands. . . ."[2]

Landlords sold in the post-war years, not because they any longer feared legislative action against their class, but because of the low returns obtainable from land-ownership. For example, on an estate of about 25,000 acres owned by Lord Leconfield, gross receipts amounted to £31,961 in 1913, gross

[1] D. K. Britton, "Sale Value of Farm Land between the Wars," *The Farm Economist*, December, 1949.
[2] *Estates Gazette*, Vol. 95, 3rd January, 1920, p. 12.

payments were £19,454, leaving a net return of £12,500, 10/- per acre. In 1920, the figures were £38,188, £31,378, and £6,800 respectively, a net return of little over 5/- per acre.[1] While the income from the land was halved, the sale value of the land had probably doubled, although there is insufficient evidence to be certain about this.

On 27th June, 1921, the reaction came. Agricultural product prices had fallen, and the government of the day, considering itself unable to afford the cost of the guarantees made in 1917, repealed the Act. Land prices fell, the demand for land shrinking rapidly. Owner-occupiers, who had bought at high prices in the expectation of continuing prosperity, often found themselves in difficulties and properties were lost to the mortgagees, or sold at reduced prices. Through the latter part of 1921 to 1923 there were few accessions to the ranks of owner-occupiers, save for landlords farming in hand unlettable farms. At the same time, owner-farmers were going out of business or becoming tenants of the former mortgagees of their farms. Bankruptcies among farmers rose from 44 in 1920 to 403 in 1922 and 472 in 1923, indicative of the difficulties of farmers and suggesting a decrease in the number of owner-farmers who, with high fixed payments, were particularly vulnerable to reductions in income. The extent of this decrease must not, however, be overstated. Despite the poor agricultural prospects, some land was still sold for owner-occupation. "Sales by auction of agricultural land have been fairly satisfactory, but in most instances the farms have been purchased by the tenants at greatly reduced prices...."[2] "The ... growth in the number of new land-owners in this district, during the past year, is remarkable."[3]

The main part of the increase in owner-occupation which occurred between 1909 and 1927 occurred in the years 1919 to 1921. The increase in this period, however, was not as large as is often supposed because increases, which are not fully recorded in the statistics, occurred in the ten years before 1919,

[1] Mr. H. T. Watson, agent to Lord Leconfield, *ibid.*, Vol. 100, 4th November, 1922.
[2] Report of Rippon, Boswell & Co., Exeter, *ibid.*, Vol. 101, 6th January, 1923, p. 13.
[3] Report of W. Brown & Co., Tring, *ibid.*, p. 14.

and because the decline in owner-occupation in 1921-23 was made good within the next few years in another short period of increasing owner-farming.

The second period of increase was the two years 1924 and 1925. Land prices had recovered somewhat from the slump of 1921-22 and farm incomes had risen.[1] Those land-owners who were pessimistic as to the future prospects of agriculture, and hence the future level of land prices, saw in the rise in land prices an opportunity to sell. In particular, the commercial and industrial rich who had bought estates in the preceding ten or twenty years appear sometimes to have found it necessary to sell them at this time to free the money to support their businesses which were in difficulties.

An alternative explanation is that the land sales were induced by the Agricultural Holdings Act, 1923, in the same way as it has been suggested the 1908 Act might have caused some land to be sold. In the way of this explanation is the fact that the 1923 Act introduced no new legislation, being merely a consolidating Act, embodying the new legislation introduced in 1920. In the few instances where the reports in the *Estates Gazette* gave reasons for the increase in land sales, the reason given was the improved conditions of agriculture, although there are oblique remarks which could be interpreted as referring to the 1923 Act. Death duties were seldom mentioned.

Farms were in demand in 1924 and 1925, both for rent and for purchase, and a good deal of land seems to have been sold. "I know of one farm where there were 60 applications for it . . ."[2] "Farms, small-holdings, and other agricultural property has had a ready sale and in most cases the tenants have . . . acquired the holdings which have been under their

---

[1] The average sale value of farm land rose from £28·6 per acre in 1921 to £30·9 in 1925. (Britton, *op. cit.*). No continuous series of income figures is available, but a pointer to an increase in income is given by the general agricultural price index which rose from 157 in 1923 (1911-13 = 100) to 161 in 1924, while agricultural wages fell from 36/11 per week in 1921 to 28/- per week in 1924. Colin Clark gives the net output of agriculture as £104 million in 1924 and £146 million in 1925. (*National Income and Outlay*, p. 78).

[2] Mr. N. E. Buxton, *House of Commons Debates*, 5s., Vol. 169, Col. 1130, 1924.

cultivation."[1] This did not apply to large farms on which there may have been some farming in hand.

After 1925, land sales practically ceased and with them the increase in owner-occupation. By 1927 over one-third of the land of England and Wales was cultivated by its owners, compared with one-eighth in 1908, just before the increase started. The rate of increase was low in pre-war years, though faster from 1909-12 than from 1912-14. During the war years the rate of increase accelerated, reaching a peak in 1919-20. In 1921 and early 1922 the increase was temporarily suspended, some owner-occupancies reverting to tenancies. By 1923 it had recovered somewhat and in 1924 and 1925 there was again a significant rate of increase. This tailed off in 1926.

(d) *Summary* : 1909 *to* 1927. The changes which occurred between 1909 and 1927 are shown in Table II.

TABLE II
CHANGE IN THE NUMBER OF HOLDINGS AND AREA OF CROPS AND GRASS AND IN THE EXTENT OF OWNER-OCCUPATION, ENGLAND AND WALES, 1909 TO 1927

Size class	1909	1927	Change : 1927 1909
All sizes			
No. of holdings	430,812	401,734	0·93
No. of owner-occupied holdings	55,920	146,887	2·63
Percentage of holdings owner-occupied	12·98%	36·56%	2·82
Area of crops and grass (acres)	27,323,464	25,590,330	0·94
Owner-occupied area (acres)	3,337,456	9,225,734	2·76
Percentage of area owner-occupied	12·21%	36·05%	2·95
Over 1, not over 5 acres			
No. of holdings	90,405	74,331	0·82
No. of owner-occupied holdings	14,877	31,358	2·11
Percentage of holdings owner-occupied	16·46%	42·19%	2·56
Over 5, not over 50 acres			
No. of holdings	197,606	186,497	0·94
No. of owner-occupied holdings	26,352	66,382	2·52
Percentage of holdings owner-occupied	13·34%	35·60%	2·67
Over 50, not over 300 acres			
No. of holdings	127,772	128,384	1·00
No. of owner-occupied holdings	12,397	44,333	3·56
Percentage of holdings owner-occupied	9·70%	34·53%	3·56
Over 300 acres			
No. of holdings	15,029	12,522	0·83
No. of owner-occupied holdings	2,294	4,814	2·09
Percentage of holdings owner-occupied	15·27%	38·44%	2·52

[1] Report of W. Easton & Son, Hull, *op. cit.*, Vol. 107, 9th January, 1926, p. 45.

The italicised figure which appears in the bottom right hand corner of each block in Table II will be referred to as the "Growth rate" of the group shown. The growth rates have been calculated by dividing the percentages of owner-occupation in 1927 by those for 1909; the same result is obtained, however, by dividing the change in owner-occupation between 1909 and 1927 by the overall change between those years.

The table shows two important things. It will be seen that the growth rate of acreage owned, 2·95, exceeds that of number of holdings owned, 2·82. This higher growth rate of acreage owned carried with it an increase in the average size of the owner-occupied holding, from 59·7 acres in 1909 to 62·7 acres in 1927, clearly indicative that larger than average sized holdings had passed from tenant occupation into owner-occupation. The average size of all holdings rose from 63·4 acres in 1909 to only 63·7 acres in 1927.

The table also shows that the number of owner-occupiers in the 50 to 300 acre size class was well below average in 1909 and that this was the main class to be affected by the increase in owner-occupation over the period. This can be attributed to the fact that, although the demand to rent farms in this size class was strong enough that few were farmed in hand in 1909, it was not strong enough to induce a farmer to purchase his farm for fear of being unable to rent another farm if served with a notice to quit. This applied particularly to farms of over 100 acres in size. The opportunities for land-owners to sell such farms were, therefore, limited. As the demand to rent farms increased and spread over the size classes, farmers lost the protection formerly enjoyed, and the farms, becoming more readily saleable, were sold. By 1927, this size class was not noticeably below average in number of owner-occupiers.

In 1909, the percentage of owner-occupation in the over 300 acre size class was high, pointing to the existence of some farming in hand in this class in 1909 and also to purchases of really large farms for extensive farming as a means of combatting the effects of depression before 1909. During the war years, when extensive arable production was profitable, large holdings sold readily and, in addition, there was probably an increase in farming in hand by landlords wishing a greater share in the agricultural prosperity than was obtainable simply by raising rents. The low growth rate, 2·52, in this size class between 1909 and 1927, was not, therefore, due to a low level of sales for owner-occupation, but to a reduction of farming in hand in 1927 as compared with 1909, some of the holdings concerned being tenanted in the later year.

The position with regard to size classes applies also to counties, those counties with a low percentage of owner-occupation in 1909 tending to have a high growth rate of numbers of owner-occupiers between 1909 and 1927. In 21 counties in England the growth rate exceeded the average for England, 2·75, and in 18 of those counties there was, in 1909, a less than average percentage of holdings owner-occupied.[1] Of these 21 counties, 15 were counties with more than 60 per cent. of their area under permanent grass, that is pasture counties, and of the other six, none were cereal producers of any great importance. Pasture counties had, on the whole, a much lower percentage of owner-occupation in 1909 than the non-pasture counties, no doubt because livestock farmers, particularly before the introduction of machine farming, needed a larger capital investment per acre than arable farmers and hence a larger capital before they could contemplate purchasing their holdings. For the same reason, they had less reason to fear losing their holdings should their landlords decide to sell. By 1927, there was no one type of farming in which owner-occupation appeared more or less important than in other types.

It is clear, therefore, that although the numerical growth in owner-occupation may have been somewhat larger in grain growing counties—which were affected by the 1917 Act—in

[1] The 21 counties are :—

County	Growth rate	County	Growth rate	County	Growth rate
Bedford	2·90	Kent (*)	2·82	Shropshire	3·81
Cheshire	4·34	Lancashire	3·16	Somerset (*)	3·06
Cornwall	3·46	Leicester	3·50	Stafford	3·21
Derby	3·03	Lincoln	2·84	Warwick	2·85
Devon (*)	3·15	Monmouth	2·83	Worcester	2·76
Dorset	3·38	Nottingham	2·78	Yorks. E.R.	3·04
Hereford	3·46	Rutland	3·02	N.R.	3·67

Counties marked (*) are those with a greater than average percentage of owner-occupation in 1909.

the 1909-27 period, the greatest proportionate increases did not occur in such counties. The main growth occurred in those counties and in that farm size group in which owner-occupation had been weakest before 1909, that is, generally, where the opportunities for land-owners to sell their land had been most restricted.

III. THE PERIOD OF CONSOLIDATION : 1928 TO 1950.

These 23 years cover depression, war, a period of post-war uncertainty and the first three years' operation of the Agricultural Act, 1947. What variations occurred in the extent of owner-occupation in these years is not known at all exactly. The only figures available relate to 1927, 1941 and 1950; they are given in Table III.

TABLE III

Year	Number of owner-occupied holdings	Percentage of holdings owner-occupied	Area of crops and grass owner-occupied (acres)	Percentage of area owner-occupied %
		(Holdings over 5 acres)		
1927	115,529	35·3	9,129,167	35·8
41	103,200	34·6	7,968,600	32·7
		(Holdings of 5 acres and over)		
41	104,600	34·7	7,980,000	32·7
50	115,300	39·0	9,100,000	38·0

Sources : 1927—Collected from the *Abstracts of Parish Returns of Acreage of Crops*, 1927.
1941—Calculated from the *National Farm Survey of England and Wales, 1941-3* and *Agricultural Statistics*, 1941.
1950—Calculated from "Tenure and Size of Holdings (England and Wales)," Press release, MAF 3088, 1952.

The figures shown for 1941 in the table were calculated by using the percentages of owner-occupation given in the Farm Survey with the statistics relating to the number and acreage of holdings given in the Agricultural Statistics for 1941. Using the percentages in this way is, in itself, a questionable procedure, necessitated by the impossibility of comparing the Survey results with any figures for other years owing to unspecified differences in definition. Further, the Survey percentages themselves may be inaccurate. The Survey results were based on a 14 per cent. sample of all returns received. For a part of eastern England covering 14·7 per cent. of the cultivated area of England and Wales, the extent of the owner-occupation of the area of crops and grass has been calculated using all the returns received from the area.[1] The differences between these results and those shown by the Survey for this area are apparent. The figures are:

County	Survey %	Cambridge Study %	County	Survey %	Cambridge Study %
Bedford	40	38·6	Lincs., Holland	39	43·8
Cambridge	29	35·4	Norfolk	37	37·6
Essex	51	53·2	Peterborough	18	24·8
Hertford	30	31·7	Suffolk, East	47	49·8
Huntingdon	30	33·5	West	48	50·5

These differences are often considerable and all bar one are in the same direction, suggesting that overall the Survey might underestimate the extent of owner-occupation in 1941 by about 2 per cent. The Survey report, in discussing the statistical techniques used, gives the maximum sampling error as about 0·21 per cent. in the overall extent of owner-occupation by area and 1·6 per cent. in the case of an average sized county. In seven of the counties shown above the error exceeds this figure, suggesting but not proving, that the overall error might be considerably greater than the figure of 0·21 per cent. For this reason the results of the Farm Survey cannot be regarded with any great confidence.

The 1950 figures are even more questionable. Rough grazings were included in the figures and had to be excluded for use here, giving opportunity for errors to occur. Further, the figures are based on incomplete data, completed returns being received from only 256,880 holdings out of 380,000 recorded. No indication is given respecting the adjustments made to take account of missing returns. There appears to be no ground for assuming that the returns received represented a fair sample of all holdings. The request to have access to the data on which the figures were based was refused on the ground that the data were not sufficiently accurate to be further worked on.

[1] *Land-ownership in the Eastern Counties*, 1941, Department of Agriculture of the University of Cambridge, pp. 28-32.

It is clear that no precision can be given to the discussion of owner-occupation for the years after 1927. The period will, therefore, be discussed in general terms under three headings.

(a) *The Pre-War years*: 1928 to 1939. The position of agriculture in these years is clearly shown in the net output figures given in Table IV.

TABLE IV

VALUE OF THE NET OUTPUT OF AGRICULTURE IN THE UNITED KINGDOM IN GROUPS OF YEARS, 1904-10 TO 1935-39

Years	Value of net output	Years	Value of net output
	£m.		£m.
1904–10	135·03	1924–29	157·34
11–13	147·09	30–34	139·57
20–22	332·97	35–39	158·53

Source: Ojala, *op. cit.*, p. 61.

These figures do not represent the incomes of farmers, two big items, wages and rent, needing to be deducted besides numerous smaller items, such as rates and depreciation, in order to yield net income.

In the early 1930's, the value of the net output was only a little higher than in the period 1904-10, years of no more than quiet prosperity. The mid-years of the two periods, 1906 and 1932, respectively, may be compared:

	1906	1932
Index of farm wage rates	51	98
Index of rents	74	80
Cost of living index	93	144
Number of holdings	431,806	390,469

It is clear that farmers' real incomes fell considerably between the two periods, despite the rise in the value of the net output. At the same time, however, the number of farmers having to share that real income fell.

Owner-occupiers were particularly hard hit by the depression as their mortgage payments, contracted in times of high land and product prices, were fixed while their incomes fell. Many, in consequence, failed and the mortgagees foreclosed.

"Several farms have been sold where farmers have been pressed by mortgagees."[1] Others sold out and cut their losses, often selling their mortgaged farms at prices "... much less than the original mortgage value of the holdings."[2] Selling owner-farmers frequently became tenants of the purchasers of their farms. The annual figures of bankruptcies among farmers for the years 1928 to 1939 tell plainly the story of the difficulties of these years. The figures are:

1928	487	1932	560	1936	215
29	345	33	428	37	258
30	350	34	288	38	252
31	497	35	224	39	201

Figures by courtesy of National Farmers Union.

After 1939, it was not until 1951 that the number of bankruptcies again exceeded 100 in any year.

After 1934, a period of purchasing of small farms for owner-occupation occurred: "... the majority of our sales ... have been to purchasers acquiring for occupation."[3] The total of land sales reported in the *Estates Gazette* rose from £4·6 million in 1931 to £6·9 million in 1935, the rise continuing until the outbreak of war, although there was a set-back in late 1937 and in 1938. Despite these purchases for owner-farming there was a decrease in the number of owner-occupied holdings for three reasons. Farmers who had hung on during the early 'thirties because they feared any such settlement of their affairs as the sale of their farms would involve, often took advantage of more buoyant conditions to sell. Mortgagees who had refrained from foreclosing on farmers during the worst of the depression, took advantage of improving conditions and higher land sale prices to enter into possession of the holdings of farmers in arrears. Thirdly, during the most depressed years, land-owners and mortgagees-in-possession often farmed land in hand, letting it later when conditions improved. By

[1] Report of G. Tarn Bainbridge, Son & Handley, Darlington, *Estates Gazette*, Vol. 111, 14th January, 1928, p. 52.

[2] Report of W. & H. Peacock, Bedford, *ibid.*, Vol. 117, 10th January, 1931, p. 56.

[3] Report of Jackson, Stops & Staff, London, *op. cit.*, Vol. 125, 19th January, 1935, p. 107.

1934, land agents could speak of "... land-owners and mortgagees who were forced to take over in the bad times (being) able to hand over again to responsible tenants..."[1] These things occurred mainly in 1934 and 1935. In 1936 it appears that the number of owner-occupiers increased slightly, although this increase was halted in 1938.

Comparing the 1927 and 1941 statistics for owner-occupation in three size classes, it is quite clear where the main decline in owner-occupation occurred. The percentages of numbers of holdings owner-occupied in the two years in England and Wales were:

Size class (acres)	1927 %	1941 %
5 – 100	35.4	35.7
100 – 300	34.8	31.3
300 plus	38.4	33.5
Total	35.3	34.6

Even making allowances for possible inaccuracies in the 1941 percentages, it is clear that owner-farming decreased most noticeably in the 100 to 300 acres size class. The decline in the over 300 acre size class was greater in terms of percentages, but represented only 800 holdings. It has already been shown that it was in the 100 acres to 300 acres farm size class that the greatest increase in owner-occupation occurred before 1927. The decline in this size class between 1927 and 1941 can mainly be attributed to the burdens of debt incurred by owners at the time of purchasing their farms; it constitutes one more example of the vulnerability of farmers with a high level of fixed charges in times of falling prices.

(b) *The War Years*: 1940 *to* 1946. After 31st December, 1941, Defence Regulation No. 62 provided tenants with security of tenure on the sale of their holdings. This removed a powerful incentive for tenants to purchase their holdings, but, by giving the tenant security, it led to a shortage of farms to rent so that only by purchasing a vacant farm could a prospective new entrant to farming gain a place. As a result, vacant farms commanded higher prices than tenanted farms, the difference,

---

[1] Report of Arthur Rutter, Sons & Co., Bury St. Edmunds, *op. cit.*, Vol. 124, 29th December, 1934, p. 1057. "Being" substituted for "have been" in the text.

the vacant possession premium, reaching on average 76 per cent. of the price of tenanted farms for the three years 1944-6.[1]

Some owner-occupiers, particularly the owners of holdings over 200 acres in size, sold to investors during the war, obtaining long-term leases and having the capital formerly invested in their land free for farming purposes. Overall, however, the prosperous war years were years of some increase in owner-farming although, tenants being secure in their tenure, prosperity did not lead to the same sort of increases in owner-occupation as occurred during the first war.

(c) *The Post-war Years*: 1947-1950. In 1947, the Agriculture Act came into operation. This guaranteed prosperity to farmers and gave them such things as security of tenure, freedom of cropping and protection against arbitrary increases in rents. Most of the effects of the Act on owner-occupation have been discussed in another place.[2] Here, only brief mention will be made of the effects of the continuing and guaranteed prosperity on owner-occupation.

Owner-occupation increased on the one hand because of increasing purchases of farms by new entrants to the industry. "The demand for properties with vacant possession still remains high . . ."[3] As a result, the vacant possession premium rose to a level of 108 per cent. on average for the years 1949-51. The existence of such a premium constitutes a strong inducement for the owner of a vacant farm to sell it rather than re-let, further reducing the supply of farms to the rental market. The rental provisions of the Act strengthened this tendency as, although an owner can ask what rent he likes for a vacant farm, he can only be sure of receiving that rent for three years, after which the tenant can appeal to arbitration on the rent.

Owner-farming also increased because of the continuing break-up of agricultural estates. "The break-up of large agricultural estates continues and has emphasised the willingness

[1] J. F. Ward, "Changes in the Sale Value of Farm Real Estate in England and Wales, 1937-9 to 1951," *Farm Economist*, August, 1953.

[2] "Owner-Farming and the 1947 and 1948 Acts," *Journal of the Agricultural Economics Society*, 1955.

[3] Report of Jackson, Stops & Staff, *Estates Gazette*, Vol. 156, 30th December, 1950, p. 488.

of tenants to buy their farms ..." [1] In part, this has been the result of death duties which fall severely on agricultural land, despite the agricultural rebate of 45 per cent. In part, it is a direct consequence of the provisions of the Acts, for, as was argued earlier, complete security for tenants is probably incompatible with a landlord/tenant system. But in part, also, the poor returns from land-ownership are responsible for the break-up of estates. This also has reference to estate duties. The value of agricultural land at present usually exceeds its earning power capitalised at the current rate of interest. This means that a man, having to sell assets to meet a claim for estate duties, can retain for himself a larger income by selling land rather than non-agricultural assets.

The low returns from land-ownership in the period are indicated by figures collected from a sample of 800,000 adjusted acres. For 1938 these show gross rent as 25/8 per adjusted acre, while expenditure on maintenance and statutory charges amounted to 11/- per adjusted acre, and expenditure on improvements to 4/2, leaving a net rent of 10/6 per adjusted acre. On the same sample in 1950, the figures were 31/6, 20/8, and 15/10 respectively, giving a negative net rent of 5/- per acre.[2] These figures must be regarded with some caution as there is reason to believe that the sample is not a representative one. Further, although it is justified to charge the whole expenditure on improvements to gross rent in arriving at net rent in a period when the annual expenditure has been of a constant amount, this is not so in a period of rising annual expenditure as in 1950. The figures can, therefore, be regarded as no more than indicative of changes which have occurred. Even if taken as only indicative, however, at a time when the sale price of tenanted land rose from an average of £22·5 per acre in 1938-40 to £46·7 per acre for 1948-50, it is small wonder that landowners wished to sell their land.

It is of interest in view of these figures to glance at net rents over the years covered by this paper. In the period

[1] Report of Chesshire, Gibson & Co., Birmingham, *ibid.*, Vol. 157, 13th January, 1951, p. 33.
[2] *An inquiry into Agricultural Rents and the Expenses of Land-owners in England and Wales*, 1950 and 1951, Country Land-owners' Association, pp. 28, 32.

1872-6 net income from land was about 57 per cent. of gross rents,[1] that is, about 16/- per acre. At the beginning of the present century net income represented 65 per cent.[2] of a smaller average gross rent, and was about 13/6 per acre. By 1928-29 the net income of land-owners had fallen to about 43 per cent. of the gross rent,[3] that is, about 10/4 per acre. This level was more or less stable until after the war.

IV. POST 1950.

The trends of the years 1947 to 1950 show no sign of being reversed. Although rents are gradually rising,[4] estate duties bring some estates into the market each year and when the farms are sold the tenants are frequent purchasers. No figures of the extent of owner-occupation have been collected since 1950; as a guess it is suggested that about one-half of the farmers of England and Wales now own their farms. Even if owner-occupation does not become the predominant tenurial form in the not too distant future, it is unlikely quickly to become again so unimportant as it was in 1908.

The post-war experiences have high-lighted two important points. The first is that farmers prefer to remain tenants so long as agricultural land is under-rented, but are willing to become owners when rents approach economic levels. The second is that security of tenure has not resulted in tenants abandoning the land market, but has stopped them paying exorbitant prices for their farms. On the other hand, new entrants to farming have paid very high prices for vacant farms[5] and are likely to be in an extremely uncomfortable position if agriculture should again become depressed.

---

[1] R. J. Thompson, "An inquiry into the rent of agricultural land in England and Wales during the 19th century," *Journal of the Royal Statistical Society*, 1907, p. 603.

[2] *Ibid.*, p. 605.

[3] W. C. D. Dampier-Whetham, "The Economics of Rural Land-owning," *Journal of the Agricultural Economics Society*, December, 1930, p. 59.

[4] The average rise in gross rents appears to have been about 15 per cent. between 1950 and 1953.

[5] In the period 1952-4 the average sale price of vacant land was £84 per acre, compared with £41 per acre for tenanted land.

INDEX

Abberley (Worcs), 93
Abbots Morton (Worcs), 94
Acts of Parliament: Agricultural (1947), 299, 304; Agricultural Gangs (1867), 159; Agricultural Holdings Act (1883), 50, 251, (1908), 290–1, (1923), 295; Agricultural Rates (1896), 253; Ballot, 50; Corn (1791), 105; Corn Production, 292; Education, 159, 170; Enclosure, 26, 91–101, 115; Finance (1909–10), 290; Ground Gain (1881), 50; Improvement of Land, 63–4, 72; Poor, 125–8; Property and Income Tax, 57; Reform, 50, 283; Settled Land (1882), 32, 49, 50, 251; Small Holdings (1908), 53; Tithe Commutation (1836), 62, 67; Union Chargeability (1865), 157
Agriculture, Board of, 12, 52, 107, 108, 113, 116, 251, 252; enquiry into rents (1804), 59; questionnaire on the state of agriculture, 108
Agricultural Rating Bill (1897), 253
Aldbourne (Wilts), 233
Alderminster (Warks), 101
Alstonefield (Staffs), 97, 98
Annals of Agriculture, 107, 108
Arable farming, 18, 19–21, 244–8, 256 (*and see* Corn growing); products, 228–9
Arch, Joseph, 130, 139n
Ashby, A. W., 266, 279
Ashworth, Prof W., 234
Aspley Guise (Beds), 97
Astley (Warks), 101
Atherstone (Warks), 100
Attercliffe (Yorks), 100
Austin, Mr, 150n

Badsey (Worcs), 95
Bailey-Denton, Mr, 78
Bakewell, Robert, 11, 21

Ballinasloe, Ireland, 201
Bankruptcies, 289, 294, 301
Barley, yield, 110, 111
Barnwell (Cambs), 99
Bassingbourne (Cambs), 99
Barrington, R. M., 201
Barton (Cambs), 94, 98, 99, 100
Beans, yield, 110, 111
Beasley, G., 243n
Beaufort, Duke of, 232
Becket, Sir John, 95
Bedford, Dukes of, 15, 57
Bedfordshire: enclosures, 91; owner occupation, 300; rents, 62, 64, 65, 66, 83; wages, 128
Beef, prices, 203, 205, 227
Beilby, O. J., 275
Bellerby, J. R., 220, 244
Beresford, M. W., 102
Berkshire: cattle, 214; cottages, 153; land sales, 45; returns, 109
Bickenhill (Warks), 97
Bloch, Marc, 219
Bloodworth family, 93
Boreham, A. J., 263, 265, 266, 267, 279
Borough Fen (Northants), 224
Bottisham (Cambs), 93, 99
Bowley, A. L., wage index, 138, 269, 270
Bread, 111, 141, 142, 143
Brewing and distilling industries, 23
Bright, Tom, 78–9
Britton, D. K., 266, 279
Buckinghamshire: enclosures, 91, 93; land sales, 45; rents, 62, 64, 65, 66, 83; wages, 126–7, 128, 131
Building, cost of, 78–9, 85; trends, 47
Building News, 41
Burke, Edmund, 111
Bury St Edmunds, 151n

Caird, Sir James, 18, 57, 64, 128,

Caird—cont.
  139n, 147, 157, 162, 169, 221, 226, 227, 243n, 247, 285
Cambridgeshire: cottages, 154; diet, 193–5; enclosures, 91, 93, 99, 100; owner occupation, 300; rents, 62, 64, 65, 66, 83, 245; sheep, 205; wages, 128, 134, 137, 188
Canterbury, Archbishop of, 107
Capital invested in improvements, 75–80; outlay and rents, 61, 63–4
Cattle, 242n; enterprises, 213–15; feeding, 206; prices, 201, 203, 205–6, 209; selective breeding, 112 (*and see under counties*)
Censuses, population, 269
Central Chamber of Agriculture, 249
Central Landowners' Association, 266
Cereal farming, 221–36, 237 (*and see* Grain growing)
Chamberlain, John, 93
Chambers, J. D., 26, 28
Channing, F. A., 251–2
Chaplin, H., 249, 251, 252, 253, 254n
Charnwood Forest, 92, 96
Cheese, 244n
Cheshire: butter, 244n; cattle, 214; high feeding, 229; rents, 65
Chesterton (Cambs), 93, 99
Churley, P. A., 117
Clapham, Sir J. H., 13, 14, 25–6, 32, 226–7, 234
Clarke, J. A., 223
Clay, J., 252
Clifford, Frederick, 153, 164, 167
Clover, 19, 20, 23, 228n
Clun Forest (Salop), 98
Clutton, John, 77, 78, 79
Cobbett, William, 18, 247
Cobham, Lord, 251, 252, 253
Coke (of Norfolk), 11, 13, 15, 19
Coleshill (Warks), 97
Collings brothers, 21
Colmworth (Beds), 97
Commissions: Agricultural Interests (1879–82), Richmond, 125, 249–51, 252; Agriculture (1872–82), 65, 71, 241; (1892–6), 57, 58, 65, 66, 73, 146, 147, 201, 241, 265; (1894–5), 154; (1919–20), 254n; Children's Employment, 154; Depressed State of the Agricultural Interest (1879), 249–54; Depression in Trade (1886), 57; Ecclesiastical, 58, 74; Employment of Children, Young Persons and Women in Agriculture (1867–9), 125, 138, 147, 148, 150–1, 152–3, 164, 166; Labour (1891–4), 125, 138, 146, 147, 148, 153, 154; Tithe Rentcharge, 266
Committees: Agricultural Distress (1836), 162, 163n; Agricultural Prices in Scotland, 202; Dearth of Provisions (1799), 114; Employment of School Children (1901), 170; Haversham (1911), 288; High Price of Provisions, 115; Inclosure (1844), 92; Labourers' Wages (1824), 125, 127, 167n; State of Agriculture (1833), 61, 125–6, 146–7, 157n; Tithe Rent Charge (1890), 57
Connington (Cambs), 99
Corn growing, 247–8, 249–50, 253–5, 276–7
Corn Law (1791), 105; repeal of, 130
Cornwall: cottages, 155; high farming, 229
Corringham R. W., 224
Cottages, cost of, 79; rents of, 155 (*and see under counties and* Labourers)
Cottenham (Cambs), 93, 99
County Councils, 51, 53
Crops, fodder, 19, 20, 284–5; root, 19, 21
Crown Estates, 74, 77, 79
Cumberland: cropping, 235; diet, 192; high farming, 224, 229; livestock, 210, 234; wages, 132, 186
Custance, 93n

Dairy farming, 22, 213–15; produce prices, 242–4, 254, 256
Dalton, C. N., 252
Davies, Rev D., 108

Davies, E., 17
Defence Regulation no 62 (1941), 303
Defoe, D., 13, 22
Delamere Forest (Cheshire), 77
Depression, 11, 65, 71, 220; The Great, 241–56
Derby, Earl of, 50, 245
Derbyshire: rents, 65; wages, 132, 186
Devonshire, Duke of, 94
Devonshire: cottages, 152, 155; female labour, 147; rents, 65; returns, 116; wages, 128, 180
Diet, 193–5; Cumbs, 192; Essex, 193–5; Hunts, 193–5
Disafforestation, cost of, 77
Donaldson, W., 107
Dorset: cattle, 213, 214; cottages, 152, 153; female labour, 147, 148; returns, 112, 116; wages, 132
Dowland, John, 94
Doyle, Sir Francis, 168n
Drainage, 16, 22, 63–4; cost of, 76, 77, 78, 85.
Drescher, L., 228
Drills, horse-drawn, 20
Drought, 204, 234, 251, 253
Druce, Mr, 249, 250
Durham: rents, 35; wages, 136, 186
Duty, on auction sales, 32–5, 36–7, 38; death, 293, 305; stamp, on land sales, 36–7, 38, 39

East Anglia, high farming, 221
Eastbourne (Sussex), 127
East Lothian, 20
Eden, Sir Frederic, 108–9
Egremont family, 15
Elliot, Arthur, 100
Ellis, William, 221
Elton, C. I., 252
Enclosure, 13, 16, 17–18, 22; Acts, 26, 91–101, 115; effects of, 11–12, 24–6, 59; House of Commons Committees, 95, 96–7; time taken over, 98–9; Beds, 91; Bucks, 91, 93; Cambs, 91, 93, 99, 100; Leics, 91; Northants, 91; Oxon, 93; Staffs, 91, 93; Warks, 91, 93; Worcs, 91, 93

Enclosure Commissioners, 91–101; choice of, 92–5; expenses and fees, 95–7; procedures, 98–101
Enquiry, Family Budget (1937–8), 265
Erdington (Warks), 96, 101
Ernle, Lord, 12–14, 26, 219, 220, 241
Estate Exchange, 33, 34, 40–1, 42–4, 45, 47
Estates Gazette, 31, 34, 37, 40, 41–6, 48, 286, 288
Estates market, *see* Land market
Essex: cattle, 214; corn growing, 255; cottages, 153; diet, 193–5; female labour, 148; land sales, 45; owner occupation, 300; rents, 60, 62, 64, 65, 66, 82, 83; returns, 112; sheep, 205; wages, 128, 129, 134, 136, 177, 188
Everett, R. L., 251, 252
Eversden (Cambs), 99
Excise Inquiry (1835), 33, 37
Export, grain, 111; livestock, Irish, 201

Famine, Irish, 130
Farmers, tenant, 51, 53, 288, 291–5, 297
Farming, hill, 204–5, 206–9, 215; methods, 19–24
Farms, size of, 17–18, 25, 250, 252, 253
Fencing, cost of, 78
Fertilizer, 221, 229 (*and see* Manure)
Fletcher, T. W., 219, 228
Food: labourers', 140–5, 192–5; riots, 105, 106, 113; supplies, 105, 107–8, 113–14
Fowler, Sir H., 252n
Frank, Howard, 53
Fraser, Rev J. (Bishop of Manchester), 153, 166
Freeholder, 40, 41
Freehold Land Times, 40, 41
Free Land League, 255
Free trade, 31n, 63
Frere, P. H., 225, 230, 232
Fulbourne (Cambs), 9
Fussell, G. E., 22–3

Galpin, W. F., 113
Giffen, R., 250n, 252, 254
Gilmour, J., 252
Girton (Cambs), 99
Glamorganshire, wages, 188
Glasgow, 47
Gloucestershire: cottages, 153, 155; crop acreage, 118; high farming, 229; rents, 65; returns, 112; yields, 110, 111
Gonner, E. C. K., 13, 14
Goshen, G. J., 249
Grain: crops for fodder, 20; export, 111; growing, see Corn growing; import, 105–6, 111, 113; prices, 105, 106, 111, 113, 115, 222–36, 242, 243, 246; high feeding, 222, 224–5
Gransden (Cambs), 99
Grasses, artificial, 19, 21
Graunt, John, 106
Grazing, 231n, 247
Guilden Morden (Cambs), 99
Guthlaxton (Leics), 117

Habakkuk, Prof H. J., 15, 16, 17
Hainault Forest (Essex), 77
Halévy, E., 241
Hall, Sir Daniel, 226
Halton (Warks), 118
Hampshire: cattle, 214; cottages, 155; wages, 128
Hammond, J. L., and Barbara, 12, 13, 14, 24, 26
Handley, H., MP, 63
Hardwick (Cambs), 99
Hardwick, Earl, 95
Hare, 93n
Harris, C. C., 228, 229
Harston (Cambs), 99
Hasbach, W., 228
Hathersage (Derby), 94, 96
Henley, J. J., 148
Herefordshire: rents, 60, 62, 64, 65, 66, 82, 83; wages, 129, 179
Hertfordshire: cottages, 156; land sales, 45; owner occupation, 300; wages, 128, 129, 175, 188

High farming ('high feeding'), 221–6, 229–31; Ches, 229; Cornwall, 229; Cumbs, 224, 229; East Anglia, 221; Glos, 229; Kent, 224; Lincs, 223; Norfolk, 223, 225, 226; Notts, 224
Homer, Rev William, 92, 96
Horses, 112, 237, 242n, 245
Hoskins, Dr W. G., 23
Houghton's *Collection of Letters*, 106–7
House purchase, 35, 47–8
Humphreys, James, 36, 37, 38
Hunt, K. E., 279
Hunter, Dr, 152
Huntingdonshire: diet, 193–5; labour, 128; owner occupation, 300; sheep, 205
Husbandry, alternate, 19, 21, 23; arable, 18, 19–21, 244–8, 256; convertible, 19–20, 23; mixed, 221–36, 237; open-field, 23–4

Import, agricultural products, 243–4, 256; cheese, 244n; grain, 105–6, 111, 113
Improvement, by landowners, 72–9
Income: aggregate wages, 268–9; capital and interest, 267, 274; farmer-labourer income ratio, 264, 269, 272–4; farmers' incentive income, 220, 244–5, 261–2, 264, 269–74, 278; farm-industry wage ratio, 270–4, 278; total factor income, 263–5, 285, 306
Income Tax: Returns, 57, 62, 66–71, 84; farmers', 292
Index, price, 63, 68–72, 203, 204, 205, 241–2, 244, 256; wage, 138, 269, 270
Industrial Revolution, 11, 22
Inland Revenue, 241, 265–6, *and see* Income Tax
Invasion, threat of (1797–8), 112
Inverness Market, 201, 202
Investment in land, 48, 54
Ireland, farm income, 265, 271–2, 273
Ireland, livestock exports, 201
Iveson, John, 96

John, Dr A. H., 221
Johnson, A. H., 13, 14, 17
Journal of Auctions, 40, 41

Kay, Dr, 150
Kent, 24; high farming, 224; land sales, 45; rents, 65; wages, 128
Kenyon, G. H., 112
Kidderminster (Worcs), 126
Kidford (Sussex), 112
Kindleberger, Prof C., 237
King, Gregory, 106
Kingscote, Mr, 251, 252
Kingston (Cambs), 99, 101
Kingston, Duke of, 94
Kingswinford (Staffs), 94
Kirk, J. H., 263

Labourers, 123–91; allowances, 133, 139, 173–80, 187, 189, 191; census (1901), 160; cottages and rent, 151–9; education, 161, 170; effect of machinery, 139, 140; employment, 25–6; food and diet, 140–5, 192–5; gang system, 158–9; harvest payments, 133, 134, 140; irregularity of work, 145–7; migration from country, 26, 160–72; piecework, 124, 133, 134, 135, 139, 174–80; revolt (1830), 24; surplus, 126, 127, 128; terms of engagement, 124–5; wages, weekly, 124, 129–32, 145–6, 173–91, 242, 245, 264, 268–72, according to price of wheat, 130–2, compared with yearly earnings, 124, 132–40, 187–91; women and children, 144, 147–51; Devon, 147; Dorset, 147, 148; Essex, 148; Norfolk, 149, 150; Northants, 149; Som, 147; Surrey, 148; Wilts, 147, 148; Worcs, 148; 1903 compared with 1850, 159–60
Lambert, G., 66, 252
Lancashire: butter, 244n; cattle, 214; wages, 132, 186
Land market, 31–54; advertising, 40, 41; auction duty, 32–5, 36; burdens on, 251, 253, 254; Estate Exchange, 33, 34, 40–1, 42–4, 45, 47; house purchase, 35, 47–8; investment, 48, 50; London control of, 42–5, 46; motives for selling, 52; prices, movement of, 35–8, 39–40, 47, 52–4; supply and demand, 49–50, 51–2, 53–4; volume of sales, 34, 36–7, 38, 42–5, 46, 49
Land: nationalization, 52; reformers, 32; sale of, 286, 287–8, 292, 294–6, 301 (*and see* Land market); tax, 290; use of, 18; valuation and price of, 293, 294, 295, 303–4, 305
Landbeach (Cambs), 99
Landowners, 283, 289–90, 291, 293–5, 305 (*and see* Owner occupation); status of, 50–1
Landownership, structure of, 15–18, 27
Lavergne, L. de, 230
Lawes, J. D., 235
Lawes and Gilbert, 228–9
Law Times, 40
Leases, 16
Leconfield, Lord, 293
Leicester, Earl of, 255
Leicester, sheep, 207
Leicestershire: crop acreage, 117–18; enclosures, 91
Leighton Buzzard (Beds), 100
Ley farming, 19–20
Leys, 23–4
Lincolnshire: cottages, 155; high farming, 223; owner occupation, 300; rents, 60, 62, 64, 65, 66, 82, 83; wages, 134, 188
Lister, S. Cunliffe, 50n
Little, H. J., 157
Little, W. C., 148, 153, 154, 166, 252
Livestock: 'high feeding', 221–6, 229–31, 237; husbandry, 21, 228–9, 232–6, 237, 244–8, 255, 256; prices, 201–9, 242, 246, 254; returns, 112, 118
London Auction Mart, 42, 44, 45, 46
London Farmers' Club, 234, 250
London market, 22; milk market, 214; property business, 47
Long, W. H., 52, 251, 252, 253
Longstanton (Cambs), 99

Longstow (Cambs), 95, 99
Low Countries, 19
Lowther, 254n
Lyttleton, Lord, 251

MacGregor, J. J., 266, 268
Machinery, agricultural, 22
Maize, 244
Malt distillery, 111
Malthus, Thomas, 109
Manchester, 251
Mangels, 234-5
Manure, 221-5, 229
Marketing, 22-3
Marlborough, Duke of, 49
Marling, 78
Marshall, William, 12, 107
Mathias, P., 23
Maxwell, George, 92-3
McCulloch, J. R., 60, 61, 62, 64
McGregor, O. R., 220n
McMullen, W. D., 279
Meat, prices, 141, 142, 203, 204, 205, 227, 243-4; production, 228n
Mechi, J. J., 221
Middlemarch, 234
Middlesex: cattle, 213; land sales, 45
Milk, 214, 247
Mill, John Stuart, 75
Mingay, G. E., 28
Monmouthshire, wages, 188
Montgomeryshire, 65
Mortgages, 52, 288, 291, 301-3
Murray, Dr Keith, 255n

Napoleonic Wars, effect on agriculture, 112, 118
Napolitan, L., 275
National Farm Survey (1941-3), 266, 299-300
National Income and Expenditure, 265
Netherlands, 19
Newbold Vernon (Leics), 101, 102
Nockold family, 93, 94
Norfolk: cottages, 153; diet, 193-5; female labour, 149, 150; four-course system, 13, 19, 20, 221, 222, 235; high farming, 223, 225, 226; owner occupation, 300; rents, 35, 65, 85; returns, 116; sheep, 205; wages, 128, 134, 146, 188
Norton, Trist & Gilbert, land sale estimate, 36n, 46
Northamptonshire: enclosures, 91; rents, 64, 65
North, Lord, 33
Northumberland: farm labourers, 168n; female labour, 149; rents, 35, 65; wages, 129, 139, 173, 186
Northumberland, Duke of, 39
North Wales, rents, 60, 62, 64, 66, 82, 83
Nottinghamshire: high farming, 224; rents, 65; returns, 116

Oakington (Cambs), 99
Oats, yield, 111
Oilcake, 221-5, 244
Ojala, Dr E. M., 228, 241, 244, 245n, 256, 263, 279
Olsen, M., 228, 229
Open-field farming, 23-4
Orwin, C. S. and Felton, 268
Output, 26-7, 228n, 245-6, 256, 263-5, 275-8, 301
Owner occupation, 17-18, 25, 283-306; by counties, 298, 300; growth rate of, 296-9
Oxfordshire: enclosures, 93; rents, 65; returns, 116; wages, 128, 188

Pasture, arable conversion to, 232-3, 234
Peas, yield, 111
Peel, Sir Robert, 33
Pelham, Lord, 116
Pell, Albert, 75-6, 77
Pemberton, Christopher, 93, 94, 95
Pennington, W., 107
Peterborough, diocese of, 116; owner occupation, 300
Pigs, 112, 242n
Pitt, William, 106
Plague, animal, 231
Poor Law, 125-8; Commissioners, 126, 127, 147, 150-1, 162

Population, 242; censuses, 269; (1901), 160n
Potato blight, 272
Porter, G., 61n
Portland, Duke of, 109, 113
Potash, 222
Press taxation, 40
Price, Bonamy, 249
Price, L. L., 57
Prices, 61, 62, 63, 66, 68–72, 108, 226–7, 262–3, 269–70; beef, 203, 205, 227, 243n; dairy produce, 242–4, 254, 256; fatstock, 223, 224; food, 140, 143–4; grain, 105, 106, 111, 113, 115, 222–36, 242, 243, 246; livestock, 201–9, 242, 246, 254; meat, 141, 142, 203, 204, 205, 227, 243, 244; mutton, 203, 204, 227, 243n; retail, 269–70; wheat, 61n; wool, 202, 203, 206–7, 209
Prosperity (1853–73), 219–37
Purdy, Mr, 138
Pusey, Philip, 63, 221–2, 223, 224

Quedgely (Glos), 110

Radnor, Earl of, 109
Railways: influence of, 204, 213, 214; and rents, 64
Rainy, Alexander, 38n, 41
Rampton (Cambs), 99, 101
Read, C. S., 223, 225
Read, S. C., MP, 249
Real estate market, *see* Land market
Rendel, Lord, 251, 252
Rents: agricultural, 245, 264, 265–6, 273, 274, 284–5, 305, 306; movement of, 35–6, 40, 48, 52, 59–66; of agricultural land, 57–86; cottages, 156–7 (*and see under* Labourers); 'economic', 79, 80; expenditure on outgoings, 72–5; Income tax returns, 66–71 (*and see under counties*)
Repairs, by landowners, 72–5
Report on Burdens of Land (1846), 128, 131, 147, 163
Retail prices, national and rural, 269–70

Returns (1800), 105–19, 242; causes necessitating, 106–9; committees on, 110, 111, 114, 115; crop acreages, 112, 116–17, 119; form of, 109–10; Home Office questionnaires, 109, 113–14, 116; information from, 111, 115, 116; livestock, 112 (*and see under counties*)
Rew, Mr, 146
Rhee, H. A., 241, 266, 279
Rhyddlan, 98
Richmond, Duke of, 249
Richmond Commission, 125, 249–51, 252
Riots: food, 105, 106, 113; labourers', 127, 130, 163, 164
Ritchie, C. T., 249
Roads, cost of, 76, 79
Rockingham, Duke of, 15
Root crops, 19, 21
Rotation, 19, 23
Rothley (Leics), 101
Royal Agricultural Society, 63, 250
Rutland: rents, 65; wages, 128
Rye, 111
Ryegrass, 20

Sainfoin, 20, 23
Sales, auction, duty on, 32–5, 36–7, 38
Salford (Beds), 101
Sanderson, James, 207
Sanston (Cambs), 99
Sauerbeck's price index, 63, 68–72, 203, 204, 205, 241–2, 244, 256
Scotland: farm incomes, 265, 266; Highland and Agricultural Society, 204; hill farms, 206, 207
Shaw-Lefevre, G. J., 251, 252, 253, 255
Sheep, 112, 201–5, 206–9, 242n, 246; selective breeding, 21; Blackface, 206, 209; Border-Leicester, 201, 204, 206, 207; Cambs, 205; Cheviot, 201, 202, 206, 207; Essex, 205; Hunts, 205; Leics, 207; Norfolk, 205; Suffolk, 205
Sheldon, Prof J. P., 254n
Shepherds, 125, 139, 144

Shropshire: rents, 35; wages, 129
Simon, Dr (Sir) J., 152, 157
Sinclair, Sir John, 59, 94, 107, 119
Small Holdings Act (1908), 53; Committee, 76
Smith, Dr E., 144, 147
Soil differences, effects on production, 19–20, 25, 61
Somerset: cottages, 152, 155; female labour, 147; rents, 65; wages, 188
South Midlands, rents, 86
Speenhamland (Berks), 105
Spencer, Earl, 63
Spencer, Mr, 148
Squarey, Elias P., 76, 77
Staffordshire, enclosures, 91, 93
Stamp, Lord, 266
Stamp Office, 37
Stamps and Taxes, Board of, 39
Stanhope, Hon Edward, 153, 166
Stapleford (Cambs), 99
Steeple Morden (Cambs), 99
Stephenson, Sir William, 249
Stetchworth (Cambs), 99
Stock rearing, 204–9
Stoneyhurst (Lancs), 251
Stow-cum-Quy (Cambs), 93, 96, 99
Street, A. G., 255n
Suffolk: cottages, 153, 155; diet, 193–5; livestock, 230; owner occupation, 300; rents, 65; returns, 116; Scottish farmers in, 168n; sheep, 205; wages, 128, 129, 132, 146, 151n, 165n, 176, 188
Swaffham (Cambs), 99
Swaffham (Norfolk), 149
Swavesey (Cambs), 99
Surrey: female labour, 148; land sales, 45; wages, 128
Surveyors' Institution, 77
Sussex: cattle, 214; cottages, 153, 155; pauperism, 24; rents, 65; returns, 112; wages, 126, 127, 136, 188

Tate, W. E., 13, 93n
Tawney, Prof R. H., 23
Taylor, F. D. W., 269, 279
Taxation, press, 40

Taxes, Board of, 114
Tenure, security of, 290–1, 303, 304, 306
Teversham (Cambs), 99
Teviotdale, 201, 202
Thirsk, Dr Joan, 117
Thomas, O., 252
Thompson, R. J., 266
Thorpe, 93n
Thurnal, Mr, 162–3
Timber, sale of, 77, 78
Townshend, Turnip, 11, 12–13, 19
Trade, Board of, 114; reports on wages, 125, 138, 146
Trow-Smith, R., 21
Truslove, 93n
Trustram-Eve, H., 288
Tull, Jethro, 11, 20–1
Turnips, 19, 20, 21, 23, 24, 228n, 235

Venn, J. A., 241
Victoria County History, 117

Wages, 123–91; allowances, 133, 139, 173–80, 187, 189, 191; cottages and rent, 151–9; harvest payments, 133, 134, 140; irregularity of work, 145–7; piecework, 124, 133–5, 139, 174–80; Poor Law administration, effect of, 125–8; sources of information, 123–4; questionnaire, 195–8; surplus labourers, 126, 127, 128; value of food, 14–15; weekly rates, 124, 129–32, 145–6, 173–91; compared with yearly earnings, 124, 132–40, 187–91; women and children, 144, 147–51 (*and see under counties and Labourers*)
Wales: diet, 194–5; owner occupation, 284; rents, 60, 62, 64, 80, 83
Walpole family, 19
Waresley (Cambs), 99
Warwickshire: enclosures, 91, 93; rents, 64; returns, 110, 114; wages, 129, 136, 174, 188
Wedge, 93n
Welsh marches, 223
West Wickham (Cambs), 99

Westmorland: cottages, 155; rents, 65; returns, 116; wages, 186
Whaddon (Cambs), 99, 100
Wheat: acreage, 228-9 (*and see* Corn, Grain)
Whichwood Forest (Oxon), 77
Whitehead, C., 252
Whittlebury Forest (Northants), 77
Whitwick (Leics), 101
Willingham (Cambs), 93, 99
Wilson, Henry, 233
Wilson Fox, A., 201
Wiltshire: cattle, 214; cottages, 152; female labour, 147, 148; rents, 65, 85; wages, 128, 129, 132, 178
Witton (Warks), 96

Wood, G. H., 268, 271
Worcestershire: cropping, 235; enclosures, 91, 93; female labour, 148; rents, 65
Worlidge, J., 20

Yeomen, 17-18, 25
Yields, barley, 110, 111; beans, 110, 111; grass, 110, 111; harvest, 105, 107, 109, 111, 113-16; oats, 111; peas, 111
Yorkshire: cattle, 214; rents, 35, 65; returns, 117; wages, 136, 186
Young, Arthur, 12, 20, 23, 35, 106, 107, 117; questionnaire on agriculture, 107-8, 118